TOP FEDERAL TAX ISSUES FOR 2013
CPE COURSE

CCH Editorial Staff Publication

.CCH

a Wolters Kluwer business

Contributors

Technical Reviewer..................................... George G. Jones, J.D., LL.M
Contributing Editors...Brant Goldwyn, J.D.
Adam R. Levine, J.D., LL.M
Larry Perlman, CPA, J.D., LLM
Jennifer J. Rodibaugh, J.D.
Leo V. Roinila, JD, LL.M
Raymond G. Suelzer Jr., J.D., LL.M
George L. Yaksick, Jr., J.D.
Production Coordinator .... Gabriel E. Santana
Design/Layout...Laila Gaidulis
Production ....Lynn J. Brown

This publication is designed to provide accurate and authoritative information in regard to the subject matter covered. It is sold with the understanding that the publisher is not engaged in rendering legal, accounting, or other professional service. If legal advice or other expert assistance is required, the services of a competent professional person should be sought.

ISBN: 978-0-8080-3078-2

No claim is made to original government works; however, within this Product or Publication, the following are subject to CCH's copyright: (1) the gathering, compilation, and arrangement of such government materials; (2) the magnetic translation and digital conversion of data, if applicable; (3) the historical, statutory and other notes and references; and (4) the commentary and other materials.

Printed in the United States of America

MIX
Paper from
responsible sources
FSC® C101537
FSC
www.fsc.org

TOP FEDERAL TAX ISSUES FOR 2013 CPE COURSE

Introduction

Each year, a handful of tax issues typically require special attention by tax practitioners. The reasons vary, from a particularly complicated new provision in the Internal Revenue Code, to a planning technique opened up by a new regulation or ruling, or the availability of a significant tax benefit with a short window of opportunity. Sometimes a developing business need creates a new set of tax problems, or pressure exerted by Congress or the Administration puts more heat on some taxpayers while giving others more slack. All these share in creating a unique mix that in turn creates special opportunities and pitfalls in the coming year and beyond. The past year has seen more than its share of these developing issues.

CCH's *Top Federal Tax Issues for 2013 CPE Course* identifies those recent events that have developed into the current "hot" issues of the day. These tax issues have been selected as particularly relevant to tax practice in 2013. They have been selected not only because of their impact on return preparation during the 2013 tax season but also because of the important role they play in developing effective tax strategies for 2013 and beyond. Some issues are outgrowths of several years of developments; others have burst onto the tax scene unexpectedly. Among the latter are issues directly related to the recent economic downturn and tax legislation designed to assist in a recovery. Some have been emphasized in IRS publications and notices; others are just being noticed by the IRS.

This course is designed to help reassure the tax practitioner that he or she is not missing out on advising clients about a hot, new tax opportunity; or that a brewing controversy does not blindside their practice. In addition to issue identification, this course provides the basic information needed for the tax practitioner to implement a plan that addresses the particular opportunities and pitfalls presented by any one of those issues. Among the topics examined in the *Top Federal Tax Issues for 2013 CPE Course* are:

- Exempt Organizations: New Restrictions on Filings, Contributions
- FATCA: Foreign Tax Compliance Requirements
- Tax Return Preparer Penalties
- IRS Audits: The Examination Process and New Developments
- Dealing with IRS Collections
- New Repair Regulations
- MACRS Asset Dispositions and General Asset Accounts Rules
- Net Operating Losses
- Health Care Reform Moves Forward
- Tax Reform: Policy and Proposals

Study Questions. Throughout the course you will find Study Questions to help you test your knowledge, and comments that are vital to understanding a particular strategy or idea. Answers to the Study Questions with feedback on both correct and incorrect responses are provided in a special section beginning on page 11.1.

Index. To assist you in your later reference and research, a detailed topical index has been included for this course beginning on page 12.1.

Quizzer. This course is divided into four Modules. Take your time and review all course Modules. When you feel confident that you thoroughly understand the material, turn to the CPE Quizzer. Complete one, or all, Module Quizzers for continuing professional education credit.

Go to **CCHGroup.com/PrintCPE** to complete your CPE Quizzers online for immediate results and no Express Grading Fee. Further information is provided in the CPE Quizzer instructions on page 13.1.

October 2012

CCH'S PLEDGE TO QUALITY

Thank you for choosing this CCH Continuing Education product. We will continue to produce high quality products that challenge your intellect and give you the best option for your Continuing Education requirements. Should you have a concern about this or any other CCH CPE product, please call our Customer Service Department at 1-800-248-3248.

COURSE OBJECTIVES

This course was prepared to provide the participant with an overview of specific tax issues that impact 2012 tax return preparation and tax planning in 2013. These are the issues that "everyone is talking about;" each impacts a significant number of taxpayers in significant ways.

Upon course completion, you will be able to:

- Explain the simplified advance ruling process for exempt organizations;
- Describe when and if Schedule K-1 information and Social Security numbers should be reported on Form 990;
- Understand the rationale behind Congress and the IRS' ongoing efforts to expand information reporting, both at home and abroad;
- Identify foreign financial and other institutions affected by FATCA;
- Understand the Code Sec. 6694(a) penalty for understatement of taxpayer's liability by tax return preparer;
- Describe the Code Sec. 6694(b) penalty for willful or reckless understatement of a taxpayer's liability by a tax return preparer;
- Describe the IRS audit examination process from selection to resolution;
- List the taxpayer's rights in an audit;
- Understand the IRS collection process;
- Describe the methods and tools the IRS employs to collect unpaid taxes;
- Understand the standards used in distinguishing a repair from an improvement;
- Distinguish among improvements that are betterments, restorations, or adaptations to a new or different use;
- Delineate what types of transactions are considered "dispositions" of MACRS assets;
- Identify MACRS assets that may be disposed of;
- Define net operating losses;
- Determine the application of NOLs to individuals and different types of entities;
- Understand the tax basics of the U.S. Supreme Court's decision in National Federation of Independent Business, et al. v. Sebelius (2012-2 USTC 50,423), which upheld the Affordable Care Act (except for certain provisions related to the expansion of Medicaid);

- Describe the individual shared responsibility provisions (individual mandate) in the Affordable Care Act;
- Name many possible reforms for corporate, small business, and individual taxation;
- List the proposals currently under debate in Congressional committee as a possible framework for tax reform in 2013 and beyond.

One **complimentary copy** of this course is provided with certain copies of CCH publications. Additional copies of this course may be downloaded from **CCHGroup.com/PrintCPE** or ordered by calling 1-800-248-3248 (ask for product 0-4281-500).

TOP FEDERAL TAX ISSUES FOR 2013 CPE COURSE

Contents

MODULE 1: REPORTING REQUIREMENTS: EXEMPT ORGANIZATIONS/
FOREIGN ASSETS

1 **Exempt Organizations: New Restrictions on Filings, Contributions**
Learning Objectives 1.1
Introduction... 1.1
Form 990 Current Issues 1.2
Form 990-N, E-Postcard Filing 1.7
More Small Tax-Exempts Can File E-Postcard 1.9
EO Select Check Online Tool Available 1.12
Application For Exemption of Qualified Nonprofit
   Health Insurance Issuers................................. 1.14
Charitable Organizations and Medicare
   Shared Service Program Participation...................... 1.15
IRS and Tax Court Crack Down on Charitable
   Conservation Easements 1.21
Conclusion... 1.26

2 **FATCA: Foreign Tax Compliance Requirements**
Learning Objectives 2.1
Introduction... 2.1
Statutory Framework 2.3
FFI Agreements 2.9
Deemed-Compliant FFIs 2.18
FATCA Timeline and Effective Dates......................... 2.22
Withholding... 2.23
Intergovermental Implementation Agreements.................. 2.24
Conclusion... 2.24

MODULE 2: IRS PROCEDURE: PENALTIES/AUDITS/COLLECTIONS

3 **Tax Return Preparer Penalties**
Learning Objectives 3.1
Introduction... 3.1
Code Sec. 6694 Penalties 3.2
Tax Shelters and Reportable Transactions 3.5
Code Sec. 6695 Penalties 3.7
Code Sec. 7216 .... 3.16
Registered Tax Return Preparers 3.18
Mandatory E-File... 3.20
Referral to IRS Office of Professional Responsibility............. 3.23
Conclusion... 3.24

4 **IRS Audits: The Examination Process and New Developments**
Learning Objectives 4.1
Introduction 4.1
The Audit Selection Process 4.2
Types of Audits 4.5
PreContact Responsibilities 4.11
The Examination Process 4.14
Audit Technique Guides 4.20
Appeals 4.22
Parallel Civil Audits and Criminal Investigations 4.24
Conclusion 4.26

5 **Dealing with IRS Collections**
Learning Objectives 5.1
Introduction 5.1
Collection Basics 5.2
Fresh Start Initiative 5.4
Liens and Levies 5.5
Collection Alternatives 5.12
Collection Appeals 5.23
Conclusion 5.27

MODULE 3: BUSINESS: DEPRECIATION/LOSSES

6 **New Repair Regulations**
Learning Objectives 6.1
Introduction 6.1
Basic Rule: Improvements are Capitalized 6.2
Unit of Property 6.3
Betterments as Improvements 6.8
Restorations as Improvements 6.12
Adaptation as Improvement 6.16
Change in Accounting Method 6.16
Routine Maintenance Safe Harbor 6.17
Optional Simplified Method
    For Certain Regulated Taxpayers 6.20
Materials And Supplies 6.20
De Minimis Expensing Rule 6.24
Optional Method For Rotable Spare Parts 6.27
Conclusion 6.30

7 **MACRS Asset Dispositions and General Asset Accounts Rules**
Learning Objectives 7.2
MACRS Dispositions 7.2
MACRS General Asset Accounts 7.10
Accounting Method Changes 7.22
Conclusion 7.25

8 Net Operating Losses

Learning Objectives 8.1
Introduction 8.1
NOL Deductions Defined 8.1
Why Allow Offsets for NOLs? 8.2
Steps in Figuring an NOL 8.3
Uses by Estates and Trusts 8.7
Uses by Partnerships 8.7
NOL Carrybacks/Carryforwards 8.10
Corporate Equity Reduction Limit on NOLs 8.18
Refund Procedures 8.19
Assessments 8.21
Transfers of NOLs 8.21
Built-In Gains and Losses 8.23
Continuity of Business 8.24
Conclusion 8.24

MODULE 4 — CHANGING LEGISLATIVE LANDSCAPE

9 Health Care Reform Moves Forward

Learning Objectives 9.1
Introduction 9.1
Court Challenges to the Affordable Care Act 9.2
Shared Responsibility For Individuals 9.5
Shared Responsibility For Employers 9.8
Code Sec. 36B Premium Assistance Tax Credit 9.11
Code Sec. 45R Small Employer Health Care Credit 9.12
Health Flexible Spending Accounts 9.15
Indoor Tanning Excise Tax 9.18
Branded Prescription Drug Fee 9.19
Medical Device Excise Tax 9.21
New Reporting Requirements 9.23
Conclusion 9.26

10 Tax Reform: Policy and Proposals

Learning Objectives 10.1
Introduction 10.1
Fundamental Tax Reform: The Building Blocks 10.3
Corporate Taxation 10.6
Small Business Taxation 10.12
Individual Taxation 10.15
Conclusion 10.20

Answers to Study Questions 11.1
Index 12.1
CPE Quizzer Instructions 13.1
Quizzer Questions: Module 1 . . . . 13.3
Quizzer Questions: Module 2 . . . . 13.9
Quizzer Questions: Module 3 . . . . 13.17
Quizzer Questions: Module 4 . . . . 13.25
Evaluation Form 13.45

Exempt Organizations: New Restrictions on Filings, Contributions

Changes and modifications in the methods and requirements related to the federal government's oversight of tax-exempt organizations have increased in both scope and frequency lately, with that trend promising to continue into the near future. This chapter provides updates on the recent government oversight with respect to exempt organizations and charitable deductions, with particular focus on several areas in which the IRS has been especially active.

LEARNING OBJECTIVES

Upon completion of this chapter, the reader should be able to:

- Explain the simplified advance ruling process for exempt organizations;
- Describe when and if Schedule K-1 information and Social Security numbers should be reported on Form 990;
- Determine when a small organization can file a Form 990-N;
- Demonstrate how to best search on Exempt Organization Select Check;
- Explain the requirements to become a qualified nonprofit health insurance issuer, and how to participate in a Medicare Shared Savings Program through an accountable care organization; and
- Illustrate some of the important requirements relating to the conservation easement deduction and provide some pointers for drafting and implementing conservation easements that will help bypass IRS scrutiny.

INTRODUCTION

The nonprofit sector continues to grow rapidly despite facing a number of substantial issues, including funding concerns in a weak economy, increasingly complex governance requirements from funding sources, and shifting reporting requirements—all of which increase the difficulty in managing tax-exempt organizations. Concern has continued to grow over the appropriateness of exempt status for some types of organizations, even as Congress has created new types of organizations to help deal with some of society's ills. Moreover, with increasing complexities comes the need for greater transparency. The IRS believes that greater transparency on the exempt organization's annual information return leads to correct reporting.

FORM 990 CURRENT ISSUES

Tax-exempt organizations that are required to file annual returns generally do so on Form 990, *Return of Organization Exempt From Income Tax.* Form 990, which was significantly revised for tax years starting in 2008, is an annual information return for exempt organizations. Form 990 provides financial and governance information, plus describes what the charity does. The form comprises 12 pages, plus 16 separate schedules that may need to be filled out.

For 2011, organizations exempt from income tax under Code Sec. 501(a) may file Form 990-EZ, *Short Form Return of Organization Exempt From Income Tax,* instead of Form 990 if they meet the following requirements:

- Their gross receipts for the year were less than $200,000; or
- Their total assets at the end of the year were less than $500,000.

Final Regulations Implement Redesigned Form 990 and Continue Simplified Application Process

The IRS has issued final regulations to implement the redesigned Form 990 (T.D. 9549). The final regulations generally track earlier proposed regulations, most notably continuing the elimination of the advance ruling process for new Code Sec. 501(c)(3) organizations.

COMMENT

Under the prior regulations, an organization seeking to be recognized by the IRS as a publicly supported charity instead of a private foundation had to complete a two-step process:

1. The organization had to declare that it expected to be publicly supported on an on-going basis.

2. After five years, the organization had to file Form 8734, *Support Schedule for Advance Ruling Period,* showing the IRS that it actually met the public support test.

According to the IRS, approximately 95 percent of the organizations that received advance rulings later received definitive rulings that they were public charities.

Application process. Under the proposed regulations, an organization would be a publicly supported organization (thus qualifying for public charity status) in its first five years if it could show, in its application for exemption, that it could reasonably be expected to receive the requisite public support during such period. The final regulations continue this treatment, eliminating the need for an advance ruling.

Public support test. The proposed regulations changed the computation period for public support from a four-year period composed of the four years prior to the tax year being tested to a five-year period ending with the tax year being tested.

An organization that meets a public support test for a tax year is treated as publicly supported for that tax year and the immediately succeeding tax year. An organization that does not meet a public support test for a tax year may be at risk of being classified as a private foundation as of the first day of the succeeding tax year if the organization also fails to meet a public support test for that succeeding tax year. Because the IRS and the Treasury Department recognized that an organization will not be able to compute its public support for a tax year under the changed computation period until the subsequent tax year, the notice of proposed rulemaking requested comments on specific situations that might warrant relief from the imposition of Chapter 42 excise taxes.

One commentator recommended treating organizations that fail a public support test for two consecutive years as private foundations. The final regulations provide that an organization that fails a public support test for two consecutive tax years will be treated as a private foundation as of the beginning of the second year of failure only for purposes of Code Secs. 507 (termination of private foundation status), 4940 (excise tax based on investment income), and 6033 (information returns of Code Sec. 501 organizations). An organization will be treated as a private foundation for all purposes beginning the first day of the third consecutive tax year.

Accounting method. When an organization computes its public support and reports the information on Form 990, Schedule A, *Public Charity and Public Support,* the proposed regulations required it to use the same accounting method used to keep its books under Code Sec. 446 (general rule for methods of accounting) and that it otherwise uses to report on its Form 990. The final regulations continue this treatment unchanged.

> **COMMENT**
>
> The IRS explained that one of the goals of the redesigned Form 990 is to implement consistent reporting throughout each organization's Form 990 and financial records.

> **COMMENT**
>
> The IRS also did not incorporate suggestions regarding the requirement of a present value calculation for multiyear grants. The IRS stated that the five-year testing period in the regulations should mitigate the impact of recognizing a larger amount of support from one source in a single year.

Reliance. The final regulations allow donors to rely on an organization's determination letter that it is a public charity unless the donor was responsible for, or aware of, any action resulting in the loss of that status.

The final regulations also restore language inadvertently deleted from the proposed regulations giving limited grantor and donor reliance based on a written statement from the grantee organization.

Additionally, the final regulations provide that sponsoring organizations of donor-advised funds, for purposes of Code Sec. 4966 (taxes on taxable distributions), may rely on an IRS determination letter or ruling.

Private foundation status. The final regulations retain the process for terminating private foundation status as described in the proposed regulations. Thus, the final regulations keep a provision requiring terminating private foundations to provide sufficient information to the IRS within 90 days of the end of the 60-month period to enable the IRS to make a determination on public charity status. Also, a terminating private foundation could request an advance ruling regarding its public charity status. The IRS declined to adopt recommendations to simplify the termination process.

COMMENT

The final regulations generally are effective September 8, 2011, and generally apply to tax years beginning on or after January 1, 2008, with transition rules governing the five-year computation period to calculate public support.

Form 990 Complexity Remains

Tax-exempt organizations complained about the difficulty of completing Form 990 at a May 16, 2012, hearing before the House Ways and Means Oversight Subcommittee. Industry officials told Subcommittee Chairman Charles W. Boustany Jr., R-La., that completing Form 990 requires too much detailed, and sometimes redundant, information from hospitals and universities. Cornell University Vice President for Finance Joanne M. DeStefano testified that many universities have to hire outside auditors to oversee their information reporting, and those costs are reducing the resources available for meeting their education mission. DeStefano testified on behalf of the National Association of College and University Business Officers.

Nevertheless, witnesses testified that the IRS has worked well with the nonprofit community to conduct adequate oversight. Diana Aviv, president of the Independent Sector, a trade group representing nonprofit organizations, said the IRS is developing risk models based on data collected from the recently revised Form 990. Moreover, Aviv said, the IRS has reported that tax compliance is higher among organizations that follow the Independent Sector's governance recommendations, including those that have a written mission statement and use comparability data to make compensation decisions.

In the upcoming legislative push for tax reform, Congress should not jeopardize income tax exemption for charitable hospitals or their tax-exempt financing, said Michael J. Regier, senior vice president of Legal and Corporate Affairs, VHA Inc. (formerly the Voluntary Hospitals of America). He said Congress should also protect the deductibility of charitable contributions and bequests for hospital donors. Regier noted that these provisions are used to provide charity care and financial assistance to uninsured and low-income persons, community health improvement services, and research and education.

Schedule K-1 Optional for 2011 990/990-EZ Filers

For tax year 2011 (forms filed in 2012), the IRS announced that it is optional for Form 990 filers to report their interests in the income, expenses, and assets of joint ventures and other partnerships in which they have an ownership interest using information from Form 1065, *U.S. Return of Partnership Income,* Schedule K-1 (Announcement 2012-19). Filers may report their interests based on their own books and records. The same optional treatment is available to filers of Form 990-EZ. The announcement follows up on a posting on the IRS website informing filers about the change.

> **COMMENT**
>
> The IRS explained that the change was made so it could more fully consider the concerns expressed by the filing organizations and so the IRS could determine how best to promote compliance and transparency while minimizing the burden in reporting of partnership interests.

Earlier in 2012, the IRS released revised instructions for the 2011 Form 990 and 2011 Form 990-EZ. Among other changes, the IRS instructed organizations to report their distributive share of assets in joint ventures and investment partnerships, using the ending capital account in the partnership as reported on Schedule K-1, rather than using the amounts from the organization's own books and records.

> **COMMENT**
>
> Schedules K-1 are often received sometime after the Form 990 due date. Of those received prior to the due date, many are subsequently amended by the issuer. As a result, complying with the guidance in the instructions would likely require a filer to extend the initial due date of its Form 990. In addition, it is foreseeable that an organization reporting joint venture information as shown on Schedule K-1 could result in a less meaningful presentation of the organization's financial status than if it were to report the joint venture based upon the organization's books and records.

Now, the IRS is making use of Schedule K-1 optional for Form 990 and Form 990-EZ for the 2011 tax year. In reporting on the 2011 Form 990 or Form 990-EZ its proportionate interests in the income, expenses, and assets of partnerships in which it has an ownership interest, an organization generally may continue to report these interests based on its books and records.

The IRS further noted, however, as in prior years, organizations that complete Form 990, Schedule H, and Form 990, Schedule R, must continue to use information from Form 1065, Schedule K-1, in reporting certain partnership information on those schedules, as explained in the instructions for 2011 Form 990, Schedule H, and 2011 Form 990, Schedule R.

Social Security Numbers

Filers of Form 990 should not enter Social Security numbers (SSNs) anywhere on the form, the IRS has cautioned in a speech to practitioners. The IRS has discovered some Forms 990 with SSNs and cannot redact them before public inspection.

Some Forms 990 have been filed by exempt organizations containing the SSNs of individuals apparently affiliated with the organization. In other cases, Forms 990 have included the SSNs of individuals who received a benefit from the organization, such as a scholarship. The IRS observations were based on a recent outside study that examined Forms 990 filed between 2001 and 2006.

All Forms 990 are open for public inspection and the IRS has no authority to redact these Social Security numbers.

> **COMMENT**
>
> Form 990 was redesigned in 2008 and includes cautions that may minimize this problem.

SSNs of return preparers are also appearing on Forms 990. Return preparers should be using their preparer tax return identification number (PTIN) and not their SSN (NPRM REG-124791-11). The concern here is potential identity theft. The IRS, the National Taxpayer Advocate, and the Treasury Inspector General for Tax Administration (TIGTA) have cautioned that identity theft is a growing problem (IR-2012-13).

> **COMMENT**
>
> The redesign of the Form 990 includes a request for the paid preparer's taxpayer identification number (PTIN) on the form and instructions.

STUDY QUESTION

> **1.** How long is an exempt organization's computation period for the public support test?
>
> **a.** Four years
> **b.** Five years
> **c.** Seven years
> **d.** This requirement was eliminated with the redesign of the Form 990

FORM 990-N, E-POSTCARD FILING

Exempt organizations whose annual gross receipts are $50,000 or less are not required to file a Form 990 or Form 990-EZ. However, for tax periods beginning after 2006, these organizations are required to file a Form 990-N, *Electronic Notice (E-Postcard) for Tax-Exempt Organization Not Required to File Form 990- or 990-EZ (Pension Protection Act of 2006* (P.L. 109-280) (PPA)). The form is due by the 15th day of the fifth month after the close of the organization's tax period (May 15 for calendar year taxpayers).

> **COMMENT**
>
> The original filing threshold of $25,000 was increased to $50,000 for tax years beginning on or after January 1, 2010, by Rev. Proc. 2011-15 (see below).

There is no paper Form 990-N. The IRS developed a simple, Internet-based electronic filing system for the e-postcard, so that organizations should not have buy computers or software to file the form.

> **COMMENT**
>
> Organizations that do not have access to a computer can use equipment at places that provide Internet access to the public, such as a local library, to file.

The form is intended to ensure that donors and the IRS have current information about exempt organizations. The e-postcard requires the following information:

- Employer identification number (EIN), also known as a taxpayer identification number (TIN);
- Tax year;
- Legal name and mailing address;
- Any other names the organization uses;
- Name and address of a principal officer;

- Website address, if the organization has one;
- Confirmation that the organization's annual gross receipts are normally $50,000 or less; and
- If applicable, a statement that the organization has terminated or is terminating (going out of business).

Filing the e-postcard is an affirmative statement by the filing entity that its gross receipts are $50,000 or less. Further, filing an e-postcard does not relieve the entity from any other filing requirements.

COMMENT

These filing requirements do not apply to organizations that are included in a group return, private foundations that must file Form 990-PF, *Return of Private Foundation*, or Section 4947(a)(1) Nonexempt Charitable Trust Treated as a Private Foundation, and supporting organizations that must file Form 990 or Form 990-EZ.

A small organization may choose to file a Form 990 or Form 990-EZ, rather than an e-postcard, but whatever form is used must be filled out completely. The IRS is required to revoke the tax-exempt status of any organization that fails to meet its annual filing requirement (including the Form 990-N) for three consecutive years (Code Sec. 6033(j)).

If a return is not filed by its due date with any extension, or an incomplete return is filed, the IRS may notify the organization in writing and give a fixed time for filing that is generally within 90 days after notice. If the completed return is not then filed by the due date, a penalty is imposed on the person responsible for filing the return in a timely fashion, unless reasonable cause is shown for not filing the return by the final due date.

Incomplete returns are processed using the earliest starting date for the statute of limitations. If designated information is omitted from the Form 990 and attachments, the organization may be penalized for failing to file a return, and the statute of limitations does not begin to run until the information is provided. However, if other nondesignated information is omitted from the return, the organization is penalized for filing an incomplete return, and the statute of limitations generally begins to run on the date the return had been filed.

The IRS has posted a list of organizations that have automatically lost their exempt status on its website (**www.irs.gov/charities/article/0,,id=240099,00.html**). Because the list is an official IRS record of organizations that lost their exempt status for failing to file for three consecutive years, an organization whose exempt status is reinstated remains on the list.

MORE SMALL TAX-EXEMPTS CAN FILE E-POSTCARD

Additional small tax-exempt organizations can file a simple annual information return, the IRS has announced (IR-2011-3, Rev. Proc. 2011-15).

In 2010, the IRS reported that many small tax-exempt organizations had missed the filing deadline for Form 990-N. The agency gave very small nonprofits additional time to file the e-postcard.

> **COMMENT**
>
> It was not a surprise that many very small exempts did not file the e-postcard. For decades, there was never a need to file with the IRS and many individuals advising, working for, or volunteering with very small exempt organizations would not be looking for a change.

The revenue procedure provided guidance on the gross receipts thresholds for filing the Form 990-N. Gross receipts are the total amounts the organization received from all sources during its annual accounting period, without subtracting any costs or expenses. Gross receipts are considered to be $50,000 or less if the organization:

- Has been in existence for one year or less and received, or donors have pledged to give, $75,000 or less during its first tax year;
- Has been in existence between one and three years and averaged $60,000 or less in gross receipts during each of its first two tax years; and
- Is at least three years old and averaged $50,000 or less in gross receipts for the immediately preceding three tax years (including the year for which calculations are being made).

990-N Filing Relief Program

The IRS has updated frequently asked questions on its website about a temporary filing relief program for small tax-exempt organizations and automatic revocation of tax-exempt status. Generally, qualified organizations must file the requisite information returns for the past three years to preserve their tax-exempt status.

> **COMMENT**
>
> If an organization's exempt status is automatically revoked, the organization could request reinstatement of its exemption retroactive to the date of revocation. The organization must show reasonable cause why it failed to file for three consecutive years.

Many small tax-exempt entities missed the May 17, 2010, filing deadline and risked automatic revocation of their tax-exempt status. The filing requirement has been in effect since the beginning of 2007, which made 2009 the third consecutive year under the new law. Any organization that failed to file for three consecutive years automatically lost its federal tax-exempt status. Form 990-series information returns are due on the 15th day of the fifth month after an organization's fiscal year ends. Many organizations use the calendar year as their fiscal year, which made May 15 the deadline for those tax-exempt organizations. May 15 fell on a Saturday in 2010, so the deadline was actually Monday, May 17.

The IRS responded with a one-time initiative to bring them into compliance. The IRS provided two types of relief to qualified organizations:

- A filing extension for tax-exempt entities required to file Form 990-N; and
- A voluntary compliance program (VCP) for small organizations eligible to file Form 990-EZ.

COMMENT

Under the filing relief program for Form 990-N filers, an organization may file Form 990 in lieu of the Form 990-N (for example, to satisfy state filing requirements), as long as the return was completed and filed by October 15, 2010.

IRS Appropriately Identified Organizations Whose Tax-Exempt Status Was Automatically Revoked

On June 8, 2011, the IRS appropriately identified 279,500 tax-exempt organizations that did not file a return or notice for three consecutive years, according to a report by the Treasury Inspector General for Tax Administration (TIGTA) *(TIGTA Report: Appropriate Actions Were Taken to Identify Thousands of Organizations Whose Tax-Exempt Status Had Been Automatically Revoked, but Improvements Are Needed (Reference Number: 2012-10-027))*. However, auditors determined that programming changes were incomplete and did not identify more than 15,000 organizations that failed to file for three consecutive years. As a result, these organizations were not informed that their tax-exempt status had been automatically revoked.

PPA requires the IRS to maintain a list of organizations whose tax-exempt status has been automatically revoked for failing to file a return or notice for three consecutive years. TIGTA reviewed the IRS's readiness for and implementation of the automatic revocation provisions of the PPA.

TIGTA found that the IRS performed extensive outreach and took actions to prepare for the automatic revocations In addition, TIGTA determined that improvements were needed to:

- Provide better guidance to organizations when their tax-exempt status is automatically revoked if they believe it was revoked in error or are looking for how to reapply for retroactive reinstatement; and
- Ensure accurate information is posted to the IRS's taxpayer database.

> **COMMENT**
>
> If an organization has had its tax-exempt status automatically revoked and seeks to have its exempt status reinstated, it must file an application for exemption and pay the appropriate user fee. Certain small organizations applying for reinstatement before December 31, 2012, could qualify for a reduced user fee and retroactive reinstatement of exempt status (Notice 2011-43).
>
> Since June 2011, 435,000 organizations have had their exempt status automatically revoked, according to Lois Lerner, Director, EO Division, TE/GE, IRS. She spoke at the American Bar Association's Section of Taxation May Meeting on May 11, 2012. Roughly 17,000 of these organizations have applied for retroactive reinstatement. The small number of organizations seeking retroactive reinstatement could indicate that many of the organizations are no longer in existence.

Throughout the review, TIGTA raised issues and the IRS took actions to address them. Specifically, computer programming issues were corrected; guidance provided on an IRS website was updated; and changes were made to an electronic filing website to reduce inaccurate address updates. In addition, TIGTA made three recommendations concerning programming changes and better guidance in the revocation notice.

> **COMMENT**
>
> The tax-exempt status of an organization is very important to its existence, stated Treasury Inspector General for Tax Administration J. Russell George. "The IRS must ensure it makes the correct call. I am pleased that, in general, the IRS is accurately identifying organizations whose tax-exempt status has been revoked. While we have identified some areas for improvement, the IRS is overall, getting the job done," added George in a May 3 press release.

IRS management agreed with the recommendations and has already taken corrective actions. Two work requests have been submitted to change the programming to more accurately identify organizations that did not file and to ensure accuracy in the accounts of tax-exempt organizations.

STUDY QUESTION

2. Which of the following information items is *not* on the Form 990-N (e-postcard)?

   a. Statement of charitable purpose
   b. Website address
   c. Address of principal officer
   d. Other names used by the organization

EO SELECT CHECK ONLINE TOOL AVAILABLE

Exempt Organizations Select Check is an online search tool that allows users to select an exempt organization and check certain information about its federal tax status and filings (IR-2012-34). It consolidates three former search sites into one. The site:

- Provides expanded search capability and a more efficient way to search for organizations that are eligible to receive tax-deductible charitable contributions (Publication 78 data);
- Shows organizations that have had their tax-exempt status automatically revoked because they have not filed Form 990 series returns or notices annually as required for three consecutive years (Auto-Revocation List); and
- Discloses organizations that have filed a Form 990-N annual electronic notice (e-postcard).

Each list must be searched separately. Users can look for organizations eligible to receive deductible charitable organizations by employer identification number (EIN), which was not possible previously. Further, the Auto-Revocation list may now be searched by EIN, name, city, state, ZIP code, country, exemption type, and revocation posting date, rather only by state.

The EO Select Check data is generally updated monthly for automatically revoked organizations and organizations eligible to receive deductible contributions, and weekly for Form 990-N (e-postcard) filings.

In addition to searching for a particular organization, users may download a complete list of each of the databases through Exempt Organizations Select Check.

The EO Select Check contains search tips that offer suggestions on how to use the search application. These tips include:

- Avoid common words such as *the* or *foundation*;
- Searching for less information may produce better results than searching for a lot of information. If the search is not producing good results, search using fewer terms or fields and then sort the results to pinpoint the result needed. For example, an individual can focus search results by sorting by city, state, or ZIP code;
- If conducting a series of searches in succession, clear the search screen after each one;
- If an organization is listed on the Auto-Revocation List, an individual can search organizations eligible to receive tax-deductible contributions (Pub. 78 data) to see whether its tax exemption has been reinstated; and
- Due to the different structure of foreign addresses, data is sometimes found in an unexpected location. For example, the province or country in which the organization is located is sometimes in the City field in the Auto-Revocation database. Thus, if you are not obtaining expected results, try searching for information in a different way.

The new tool can be found at **www.irs.gov/charities/article/0,,id=249767,00. html**.

Exempt Status Is Reinstated

On its website, the IRS addressed a situation in which an organization's tax-exempt status was reinstated, but that information was not in Exempt Organizations Select Check (Pub. 78 Data) or the Exempt Organizations Business Master File extract (EO BMF). The IRS Business Master File lists and contains descriptive information for all active organizations that have registered for tax-exempt status with the IRS.

The IRS replied that although Select Check has been a major improvement in its search function, there still will be a delay between the time the organization is reinstated (or receives its initial exemption determination) and the time it shows up on Select Check and EO BMF.

Select Check and EO BMF information is drawn from the IRS Master File. Once a month a computer program automatically pulls updated data from the Master File and transfers it to Select Check and EO BMF. Therefore, if an organization's record was updated in the Master File prior to the date the program is run, that information will appear in that month's update of Select Check and EO BMF. If, on the other hand, the organization's information is updated in the Master File after the date the program is run, that information won't be included in Select Check and EO BMF until the following month's update.

Between updates to Select Check and EO BMF, donors can rely on the organization's determination letter from the IRS as proof of exempt status. Even if the organization remains on the list of automatically revoked organizations, donors can rely on an IRS determination letter dated on or after the effective revocation date. Donors also can confirm an organization's status by calling the IRS (toll-free) at 877–829–5500.

STUDY QUESTION

3. What information is *not* part of Exempt Organization Select Check?

a. Exempt organizations that have been revoked
b. Organizations that have filed Form 990-N
c. Organizations that have applied for recognition of exempt status
d. Effective revocation date of the organization's exempt status

APPLICATION FOR EXEMPTION OF QUALIFIED NONPROFIT HEALTH INSURANCE ISSUERS

The IRS has issued temporary and proposed regulations under Code Sec. 501(c)(29) authorizing the IRS to prescribe the procedures by which qualified nonprofit health insurance issuers (QNHII) that participate in the consumer-operated and oriented plan (CO-OP) Program established by the Centers for Medicare and Medicaid Services (CMS) may seek exemption from federal income tax (T.D. 9574, NPRM REG-135071-11). Code Sec. 501(c)(29) was added to the tax code by the *Patient Protection and Affordable Care Act* (P.L. 111-148).

Code Sec. 501(c)(29)(B)(i) provides that a QNHII that has received a loan through the CO-OP program generally may be recognized as exempt from taxation under Code Sec. 501(a) only if the QNHII gives notice to the IRS that it is applying for recognition as a *Section 501(c)(29) organization*. The temporary regulations provide that the IRS may issue procedures that a QNHII seeking such recognition must follow. The temporary regulations also expressly authorize the IRS to recognize a QNHII as exempt effective as of a date prior to the date of its application. However, the application must be submitted in the manner and within the time prescribed by the regulations, and the QNHII's prior purposes and activities met the requirements for exempt status under Code Sec. 501(c)(29).

Guidance on Determination Letters

The IRS has provided guidance setting forth the procedures for issuing determination letters and rulings on the exempt status of qualified nonprofit health insurance issuers described in Code Sec. 501(c)(29) (Rev. Proc.

2012-11). The *Patient Protection and Affordable Care Act* (P.L. 111-148) (PPACA) directs the CMS to establish the CO-OP Program, the purpose of which is to foster the creation of member-governed QNHIIs that will operate with a consumer focus. CMS provides loans to organizations applying to become QNHIIs.

Under Code Sec. 501(c)(29), a QNHII that has received a CO-OP loan may be recognized as exempt from taxation under Code Sec. 501(a) for the period during which it is in compliance with Code Sec. 1322. The QNHII, in order to qualify for tax exemption, must also meet additional requirements. The IRS is authorized to prescribe procedures by which QNHIIs may apply for recognition as exempt. In addition to the new guidance, QNHIIs seeking exemption should also follow Rev. Proc. 2012-9 (or its successor) and may find information on user fees in Rev. Proc. 2012-8.

A QNHII seeking recognition of exemption must submit a letter application along with Form 8718, *User Fee for Exempt Organization Determination Letter Request.* The application must be signed under penalty of perjury and must include:

- The QNHII's employer identification number;
- A statement of receipts and expenditures and a balance sheet for the current year and the three preceding years;
- A detailed narrative statement of the QNHII's past and proposed activities, as well as of the QNHII's actual and anticipated receipts and contemplated expenditures;
- A copy of the QNHII's organizing document;
- A copy of the current bylaws;
- A copy of the award notice issued by CMS and the fully executed loan agreement with CMS;
- A number of other representations;
- A subject line with "SECTION 501(c)(29) CO-OP HEALTH INSURANCE ISSUER" in bold, underlined, and/or all uppercase font; and
- The correct user fee.

CHARITABLE ORGANIZATIONS AND MEDICARE SHARED SERVICE PROGRAM PARTICIPATION

The IRS has released a fact sheet that provides additional information for charitable organizations that may want to participate in the Medicare Shared Savings Program (MSSP) and confirms that Notice 2011-20 continues to reflect IRS expectations regarding the MSSP and accountable care organizations (ACOs) (FS-2011-11). The fact sheet is the most recent IRS guidance in the area.

The guidance may apply to Code Sec. 501(c)(3) tax-exempt organizations, such as charitable hospitals, that participate in the MSSP through ACOs.

Type of Legal Entity

An ACO may be structured as a particular type of legal entity (for example, a corporation or partnership) to participate in the MSSP. The CMS final regulations do not require an ACO to be any particular type of legal entity. The CMS final regulations generally require an ACO to be organized as a legal entity separate from its participants. However, a single, clinically-integrated organization—for example, a hospital employing physicians—may qualify as an ACO under the Shared Savings Program. The tax consequences for the ACO and its tax-exempt participants will vary depending on the type of entity.

Consequences for Tax-Exempt Participants

An ACO structured as a corporation for federal tax purposes generally will be treated as a separate taxable entity from its participants.

If an ACO is structured as a partnership for federal tax purposes, its activities will generally be attributed to its partners. An ACO structured as an LLC generally may choose to be treated as a corporation, a partnership, or an entity that is disregarded for tax purposes.

Charitable Organization Participation

A charitable organization can participate in the Shared Savings Program through an ACO. If charitable organizations participate in the Shared Savings Program through an ACO along with private parties, the charitable organization must be sure that it continues to meet the requirements for tax exemption to avoid adverse tax consequences. For example, its participation must not result in:

- Its net earnings inuring to the benefit of private shareholders or individuals; and
- Its being operated for the benefit of private parties participating in the ACO.

The IRS determines whether prohibited inurement or impermissible private benefit has occurred based on all the facts and circumstances.

Activities Unrelated to the Shared Savings Program

In some circumstances, an ACO can conduct activities unrelated to the Shared Savings Program (non-Shared Savings Program activities) without jeopardizing the status of its tax-exempt participants. An ACO's conduct of non-Shared Savings Program activities may jeopardize the status of a tax-exempt participant. This determination is analyzed under the general tax rules applicable to charitable organizations and depends on all of the facts and circumstances. Some facts and circumstances to be considered include whether the non-Shared Savings Program activities:

- Further an exempt purpose described in Section 501(c)(3) (charitable purpose);
- Are attributed to the tax-exempt participant; or
- Represent an insubstantial part of the participant's total activities; and
- Do not result in inurement of the tax-exempt participant's net earnings or in the participant conferring impermissible private benefit.

Furthering Charitable Purpose

In some circumstances the IRS recognizes that an ACO's non-Shared Savings Program activities can further a charitable purpose. For example, an ACO's activities related to serving Medicaid or indigent populations might further the charitable purpose of relieving the poor and distressed or the underprivileged. However, if an ACO is treated as a partnership, the ACO and its tax-exempt participants should consult IRS guidance regarding joint ventures—specifically, Rev. Rul. 2004-51 and Rev. Rul. 98-15—for examples of partnerships conducting activities that further a charitable purpose of a tax-exempt participant.

Unrelated Business Income

An ACO's non-Shared Savings Program activities, when approved, will also not always generate unrelated business income (UBI) for its tax-exempt participants. The IRS recognizes that certain non-Shared Savings Program activities may be substantially related to the exercise or performance of a charitable purpose.

Generally, non-Shared Savings Program activities that are substantially related to a tax-exempt participant's charitable purposes will not generate UBI for that participant. Tax-exempt participants in ACOs treated as partnerships should consult IRS guidance regarding joint ventures and UBI.

Whether an ACO's activities not substantially related to a charitable purpose will generate UBI for their tax-exempt participants depend on various factors. For example, certain kinds of income from the ACO, including dividends and interest, may be excluded from UBI under one of the modifications described in Code Sec. 512(b) (for example, dividends, interest, and royalties). Therefore, if an ACO pays a charitable organization royalties, these payments will not be considered unrelated business income.

In addition, if the ACO is treated as a partnership, whether a tax-exempt partner of the ACO will have to include its share of income derived from an activity in UBI will depend on a variety factors. These factors include whether:

- The activity constitutes a trade or business;
- Is regularly carried on; or
- Is specifically excluded from the definition of an unrelated trade or business under Code Sec. 513.

Tax Status of ACOs

An ACO engaged exclusively in Shared Savings Program activities can qualify for tax exemption under Code Sec. 501(c)(3), provided that it meets all of the requirements for tax exemption under Code Sec. 501(c)(3).

One requirement for tax exemption in general is that the organization engages exclusively in activities that accomplish one or more charitable purposes. As noted in Notice 2011-20, the IRS expects that Shared Savings Program activities generally will further the charitable purpose of lessening the burdens of government (Reg. § 1.501(c)(3)-1(d)(2)). Thus, an ACO engaged exclusively in Shared Savings Program activities could qualify for tax exemption under Code Sec. 501(c)(3), as long as the ACO also meets all of the other requirements for tax exemption under that section.

> **COMMENT**
>
> An ACO that is treated as a partnership or is disregarded for federal tax purposes is not eligible to apply for tax-exempt status under Code Sec. 501(c)(3). Therefore, ACOs that want to apply for exempt status should be formed as corporations.

In addition, an ACO engaged in both Shared Savings Program and non-Shared Savings Program activities can qualify for tax exemption under Code Sec. 501(c)(3), provided it engages exclusively in activities that accomplish one or more charitable purposes and meets all of the other requirements for tax exemption under Code Sec. 501(c)(3).

The IRS recognizes that certain non-Shared Savings Program activities conducted by an ACO may further a charitable purpose.

Electronic Health Records Technology

Fact Sheet 2011-11 explains that a 2007 IRS memorandum relating to electronic health records (EHRs) applies to a charitable organization participating in the Shared Savings Program through an ACO.

A May 2007 Memorandum from the Director of Exempt Organizations to the Directors of EO Examinations and EO Rulings and Agreements (**www.irs.gov/pub/irs-tege/ehr_qa_062007.pdf**) states that the IRS will not treat the benefits a hospital provides to its medical staff physicians as inurement or impermissible private benefit if:

- The benefits fall within the range of EHR software and technical support services ("Health IT Items and Services") that are permissible under regulations issued by the U.S. Department of Health and Human Services;
- The hospital ensures that the Health IT Items and Services are available to all of its medical staff physicians; and
- The hospital provides the same level of subsidy to all of its medical staff physicians or varies the level of subsidy by applying criteria related to meeting the healthcare needs of the community.

EXAMPLE

Best Care Hospital develops Personal Health Login software so that patients can log on to view their own records and see the trend of lab results from the last year. If the hospital provides this software to its physicians, the IRS will not consider it inurement or an impermissible private benefit.

The IRS will continue to follow the memorandum with respect to all hospitals described in Section 501(c)(3), including those participating in an ACO.

STUDY QUESTION

4. If an ACO pays a charitable organization royalties, these payments will:

    a. Not be considered unrelated business income
    b. Be treated as taxable at the dividends and interest tax rate
    c. Be taxable because charitable organizations are ineligible to receive royalties
    d. Be taxable as unrelated business income, unless they accrue from conduct of the organization's primary charitable purpose

Proposed Reliance Regulations Illustrate Program-Related Investments

Recently released proposed regulations provide new examples illustrating investments that qualify as program-related investments (PRIs) under the private foundation rules (NPRM REG-144267-11, April 19, 2012). The charitable activities described in the new examples are based on published guidance and on financial structures described in private letter rulings.

> **COMMENT**
>
> The proposed regulations do not make any changes in the rules but add examples, which private foundations had requested. Some foundations were hesitating to use PRIs because the existing regulations had not been updated in 40 years.

Background. Code Sec. 4944(a) imposes an excise tax on a private foundation that makes an investment that jeopardizes the carrying out of any of the private foundation's exempt purposes. Foundation managers who knowingly participate in the making of a jeopardizing investment are also liable for the tax. Moreover, Code Sec. 4944(b) imposes additional excise taxes on private foundations and foundation managers when investments are not timely removed from jeopardy.

A PRI is not considered a jeopardy investment. A PRI is an investment whose primary purpose is to accomplish a charitable, religious, scientific, or other qualified purpose (even if the purposes are carried out by noncharitable organizations) with no significant purpose either to produce income or capital appreciation or to accomplish legislative or political activity. The IRS issued regulations with examples of PRIs in 1972.

Proposed regulations. The new examples reflect current investment practices, the IRS explained. They illustrate that:

- An activity conducted in a foreign country furthers a charitable purpose if the same activity would further a charitable purpose if conducted in the United States;
- The charitable purposes served by a PRI are not limited to situations involving economically disadvantaged individuals and deteriorated urban areas;
- The recipients of PRIs need not be within a charitable class if they are the instruments for furthering a charitable purpose;
- A potentially high rate of return does not automatically prevent an investment from qualifying as program-related;
- PRIs can be achieved through a variety of investments, including loans to individuals, tax-exempt organizations and for-profit organizations, and equity investments in for-profit organizations;
- A credit enhancement arrangement may qualify as a PRI; and

- A private foundation's acceptance of an equity position in conjunction with making a loan does not necessarily prevent the investment from qualifying as a PRI.

The new examples show that a PRI may accomplish a variety of charitable purposes, such as advancing science, combating environmental deterioration, and promoting the arts. The examples also demonstrate that an investment that funds activities in one or more foreign countries, including investments that alleviate the impact of a natural disaster or that fund educational programs, may further the accomplishment of charitable purposes and qualify as a PRI.

> **COMMENT**
>
> Taxpayers may rely on the examples before the proposed regulations are finalized.

STUDY QUESTION

5. Which of the following applies to the new program-related investment examples?
   a. The PRI examples do not reflect investment options that are used in today's market
   b. The examples replace old examples that had not been updated in 40 years
   c. The examples show that PRI can have a high rate of return
   d. The examples illustrate how a PRI often is a jeopardy investment undertaken to maximize returns

IRS AND TAX COURT CRACK DOWN ON CHARITABLE CONSERVATION EASEMENTS

The Tax Court is currently facing more than 200 cases on its docket relating to the popular charitable conservation easement deduction, which was established to offset certain costs and losses associated with preserving property of historical, educational, or other public value. The increasing use (and often abuse) of the deduction by some taxpayers, however, has caused the IRS and Tax Court to heighten their scrutiny of charitable tax deductions for contributions of conservation easements. The Tax Court has controversially upheld deductions claimed for contributions of property that arguably benefit mostly high-income taxpayers.

Background

Under Code Sec. 170(h) a *qualified conservation contribution* for conservation easements is defined as a contribution of a qualified real property interest to a qualified organization exclusively for conservation purposes. A *qualified real property interest* is defined as:

- The entire interest of the donor other than a qualified mineral interest;
- A remainder interest; and
- A restriction granted in perpetuity on the use that may be made of the real property.

COMMENT

Code Sec. 170(h) provides for a charitable contribution made during the tax year, which generally is not available to contributions of partial property interests. Conservation easements are in effect partial interests in property. However, charitable "qualified conservation contributions" to qualified organizations are excepted from this general rule against contributions of partial property interests under Code Sec. 170(f)(3)(B)(iii).

A qualified conservation contribution must fulfill one of four conservation purposes. These include:

- The preservation of land areas for outdoor recreation by, or for the education of, the general public;
- The protection of a relatively natural habitat of fish, wildlife, or plants, or similar ecosystem;
- The preservation of open space where such preservation will yield a significant public benefit and is either for the scenic enjoyment of the general public or pursuant to a clearly delineated federal, state, or local governmental conservation policy; and
- The preservation of a historically important land area or certified historic structure.

Policy Debate

As of January 1, 2012, the conservation deduction is limited to 30 percent of a donor's adjusted gross income (AGI), a decrease from the enhanced 50-percent AGI deduction in effect from 2006 until the end of 2011. The enhanced deduction was first written into law in 2006 as part of the *Pension Protection Act of 2006* (P.L. 109-280). The provision was scheduled to end in 2008 but has been extended multiple times. The enhanced deduction had resulted in an increase of donations.

Critics of the deduction recognize that conservation easements represent an important public value for preservation, but argue that the costs far outweighed the benefits. They cite $3.8 billion in federal revenue loss between 2003 and 2008 because of the deduction, along with $10 billion lost in development opportunities. Other costs include reputational costs and the transactional costs of administering the deduction.

At the same time, the benefits derived from charitable contributions of conservation easements are largely unquantifiable.

Tax Court Cases

As of May 2012, about 216 conservation easement cases have been docketed with the Tax Court. In recent years, the Tax Court rulings reflected a more sophisticated approach to deductions for charitable conservations easements than previously. The IRS is winning the cases for the most part.

> **COMMENT**
>
> The IRS had won all of the Tax Court cases on conservation easement deduction cases since the beginning of 2012 (*K.M. Carpenter*, TC Memo. 2012-1; *M.J. Cohan*, TC Memo. 2012-8; *Esgar Corp.* TC Memo. 2012-35; *J.E. Butler*, TC Memo. 2012-72; *L. Dunlap*, TC Memo. 2012-126, and *R.L. Mitchell*, 138 TC No. 16).

Golf courses. Although it has become stricter in accepting historical façade and other common types of conservation easements, the Tax Court has been perceived as showing leniency for conservation easements on land that is or is intended to be used as a golf course as the result of the outcome of several cases.

Meanwhile, the supposedly favorable Tax Court treatment of conservation easements for golf courses has become a point of contention among legislators. Although on the one hand conservation easements may preserve large tracts of land, they can also be used to reap unfair tax benefits for high-income taxpayers, particularly where golf courses surrounded by luxury housing developments are concerned. In February 2012, President Obama announced in his fiscal year (FY) 2013 budget that he would pursue an amendment to the charitable contribution deduction provision that would prohibit a deduction for any contribution of property that is, or is intended to be, used as a golf course.

> **COMMENT**
>
> The president's FY 2013 budget reports that:
>
> These contributions have raised concerns both that the deduction amounts claimed for such easements (often by the developers of the private home sites) are excessive, and also that the conservation easement deduction is not narrowly tailored to promote only bona fide conservation activities, as opposed to the private interests of donors.... Easements on golf courses are particularly susceptible to overvaluation...because of the difficulty determining both the value of the easement and the value of the return benefits provided to the donor—including indirect benefits, such as the increase in the value of home sites surrounding the golf course.

Substantiation requirements. Substantiation issues are common means through which courts will disallow tax deductions. They are simpler to rule on than valuation of fair market value and benefits. And because the charitable contributions of conservation easements are so often subject to abuse (for example, the façade easement), courts are more apt to be suspicious and to disallow deductions based on faulty Forms 8283, Noncash Charitable Contributions; lack of or an insufficient contemporaneous written acknowledgments of contributions; and nonqualifying appraisals.

> **PLANNING POINTER**
>
> In drafting their documents, potential donors should hire attorneys, specialists, and accountants experienced in the area of conservation easements.

Using experts may result in a considerable expense for taxpayers. However, such costs could be itemized as a miscellaneous deduction. The IRS may soon finalize its proposed regulations for qualified appraisers, providing more certainty in this complicated area.

In an area governed by nearly 100 pages of regulations and in which many IRS agents who review the deduction may not have extensive experience with conservation easements, however, it is clearly important to provide as much information on the contributed property as possible and in an upfront manner.

Other drafting recommendations include:

- Form 8283 should be properly completed and accompanied by a detailed baseline report;
- A copy of the conservation easement deed describing the property should be attached, as should the contemporaneous written acknowledgment letter from the donee (because the deduction for charitable contributions conservation easements is, in essence, another layer of the deduction for noncash charitable contributions, conservation easement donors

are subject to the requirement that they provide a contemporaneous written acknowledgment of their contribution); and

- The letters, as with all noncash donations of more than $250, should state whether the donee provided any goods or services in consideration for the contribution, and if so, the value of those goods or services.

Valuation

Finding good, qualified appraisers is important for donors who do not want their contribution deductions challenged. In nearly every case, overvaluation is an issue; the IRS has seen many problems with improper or inflated appraisals of the fair market value of donated property.

Generally, if the claimed deduction for an item or group of similar items of donated property is more than $5,000, the donor must get a qualified appraisal made by a qualified appraiser.

A *qualified appraisal* is an appraisal document that:

- Is made, signed, and dated by a qualified appraiser (defined later) in accordance with generally accepted appraisal standards;
- Meets the relevant requirements of Reg. § 1.170A-13(c)(3) and Notice 2006-96;
- Relates to an appraisal made not earlier than 60 days before the date of contribution of the appraised property;
- Does not involve a prohibited appraisal fee; and
- Includes certain information (for example, description of the property, date of contribution, etc.).

A qualified appraiser with local expertise is generally recommended because of the local comparables required to substantiate the valuation. Even if an appraiser arrives at the correct amount and fulfills every requirement, if he or she is not qualified, the deduction would not be allowed.

A *qualified appraiser* is an individual who meets all the following requirements:

- The individual either:
  - Has earned an appraisal designation from a recognized professional appraiser organization for demonstrated competency in valuing the type of property being appraised, or
  - Has met certain minimum education and experience requirements. For real property, the appraiser must be licensed or certified for the type of property being appraised in the state in which the property is located. For property other than real property, the appraiser must have successfully completed college or professional-level coursework relevant to the property being valued, must have at least two years of experience in the trade or business of buying, selling, or valuing

the type of property being valued, and must fully describe in the appraisal his or her qualifying education and experience;

- The individual regularly prepares appraisals for which he or she is paid;
- The individual demonstrates verifiable education and experience in valuing the type of property being appraised. To do this, the appraiser can make a declaration in the appraisal that, because of his or her background, experience, education, and membership in professional associations, he or she is qualified to make appraisals of the type of property being valued; and
- The individual has not been prohibited from practicing before the IRS under Section 330(c) of Title 31 of the United States Code at any time during the three-year period ending on the date of the appraisal.
- The individual is not an excluded individual.

STUDY QUESTION

6. Which of the following is *not* a requirement of a qualified appraiser?

   a. He or she must be a member of Appraisers Association of America
   b. He or she must regularly prepares paid appraisals
   c. He or she must be eligible to practice before the IRS
   d. He or she must have both education and experience in valuing the type of property being appraised

CONCLUSION

The IRS is responsible for ensuring that organizations are not abusing the tax exemptions, but it is also responsible for providing exempt organizations with clear guidance and details regarding the specific compliance requirements each of the many varieties of exempt organization must follow. Legislative changes to the tax code provisions keep the IRS busy on one hand, whereas ever-inventive individuals and organizations challenge the IRS oversight abilities on the other hand. As a result, constant attention to change is essential for any practitioner in the exempt organizations area.

FATCA: Foreign Tax Compliance Requirements

As part of what seems an ever-expanding effort to close the "tax gap," Congress and the Internal Revenue Service continue to extend the information reporting requirements, both at home and abroad. With an estimated $395 billion falling into the gap every year, it is easy to understand why. By being able to locate and collect excess monies already owed, Congress can, in effect, increase revenues without having to deal with the messy politics of tax hikes. Information reporting is useful to the IRS, meanwhile, because collecting such data provides the agency with the ability to match what is reported by one taxpayer with that provided by another and pounce upon discrepancies. As a result, these efforts are likely to expand even further. In keeping with this trend, this chapter examines the far-reaching information-reporting requirements imposed by the *Foreign Account Tax Compliance Act* (FATCA).

LEARNING OBJECTIVES

Upon completion of this chapter, you will be able to:

- Understand the rationale behind Congress and the IRS' ongoing efforts to expand information reporting, both at home and abroad;
- Identify foreign financial and other institutions affected by FATCA;
- Articulate the obligations placed upon domestic and foreign withholding agents by the new rules;
- Understand the requirements and significance of foreign financial institution agreements, as well as the consequences both of entering into such an agreement and the failure of so doing;
- Relate key provisions of the due diligence, verification, reporting, and withholding requirements required of participating foreign financial institutions going forward;
- Articulate what membership in an expanded affiliate group means with respect to the new requirements;
- Identify the categories qualifying for deemed-compliant status; and
- Discuss the implementation timeline for the new provisions.

INTRODUCTION

FATCA, enacted as part of the *Hiring Incentives to Restore Employment Act of 2010* (hereafter the HIRE Act), was designed to prevent tax evasion by U.S. citizens and residents via the use of offshore accounts.

FATCA attempts to accomplishes this goal in two ways: (1) requiring U.S. taxpayers to disclose on a separate form (Form 8938, *Statement of Specified Foreign Financial Assets*) attached to their annual income tax return any interest in specified foreign assets that in the aggregate exceeds $50,000; and (2) effectively requiring foreign financial institutions through withholding and information reporting rules to identify for the IRS those U.S. taxpayer that may not self-disclose foreign assets. This chapter focuses on the second method, which involves foreign financial institutions.

FATCA takes direct aim at foreign financial institutions (FFIs) and other financial intermediaries that either knowingly or unknowingly might facilitate offshore tax evasion. FATCA has done so by adding a new Chapter 4 to the tax code. Specifically, in a significant extension of long-arm jurisdiction, Congress has, via Chapter 4:

- Extended the scope of the U.S. information-reporting regime to reach foreign financial institutions (FFIs) that maintain U.S. accounts;
- Imposed increased disclosure obligations on certain nonfinancial foreign entities (NFFEs) deemed to present a high risk of U.S. tax avoidance; and
- Provided for withholding tax on those FFIs and NFFEs that fail to comply with the reporting and other requirements of Chapter 4.

This withholding may generally be credited against the U.S. income tax liability of the beneficial owner of the payment to which the withholding is attributable and generally may be refunded to the extent the withholding exceeds such liability. An FFI that does not comply with the requirements of Code Sec. 1471(b), however, and that beneficially owns the payment from which tax is withheld under Chapter 4, may not receive a credit or refund of such tax except to the extent required by a treaty obligation of the United States.

COMMENT

Under FACTA, taxpayers who hold any interest in specified foreign financial assets during the tax year must attach to their income tax returns for the year, using Form 8938, certain information with respect to each asset if the aggregate value of all the assets exceeds $50,000. A specified foreign financial asset includes: any depository, custodial, or other financial account maintained by a foreign financial institution, and certain assets issued by other than a U.S. person, such as stock or securities, as well as any interest in a foreign entity.

> **NOTE**
>
> U.S. persons also must generally disclose any account in which they have a financial interest or as to which they have signature or other authority on Form TD F 90-22.1, Report of Foreign Bank and Financial Accounts, (the FBAR). Although the nature of the information required to be disclosed in Form 8938 is similar to the information disclosed on an FBAR, it is not identical and compliance with one does not fulfill reporting under the other. The FBAR must be filed by June 30 of the year following the year in which a $10,000 filing threshold is met. Although the nature of the information required to be disclosed on Form 8938 is similar to the information disclosed on an FBAR, it is not identical and compliance with one does not fulfill the reporting obligation under the other.

STATUTORY FRAMEWORK

FATCA obligates any withholding agent to withhold 30 percent of any "withholdable payment" made to an FFI unless the FFI meets certain requirements. These requirements will be met if the FFI either:

- Enters into an agreement (an FFI agreement) with the IRS in which it agrees to identify its U.S. accounts and comply with certain verification and due diligence requirements; or
- Meets requirements prescribed by the Treasury Department and the IRS deemed to comply with the requirements of the new law.

> **COMMENT**
>
> FFIs that meet these requirements are termed *participating FFIs*, whereas those that do not are referred to as *nonparticipating FFIs*.

> **COMMENT**
>
> FATCA's mandates are stringent, requiring any person who, in any capacity, has control, receipt, disposal, or payment of any withholdable payment to apply the 30 percent withholding.

> **COMMENT**
>
> Participating FFIs and grantor trusts are specifically included within the definition of withholding agent, whereas individuals making payments not in the ordinary course of business are specifically excluded.

Foreign Financial Institution

FATCA's broad definition of *foreign financial institution* includes virtually any foreign institution, other than a financial institution organized under the laws of a possession of the United States, engaged in financial activity of any sort, including:

- Any deposit-accepting entity ordinarily engaged in the business of banking;
- Any entity that, as a substantial portion of its business, holds financial assets on account for others; and
- Any entity engaged primarily in the business of investing, reinvesting, or trading in securities, partnership interests, commodities, or derivatives of any of these.

Nonfinancial Foreign Entities

FATCA defines a *nonfinancial foreign entity* as any foreign entity that is not a financial institution, as delineated above. These entities nevertheless will also be subject to the 30 percent withholding requirement unless the entity (or another nonfinancial foreign entity that is the beneficial owner of the payment) provides the withholding agent with a certification that the beneficial owner does not have any "substantial United States owners" or, if it does, each owner's name, address, and tax identification number (TIN).

COMMENT

In general, a *substantial United States owner* is a U.S. person who owns, directly or indirectly:

- More than 10 percent of the stock of a corporation, by vote or value; or
- More than 10 percent of the capital or profits interest of a partnership.

However, in the case of a financial institution that is engaged primarily in the business of investing, reinvesting, or trading in securities, or the like—including, notably, hedge or equity funds—any United States person with *any* interest is a substantial United States person.

Withholdable Payments

To trigger the FATCA requirements, the payment must be a *withholdable payment,* defined to mean, subject to certain exceptions:

- Any payment of interest, dividends, rents, salaries, wages, premiums, annuities, compensations, remunerations, emoluments, and other fixed or determinable annual or periodical gains, profits, and fixed, determinable, annual, or periodical (FDAP) income, if such payment is from sources within the United States; and

- Any gross proceeds of any sale or disposition of any property capable of producing U.S source interest or dividends also qualify, as long as the income is not effectively connected to the conduct of a U.S. trade or business.

> **CAUTION**
>
> Though *FDAP income* is given the same meaning as in Chapter 3 of the tax code, an exclusion from withholding under Chapter 3 or from taxation under Code Sec. 881 does not exclude the amount from the definition of U.S. source FDAP income for purposes of determining whether a payment is withholdable under FATCA.

Among payments that are excluded from the definition of withholdable payments are:
- Certain short-term original issue discounts;
- Income effectively connected to the conduct of a U.S. trade or business;
- Some payments made in the ordinary course of the withholding agent's business;
- Certain broker transactions involving the sale of fractional shares; and
- Gross proceeds from property sales producing excluded income.

> **COMMENT**
>
> Code Sec. 103-exempt payments with respect to state and local bonds are also not withholdable payments.

Withholding Agents

Under the FATCA requirements as implemented by IRS guidance, withholding agents must withhold 30 percent of any withholdable payment made after December 31, 2013, to a payee that is an FFI unless:
- The withholding agent can reliably associate the payment with documentation upon which it is permitted to rely to treat the payment as exempt from withholding;
- The payment is made under a grandfathered obligation, as discussed below; or
- The payment constitutes gross proceeds from the disposition of such a grandfathered obligation.

In general, and absent an exception, withholding agents must withhold under FATCA on any withholdable payments made after December 31, 2013, to an FFI regardless of whether the FFI receives the payment as a beneficial owner or as an intermediary.

COMMENT

The FATCA rules relating to the requirement to withhold U.S. tax on certain payments apply primarily to U.S. financial institutions or withholding agents. With the exception of those acting as intermediaries with respect to withholdable payments, FFIs will generally not be required to withhold tax on payments made to account holders or nonparticipating FFIs before January 1, 2017.

COMMENT

The Treasury Department and the IRS hope to coordinate withholding requirements under Chapters 3 and 4 by requiring withholding agents to withhold on payments of U.S. source FDAP income under Chapter 4 when the agent would be responsible for withholding under Chapter 3.

COMMENT

Special rules apply with respect to payments of U.S source FDAP income to participating FFIs that are not qualified intermediaries but are acting as intermediaries or that are nonwithholding flow-through entities for purposes of Chapter 3, unless the participating FFI provides certain documentation necessary to determine the portion of the payment for which no withholding is required under Chapter 4.

Withholding agents must withhold 30 percent of any withholdable payment to an NFFE if the payment is beneficially owned by the NFFE, or another NFFE, unless FATCA requirements are met with respect to the beneficial owner of the payment. These requirements will be met with respect to the beneficial owner of a payment if:

- The beneficial owner or payee provides the withholding agent with either a certification that such beneficial owner does not have any substantial U.S. owners, or the name, address, and TIN of each substantial U.S. owner;
- The withholding agent does not know or have reason to know that any information provided by the beneficial owner or payee is incorrect; and
- The withholding agent reports the information provided to the Secretary.

COMMENT

The withholding requirements do not apply to payments beneficially owned by certain classes of persons or to any class of payment identified as posing a low risk of tax evasion. Thus, exempt from withholding, for example, are payments beneficially owned by certain persons, including any foreign government, international organization, foreign central bank of issue, or any other class of persons identified by the secretary of the U.S. Treasury as posing a low risk of tax evasion.

In the case of payments for which a withholding agent lacks control, custody, or knowledge, no withholding is required. Withholding is also not required for certain payments made to participating FFIs or *territory financial institutions,* defined as financial institutions organized under the laws of one of the U.S. territories. Transitional rules exempt from the withholding requirements certain payments made prior to January 1, 2015, with respect to certain preexisting accounts for which the withholding agent does not have documentation establishing the payee's status as a nonparticipating FFI.

Although the HIRE Act provides that no withholding or deduction will be required for any payment made under any obligation outstanding on March 18, 2012, the Treasury Department and the IRS, in an effort to facilitate implementation by withholding agents and FFIs, have proposed regulations that would exclude from the definition of withholdable payment and passthrough payment those made under an obligation outstanding on January 1, 2013. Thus, a *grandfathered obligation* is any obligation outstanding on January 1, 2013, with *obligation* being any legal agreement that produces or could produce a withholdable payment or passthrough payment, with the notable exceptions of instruments treated as equity for U.S. tax purposes or lacking a stated expiration.

Under FATCA, whether an obligation is outstanding on January 1, 2013, depends on the type of instrument in question:

- A debt instrument is deemed outstanding on that date if it has an issue date before January 1, 2013, under U.S. tax law;
- A significant modification of the instrument, as determined under the rules set forth in Reg. § 1-1001-3, will result in the obligation being treated as newly issued as of the date of the significant modification;
- An obligation that is not a debt instrument is deemed outstanding on January 1, 2013, if a legally binding agreement commemorating the obligation was executed before that date; and
- Similar to debt instruments, any material modification of the obligation will result in the obligation being treated as newly executed or issued as of the effective date of that modification.

COMMENT

Whether a material modification has occurred is dependent upon all relevant facts and circumstances.

Establishing Payee Status

In general, the FATCA rules for determining the status of a payee track those set forth in Reg. § 1.1441-1(b)(2). However, FATCA does modify these rules in several significant ways. Specifically, modifications have been made to account for the requirement imposed upon withholding agents to determine an FFI's status for FATCA purposes and to determine the status of certain NFFEs.

> **COMMENT**
>
> The Treasury Department and the IRS plan to revise Forms W-8 and W-9 to permit payees to establish their status both for FATCA and Chapter 3 purposes.

In addition, the FATCA rules provide that, in certain cases, withholding agents may reliably associate a withholdable payment with valid documentation. Specifically, a withholding agent can reliably associate a withholdable payment with valid documentation if, prior to the payment, the agent:

- Holds such documentation appropriate to the payee's FATCA status;
- Can reliably determine how much of the payment relates to the valid documentation; and
- Does not know or have reason to know that any of the information, certifications, or statements in, or associated with, the documentation are unreliable or incorrect.

A withholding agent may also rely on information and certifications contained in withholding certificates or other documentation without having to inquire into the truthfulness of the information or certifications, unless it knows or has reason to know that the information or certifications are untrue.

> **COMMENT**
>
> In an effort to minimize the burden on withholding agents to collect new documentation, in the case of withholdable payments made prior to January 1, 2017, with respect to a preexisting account, withholding agents may treat a payee as a participating FFI or a registered deemed-compliant FFI if it possesses a valid withholding certificate establishing the payee's foreign status and the agent has verified the payee's employer identification number (FFI-EIN).

Recalcitrant Account Holders

Generally, a *recalcitrant account holder* is any holder of an account maintained by a participating FFI if the account holder is not an FFI and the account holder fails to:

- Comply with the participating FFI's request for documentation or information to establish whether the account is a U.S. account;
- Provide a valid Form W-9 upon the request of the participating FFI;
- Provide a correct name and TIN upon request of the FFI after the

participating FFI receives notice from the IRS indicating a name/TIN mismatch; or

- Provide a valid and effective waiver of foreign law if foreign law prevents reporting with respect to the account holder by the participating FFI.

STUDY QUESTIONS

---

1. All of the following are fixed, determinable, annual, or periodical (FDAP) income considered withholdable payments that trigger FATCA requirements *except:*

   a. Payments of annuities from sources within the United States
   b. U.S. source payments of interest and dividends
   c. Premiums paid from sources within the United States
   d. Gross proceeds of a disposition of property that could produce U.S. source interest but whose income is not effectively connected to conduct of a U.S. trade or busines

2. FATCA withholding requirements apply to:

   a. Foreign financial institutions outside of FFI agreements
   b. Foreign governments
   c. Grandfathered obligations
   d. Payments for which the withholding agent lacks control, custody, or knowledge

---

FFI AGREEMENTS

By the terms of the FATCA rules, an FFI will be subjected to the 30 percent withholding tax unless the institution enters into an agreement with the IRS, becoming a "participating FFI," in which it agrees to:

- Obtain sufficient information regarding its account holders to ascertain whether any of the accounts it holds are "United States accounts;"
- Comply with certain verification procedures;
- Comply with annual reporting requirements with respect to "specified U.S. persons;" and
- Deduct and withhold the 30 percent tax on any "passthrough payment" made to recalcitrant account holders and others.

United States Accounts

A *United States account* is any financial account held by one or more "specified U.S. persons" or, subject to certain exceptions discussed below, "United States owned foreign entities."

A *financial account,* meanwhile, is any depository or custodial account, as well as any debt or equity interest in an FFI, except for interests regularly traded on an established securities market.

COMMENT

Commercial, checking, savings, time, or thrift accounts all qualify as depository accounts, as do accounts evidenced by a certificate of deposit (CD) or the like, and interest-bearing amounts held by an insurance company.

COMMENT

Custodial accounts include accounts that hold for investment for the benefit of another person any financial instrument or contract.

NOTE

The U.S. Treasury and the IRS have proposed excluding from the definition of financial accounts some savings accounts, including both retirement and pension accounts, as well as nonretirement savings accounts that satisfy certain requirements with respect to contribution limits and tax treatment. In addition, financial accounts held solely by one or more exempt beneficial owners, or by a nonparticipating FFI solely as an intermediary for such owners, may also be excluded.

By the terms of the new law, a *specified U.S. person* is any U.S. person, subject to certain exceptions. Among those excluded are:

- Corporations whose stock is regularly traded on an established securities market and their affiliates;
- Organizations exempt under Code Sec. 501(a);
- Individual retirement plans;
- REITS;
- RICS;
- Common trust funds;
- Dealers in securities, commodities, and notional principal contracts;
- Brokers; and
- The United States and its agencies.

Similarly, a *U.S.-owned foreign entity* is any foreign entity with one or more *substantial U.S. owners,* defined, in turn, as any specified U.S. person that owns, either directly or indirectly, more than 10 percent of the stock of a corporation or more than 10 percent of the profits or capital interests in a partnership. In the case of trusts, a substantial U.S. owner is a specified U.S. person directly or indirectly holding more than 10 percent of the beneficial interests in the trust.

COMMENT

Attribution rules are applied based on those found in Reg. § 1.958-1 and applicable in determining stock ownership for purposes of the controlled foreign corporation (CFC) rules.

Due Diligence Requirements

A foreign financial institution that enters into an FFI agreement (participating FFI) must identify its U.S. accounts and comply with certain due diligence and verification requirements. These requirements vary depending upon whether the accounts in question are individual accounts or entity accounts. In addition, preexisting accounts and new accounts are subject to different levels of diligence. FFIs that adhere to the guidelines set forth below will be treated as compliant and, thus, will not be held to a strict liability standard.

Preexisting individual accounts. Accounts with a value or balance not exceeding $50,000 are exempt from review, as are certain cash value insurance or annuity contracts with a value or balance of $250,000 or less. Accounts with a value in excess of $50,000 ($250,000 in the case of insurance or annuity contracts) but $1 million or less, meanwhile, are subject to a review of "electronically searchable data" only for any indicia of U.S. status. For these purposes, U.S. indicia include:

- Identification of an account holder as a U.S. person;
- A U.S birthplace;
- A U.S address;
- A U.S. telephone number;
- Standing instructions to transfer funds to an account maintained in the United States;
- A power of attorney or signatory authority granted to a person with a U.S. address; or
- A U.S. "in-care-of" or "hold-mail" address representing the only address on file for the account holder.

When an account balance exceeds $1 million, a review of both electronic and nonelectronic files must be conducted in search of U.S. indicia. This review includes an inquiry into actual knowledge possessed by any relationship manager associated with the account.

> **COMMENT**
>
> Out of concern over the level of administrative burden being imposed, the IRS has stated that the requisite review of nonelectronic files is limited to current customer files and only to the extent that electronically searchable files contain insufficient information with respect to the account holder.

New individual accounts. For individual accounts opened after the effective date of the FFI's agreement, the FFI will be required to review the information provided at the time the account is opened, including any collected under antimoney-laundering/know-your-customer (AML/KYC) rules. In the event that any U.S. indicia are located during this review, the FFI will then be required to obtain additional documentation or treat the account as held by a recalcitrant account holder.

Preexisting entity accounts. Preexisting entity accounts with balances of $250,000 or less are exempt from review until the balance exceeds $1 million. In the case of all other preexisting entity accounts, participating FFIs can rely on AML/KYC records as well as other existing account information to determine whether the entity is an FFI, a U.S. person, or excepted from being required to document its substantial U.S. owners.

For preexisting accounts of passive investment entities, FFIs may generally rely on information collected for AML/KYC purposes to identify substantial U.S. owners when the account balances in question do not exceed $1 million. If an account balance exceeds that amount, however, FFIs must obtain information regarding all substantial U.S. owners or receive a certification that the entity has no such owners.

New entity accounts. New entity accounts of another FFI, as well as those of an entity engaged in an active, nonfinancial trade or business, or otherwise excepted, are exempt from FATCA's documentation requirements. FFIs will, however, be required to determine whether all other remaining new entity accounts have any substantial U.S. owners, generally by obtaining a certification from the account holder.

Verification Procedures

In addition to adhering to due diligence requirements to identify U.S. accounts, a foreign financial institution entering into an FFI agreement must also comply with certain IRS verification requirements designed to assess the FFI's compliance with the FFA agreement. These requirements will, among other such necessities:

- Obligate the FFI to adopt written policies and procedures governing the participating FFI's compliance;

- Conduct periodic internal reviews; and
- Call for periodic provision of information to the IRS that will allow it to determine whether the participating FFI has satisfied its obligations under the agreement.

> **COMMENT**
>
> Responsible FFI officers will be expected to certify that the FFI has complied with the terms of the FFI agreement. Thus, barring extenuating circumstances, verification through third-party audits is not required.

> **COMMENT**
>
> The IRS anticipates that repetitive or systematic failures of the participating FFI's processes related to compliance with its FFI agreement may result in enhanced compliance verification and that certain egregious circumstances could cause the participating FFI to default on its FFI agreement.

Reporting Requirements

Participating FFIs are required to report, by March 31 of the year following the reporting year, certain information on an annual basis to the IRS about each U.S. account and to comply with requests for additional information pertaining to any U.S. account. The information that must be reported with respect to each U.S. account includes:

- The name, address, and taxpayer identifying number (TIN) of each account holder who is a specified U.S. person (or, in the case of an account holder that is a U.S.-owned foreign entity, the name, address, and TIN of each specified U.S. person that is a substantial U.S. owner of such entity);
- The account number;
- The account balance or value; and
- Any payments made with respect to the account during the calendar year.

> **COMMENT**
>
> Although it initially considered requiring the reporting of the highest of a given account's month's-end balances, the IRS ultimately decided to require only an account's year-end balance. Additionally, this amount may be reported in the currency in which the account is maintained. Should the participating FFI elect to report balance information in U.S. dollars, the participating FFI must calculate the account balance or value of the account by applying the spot rate at the close of the year or, if the account was closed during the year, the rate on the date of closure.

Payment information required to be reported during the year by participating FFIs varies depending on the type of account:

- For depository accounts, "payments" consist of the aggregate gross amount of interest paid or credited to the account during the year;
- In the case of custodial accounts, "payments" consist of
    - The aggregate gross amount of dividends paid or credited to the account during the calendar year,
    - The aggregate gross amount of interest paid or credited to the account during the calendar year,
    - The gross proceeds from the sale or redemption of property paid or credited to the account during the calendar year with respect to which the FFI acted as a custodian, broker, nominee, or otherwise as an agent for the account holder, and
    - The aggregate gross amount of all other income paid or credited to the account during the calendar year; and
- For all other accounts, gross amounts paid or credited to the account holder during the calendar year must be reported, including the aggregate amount of redemption payments made to the account holder during the calendar year.

> **COMMENT**
>
> For purposes of payment reporting, the amount and characterization of payments made for an account may be determined under the same principles that the participating FFI uses to report information on its resident account holders to the tax administration of the jurisdiction in which the FFI is located. Thus, the amount and characterization of items of income need not be determined in accordance with U.S. federal income tax principles.

In lieu of reporting the account balance or value, gross receipts, and gross withdrawals or payments, a participating FFI may elect to report the information required under Code Secs. 6041, 6042, 6045, and 6049 as if such institution were a U.S. person, and each holder of such U.S. account that is a specified U.S. person or U.S. owned foreign entity as if it were a natural person and citizen of the United States. If foreign law would prevent the FFI from reporting the required information absent a waiver from the account holder, and the account holder fails to provide that waiver within a reasonable period of time, the FFI is required to close the account.

> **COMMENT**
>
> This option does not apply to cash value insurance or annuity contract financial accounts that would otherwise be subject to the reporting requirements of Code Sec. 6047.

For accounts held by recalcitrant account holders, reporting is to be made separately for each of three categories of accounts. The separate categories of accounts held by recalcitrant account holders subject to reporting are:

- Accounts with U.S. indicia;
- Accounts of other recalcitrant holders; and
- Dormant accounts.

COMMENT

In general, *dormant accounts* are those treated as inactive accounts under applicable laws or regulations or the normal operating procedures of the participating FFI that are consistently applied for all accounts maintained by such institution in a particular jurisdiction.

Transitional reporting rules exist for accounts maintained during the 2013–2015 calendar years. Thus, for the 2013 and 2014 calendar years, participating FFIs may report only:

- The name, address, and TIN of each specified U.S. person who is an account holder and, in the case of any account holder that is an NFFE that is a U.S. owned foreign entity, the name, address, and TIN (if any) of such entity and each substantial U.S. owner of such entity;
- The account balance or value as of the end of the relevant calendar year, or, if the account was closed after the effective date of the FFI agreement, the balance or value of such account immediately before closure; and
- The account number of the account.

Added to this information required for the 2015 calendar year is data about most payments made for the account.

Withholding Requirements

In addition to the requirements just delineated, FATCA also obligates participating FFIs to withhold 30 percent of any passthrough payment made after December 31, 2013, to recalcitrant account holders or to FFIs that neither enter an FFI agreement nor otherwise qualify as a deemed-compliant entity (nonparticipating FFI). A *passthrough payment* is any withholdable payment or other payment to the extent attributable to a withholdable payment.

A participating FFI may elect not to withhold on passthrough payments, instead withholding on payments it receives, to the extent those payments are allocable to recalcitrant account holders or nonparticipating FFIs. A participating FFI that does not make such an election must withhold on passthrough payments it makes to any participating FFI that does make such an election.

Finally, participating FFIs that comply with the withholding requirements applicable to certain passthrough payments and FFI agreements will be deemed to have satisfied the withholding requirements.

> **COMMENT**
>
> Regarding the scope and ultimate implementation of withholding on foreign passthrough payments, the Treasury Department and the IRS are considering various approaches to reduce the administrative burden, for example, by providing a *de minimis* exception from foreign passthrough payment withholding.

Expanded Affiliate Groups

The FATCA rules provide that the requirements of the FFI agreement apply to the U.S. accounts of not only the participating FFI but to the U.S. accounts of every other FFI that is a member of the same expanded affiliate group, as well.

Subject to exceptions for certain branches, FFI affiliates and qualified intermediaries, for any member of an expanded affiliate group to be a participating FFI or registered deemed-compliant FFI, each FFI that is a member of the group must be either a participating FFI or registered deemed-compliant FFI. An FFI may be considered a participating FFI even though all of its branches might not be able to satisfy all of the requirements set forth in the FFI agreement.

A *branch* is a unit, business, or office of the FFI that is treated as a branch under the regulatory regime of the nation in which it is located, or otherwise regulated as separate from other branches, units or offices of the FFI, and that keeps its books and records separate from those of the FFI.

> **NOTE**
>
> All units, businesses, or offices of a participating FFI in a single country are treated as a single branch.

Likewise, a *limited branch* is a branch that is unable to report the information required with respect to U.S. accounts or that cannot withhold on its recalcitrant account holders or nonparticipating FFIs and cannot close or transfer these accounts. To qualify for limited branch status, the FFI must, as part of its registration process:

- Identify the relevant jurisdiction of each branch for which it seeks limited branch status;
- Agree that each of these branches will identify its account holders under the due diligence requirements applicable to participating FFIs;

- Retain documentation with respect to these identification requirements for six years;
- Report to the IRS in connection with those accounts it is required to treat as U.S. accounts;
- Treat each such branch as a separate entity for withholding purposes;
- Agree that the branches will not open any new accounts that it would be required to treat as U.S. or nonparticipating FFI accounts; and
- Agree that each limited branch will identify itself to withholding agents as a nonparticipating FFI.

Similarly, the expanded affiliate group rules also provide that an FFI that is a member of such a group may obtain status as a participating FFI even if one, or more, of its members cannot satisfy the requirements of the FFI agreement. *Limited FFIs* are FFIs that cannot, under local law, report or withhold as required by the FFI agreement. Nevertheless, participating and deemed-compliant FFIs must treat limited FFIs as nonparticipating FFIs with respect to withholdable payments made to these affiliates.

COMMENT

No withholding, however, will be required with respect to foreign passthrough payments made to a limited FFI.

STUDY QUESTIONS

3. A participating FFI is required to report all of the following account information *except:*

   a. The highest of a given account's month's-end balances
   b. The TIN of each account holder that is a specified U.S. person
   c. The year-end balance of the account
   d. Any payments made throughout the calendar year to the U.S. account

4. Which of the following is *not* one of the separate categories of accounts held by recalcitrant account holders that must be reported by participating FFIs?

   a. Dormant accounts
   b. All corporate accounts
   c. Accounts of other recalcitrant holders
   d. Accounts with U.S. indicia

DEEMED-COMPLIANT FFIS

FFIs will be deemed compliant with the requirements of FATCA—and therefore exempt from withholding tax—if they are either registered or certified deemed-compliant FFIs. Generally, a registered deemed-compliant FFI must register with the IRS to both declare its status and to attest that it satisfies certain procedural requirements.

Registered Deemed-Compliant FFIs

The following categories of FFIs, all of which will be addressed in turn, may qualify as registered deemed-compliant FFIs:

- Local FFIs;
- Nonreporting members of participating FFI groups;
- Qualified collective investment vehicles;
- Restricted funds; and
- FFIs that comply with the requirements of FATCA under an agreement between the United States and a foreign government.

Local FFIs. To qualify as a *local FFI,* each FFI in the group or, in the case of a standalone FFI, the FFI, itself, must meet certain licensing and regulation requirements. In addition, it must have no fixed place of business outside its country of organization and must not solicit account holders beyond its own borders. Finally, 98 percent of the accounts maintained by the FFI must be held by residents of the FFI's country of organization, and the FFI must be subject to withholding or reporting requirements in its country of organization with respect to resident accounts.

> **COMMENT**
>
> An FFI organized in a European Union (EU) member state may treat account holders that are residents of another EU member state as residents of the FFIs country of origin for this purpose.

Local FFIs must also establish procedures to ensure they do not open or maintain accounts for specified U.S. persons that are not residents of the country in which the FFIs are organized, for nonparticipating FFIs, or for entities controlled or beneficially owned by specified U.S. persons, and must perform due diligence with respect to their entity, and certain individual, accounts.

Nonreporting members of participating FFI groups. *Nonreporting members of participating FFI groups* that are members of an expanded affiliate group satisfy the requirements of the registered deemed-compliant category as long as they transfer any preexisting accounts that are identified under specified procedures as U.S. accounts, or accounts held by nonparticipating FFIs to an affiliate that is a participating FFI or U.S. financial institution. The nonreporting member(s) must also implement policies and procedures to ensure that if it opens or maintains and U.S. accounts or accounts held by nonparticipating FFIs, it either transfers the accounts to an affiliate that is a participating FFI, to a U.S. financial institution or itself becomes a participating FFI.

> **COMMENT**
>
> In such cases, the entity will have 90 days from the date on which the account is opened or on which it has knowledge, or reason to know, of a change in circumstance resulting in an account becoming a U.S. account or an account held by a nonparticpating FFI to make the transfer.

Qualified collective investment vehicles. Generally, an FFI regulated as a *qualified collective investment vehicle* is eligible to become a registered deemed-compliant FFI if all holders of record of a direct interest are participating FFIs, deemed FFIs, or exempt beneficial owners.

Restricted funds. Investment funds regulated under the laws of their country of organization are eligible to become registered deemed-compliant FFIs as *restricted funds*, as long as each distributor of the investment fund's interests is either a participating FFI, a registered deemed-compliant FFI, a nonregistering local bank, or a restricted distributor. In addition, each agreement governing the distribution of the fund's equity or debt interests must prohibit the sale of such interests to U.S. persons, nonparticipating FFIs, or passive NFFEs with one or more substantial U.S. owners. Also, the prospectus must indicate that sales to these classes of persons are prohibited. Finally, the FFI must also establish policies and procedures to review accounts and ensure the proper treatment of new accounts.

> **NOTE**
>
> Each registered deemed-compliant FFI, of all categories, must certify to the IRS that it:
>
> - Meets the requirements of the applicable category;
> - Agrees to the conditions for deemed-compliant status; and
> - Agrees to renew its certification every three years, or earlier in the event of a change in circumstance.

Certified Deemed-Compliant FFIs

FFIs may qualify as certified deemed-compliant FFIs in the following categories:

- Local banks;
- Retirement plans;
- Nonprofit organizations;
- FFIs maintaining only low-value accounts; and
- Certain owner-documented FFIs.

> **COMMENT**
>
> An institution that satisfies the requirements of these categories need not register with the IRS but must certify to withholding agents that it meets the requirements of the applicable certified deemed-compliant category on Form W-8.

In general, to qualify as a nonregistering local bank, a bank must offer basic banking services, operate solely in its country of incorporation, or in the case of members of expanded affiliate groups, that all members operate in the same country and that the assets on each member's balance sheet do not exceed $175 million.

> **COMMENT**
>
> Regarding members of expanded affiliate groups, their combined balance sheet for the expanded affiliate group as a whole cannot have more than $500 million in assets.

To qualify for certified deemed-compliant status as a retirement plan, the FFI must be organized for the provision of retirement or pension benefits under the law of each country in which it is established or operates. Contributions to the FFI may consist of only employer, government, or employee contributions and must be limited by reference to earned income. No single beneficiary may have a right to more than 5 percent of the FFI's assets. Contributions to the FFI must either be excluded from the income of the beneficiary and/or taxation of the income attributable to the beneficiary must be deferred or the FFI must receive 50 percent or more of its contributions from the government or employers.

> **NOTE**
>
> For those FFIs that provide retirement or pension benefits, but have fewer than 20 participants, FATCA provides alternative procedures.

A nonprofit organization will qualify for certified deemed-compliant status if the organization:

- Is established and maintained in its country of residence for religious, charitable, scientific, artistic, or educational purposes exclusively;
- Is exempt from income tax in its country of residence;
- Has no shareholders or members that have a proprietary interest in its income or assets; and
- Is subject to restrictions preventing the private inurement of its income or assets.

FFIs with only low-value accounts will qualify for certified deemed-compliant status if:

- The FFI qualifies as an FFI only because it accepts deposits in the ordinary course of a banking or similar business, or holds financial assets for the account of others as a substantial portion of it business;
- No financial account maintained by the FFI has a balance of more than $50,000 or, in the case of a member of an expanded affiliate group, by any member of the group; and
- Has no greater than $50 million in assets on its balance sheet, or as a whole in the case of members of expanded affiliate groups.

Finally, an owner-documented FFI is eligible for certified deemed-compliant status if it:

- Does not accept deposits in the ordinary course of a banking or similar business, holds, as a substantial portion of its business, financial assets for the account of others, or is not an insurance company that issues or is obligated to make payments with respect to a financial account;
- Does not maintain financial accounts for nonparticipating FFIs;
- Does not issue debt constituting a financial account in excess of $50,000 to any person; and
- Provides a withholding agent with all required documentation regarding its owners and that withholding agent agrees to report to the IRS regarding any owners that are specified U.S. persons.

COMMENT

Because an owner-documented, certified deemed-compliant FFI is required to provide each withholding agent such documentation, and the agent must agree to report on behalf of the owner-documented FFI, such FFIs may only have certified deemed-compliant status only with respect to a specific withholding agent(s).

FATCA TIMELINE AND EFFECTIVE DATES

Registration of FFIs Beginning in 2013

The IRS will begin accepting FFI applications through its electronic submissions process no later than January 1, 2013. An FFI must enter into an FFI agreement by June 30, 2013, to ensure that it will be identified as a participating FFI in time to allow U.S. withholding agents to refrain from withholding beginning on January 1, 2014. The effective date of an FFI agreement entered into any time before July 1, 2013, will be July 1, 2013. The effective date of an FFI agreement entered into after June 30, 2013, will be the date the FFI enters into the FFI agreement.

Participating FFI Due Diligence

New accounts. A participating FFI must put in place account opening procedures to identify U.S. accounts among accounts opened on or after the effective date of its FFI agreement.

Preexisting accounts. Table 1 lists the due diligence procedures for the three types of preexisting accounts.

Table 1. Due Diligence Mandates for Preexisting Accounts

Account Type	Requirements and Deadlines for FFI
Certain preexisting private banking accounts (≥ $500,000)	Within 1 year of the effective date of its FFI agreement, to have in place certain preexisting account due diligence procedures for all accounts opened before the effective date of its FFI agreement that are associated with a private banking relationship (including individual and entity accounts) and that have a balance or value of at least $500,000
Private banking accounts of < $500,000	By the later of December 31, 2014, or 1 year after the effective date of its FFI agreement, to complete the private banking procedures for all accounts opened before the effective date of its FFI agreement
All other preexisting accounts	To complete due diligence procedures within 2 years of the effective date of its FFI agreement

Reporting

New accounts, documented U.S. accounts, and private banking accounts. A participating FFI that has, by June 30, 2014, received a Form W-9 from the account holder (or, in cases of accounts held by U.S.-owned foreign entity, from a substantial U.S. owner of such entity) must identify and report the account to the IRS as a U.S. account by September 30, 2014. With respect to these identified U.S. accounts, certain participating FFIs will, for, this first year of reporting, only be required to report the following information:

- The name, address, and U.S. TIN of each specified U.S. person who is an account holder and, in the case of any account holder that is a U.S.-owned foreign entity, the name, address, and U.S. TIN of each substantial U.S. owner of such entity;
- The account balance as of December 31, 2013, or, if the account was closed after the effective date of the FFI's FFI agreement, the balance of such account immediately before closure; and
- The account number.

Reporting for post-2013 years. Reporting with respect to 2014 and subsequent years will be required as delineated elsewhere in this chapter and as implemented by future regulations.

WITHHOLDING

Withholdable Payments

For payments made on or after January 1, 2014, withholding agents (both domestic or foreign, including participating FFIs) will be obligated to withhold tax on U.S. source FDAP payments. For payments made on or after January 1, 2015, withholding agents will be obligated to withhold tax on all withholdable payments.

Passthrough Payments

FFIs are obligated to withhold tax on withholdable payments of U.S. source FDAP for payments made on or after January 1, 2014, but will not be required to withhold on other passthrough payments made before January 1, 2015.

STUDY QUESTIONS

---

5. A local FFI as a registered deemed-compliant FFI:

    a. Is exempt from registration to be considered deemed compliant

    b. Must have no fixed place of business outside its country of organization

    c. May solicit account holders outside of its country's borders

    d. Must have at least a simple majority of accounts held by residents of its country of organization

6. For an FFI having only low-value accounts to be certified deemed compliant:

    a. No financial account or expanded affiliate group member account maintained by the FFI may have a balance of more than $50,000

    b. The FFI's balance sheet may not have a balance of more than $1 million on its balance sheet

    c. The FFI may not accept deposits as part of its ordinary course of financial business or hold financial assets for others' accounts

    d. The FFI may not be owner-documented

INTERGOVERMENTAL IMPLEMENTATION AGREEMENTS

The U.S. government is actively pursuing efforts to team with other nations to facilitate the implementation of FATCA on a government-to-government basis. The United States is, for example, open to adopting either an intergovernmental approach that would involve reporting by FFIs to their own governments, followed by an automatic exchange of this information with the United States, or a framework for intergovernmental cooperation to facilitate FATCA implementation that would provide for direct reporting by the FFIs to the United States according to the FATCA rules, supplemented by exchange of information on request. The Treasury Department on July 26, 2012, released a model intergovernmental agreement to facilitate FACTA compliance. The model agreement was developed in consultation with France, Germany, Italy, Spain and the United Kingdom (U.K.). The U.S. and the five countries issued a joint statement welcoming the model intergovernmental agreement and anticipating its speedy implementation. "Now that we have a model intergovernmental agreement, we are looking to move forward with other countries," a Treasury official commented.

CONCLUSION

On one hand, FATCA requires certain U.S. taxpayers holding foreign financial assets with an aggregate value exceeding $50,000 to report certain information about those assets on a new form (Form 8938) that must be attached to the taxpayer's annual tax return. At the same time, the FATCA requirements directed toward financial institutions, as discussed in this chapter, operate to assure that these taxpayers do not avoid their U.S. tax obligations. These requirements were designed to enlist the aid of financial institutions the world over to help identify noncompliant US taxpayers. As a result, however, compliance costs both for taxpayers with foreign accounts and for financial institutions are expected to increase significantly.

Together, these new far-reaching requirements demonstrate the U.S. government's continuing commitment to closing the tax gap at least in part by closing opportunities for offshore tax avoidance. By all estimates, these efforts will persist in the years ahead.

CPE NOTE: When you have completed your study and review of chapters 1–2, which comprise Module 1, you may wish to take the Quizzer for this Module.

Go to **CCHGroup.com/PrintCPE** to take this Quizzer online.

Tax Return Preparer Penalties

This chapter explores the various penalties the IRS may impose on tax return preparers who engage in certain behaviors. The IRS may penalize a tax return preparer for, among other offenses, understating a taxpayer's liability, failing to provide a completed copy of return to the taxpayer, and failing to use a preparer tax identification number (PTIN). The tax code also provides for criminal sanctions for unauthorized disclosure of a taxpayer's return information. Additionally, failing to follow the new rules for registered tax return preparers (RTRPs) and the new mandatory e-filing rules may expose a preparer to sanctions.

LEARNING OBJECTIVES

Upon completion of the chapter, you will be able to:

- Understand the Code Sec. 6694(a) penalty for understatement of taxpayer's liability by tax return preparer;
- Describe the Code Sec. 6694(b) penalty for willful or reckless understatement of a taxpayer's liability by a tax return preparer;
- Identify the various Code Sec. 6695 penalties;
- List the new requirements for registered tax return preparers (RTRPs) and the consequences of failing to follow the RTRP requirements;
- Describe the Code Sec. 7216 penalty for unauthorized disclosure of taxpayer return information; and
- Differentiate among the sanctions the IRS may impose for failing to adhere to mandatory e-filing requirements for specified tax return preparers.

INTRODUCTION

The Internal Revenue Code contains penalties to stop the practices of fraudulent, unscrupulous, and/or incompetent tax return preparers. The penalties are intended to curb misbehavior and boost compliance with the tax laws. The penalties discussed in this chapter are related to the preparer's principal work activity: the preparation and filing of federal tax returns. In some cases, a preparer may be able to show reasonable cause why a penalty should not be imposed; in other cases, there is no reasonable cause exception.

CODE SEC. 6694 PENALTIES

Code Sec. 6694 provides for penalties against tax return preparers due to certain understatements of a taxpayer's liability. Code Sec. 6694(a) applies to an understatement due to unreasonable positions. If a tax return preparer prepares any return or claim for refund with respect to which any part of an understatement of liability is due to an unreasonable position and the preparer knew (or reasonably should have known) of the position, the preparer can be subject to a penalty with respect to that return. Code Sec. 6694(b) provides for increased penalties where the understatement was due to willful or reckless conduct of the tax return preparer.

Tax Return Preparer

A *tax return preparer* for purposes of the Code Sec. 6694 penalties is any person (including a partnership or corporation) who prepares for compensation, or who employs one or more persons to prepare for compensation, all or a substantial portion of a tax return or claim for refund.

> **COMMENT**
>
> Before May 26, 2007 (the effective date of the *Small Business and Work Opportunity Tax Act,* hereafter the 2007 Small Business Tax Act), the definition of a tax return preparer was limited to income tax return preparers. That act extended the definition to encompass preparers of all returns and not just preparers of income tax returns.

Categories of Returns

In Rev. Proc. 2009-11, the IRS identified categories of returns to which the penalties under Code Sec. 6694 applies, namely:

- Income tax returns—Subtitle A (such as Form 1040, *U.S. Income Tax Return,* Form 1041, *U.S. Income Tax Return for Estates and Trusts,* and Form 1120, *U.S. Corporation Income Tax Return*);
- Estate and gift tax returns—Subtitle B (such as Form 706, *U.S. Estate Tax Return,* and Form 709, *United States Gift (and Generation-Skipping Transfer) Tax Return;*
- Employment tax returns—Subtitle C (such as Form 940, *Employer's Annual Federal Unemployment (FUTA) Tax Return,* Form 941, *Employer's Quarterly Federal Tax Return,* and Form 943, *Employer's Annual Tax Return for Agricultural Employees*);
- Miscellaneous excise tax returns—Subtitle D (such as Form 720, *Quarterly Federal Excise Tax Return,* Form 2290, *Heavy Highway Vehicle Use Tax Return*); and
- Alcohol, tobacco, and certain other excise taxes–Subtitle E (such as Form 8725, *Excise Tax on Greenmail*).

Code Sec. 6694(a)

Code Sec. 6694(a) imposes a penalty in an amount equal to the greater of $1,000 or 50 percent of the income derived—or to be derived—by the tax return preparer from the preparation of the return. The penalty applies where there is an understatement of a client's tax liability that results from an undisclosed, nonabusive position for which the tax return preparer did not have substantial authority under the tax laws to back up that position. If the position was disclosed on the return, then only a reasonable basis under existing authority is required to avoid the penalty. However, if an undisclosed position is with respect to a tax shelter, listed transaction, or reportable transaction with significant avoidance or evasion, the tax return preparer must have a reasonable belief that the transaction would be more likely than not sustained on the merits to avoid the penalty.

Standards. If the tax position is disclosed, the preparer must have a reasonable basis for the position. *Reasonable basis* is a high standard; it is higher than not frivolous or not patently improper. However, reasonable basis is not satisfied merely because a return position is arguable or presents a colorable claim. The *substantial authority standard* is less stringent than the *more likely than not standard* but more stringent than the reasonable basis standard.

Reasonable cause exception. The Code Sec. 6694(a) penalty will not be imposed if, considering all the facts and circumstances, it is determined that the understatement was due to reasonable cause and the tax return preparer acted in good faith. A tax return preparer has acted in good faith where the tax return preparer relied on the advice of a third party who is not in the same firm as the tax return preparer and who the tax return preparer had reason to believe was competent to render the advice. The advice may be written or oral, but in either case the burden of establishing that the advice was received is on the tax return preparer.

A tax return preparer is not considered to have relied in good faith if:

- The advice is unreasonable on its face;
- The tax return preparer knew or should have known that the third party advisor was not aware of all relevant facts; or
- The tax return preparer knew or should have known (given the nature of the tax return preparer's practice), at the time the tax return or claim for refund was prepared, that the advice was no longer reliable due to developments in the law since the time the advice was given.

Other factors to consider are (not an exhaustive list):
- *Nature of the error* causing the understatement;
- *Complexity of provision.* Whether the error resulted from a provision that was so complex, uncommon, or highly technical that a competent preparer of returns or claims of the type at issue reasonably could have made the error;
- *Frequency of errors.* Whether the understatement was the result of an isolated error (such as an inadvertent mathematical or clerical error) rather than a number of errors;
- *Materiality of errors.* Whether the understatement was material in relation to the correct tax liability. The reasonable cause and good faith exception generally applies if the understatement is of a relatively immaterial amount. Nevertheless, even an immaterial understatement may not qualify for the reasonable cause and good faith exception if the error or errors creating the understatement are sufficiently obvious or numerous; and
- *Preparer's normal office practice.* Whether the preparer's normal office practice, when considered together with other facts and circumstances, such as the knowledge of the preparer, indicates that the error in question would rarely occur and the normal office practice was followed in preparing the return or claim in question.

Firm liability. Traditionally, the IRS regulations under Code Sec. 6694 set out a "one preparer per firm" rule, which generally treated the signing tax return preparer as the preparer subject to a penalty. If there was no signer in a firm, the individual with overall supervisory responsibility for the advice given by the firm regarding the return or claim was the nonsigning preparer subject to penalty.

The *2007 Small Business Tax Act* modified the traditional approach. In the course of identifying the individual who is primarily responsible for the tax position, the IRS may advise multiple individuals within the firm that "it may be concluded that they are the individual within the firm who is primarily responsible for the position," according to the regulations. A penalty, however, may only be assessed against the individual in the firm who is the primarily responsible tax return preparer. Nevertheless, the regulations further advise that there may be more than one tax return preparer who is primarily responsible for the position(s) giving rise to an understatement if multiple tax return preparers are employed by, or associated with, different firms. In addition, firms may also be subject to penalty under Reg. §1.669401(b)(5) in certain situations when appropriate procedures for review have not been set up or required to be followed.

STUDY QUESTIONS

---

1. The 2007 Small Business Tax Act:

    a. Imposed fines only for untenable tax positions of tax shelters, listed transactions, or reportable transactions

    b. Extended the definition of tax return preparer to encompass preparers of all types of returns

    c. Applied the Code Sec. 6694 penalties to firms rather than individual return preparers

    d. Extended the scope of penalties to apply to registered tax return preparers

2. To avoid a Code Sec. 6694(a) penalty on a disclosed tax position, a tax preparer must meet the:

    a. Reasonable basis standard

    b. More likely than not standard

    c. Substantial authority standard

    d Good faith standard

TAX SHELTERS AND REPORTABLE TRANSACTIONS

In Notice 2009-5, the IRS explained that it is reasonable to believe that positions have a more likely than not chance of being upheld on their merits if a preparer has:

- Analyzed the pertinent facts and authorities; and
- Concluded, in good faith, that there is greater than 50 percent likelihood that the tax treatment will be upheld if the IRS challenges it.

Notice 2009-5 also provides interim compliance rules for tax shelter transactions that are not listed or otherwise reportable under Code Sec. 6662A, Imposition of Accuracy-related Penalty on Understatements with Respect to Reportable Transactions. A position will not be deemed an *unreasonable position* if:

- There is substantial authority for the position; and
- The tax return preparer advises the taxpayer of the penalty standards applicable to the taxpayer.

However, the interim compliance rules do not apply to a position, described in Code Sec. 6662A, that is a reportable transaction with a significant purpose of federal tax avoidance or evasion or a listed transaction.

> **COMMENT**
>
> Code Sec. 6700 and Code Sec. 6701 impose penalties on individuals who promote abusive tax transactions. These penalties are beyond the scope of this chapter.

STUDY QUESTIONS

---

3. Under interim compliance rules for tax shelter transactions that are not listed or otherwise reportable under Code Sec. 6662A, a position will **not** be deemed an unreasonable position if:

    a. There is substantial authority for the position; and the tax return preparer advises the taxpayer of the penalty standards applicable to the taxpayer

    b. The position has no precedent

    c. The tax return preparer advises the taxpayer that the position will not be sustainable

    d. The tax return preparer does not make accuracy-related errors on the return

---

Code Sec. 6694(b) Willful or Reckless Conduct

Code Sec. 6694(b) imposes a penalty in an amount equal to the greater of $5,000 or 50 percent of the income derived—or to be derived—by the tax return preparer from preparation of a return that understates a client's tax liability resulting from the preparer's willful attempt to understate the client's tax liability or the preparer's reckless or intentional disregard of rules and regulations. A tax return preparer generally is not considered to have recklessly or intentionally disregarded a rule or regulation if the position:

- Has a reasonable basis and is adequately disclosed; and
- Represents a good faith challenge to the regulation and the regulation being challenged is identified.

In the case of a position contrary to a revenue ruling or notice (other than a notice of proposed rule making), a tax return preparer is not considered to have recklessly or intentionally disregarded the ruling or notice if he or she reasonably believes that the position would more likely than not be sustained on its merits.

Burden of proof. The IRS bears the burden of proof on the issue of whether a tax return preparer willfully attempted to understate the tax liability under Code Sec. 6694(b). Reckless conduct is a highly unreasonable omission or misrepresentation involving an extreme departure from the standards of ordinary care that a practitioner should observe under the circumstances.

> **COMMENT**
>
> If both the Code Sec. 6694(a) and Code Sec. 6694(b) penalties apply to a tax return preparer, the 6694(b) penalty amount must be reduced by the 6694(a) penalty amount.

The IRS has advised its examiners to ensure that the combined assessment of Code Sec. 6694(a) and Code Sec. 6694(b) penalties against a preparer does not exceed the greater of $5,000 or 50 percent of the income derived (or to be derived) by the tax return preparer with respect to returns, amended returns, and claims for refund prepared on or after May 26, 2007.

> **COMMENT**
>
> Because the Code Sec. 6694(b) penalty involves willfulness, there is no statutory period for assessment of the penalty. There is a three-year limitation period for assessment of the Code Sec. 6694(a) penalty, which begins to run on the statutory due date of the return or, if filed late, the filing date of the return. Code Sec. 6501(c)(4) allows for extension of the limitation period.

CODE SEC. 6695 PENALTIES

Penalties under Code Sec. 6695 may only apply to a tax return preparer. A *tax return preparer* for purposes of the Code Sec. 6695 penalties is any person (including a partnership or corporation) who prepares for compensation, or who employs one or more persons to prepare for compensation, all or a substantial portion of a tax return or claim for refund.

The penalties under Code Sec. 6695 are:

- Code Sec. 6695(a), Failure to Furnish Completed Copy of Return or Claim for Refund to Taxpayer: $50 penalty will be asserted for each failure, with a maximum of $25,000 per preparer per calendar year;
- Code Sec. 6695(b), Failure to Sign Return or Claim for Refund: $50 penalty will be asserted for each failure, with a maximum of $25,000 per preparer, per calendar year;
- Code Sec. 6695(c), Failure to Furnish Identifying Number: $50 penalty will be asserted for each failure, with a maximum of $25,000 per preparer, per calendar year;
- Code Sec. 6695(d), Failure to Retain Copy or List: $50 penalty will be asserted for each failure, with a maximum of $25,000 to any return period;
- Code Sec. 6695(e), Failure of Preparer Employer to File Information Returns: $50 for each failure to file a return as required by Code Sec. 6060, and $50 for each failure to include a required item in the return. The maximum amount for any return period is $25,000;

- Code Sec. 6695(f), Negotiation of a Taxpayer's Refund Check: $500 for each negotiated check. There is no maximum amount;
- Code Sec. 6695(g), EIC Due Diligence: Any return preparer who fails to comply with the earned income tax credit (EIC) due diligence requirements of Code Sec. 6695(g) will be charged a penalty for each failure. For any tax returns or claims for refund for tax years ending before December 31, 2011, the penalty is $100 per failure. There is no maximum amount. For any tax returns or claims for refund for tax years ending on or after December 31, 2011 the penalty is $500 per failure. There is no maximum amount.

> **COMMENT**
>
> Taxpayers who have a complaint against a preparer file Form 14157, *Complaint: Tax Return Preparer*. Form 14157 asks for information about the preparer, such as his or her name, address, telephone, and email address. Form 14157 also asks for information about the nature of the complaint, such as whether the preparer allegedly failed to file the return, failed to sign the return, or diverted the taxpayer's refund. Form 14157 is submitted to the IRS Return Preparer Office in Chesterfield, Missouri.

Code Sec. 6695(a) Penalty: Failure to Furnish Completed Copy of Return or Claim for Refund to Taxpayer

Code Sec. 6695(a) imposes a penalty on a tax return preparer who fails to comply with Code Sec. 6107(a), Failure to Furnish Completed Copy of Return or Claim for Refund to Taxpayer. Code Sec. 6107(a) requires a tax return preparer to provide a completed copy of the return or claim for refund to the taxpayer before (or at the same time as) the return or claim for refund is presented to the taxpayer for signature.

Medium used for copy. The copy of the return or claim for refund may be given to the taxpayer in any medium, including an electronic form, that is acceptable to both the taxpayer and the tax return preparer. In the case of an electronically filed return, a complete copy of a taxpayer's return or claim for refund consists of the electronic portion of the return or claim for refund, including all schedules, forms, .pdf attachments, and jurats (affidavits or attestations), that were filed with the IRS. The copy provided to the taxpayer must include all information submitted to the IRS to enable the taxpayer to determine what schedules, forms, electronic files, and other supporting materials have been filed with the return.

> **COMMENT**
>
> The copy, however, need not contain the identification number of the paid tax return preparer.

Reasonable cause. The Code Sec. 6695(a) penalty does not apply if failure to provide a copy of the return or claim for refund on the part of the tax return preparer is due to reasonable cause and not due to willful neglect.

> **COMMENT**
>
> The Code Sec. 6695(a) penalty also will not be imposed when a tax return preparer deletes certain information from the copy furnished to the taxpayer if the taxpayer holds an elected or politically appointed position with the government of the United States or a state or political subdivision thereof and who in order to carry out official duties, has arranged their affairs to have less than full knowledge of the property or the debts for which the taxpayer is responsible.

Code Sec. 6695(b): Failure to Sign Return or Claim for Refund

A tax return preparer may be liable for the Code Sec. 6695(b) penalty if the preparer, who is required by regulations to sign the taxpayer's return or claim for refund, fails to sign the return or claim for refund. Tax return preparers must sign the return or claim for refund that are not signed electronically using the appropriate method prescribed by the IRS after the return or claim for refund is completed and before it is presented to the taxpayer for signature. If more than one preparer is involved in the preparation of the return or claim for refund, the preparer with primary responsibility for the overall substantive accuracy of the return/claim for refund is the preparer who must sign it.

A special rule applies in the case of electronically signed tax returns. The signing tax return preparer need not sign the return prior to presenting a completed copy of the return to the taxpayer. However, the signing tax return preparer must provide all of the information that will be transmitted as the electronically signed tax return to the taxpayer contemporaneously with furnishing the Form 8879, *IRS e-file Signature Authorization.* The information may be furnished on a replica of an official form. The signing tax return preparer shall electronically sign the return in the manner prescribed by the IRS.

> **COMMENT**
>
> The return must be signed using the tax return preparer's PTIN. If the preparer required to sign the return or claim for refund is unavailable to sign it, another preparer must review it and then sign the return or claim for refund. If a preparer is physically unable to sign a return because of a temporary or permanent disability, the IRS has advised its examiners that the Code Sec. 6695(b) penalty should not be imposed if the words "Unable to Sign" are printed, typed, or stamped on the preparer signature line. Also, the preparer's name should be printed, typed, or stamped under the signature line after the return is completed and before it is presented to the taxpayer for signature.

> **EXAMPLE**
>
> The Johnston, Hunt, and Peak law firm employs lawyer Barry McCall to prepare for compensation estate tax returns and claims for refund of taxes. The firm is engaged by Claudio Arrigio to prepare a federal estate tax return. Firm A assigns Barry to prepare the return. Barry obtains the information necessary for completing the return from Claudio and makes determinations with respect to the proper application of the tax laws to such information in order to determine the estate's tax liability. Barry then forwards the information to Dexter Chase, who performs the mathematical computations and prints the return by means of computer processing. Dexter then sends the completed estate tax return to Barry who reviews the accuracy of the return. Barry is the individual tax return preparer who is primarily responsible for the overall accuracy of the estate tax return. Barry must sign the return as tax return preparer in order to not be subject to the Code Sec. 6695(b) penalty.

Circular 230. Willfully failing to sign a tax return prepared by the practitioner where the practitioner's signature is required constitutes disreputable conduct under Circular 230, Rules of Practice Before the IRS. Sanctions under Circular 230 include censure, suspension from practice before the IRS, or disbarment.

Reasonable cause. If failure to sign the return or claim for refund was due to reasonable cause and not due to willful neglect, the penalty will not apply. The tax return preparer must provide a written statement to substantiate the preparer's claim of reasonable cause.

Code Sec. 6695(c) Penalty for Failure to Furnish Identifying Number

The Code Sec. 6695(c) penalty applies if the tax return preparer fails to comply with Code Sec. 6109(a)(4), Furnishing Identifying Number of Tax Return Preparer. Code Sec. 6109(a)(4) requires that a return or claim for refund must contain the identifying number of the tax return preparer required to sign the return or claim for refund under Code Sec. 6695(b); and the identifying number of the partnership or employer (if there is a partnership or employment arrangement between two or more preparers).

PTINs. All tax return preparers who prepare returns for compensation must obtain and use a PTIN. The PTIN requirement applies as of January 1, 2011, to certified public accountants (CPAs), enrolled agents (EAs), registered tax return preparers, attorneys, supervised preparers, and non-Form 1040 series preparers if the individual prepares returns for compensation unless the returns are expressly exempt. Each preparer must have his or her own PTIN and may only obtain one PTIN.

The IRS has launched an online PTIN registration system. Alternatively, practitioners can apply for a PTIN using paper Form W-12, *IRS Paid Preparer Tax Identification Number (PTIN) Application*. All PTIN applicants must attest they are compliant with their personal and business tax obligations, or provide an explanation if they are not. The IRS has explained on its website that for purposes of obtaining a PTIN, an individual is in tax compliance if:

All individual and business returns that are due have been filed (or an extension requested); and

All taxes that are due have been paid (or acceptable payment arrangements have been established).

> **COMMENT**
>
> A PTIN is not the same as an electronic filing identification number (EFIN). An EFIN is issued by the IRS to individuals or firms that have been approved as authorized IRS e-file providers. It is included with all electronic return data transmitted to the IRS.

Individuals generally are required to provide their Social Security numbers when they obtain a PTIN. However, U.S. citizens who have a conscientious objection to obtaining a Social Security number for religious reasons and foreign persons who are not eligible to obtain a Social Security number and have a permanent non-U.S. address may obtain a PTIN without a Social Security number. These individuals are required to provide supplemental documentation to verify their identity and substantiate their eligibility for a PTIN.

U.S. citizens who have a conscientious objection to obtaining a Social Security number for religious reasons must complete Form W-12, *IRS Paid Preparer Tax Identification Number (PTIN) Application,* either online or on paper, and a paper Form 8945, *PTIN Supplemental Application For U.S. Citizens Without a Social Security Number Due To Conscientious Religious Objection.* Documentation to substantiate identity, U.S. citizenship, and status as a member of a recognized religious group must accompany the Form 8945.

Penalty. Willful preparing all or substantially all of, or signing, a tax return or claim for refund when the practitioner does not possess a valid PTIN constitutes disreputable conduct under Circular 230, Rules of Practice Before the IRS.

Reasonable cause. However, a preparer will not be subject to penalty if failure to comply with the PTIN requirements was due to reasonable cause and not due to willful neglect. Under Circular 230, the IRS may censure, suspend from practice, or disbar a practitioner for engaging in disreputable conduct.

Code Sec. 6695(d) Penalty for Failure to Retain Copy or List

Code Sec. 6107(b) requires a tax return preparer to retain a completed copy of the return or claim for refund, or alternatively retain a record (by list, card file, electronically, or otherwise) of all the taxpayers, their taxpayer identification numbers, the tax years, and the type of returns or claims for refund prepared. A tax return preparer who fails to comply with Code Sec. 6107(b) is liable for a $50 per-failure penalty under Code Sec. 6695(d).

Reasonable cause. The Code Sec. 6695(d) penalty does not apply if the tax return preparer's failure to comply was due to reasonable cause and not due to willful neglect.

Code Sec. 6695(e): Failure of Preparer Employer to File Information Returns

The Code Sec. 6695(e) penalty applies if a tax return preparer fails to comply with Code Sec. 6060, Information Returns of Tax Return Preparers. Under Code Sec. 6060(a), each person who employs (or engages) one or more tax return preparers must retain a record of the name, taxpayer identification number, and place of work of each tax return preparer employed (or engaged) by him or her. The Code Sec. 6695(e) penalty must be assessed within three years after the return or claim for refund was filed.

Reasonable cause. The Code Sec. 6695(e) penalty does not apply if the failure was due to reasonable cause and not due to willful neglect.

Code Sec. 6695(f) Penalty: Negotiation of a Taxpayer's Refund Check

If a tax return preparer endorses or otherwise negotiates (directly or through an agent) a refund check issued to a taxpayer (other than the preparer), the Code Sec. 6695(f) penalty applies, subject to certain exceptions. A tax return preparer may not endorse or negotiate a check for a taxpayer even though the preparer was designated as the taxpayer's representative on a Form 2848, *Power of Attorney and Declaration of Representative.*

Exceptions. A tax return preparer will not be considered to have endorsed or otherwise negotiated a check as a result of having affixed the taxpayer's name to a refund check for the purpose of depositing the check into an account in the name of the taxpayer or in the joint names of the taxpayer and one or more other persons (excluding the tax return preparer). In certain circumstances, a preparer-bank may cash a refund check and remit the cash to the taxpayer or may accept a refund check for deposit to the taxpayer's account.

A preparer-bank may:
- Cash a refund check and remit all the cash to the taxpayer;
- Accept a refund check for deposit in full to the taxpayer's account, provided the bank does not initially endorse or negotiate the check (unless the bank has made a loan to a taxpayer on the basis of the anticipated refund);
- Endorse a refund check for deposit in full to the taxpayer's account pursuant to a written authorization of the taxpayer (unless the bank has made a loan to the taxpayer on the basis of the anticipated refund); and
- Endorse or negotiate a refund check as part of the check-clearing process after initial endorsement or negotiation (Reg. 1.6695-1(f)(2)).

Reasonable cause. There is *no* reasonable cause exception to the Code Sec. 6695(f) penalty.

Code Sec. 6695(g) Penalty: EIC Due Diligence

The Code Sec. 6695(g) penalty applies if tax return preparer fails to comply with due diligence requirements with respect to determining eligibility for, or the amount of, the taxpayer's earned income credit (EIC). The framework for the Code Sec. 6695(g) penalty differs if failure to comply with the EIC due diligence requirements occurs for returns or claims for refunds for tax years ending before December 31, 2011, or tax years on or after December 31, 2011. Note also that the penalty rose from $100 to $500 per return for such failure for returns required to be filed on or after December 31, 2011.

Before December 31, 2011. The following due diligence requirements applied to tax returns or claims for refund for tax years ending before December 31, 2011:

- Complete an eligibility checklist. Preparers could use Form 8867, *Paid Preparers Earned Income Credit Checklist,* or their own form as long as it provided the same information;
- Compute the credit using either the EIC worksheet in the Form 1040, Form 1040A, *U.S. Individual Income Tax Return,* Form 1040EZ, *Income Tax Return for Single and Joint Filers With No Dependents,* instructions, or Publication 596, "Earned Income Credit," or the preparer's own worksheet that contained the same information;
- Have no knowledge or reason to know that any information used to determine the taxpayer's eligibility for the credit and the credit amount was incorrect. The preparer could not ignore the implications of information furnished to, or known by, the preparer, and must have made reasonable inquiries if the information furnished to, or known by, the preparer appeared to be incorrect, inconsistent, or incomplete; and
- Retain copies of Form 8867, *Paid Preparers Earned Income Credit Checklist* (or its successor), computation worksheet, and record of how and when the information used to determine eligibility and compute the EIC, was obtained by the preparer. The items must be retained for three years from June 30th following the date the return or claim was given to the taxpayer for signature. The items could be retained either on paper or electronically.

On or After December 31, 2011 A preparer must comply with the following due diligence requirements for tax returns or claims for refund for tax years ending on or after December 31, 2011:

- Complete and submit Form 8867, *Paid Preparer's Earned Income Credit Checklist.* The tax return preparer must complete Form 8867 or such other form and such other information as may be required by the IRS to be submitted in the manner required by forms, instructions, or other appropriate guidance. The preparer's completion of Form 8867 (or successor form) must be based on information provided to the tax return preparer or otherwise reasonably obtained by the tax return preparer;
- Complete the EIC worksheet in the Form 1040 instructions or such other form and such other information as may be prescribed by the IRS or otherwise record in one or more documents in the tax preparer's paper or electronic files the EIC computation, including the method and information used to make the computation. The completion of

the worksheet or other permitted record must be based on information provided by the taxpayer to the tax return preparer or otherwise reasonably obtained by the tax return preparer; and

- Must not know, or have reason to know, that any information used by the tax return preparer in determining the taxpayer's eligibility for, or the amount of, the EIC is incorrect. The tax return preparer may not ignore the implications of information furnished to, or known by, the tax return preparer, and *must make reasonable inquiries* if the information furnished him or her appears to be incorrect, inconsistent, or incomplete. The preparer must make reasonable inquiries if a reasonable and well-informed tax return preparer knowledgeable in the law would conclude that the information furnished appears to be incorrect, inconsistent, or incomplete. Additionally, the preparer must also contemporaneously document in the files the reasonable inquiries made and the responses to these inquiries.

PLANNING POINTER

Under the new requirements, the tax return preparer should verify the identify of the person supplying the eligibility information for the return, plus keep a copy (print or electronic) of the Form 8867 and EIC worksheet, and a record of any additional questions asked of the taxpayer to comply with the due diligence requirements and the taxpayer's answers to those questions. The retention period is three years from the date the return is filed electronically or given to the taxpayer.

COMMENT

The *United States-Republic of Korea Free Trade Agreement Implementation Act of 2011* raised the penalty for failing to comply with the Code Sec. 6695(g) EIC due diligence requirements from $100 to $500 per failure for any tax returns or claims for refund for tax years ending on or after December 31, 2011.

STUDY QUESTIONS

4. Who bears the burden of proof in determining whether a return preparer made a willful attempt to understate a tax liability under Code Sec. 6694(b)?

   a. The IRS
   b. The return preparer
   c. The return preparer's firm
   d. The taxpayer

5. The reasonable cause exception to most Code Sec. 6695 preparer penalties does *not* apply to violations of:

   a. Code Sec. 6695(b), Failure to Sign Return or Claim for Refund to Taxpayer
   b. Code Sec. 6695(e), Failure of Preparer Employer to File Information Returns
   c. Code Sec. 6695(d), Failure to Retain Copy or List
   d. Code Sec. 6695(f), Negotiation of a Taxpayer's Refund Check

---

6. Under changes to the EIC due diligence requirements of Code Sec. 6695(g), starting in 2012, the tax return preparer is now required to:

   a. Decrease the extent to which he or she seeks substantiation of the taxpayer's eligibility for the EIC
   b. Make reasonable inquiries if the information furnished him or her appears to be incorrect, inconsistent, or incomplete
   c. Complete and file additional forms with the taxpayer's return to substantiate the taxpayer's eligibility for the EIC
   d. Refuse to sign the return

CODE SEC. 7216

Code Sec. 7216(a) imposes criminal penalties on tax return preparers who knowingly or recklessly make unauthorized disclosures or uses of information furnished in connection with the preparation of an income tax return. Preparers who violate Code Sec. 7216 may face a maximum penalty of up to one year imprisonment or a fine of not more than $1,000, or both, together with the costs of prosecution.

> **COMMENT**
>
> Code Sec. 6713(a) provides a related civil penalty for unauthorized disclosures or uses of information furnished in connection with the preparation of an income tax return. The penalty for violating section Code Sec. 6713 is $250 for each disclosure or use, not to exceed a total of $10,000 for a calendar year.

Tax Return Preparer

A *tax return preparer* for purposes of Code Sec. 7216 is:

- Any person who is engaged in the business of preparing or assisting in preparing tax returns;
- Any person who is engaged in the business of providing auxiliary services in connection with the preparation of tax returns, including a person who develops software that is used to prepare or file a tax return and any Authorized IRS e-file Provider;
- Any person who is otherwise compensated for preparing, or assisting in preparing, a tax return for any other person; or
- Any individual who, as part of his or her duties of employment with a tax return preparer performs services that assist in the preparation of, or assist in providing auxiliary services in connection with the preparation of, a tax return.

Tax Return

Definition. For purposes of Code Sec. 7216, a *tax return* means any return (or amended return) of income tax imposed by chapter 1 of the Internal Revenue Code.

Tax return information. Tax return information encompasses any information, including, but not limited to, a taxpayer's name, address, or identifying number, which is furnished in any form or manner for, or in connection with, the preparation of a tax return of the taxpayer. This information includes information that the taxpayer furnishes to a tax return preparer and information furnished to the tax return preparer by a third party. Tax return information also includes information the tax return preparer derives or generates from tax return information in connection with the preparation of a taxpayer's return.

> **COMMENT**
>
> Tax return information includes statistical compilations of tax return information, even in a form that cannot be associated with, or otherwise identify, directly or indirectly, a particular taxpayer. However, preparers may make limited use of tax return information to make statistical compilations without taxpayer consent and to use the statistical compilations for limited purposes.

> **COMMENT**
>
> Information is considered "in connection with tax return preparation," and therefore tax return information, if the taxpayer would not have furnished the information to the tax return preparer but for the intention to engage, or the engagement of, the tax return preparer to prepare the tax return.

Permissible Disclosures or Uses Without Consent of Taxpayer

A number of disclosures or uses are authorized without the consent of the taxpayer. They are generally (and include but are not limited to):

- Disclosure under other provisions of the Internal Revenue Code;
- Disclosure to the IRS;
- Disclosure under an order of a court;
- Disclosure to report the commission of a crime; and
- Disclosure of tax return information due to a tax return preparer's incapacity or death.

> **COMMENT**
>
> Special rules apply for disclosures to preparers outside of the United States and disclosures in the case of related taxpayers.

Taxpayer Consent

A tax return preparer may disclose or use tax return information as the taxpayer directs as long as the preparer obtains a written consent from the taxpayer as provided in the Code Sec. 7216 rules. The consent must be knowing and voluntary. A tax return preparer may condition the provision of preparation services upon a taxpayer's consent to disclosure of the taxpayer's tax return information to another tax return preparer for the purpose of performing services that assist in the preparation of, or provide auxiliary services in connection with the preparation of, the tax return of the taxpayer.

> **COMMENT**
>
> The IRS described the form and contents of taxpayer consents in TD 9357 and Rev. Proc. 2008-35.

Circular 230. Willfully disclosing or otherwise using a tax return or tax return information in a manner not authorized by the Internal Revenue Code, contrary to an order of court, or contrary to an order of an administrative law judge in certain cases, constitutes disreputable conduct under Circular 230. Sanctions under Circular 230 include censure, suspension from practice before the IRS, or disbarment.

REGISTERED TAX RETURN PREPARERS

In 2009, the IRS launched a study of its oversight of tax return preparers. The IRS held a number of public meetings, hearing comments from representatives of tax professional associations, the tax return software industry, and state governments. The IRS discovered that the level of preparer oversight varied significantly on whether the preparer held a professional license, had been enrolled to practice before the IRS, and the requirements, if any, of the jurisdiction in which he or she prepared returns.

At the end of its study, the IRS announced a multipronged initiative to strengthen its oversight of preparers. The IRS recommended mandatory PTINs for all paid preparers, competency testing for unenrolled preparers (individuals who are not CPAs, EAs, or attorneys), and continuing education for unenrolled preparers. The IRS developed a new designation, registered tax return preparer (RTRP), for individuals who complete competency testing, continuing education, and other requirements.

COMMENT

CPAs, EAs, attorneys, certain supervised preparers, and individuals who do not prepare Form 1040 series returns are not required to take the RTRP test. Supervised preparers are individuals who do not sign, and are not required to sign, tax returns as a paid return preparer but are:

- Employed by CPA or attorney firms; or
- Employed by other recognized firms that are at least 80 percent owned by attorneys, CPAs, or EAs; and
- Who are supervised by an attorney, CPA, EA, enrolled retirement plan agent, or enrolled actuary who signs the returns prepared by the supervised preparer as the paid tax return preparer.

Practice Rights of RTRPs

Registered tax return preparers have limited practice rights before the IRS. RTRPs have the right to prepare and sign tax returns and claims for refund. RTRPs also may represent clients before revenue agents, customer service representatives, or similar officers and employees of the IRS (including the Taxpayer Advocate Service) during an examination if they signed the tax return or claim for refund for the tax period under examination.

PLANNING POINTER

Federal tax return preparers must have a current preparer tax identification number. PTINs expired on December 31, 2011, but the system continues to accept renewals.

Testing and Continuing Education for RTRPs

The IRS launched the RTRP examination in November 2011. The examination consists of 120 questions. Beginning April 16, 2012, all references on the test are to the Internal Revenue Code, as amended through December 31, 2011. The IRS explained on its website that there is no exact number of questions to obtain a passing score. Test questions are weighted in value to arrive at an overall pass/fail score. The test's potential scaled scores range from 50 to 500. Scaled scores of 350 and above are passing scores. RTRPs also must complete 15 hours of continuing education each year.

RTRP Sanctions

Individuals who are required to take the RTRP and who do not take the exam and satisfy the other requirements may not hold themselves out as a RTRP and cannot prepare returns for compensation. If they hold themselves out as RTRPs and preparer returns for compensation, they open themselves to sanctions under Circular 230. Willfully representing a taxpayer before the

IRS unless the practitioner is authorized to do so constitutes disreputable conduct under Circular 230. Sanctions under Circular 230 include censure, suspension from practice before the IRS, or disbarment.

STUDY QUESTIONS

7. Registered tax return preparers (RTRPs):

   a. Have unlimited practice rights before the IRS

   b. Have limited practice rights before the IRS

   c. Can only practice before the IRS with the assistance of a CPA, attorney, or EA

   d. Must transfer representation of a taxpayer to a CPA, attorney, or EA when cases are to come before the IRS

8. Which of the following is **not** a requirement for the registered tax return preparer (RTRP) designation?

   a. Supervision by an attorney, CPA, enrolled agent, enrolled plan agent, or enrolled actuary

   b. A passing score on the RTRP examination

   c. Completion of a minimum of 15 hours of continuing education credits per year

   d. Obtaining and renewing a preparer tax identification number (PTIN)

MANDATORY E-FILE

The *Worker, Homeownership, and Business Assistance Act of 2009* (2009 Worker Act) imposed mandatory electronic filing requirements on specified tax return preparers.

A *specified tax return preparer* is any person who prepares covered returns for compensation unless that person reasonably expects to file 10 or fewer individual income tax returns in a calendar year. If a person who is a tax return preparer is a member of a firm, that person is a specified tax return preparer unless the person's firm members in the aggregate reasonably expect to file 10 or fewer individual income tax returns in a calendar year.

> **COMMENT**
>
> The IRS provided transition relief for calendar year 2011. A preparer was not be considered a specified tax return preparer if that person reasonably expected, or if the person is a member of a firm, the firm's members in the aggregate reasonably expected, to file fewer than 100 individual income tax returns in the 2011 calendar year.

Covered Returns

The requirement applies to any return of income tax imposed by Subtitle A of the Internal Revenue Code on individuals, trusts, or estates, such as Forms 1040, 1040A, 1040EZ, and 1041. However, Forms 1040-NR, 1041QFT, and 990T (when the exempt organization is a trust subject to tax on unrelated business taxable income under Code Sec. 511(b)) cannot be electronically filed at this time and they are not deemed covered returns for purposes of mandatory e-filing by specified tax return preparers.

> **COMMENT**
>
> The electronic filing requirement for specified tax return preparers does not apply to payroll tax returns.

Filing

A return is considered filed by a specified tax return preparer if the preparer or any member, employee, or agent of the preparer or the preparer's firm submits the tax return to the IRS on the taxpayer's behalf, either electronically or in nonelectronic (paper) form. This includes the preparer or a member of the preparer's firm dropping the return in the mailbox for the taxpayer. However, acts such as providing filing or delivery instructions, an addressed envelope, postage estimates, stamps, or similar acts designed to assist the taxpayer in the taxpayer's efforts to correctly mail or otherwise deliver an individual income tax return to the IRS do not constitute filing by the tax return preparer or specified tax return preparer as long as the taxpayer actually mails or otherwise delivers the paper individual income tax return to the IRS.

Administrative exceptions. The IRS may provide administrative exemptions from the requirement of this section for certain classes of specified tax return preparers, or regarding certain types of individual income tax returns, as the IRS determines necessary to promote effective and efficient tax administration.

Waivers. The IRS may grant a waiver of the mandatory e-file requirement in cases of undue hardship. An undue hardship waiver may be granted upon application by a specified tax return preparer consistent with instructions provided in published guidance and as prescribed in relevant forms and instructions. A determination of undue hardship will be based upon all facts and circumstances. The undue hardship waiver provided to a specified tax return preparer may apply to a series or class of individual income tax returns or for a specified period of time, subject to the terms and conditions regarding the method of filing prescribed in such waiver.

Client choice. A client of a specified tax return preparer may request to independently file a return on paper. Starting in 2012, the client who insists on filing a return on paper—and not the specified tax return preparer—must physically mail or otherwise deliver the paper return to the IRS after the specified tax return preparer has prepared the return. Further, a client's request to independently file a return on paper must be made in writing. The IRS has instructed specified tax return preparers to attach Form 8948, *Preparer Explanation for Not Filing Electronically,* to the client's return. The IRS has posted sample language on its website.

Compliance. The IRS has identified three types of specified tax return preparers who may not comply with the e-file mandate:

- Preparers who are unaware of the mandate or do not fully understand the mandate;
- Preparers who know about the mandate, sign the tax return, but intentionally choose not to e-file; and
- Preparers who complete tax returns but do not sign the returns or submit them electronically.

Penalties

Disciplinary proceedings. The IRS does not have authority under the Internal Revenue Code to impose penalties on specified tax return preparers who fail to comply with the e-file mandate. However, the IRS can discipline specified tax returns under Circular 230, Rules of Practice Before the IRS. Under Circular 230, the IRS can initiate disciplinary proceedings against practitioners who engage in disreputable conduct. Circular 230 includes willfully failing to e-file in the definition of disreputable conduct for which a person can be sanctioned.

Reasonable cause. However, no sanction will be imposed if failure to e-file is due to reasonable cause and not due to willful neglect. Sanctions under Circular 230 include censure, suspension from practice before the IRS, or disbarment.

COMMENT

In 2011, the Government Accountability Office (GAO) told Congress that granting the IRS authority to penalize specified tax return preparers would provide a more commensurate sanction than those that can be imposed under Circular 230. GAO noted that prior to imposing sanctions on a preparer, the IRS must provide the preparer with notice and an opportunity for a hearing. Building a case against a preparer is time-consuming, often taking longer than a filing season.

REFERRAL TO IRS OFFICE OF PROFESSIONAL RESPONSIBILITY

The IRS Office of Professional Responsibility (OPR) enforces the Circular 230 rules of practice before the agency. Certain preparer penalties trigger referral to OPR. In other cases, referral to OPR is at the discretion of the IRS employee who discovered the alleged inappropriate behavior.

> **COMMENT**
>
> Each referral to OPR should describe and document the practitioner's action to support disciplinary action. The IRS has instructed its employees to include a summary of the suspected misconduct and provide as much detail as possible regarding the misconduct in question along with supporting documentation.

Discretionary and Mandatory Referrals

Code Sec. 6694(a). The IRS has instructed its employees to exercise discretion in making referrals of asserted Code Sec. 6694(a) penalties to OPR. Referrals of asserted Code Sec. 6694(a) penalties to OPR should be based on a pattern of failing to meet the required penalty standards under Code Sec. 6694(a).

Code Sec. 6694(b). Asserted preparer penalties under Code Sec. 6694(b) are mandatory referrals to OPR.

Code Sec. 6695(a), (b), (c), (d), (e), (f), and (g). The IRS has instructed its employees to exercise discretion in making referrals to OPR. However, in matters where preparer penalties are asserted when there is willful neglect, examiners should consider making a referral to OPR.

Interviews

The IRS has outlined procedures for its personnel to follow in cases of alleged preparer misconduct. IRS personnel should conduct an interview to develop facts and circumstances to determine whether a return preparer penalty case is warranted. During the interview process, the examiner should ask the taxpayer the following questions:

- Did the taxpayer meet with the preparer?
- Did the taxpayer complete a questionnaire and/or have a face-to-face meeting with the preparer?
- What documentation was provided to the preparer?
- Did the taxpayer receive a copy of the return?
- Was the preparer compensated?

The questions asked of the preparer are important to determine whether additional development regarding the return preparation is warranted. If the preparer is the taxpayer's representative, examiners may want to ask:

- What was discussed in the "interview" with the taxpayer?
- What documentation was provided to prepare the return?
- Was a copy of the return provided to the taxpayer?
- Was the preparer aware of any errors, omissions, or mistakes on the return under examination?
- Was the preparer compensated for the tax return preparation?

COMMENT

All information regarding the return preparer's activities and the applicability of any penalties relating to the return preparer is retained separate from the taxpayer's case file.

STUDY QUESTIONS

9. The willful failure of a specified tax return preparer to adhere to the mandatory e-filing rules may constitute:

  a. Disreputable conduct under Circular 230
  b. Improper conduct under international rules of tax return practice
  c. Conduct subject to a $1,000 fine under the federal rules of criminal procedure
  d. An automatic $100 per-violation fine under IRS rules of practice.

10. Violation of which of the following triggers a mandatory referral to the IRS Office of Professional Responsibility (OPR)?

  a. Code Sec. 6694(a)
  b. Code Sec. 6694(b)
  c. Code Sec. 6695(c)
  d. Code Sec. 6695(d)

CONCLUSION

The IRS has a variety of tools to sanction tax return preparers who engage in improper behavior. These tools are designed to encourage compliance and sanction behaviors that impair tax collection. Preparers need to be aware of the penalties and the reasonable cause exceptions to some of the penalties to avoid engaging in behaviors that the IRS deems contrary to the best interests of taxpayers and the tax preparation industry.

IRS Audits: The Examination Process and New Developments

This chapter provides an overview of the Internal Revenue Service's examination process, covering the types of audits the IRS has in its arsenal and what taxpayers can expect while facing an exam. In addition this chapter discusses some recent changes to how the IRS conducts audits, including how it selects taxpayers and how it has addressed the increasing volume of audits in its backlog.

LEARNING OBJECTIVES

Upon completion of this chapter you will be able to:

- Describe the IRS audit examination process from selection to resolution;
- List the taxpayer's rights in an audit;
- Identify the types of IRS audits;
- Understand the problems inherent with IRS correspondence audits; and
- Explain the latest developments in IRS audits.

INTRODUCTION

The tax code is a complicated document that is confusing to many taxpayers, and often as a consequence some taxpayers may inadvertently commit an error on their tax returns. Other times a taxpayer intentionally makes an incorrect entry on a return in an attempt to skirt full tax liability. Regardless of the reason for the error, it is the IRS's duty to administer the U.S. tax code as enacted by Congress and to ensure compliance among taxpayers with impartiality toward the government and the taxpayer. Mistakes may cause the IRS to deem that a tax return requires further investigation. In such cases, the IRS may initiate an *audit examination,* which is a review of a business's or individual's accounts and financial information to ensure that the taxpayer is reporting its information correctly and accurately. Returns are also selected for examination randomly or through a process using complex computer algorithms designed to maximize audit revenues.

The IRS has numerous enforcement tools at its disposal, and audits are only one means of ensuring compliance with the tax law. For example, instead of initiating a potentially time-consuming audit, the IRS will usually resort to using its math error authority to correct minor mathematical or clerical errors on a return, statement, schedule, or other supplement (a process not technically classified as an "audit"). *Audits,* as the term is used by the IRS, however, not only involve face-to-face encounters with IRS revenue agents but may also take the form of *correspondence audits* conducted entirely through U.S. mail.

According to the IRS's Fiscal Year 2011 Enforcement and Service Results, the actual percentage of tax returns audited is low. In fiscal year (FY) 2011, for example, the IRS examined only 1.11 percent of all the individual returns filed that year, and this represented a 12-year high. (In FY 2000, the percentage of individual returns audited was a scant 0.49 percent). The total audit coverage for business and corporate returns in FY 2011 was 0.63 percent. Despite the seemingly low coverage rate, however, revenue gained from examination is significant. In FY 2011, the IRS collected $124 billion from examinations.

IRS audits can be time-consuming and stressful for taxpayers and their return preparers, even when the result does not change the reported tax liability (a "no-change outcome"). The goal of taxpayers faced with audits should be to resolve the dispute efficiently and quickly, without resorting to delay tactics that would taint their relationship with the IRS audit agent or increase the agent's suspicion and scrutiny of sensitive issues that could generate additional tax deficiencies or penalties. Taxpayers should remember that an IRS agent's primary concern is to process as many audits as he or she can without sacrificing the quality and efficiency of the examination of a taxpayer's books and records. However, the IRS's budgetary constraints limit the agency's resources, and IRS agents are faced with an ever-mounting workload. As a result, most agents welcome an expeditious conclusion to an audit, whether on an agreed or unagreed basis. Practitioners and taxpayers benefit from a better understanding of the IRS audit process. Such knowledge not only reduces confusion but can speed along a complex process.

THE AUDIT SELECTION PROCESS

The examination process begins with the selection of tax returns for audit. The IRS selects tax returns for audit for numerous reasons, but selection of a return at random is rare. Generally something in the return triggers the audit, for example a claimed deduction or loss disproportionate to the taxpayer's income, a large amount of noncash charitable contributions, or a low amount of reported self-employment income. Overall, IRS statistics demonstrate individual income tax returns in higher adjusted gross income (AGI) classes are more likely to be examined compared to returns in lower AGI classes. This makes sense because examination of higher-income taxpayers is more likely to produce enough additional revenue to make the use of an IRS agent's time cost-effective. Nevertheless, the IRS makes it a point not to ignore any income class entirely. Also notable in recent years is the uptick in audits of lower-income taxpayers who may claim the earned income credit (EIC), which has been subject to more fraudulent claims than has been typically the case in the past.

The scope of an audit can vary markedly, from an inquiry into the size of a specific charitable deduction all the way up to a full-blown examination into every line of a tax return. To conserve resources, an examiner generally investigates only one or several deductions, credits, or missing income items, which are generally flagged for the examiners through computer processing (during the "preselection process"). *Field audits* of small businesses present another model for examinations, in which the IRS agent is trained to examine certain books and records, or even the physical layout of a business (for example, a restaurant). No "one-size-fits-all" audit exists although, as already mentioned, strained IRS resources generally require the "average" audit to focus only on certain items. Income is not the number one determining factor in selection, however. The IRS selects returns using a variety of methods, including those described here.

Discriminant Index Function System

The Discriminant Index Function (DIF) system selects returns through a computer scoring system involving a numerical score assignment designed to indicate the potential for revealing additional tax liability upon audit.

> **EXAMPLE**
>
> The index indicates there is a particular range of business expenses or charitable contributions that is acceptable for taxpayers with a certain income. If the claimed amount falls above this acceptable range, the DIF system will enter a higher score than otherwise, indicating greater audit potential.

The Internal Revenue Manual (IRM) requires that an experienced examiner screen each selected DIF return to eliminate those returns not worthy of examination.

According to a report issued on September 29, 2011 (Reference Number 2011-30-113), by the Treasury Inspector General for Tax Administration (TIGTA), the DIF has not been particularly useful for selecting small corporate returns due to the number of changes in the tax law since calendar year 1988, the last year from which the IRS drew on corporate return data to update the DIF formulas. TIGTA mentioned, however, that an upcoming study by the National Research Program (NRP) on corporate and shareholder tax compliance is intended to provide the necessary data to update the formulas again. Treasury Department and IRS officials anticipate the upcoming study will involve the identification, selection, and examination of approximately 2,500 tax year 2010 returns from corporations with assets of less than $250,000.

Unreported Income DIF

Closely related to the DIF, the Unreported Income DIF (UI DIF) system assigns a score to tax returns and rates them in accordance with their potential as indicators that unreported income exists. The IRS first applied UI DIF formulas to tax returns in 2002.

Coordinated Industry Case Program

The IRS examines many large corporate returns from businesses having more than $10 million in assets on an annual basis through its Coordinated Industry Case (CIC) Program. A tax return is assigned a certain number of points based upon factors, such as gross receipts, gross assets, and number operating entities. Once a return is assigned 12 or more points, it may be considered a CIC case, depending on the specific facts and circumstances for a particular taxpayer.

> **COMMENT**
>
> IRS deputy Commissioner Stephen T. Miller addressed corporate executives on March 26, 2012, stating, "It is my hope to reduce the resources we spend in CIC. I want to do that by becoming comfortable with the compliance levels of more taxpayers, thereby reducing the level of our involvement with these taxpayers. For those taxpayers that remain under audit or even cyclical audit, we still need to revise the CIC process. In short, my goal is to move the IRS away from a paradigm that has us permanently ensconced in most of your offices year after year, cycle after cycle" (**www.irs.gov/newsroom/article/0,,id=255996,00.html**).

Document Matching

The IRS examines some returns when it finds discrepancies between the income a taxpayer reported and other income information provided by third parties, such as on Forms W-2 filed by employers or Form 1099 interest statements from banks.

> **EXAMPLE**
>
> Readwell, a publishing company that has issued more than $10 in copyright royalties to Susan McCleary, Ltd., a literary agency, timely files a Form 1099-MISC reporting the payments. The literary agency, however, does not report the income on its tax return. While processing the tax return, the IRS computer system automatically notes the omission. This omission increases the chances that the literary agency will be audited more generally in addition to having an IRS computer-generated letter automatically sent to the taxpayer for the shortfall.

Related Taxpayers

Often the IRS audits taxpayers that have significant interactions with another taxpayer currently under audit. This "lateral entry" return selection process can be damaging to the taxpayer because the examining agent commences the audit with a substantial amount of information.

> **EXAMPLE**
>
> In the process of auditing ReadiCash, a local check-cashing agency, the IRS receives substantial information about ReadiCash's customers. The IRS examiner may conclude that some of the proceeds from cashed checks likely were not appropriately reported as gross receipts by the customers.

TYPES OF AUDITS

Not all tax return issues involve the same complexity or require the same level of scrutiny. As such, not all IRS examinations are the same. For example, it would be highly inefficient to send out an IRS examiner to visit an individual taxpayer's home in Tulsa, Oklahoma, and interview all his associates if all the IRS requires is a document substantiating a deduction for a charitable donation. Consequently, there are three different types of audit examinations that the IRS has to pick among in its arsenal:

- Correspondence examinations
- Office examinations
- Field examinations

Correspondence Examinations

Correspondence (corr) examinations, as the name suggests, are conducted entirely through the U.S. mail. (The IRS *never* uses e-mail to correspond with taxpayers.) Correspondence examinations require less involvement from IRS examiners and are therefore used more frequently by the budget-strapped IRS. Because corr examinations make up such a large percentage of the total examinations the IRS conducts, they are considered the "work horse" of the IRS audit tools.

The IRS routinely uses corr examinations for issues that it generally deems more efficient and less burdensome to handle by mail, for example questionable claims for earned income tax credits (EITCs) or inconsistent line items.

Although the taxpayer or its representative may speak with an IRS agent over the telephone, routinely no face-to-face communication will occur at any point during a corr audit. Instead, during a correspondence audit, the selection, the actual audit, and the closing of the case are generally conducted through "batch processing." *Batch processing* is a fully automated system that functions with minimal involvement from an actual tax examiner up until the point where a taxpayer or its representative responds by mail to the initial contact letter.

> ### COMMENT
>
> National Taxpayer Advocate Nina Olson has critiqued what she called the "ailing" correspondence audit program, advocating its replacement by a virtual face-to-face audit. The Taxpayer Advocate Service (TAS) launched a pilot program that enables taxpayers in Tampa, Florida, to speak face-to-face with a case advocate in Jacksonville and obtain a real-time documentation review by the advocate representative. Olson envisions a system that would assign PIN numbers to taxpayers under audit, connect taxpayers to a tax examiner through online means, record tax documentation with a digital camera, and retain digitized documents relevant to the case. Olson stated that this approach would offer "benefits of face-to-face office audits (i.e. higher response and agreement rates, higher customer satisfaction) while preserving some of the cost savings of correspondence exam (centralized locations, automated processing before and after the online audit)" NTA Blog (**http://www.taxpayeradvocate.irs.gov/Blog/virtual-face-to-face-audits**).

Initial contact letter. At the beginning of a correspondence examination, the IRS sends an initial contact letter that notifies a taxpayer of the opening of an audit. It generally does not propose that a specific balance is due. Rather, the initial contact letter describes the issue or issues under examination and frequently contains an information document request. This request essentially asks for the documentation the examiner needs to resolve the dispute. The taxpayer has 30 days to respond to the initial contact letter. The taxpayer should respond by mail. Phone calls are usually relayed to any available IRS employee, meaning that if the taxpayer calls several times, it may talk to different IRS employees each time, none of whom are acquainted with the subject of the previous phone calls.

Sometimes the initial contact letter for a corr audit will contain a report that proposes adjustments to items with respect to which the IRS believes it has a reasonable certainty of proving a potential liability. This is called a "combo letter," and it is generally an IRS Letter 525. In contrast with the regular initial contact letter, a combo letter includes the IRS's upfront determination of a taxpayer's adjusted tax liability and gives the taxpayer 30 days to either agree with the adjustment or to disagree and file a protest with the IRS Office of Appeals. The IRS believes combo letters significantly reduce the audit cycle duration and present the taxpayer with a clearer understanding of the changes being proposed.

Failure to respond. Because the IRS makes extensive use of automation in the corr examination program, time deadlines are automatically programmed into the system. During the audit, attempted correspondence contacts that do not receive a response are systemically advanced through the examination process. If the IRS receives mail from the taxpayer, that mailing (once processed as received) precludes subsequent notices from being issued.

If the taxpayer does not respond to the initial contact letter within the requisite 30 days, the IRS will automatically issue a second letter informing the taxpayer of the proposed tax assessment. If the taxpayer does not respond to the second letter or if the response is insufficient to address the items in question, the IRS will issue Letter 3219, the Notice of Deficiency. This notice requires the taxpayer to pay the tax assessment or file a petition with the Tax Court within 90 days. If a resolution has not occurred by the end of the 90-day period (or any extensions given in response to the notice), the program examination is closed and the assessed tax is posted to the taxpayer's account.

Correspondence audits increasing. The IRS considers corr audits to be "cost-effective," meaning they generally yield more tax revenue than they require in IRS employee labor costs. As such, the number of corr audits has risen steadily over the past decade. The IRS Oversight Board reported in its "Annual Report to Congress 2011" that the volume of taxpayers audited by correspondence exam has grown from 72 percent of all IRS examinations of individual tax returns in FY 2001 to 78 percent of all individual tax returns in FY 2010. More specifically, in FY 2000, the IRS conducted 366,657 automated correspondence exams. In FY 2011, the IRS conducted 1,179,069, representing an increase of 220 percent from FY 2000.

Recently, the economic downturn has forced lawmakers to make tough decisions concerning funding for government agencies and programs. The IRS FY 2012 budget was reduced by $305 million from FY 2011, and the IRS will most likely enter FY 2013 on the same budget or only slightly higher. As such, the number of correspondence audits (as opposed to other types) is expected to increase further in the near future. Unfortunately, this trend has provoked concerns from IRS employees, practitioners, and taxpayers concerning the burden correspondence audits place on taxpayers, which includes the duration of time it often takes the IRS to close the audit.

One recurring complaint is that the IRS workforce is not large enough and lacks the resources to enable timely responses to taxpayers who respond to the initial contact letter. Another is that the IRS combo letters initiating a correspondence audit with an already determined amount of tax liability do not give taxpayers enough time to respond adequately to the adjustments before the IRS issues the taxpayer a default.

Office Examinations

Generally, office examinations involve small businesses or individual income tax returns that predominantly include sole proprietorships. In addition, if a taxpayer previously selected for a correspondence audit requests an interview to discuss the IRS's proposed adjustments, the case may be moved to the taxpayer's district office. Conversely, an examiner may sometimes determine that a tax return selected for an office audit examination would be better handled through a correspondence audit.

Office examinations generally take place at the IRS office located nearest to where the taxpayer maintains its financial books and records, which is generally its residence or place of business. However, on a case-by-case basis the IRS will consider written requests from taxpayers or their representatives to change the office examination location. A request by a taxpayer to transfer the place of an office examination will generally be granted if the current residence of the taxpayer or the location of the taxpayer's books, records, and source documents is closer to a different IRS office than the one originally designated for the examination. Additionally, Treasury Reg. §301.7605-1(e)(1) directs the IRS to consider several factors, which include whether the selected office audit location would cause undue inconvenience to the taxpayer.

After considering these factors, the IRS may exercise its discretion to relocate an office examination. The factors under Treasury Reg. § 301.7605-1(e)(1) do not include consideration of the location of the place of business of a taxpayer's representative. However, the IRS agent may determine, based on the factors listed in Treasury Reg. § 301.7605-1(e)(1)(1), that the examination should take place at the representative's office.

Office examinations involve issues that are too complex for a correspondence audit, which involves only the exchange of mail and (sometimes) a few telephone calls. Issues subject to an office audit, however, are usually not complex enough to warrant a full-scale field audit examination. Common issues include the substantiation of a business purpose, travel and entertainment expenses, Schedule C items, or certain itemized deductions.

Initial contact. After the IRS has selected a tax return for office examination, the return is assigned to an examiner and scheduled for examination. Following assignment, office audits often are initiated by a letter (usually Letter 3572) mailed from the IRS, but the IRS examiner may also initiate the office audit by a telephone call requesting that the taxpayer bring certain information and records to the IRS office.

Office examinations are conducted primarily by the interview method. Basically, the IRS examiner requests the taxpayer and/or its representatives to come to the district director's office and bring certain tax and financial records to support the items on the tax return. An examining agent generally conducts an interview of the taxpayer or its representative and reviews the records and other relevant information brought to the IRS office in support of items reported on the tax return(s). During this process, an examiner might ask a taxpayer to explain certain items, for example, insufficiently substantiated charitable contributions or certain itemized deductions that appear disproportionate to the taxpayer's reported gross income. Also during the examination interview, the taxpayer has an opportunity and the right to point out to the examining officer any amounts included in the return that are not taxable or any deductions that the taxpayer failed to claim on the return.

During discussions between the taxpayer and the IRS examiner at an office examination interview, additional issues may arise. Therefore, taxpayers may find it wise to obtain a representative who can be directly involved during an office examination. Taxpayers and representatives should take steps to limit the scope of the examiner's inquiry. The scope of an office examination generally is limited to the issues that were specified in the initial contact letter to the taxpayer. If an issue arises and it seems that there might be a reason to expand the scope of the office audit examination, such expansion generally requires the permission of the group manager.

Field Examinations

The IRS initiates a field exam audit by sending either a Letter 2205 or Letter 3572, which lays out the issues to be examined and lists a specific IRS agent as the point of contact. Sometimes the taxpayer receives a telephone call from the field exam agent prior to receiving the letter. Taxpayers must contact that agent within 10 days of receiving the initial contact letter in order to schedule an interview. Generally a Form 4564, *Information Document Request,* also accompanies the initial contact letter and contains the IRS examiner's description of the audit-related documents it wants to review.

Conducting a field examination of a tax return requires the agent to have far greater knowledge of tax law and accounting principles than do correspondence or office audits, and therefore, field examiners are generally much more experienced. Field audits almost always take place where the taxpayer's books, records, and other relevant data are maintained, which generally means the taxpayer's residence or place of business. However, if a business is so small that a field examination would essentially require the taxpayer to close the business or would unduly disrupt the operation of the business, the IRS examiner can conduct the field examination at the closest IRS office or at the office of the taxpayer's representative.

Factors most commonly triggering field examinations. Generally, business returns are selected for field examination if a number of factors exist. These may include those listed in IRM 4.1.5.1.3 (Sorting of Classified Returns) (10-24-2006):

- The company files a corporate return such as Form 1120, 1120S 1120F, 1041, or 1065;
- Returns or records show significant business activity at a place other than the taxpayer's residence;

- Returns show significant income or losses from related entities;
- Schedule C or F shows unusual accounting methods, complex issues, and/or a need for a significant amount of accounting and auditing skills;
- The issues are complex enough that an audit would likely take an extensive amount of time to complete;
- Issues indicate that an on-site inspection of records or assets is required; and
- Individuals have received wages from closely held C corporations and claimed employee business expenses or Schedule C expenses.

Field audits and fraud. The IRS has faced recent criticism that its field exams are ineffective in turning up additional taxes related to tax fraud. The Treasury Inspector General for Tax Administration (TIGTA) recently published the results of its review of a statistical sample of 116 field audits closed between June 2009 and June 2010. The review found 26 audits with fraud indicators that were not recognized and investigated in accordance with IRS procedures and guidelines. The 26 field audits in question each involved income and/or overstated expenses that resulted in the taxpayers agreeing they owed additional taxes of at least $10,000. The IRS disagreed with TIGTA's recommendations but has stated it will address the matter in the future.

Large Business and Coordinated Industry Case Audits

In addition to correspondence, office, and field audit examinations, the IRS routinely audits certain large businesses. Some of the largest and most complex taxpayers are audited under the Coordinated Industry Case (CIC) program, commonly referred to as the large case program. Cases in the CIC program involve large business taxpayers and their effectively controlled entities. Examinations are conducted by an IRS audit team of agents, who are generally present physically at the taxpayer's place of business. Examinations generally cover certain complex issues and involve the routine review of gross receipts, gross assets, and number of operating entities.

Returns involving a significant number of complex issues are often audited by an examination team of the most experienced agents who remain physically present at the taxpayer's business and conduct audits on a somewhat permanent basis. The taxpayer is often required to provide examining agents with office space, equipment, and files.

Recently, top IRS officials have disclosed that the agency intends to move some of its resources away from the traditional CIC program and concentrate compliance efforts on different areas, such as the Industry Issue Resolution (IIR), Compliance Assurance Process (CAP), and Schedule UTP, Uncertain Tax Positions, programs. These programs are designed to increase compliance and resolution of issues *prior* to filing and also to pinpoint the most important issues behind noncompliant audits so that IRS Large Business and International (LB&I) Division examiners can focus on them and eliminate unproductive steps in the examination process.

> **COMMENT**
>
> As part of the shift away from the CIC program as it currently is, the IRS has expressed a goal of paying more attention to passthrough entities. Paul DeNard, LB&I Operations's deputy commissioner, recently stated that 75 percent of the approximately 260,000 taxpayers under LB&I's jurisdiction are passthrough entities. Heather Maloy, commissioner of LB&I, also stated at a conference in April 2012 that the IRS plans in the future to focus its limited resources on decreasing noncompliance among individuals with large personal networks of foreign and passthrough dealings.

PRECONTACT RESPONSIBILITIES

Once a tax return has been selected for potential audit and assigned to an IRS examiner, he or she must consider whether to proceed with an examination. At this stage in the process, the examiner is required to consider factors that might prevent an exam. For example, the examiner must take into account the time remaining in the statute of limitations period since the tax return in question was filed. The examiner must also assess whether there are any conflicts of interest or other disqualifying factors that would prevent him or her from conducting the examination.

Statute of Limitations

While considering the propriety of an exam, the examiner will look to the statute of limitations. Under Code Sec. 6501(a), the statute of limitations for assessing a deficiency of tax liability is three years, which runs from the date on which the tax return was filed (or from the return's due date if filed early). In cases where fraud-related issues are present, however, there is no limitations period.

If the statute of limitations is scheduled to expire imminently or within 12 months, the examining agent must obtain his or her relevant group manager's approval before starting the audit. If the examiner determines that he or she cannot meet the IRS's guideline requirements within the period of time allotted for an examination, then the group manager must decide whether to begin or forego the examination. The guidelines require generally that examinations of individual returns should be completed within 26 months after the return was due or filed, whichever is later. For business returns, the cycle is 27 months.

If the group manager and examiner decide to begin the examination, they must document the group manager's approval for a deviation from the examination cycle requirements in the record. The IRM specifies that the group manager may take into account factors that might support exceeding the examination cycle, namely whether an examination:

- Would result in a serious criticism of the IRS's administration of tax laws;
- Would establish a precedent that would seriously hamper subsequent attempts by the IRS to take corrective action;
- Would result in inconsistent treatment of similarly situated taxpayers; or
- Would be contrary to an established IRS position.

Extensions to the Statute of Limitations

The IRS at times may request that a taxpayer extend the statute of limitations so that the examiner will have time to examine the tax return and assess tax. The taxpayer is not required to consent to an extension, but doing so may be to the taxpayer's benefit. Without an extension, the IRS may rush to assess tax without considering further documentation that would have been beneficial in a taxpayer's case. Also if the examiner makes an adjustment to the tax return, the taxpayer cannot appeal the results of the audit within the IRS unless sufficient time remains in the statute of limitations period.

Other Disqualifying Factors

In some cases the examiner must recuse himself or herself from handling an audit. This can occur when there is a conflict of interest, such as if the examiner has a personal relationship of some kind with the taxpayer or a financial or professional interest with the taxpayer. The IRM instructs examiners to avoid any situation that might create a conflict of interest. If an examiner is assigned a return that might create a real or apparent conflict of interest, he or she must immediately inform the group manager. The taxpayer also has a right to ask the group manager for review by another agent, which the manager must approve if the facts warrant.

Assessment of Audit Potential

Following the initial review for disqualifying factors, the examiner will assess the taxpayer's return on its audit potential in a precontact analysis. The examiner is responsible for determining the scope of the audit, beginning with the issues identified by the classifier on the classification check sheet. The examiner must perform a precontact analysis including a thorough review of the case file to identify large, unusual, or questionable items (LUQs) beyond those selected on the classification check sheet.

Analysis process. While assessing audit potential during this stage, the examiner is instructed to review the complete tax return including line items, credits, the balance sheet, elections, schedules, and any other items attached to the return. Time given to the IRS may not always allow for a thorough review. Further, the examiner is instructed to review internal and external data from the various IRS case file programs, the Internet, and other sources specified in the IRM. The examiner determines from this information whether an employee from another IRS function is working with the taxpayer. If so, the IRM instructs the examiner to contact the employee assigned the case and determine the extent of that involvement.

The IRM advises examiners to check appropriate internal records to determine whether a valid power of attorney is on file for the year(s) under examination. The IRM also instructs them to perform preliminary research, including reviewing code sections, regulations, court cases, revenue rulings and procedures, Coordinated Issue Papers (ISPs), Audit Technique Guides (ATGs), and/or business units' web pages as necessary to become familiar with the issues.

Large, unusual, or questionable items. What the examiner will determine to be an LUQ item depends on the examiner's analysis of the return as a whole and the separate items listed there. The amounts listed for some items may seem questionable in certain circumstances, but not in others. The IRM advises examiners to consider multiple factors in assessing a return's audit potential and worthiness for an exam, including:

- *The size of the item compared to the total*—The amount of a claimed deduction for business expenses compared to the total amount of business expenses;
- *Absolute size of the item*—The size of an item in and of itself may appear unusual or questionable;
- *Inherent character of the item*—The nature of an item may seem out of context, for example a claim for airplane travel on a plumber's return;
- *Evidence of intent to mislead*—Such evidence may include missing or incomplete schedules or obviously incorrect items;
- *Beneficial effect of the manner in which an item is reported*—For example, expenses claimed on a business schedule rather than claimed as an itemized deduction;
- *Relationship to other items*—Incomplete transactions identified on the tax return may relate to other items, for example, when a taxpayer has reported sales of stock but no dividend income;
- *Whipsaw issues*—These occur when there is a transaction between two parties and characteristics of the transaction will benefit one party and harm the other; and
- *Missing items whose absence benefit the taxpayer*—Examiners will consider items that are not shown on the return but would normally appear on the returns of similar taxpayers, including income, expenses, deductions, and credits.

STUDY QUESTIONS

1. All of the following are methods the IRS uses to select returns for audit *except:*
   a. Comparing interactions of a taxpayer with related taxpayers
   b. Matching income of a taxpayer with information from third parties
   c. Reviewing the pool of taxpayers who request extensions of time to file their returns
   d. Scoring returns for their potential for revealing additional tax liability

2. After returns are initially reviewed for their audit potential, the following step is performed next::
   a. Preselection examination
   b. Precontact analysis
   c. Predetermination conference
   d. Group manager determination

THE EXAMINATION PROCESS

Notification

After the IRS selects a taxpayer's account for an audit examination, the IRS notifies the taxpayer in an initial contact letter sent by U.S. mail. The type of letter the IRS sends to a taxpayer in notification of an audit depends on the type of audit:

- For correspondence audits, the IRS generally sends either a Letter 566 (CG) or a Notice CP2000;
- For field audits, the initial contact generally is either IRS Letter 2205 or Letter 3572 and is often preceded by a telephone call from the examining agent; and
- For office audits, initial contact is generally made through a telephone call and/or a letter, which is generally Letter 3572.

The IRS does not currently use e-mail notification to alert taxpayers that they are under audit. Nor does it use e-mail as a means of corresponding during an audit. At present, e-mail is considered subject to too much potential fraud to accept it as a means of communication. Further, the IRS has warned that any correspondence-mail asking for confidential information such as Social Security numbers should trigger suspicions that someone not from the IRS may be attempting to steal the taxpayer's identity.

An initial contact letter contains the examiner's name and contact information in the upper right-hand corner. Additionally, the initial contact letter may be accompanied by IRS Publication 1, "Your Rights as a Taxpayer," and Notice 609, Privacy Act Notice. The letter may also include a Form 4564, *Information Document Request,* if the taxpayer has been selected for a field or office audit.

Initial Contact by Taxpayer

Because an audit, once begun, is rarely "lost in the system" by the IRS and because examiners are usually undeterred by delay tactics, taxpayers should make the initial contact with examining agent as soon as possible to begin the audit process in earnest, according to the IRS. For noncorrespondence audits that will take place either in an IRS office or the taxpayer's home or place of business, the examiner generally prefers to schedule the date and location for an initial appointment to meet the taxpayer within 14 days of the initial contact. Delaying an appointment for 45 days or longer requires the approval by the examining agent's group manager.

In addition to scheduling the initial appointment for a noncorrespondence audit, during the initial contact call the examiner and taxpayer should identify the persons who will be present at the initial interview. The examiner should also identify the issues subject to the exam, the information, documents, and other records he or she needs, and should answer the taxpayer's questions about the audit process.

Taxpayer Rights

At the beginning of the examination process, IRS examiners are instructed to inform the taxpayer of the existence of the Taxpayer Bill of Rights 2 (P.L. 104-168) and the examination and the appellate processes. Generally, examiners convey this information during the initial contact phone call or the initial interview.

Among the rights a taxpayer has during an audit are:

- The right to privacy and confidentiality about tax matters, which includes the right to know why the IRS is asking for information, how it will use it, and what the consequences are for failure to provide requested information;
- The right to professional and courteous treatment by IRS employees;
- The right to representation, by oneself or an authorized representative;
- The right to appeal disagreements, both within the IRS and before the courts;
- The right to relief from penalties if the taxpayer can prove it acted reasonably and in good faith or relied on the incorrect advice of an IRS employee.

Representation

Following notification, the taxpayer should decide whether to exercise the right to obtain representation. A taxpayer may elect to represent him or herself or obtain representation to appear at the audit with the taxpayer or in place of the taxpayer. Generally a representative may be an attorney, a certified public accountant, an enrolled agent, or the unenrolled tax return preparer who prepared the return.

Should the taxpayer ask for representation during an initial telephone call or interview for an office or field audit with an IRS examiner, in most cases the examiner must stop and reschedule in order to give the taxpayer a reasonable amount of time to obtain representation. However, the taxpayer cannot use this suspension to needlessly delay the exam interview process. If the IRS examiner deems there is such an abuse, the IRS may issue an administrative summons. A taxpayer under an administrative summons must be physically present at the interview.

Unlike situations involving criminal matters, the right to be represented at an audit does not include the right to be provided representation free of charge. If the audit results in litigation, however, a judge may at times decide to award certain court costs to a petitioner, which could include the cost of representation in connection with litigation of an issue.

A taxpayer who has decided to find an attorney, enrolled agent, certified public accountant, or other qualified person for representation before the IRS, must have that representative complete and file with the IRS a Form 2848, *Power of Attorney and Declaration of Representative*. If a taxpayer wants assistance with the audit but does not want to obtain a representative to act on its behalf, the taxpayer should complete a Form 8821, *Tax Information Authorization (TIA)*. By submitting Form 8821, the taxpayer can designate any individual, corporation, firm, organization, or partnership to receive and inspect any confidential information in any IRS office relating to the audit.

Ultimately, the examiner is responsible for ensuring that the authorizations in Form 2848 and Form 8821 are properly executed. IRS examiners cannot disclose confidential tax information to an unauthorized person.

Examination Techniques for Gathering Evidence

At the beginning of the audit, examiners will accumulate the evidence they require to evaluate the accuracy of the taxpayer's tax return or returns in question. The evidence will most likely include the taxpayer's testimony, the taxpayer's books and records, documents from third parties, and the examiner's own observations.

The IRS may use several means of acquiring evidence, called *examination techniques* in the IRM. Before deciding to use a particular examination technique, agents may consider whether its use will provide the necessary evidence, whether any benefit gained will justify the costs and burden to the examiner and taxpayer, and whether there a less expensive alternative if costs will run too high.

The IRM specifies several examination techniques in connection with business taxpayers, including:

- Analyzing balance sheets, financial accounts, and transactions that might reveal questionable items that require further examination;
- Reviewing documentation, such as business books and records, for content and accuracy to substantiate LUQ items claimed on the tax return;
- Submitting to the taxpayer and/or its representative a written questionnaire soliciting detailed responses;
- Interviewing the taxpayer or third parties in attempt to verify the accuracy of information presented by the taxpayer;
- Inspecting the taxpayer's inventory, securities, or other assets; and
- Touring the taxpayer's business to observe daily business operations.

Examination of Income

As an examiner compiles documentation and tax information from the taxpayer using the various examination techniques, he or she will also analyze the documents and compare them to the taxpayer's calculation of the income it reported on the tax return(s) under audit.

Minimum income probes. First, the examiner will conduct certain minimum probes into the taxpayer's income. This is done regardless of the type of return filed by the taxpayer. The IRM specifies that minimum income probes are a set of analytical tests to determine whether the taxpayer accurately reported income. If the taxpayer underreported income, the probes should reveal at least a portion of the understatement. These minimum income probes vary according to the type of return (nonbusiness or business) and the method of the examination (office audit or field examination). LUQ income items will also be considered as the examiner reviews the return's accuracy.

In-depth income examination. If, resulting from the minimum income probes, the examiner determines that the taxpayer has reported all taxable income from known sources, that the taxpayer can reconcile its books and records with the tax return, and that all else appears to be in order and legitimate, the examiner may conclude its review without making an adjustment.

If, on the other hand, after conducting the minimum income probes the examiner has turned up indications of inaccuracies, items that cannot be explained or substantiated, or other signs that there may be unreported income, then the examiner will conduct a more in-depth examination of the taxpayer's income. It is at this point during the audit that the examiner may resort to gathering evidence from third parties, such as business associates. Examiners may also expand the scope of the examination to include tax returns for prior or subsequent tax years.

EXAMPLE

During an office audit of one tax year, the examiner sees that Justin and Amanda Pfeiffer, joint taxpayers, have deducted the amount paid for their son Aidan's college tuition as contributions to charity. Aidan is a junior at a four-year college. After learning during the interview that there is a possibility that Justin and Amanda similarly deducted Aidan's tuition amount in prior years, the examiner decides to conduct minimum income probes into the Pfeiffers; returns for the two tax years prior to the year currently under audit.

Reconstruction of income. If the taxpayer does not, or is not able to, provide the examiner with all the requested documentation needed for the audit, the IRS has broad authority to reconstruct a taxpayer's income. This step occurs when the taxpayer has not adequately kept the required books and records necessary to determine its taxable income. Among the commonly used methods of reconstructing income are the net worth method, bank deposit method, specific item method, cash expenditures method, and the percentage markup method. Any deficiency determination based on reconstruction is presumptively correct in a civil audit, and taxpayers have the burden of proof to rebut the presumption.

Formal indirect methods. If the taxpayer does not agree with the examiner's adjustments after the in-depth examination, in certain cases the examiner is authorized to use indirect methods of determining the actual amount of unreported income. This is appropriate when, after the in-depth examination, the examiner has established a reasonable likelihood of unreported income. The formal indirect methods involve the development of circumstantial proof of income, for example, through the use of bank deposits, source and application of funds, ratio analyses, or changes in net worth.

Because the IRS is limited by law in its ability to use formal indirect methods, examiners are instructed to document their rationale for resorting to a formal indirect method of proving unreported income. The documentation must contain:

- A summary of the facts relevant to the decision to use a formal indirect method of proof;
- A description of the procedures and audit techniques;
- The group manager's comments, if appropriate;
- Any other information relevant to the decision; and
- The examiner's conclusions.

If the in-depth examination has provided an explanation to the understatement of tax, the examiner may conclude the examination without making an adjustment.

If the examination has turned up indicators of criminal fraud or has otherwise met the criteria for a referral to the Criminal Investigation (CI) division, the IRM directs the examiner to make the referral.

If the examiner does make an adjustment to income, then the next steps in the audit hinge on whether the taxpayer agrees with the examiner.

Determination of Penalties

Whenever an examiner decides to make adjustments to a tax return, he or she will also consider whether to add penalties. Throughout the audit the examiner will have assessed the appropriateness of penalties based on the existence of any indicators of noncompliant behavior. Examiners may impose penalties for numerous reasons, which include:

- Aiding and abetting the understatement of tax liability;
- Estimated tax understatement;
- Failure to file;
- Failure to pay (on returns secured by the examiner);
- Fraud;
- Frivolous returns;
- Negligence;
- Paid tax return preparer errors or malfeasance;
- Promotion of abusive tax shelters;
- Substantial understatement of income; and
- Valuation overstatement (such as the basis of a capital asset that would reduce the amount of sale proceeds reported as income).

In general, certain penalties may not be assessed until after the examiner has obtained the written approval of his or her immediate supervisor. For example, written approval is required for assessment of any fraud penalty, which includes the Code Sec. 6651 penalty for the fraudulent failure to file. The approval requirement is relaxed, however, for some penalties that are automatically calculated by electronic means, independently of an examiner. These include the Code Secs. 6654 and 6655 penalties for, respectively, the failure by an individual or corporation to pay estimated income tax.

Penalties, once applied, may also be reduced or waived under certain circumstances. These circumstances would include, for example, an instance where the taxpayer showed he or she had reasonable cause or acted in good faith when omitting an item of income.

EXAMPLE

An IRS examiner assesses an accuracy-related penalty for a substantial understatement of tax liability after Davis McCauliffe, a single taxpayer, failed to include the nonexcludable proceeds from a tort settlement in her gross income. However, Davis can prove that she acted in good faith and had reasonable cause to omit the settlement proceeds because she relied on the advice of her attorney, also a CPA, in excluding the proceeds. The penalty likely will be waived by the IRS. Absent this waiver, Davis could contest application on the penalty in court.

Making Audit Determinations

After the examining agent has reviewed all the evidence and assessed the appropriateness of penalties, he or she will conclude the case. The taxpayer will receive an audit report from the IRS, which states the examiner's conclusion. An audit can be concluded in three ways:

- No change—The taxpayer has substantiated all of the items under review during the audit, and the examiner concludes the case as a no change and sends a form letter to the taxpayer (i.e., Letter 3581 for correspondence exams or Letter 3401, *No-Change Report Transmittal Letter,* for field and office exams;
- Agreed—The IRS has proposed adjustments in its audit report, and the taxpayer understands and agrees with the changes to its tax liability;
- Disagreed—The IRS has proposed adjustments in its audit report, and the taxpayer understands, but disagrees with the changes. In such cases, the taxpayer may choose to exercise its right to appeal.

Whatever the conclusion may be, it must reflect a correct application of the law, regulations, court cases, revenue rulings, and other applicable resources. Examiners are responsible for correctly determining the meaning of statutory provisions and not adopting strained interpretations. "No change" on certain issues does not restrict the IRS from auditing other issues or relevant items on the same return.

AUDIT TECHNIQUE GUIDES

Examiners do not always have experience with the particular business practices or accounting methods commonly used by the business taxpayers whose returns they must audit. To close this knowledge gap and to improve tax compliance by focusing on the particular issues that frequently arise during audits of taxpayers in certain industry groups, the IRS publishes and regularly updates Audit Technique Guides (ATGs). These guides provide IRS examining agents with necessary insight into the common or unique business practices, accounting methods, and other information specific to certain industries.

ATGs explain and lay out examination techniques, audit methods, typical sources of income, and questions that are designed for use in audits of taxpayers from a particular industry. For example, the ATG on fishing audits directs IRS examiners to question third parties such as bait sellers, regulatory agencies, and boat owners in order to more completely develop the details of the taxpayer's income and expenses. ATGs may also focus on a particular issue, such as compensation or a tax credit, rather than a specific industry. For example, the IRS published an ATG on how to conduct examinations involving charitable contributions of conservation easements.

PLANNING POINTER

The examiner is responsible for reviewing a relevant ATG before commencing an audit. ATGs can also help taxpayers and their representatives to prepare for an audit. Because ATGs provide guidance for examiners on what income sources to examine, what questions to ask in interviews, and what evidence to consider, the guides may also be helpful for individual taxpayers, small business owners, and tax professionals within the industry during the stages of their financial and tax planning.

Market Segment Specialization Program

ATGs are prepared under the purview of the IRS Market Segment Specialization Program (MSSP). The MSSP is an examination program under which IRS teams research and conduct detailed studies of particular market segments where necessary. A market segment consists of an industry, issue, or profession that is selected by the chief of the IRS Examination Division.

The MSSP teams use their studies of a market segment to develop guidelines that are specific to that particular business environment. Historically, the IRS has singled out for study many industries in which issues have regularly given rise to compliance problems. As IRS agents in an MSSP team study the tax compliance practices of a particular group they learn what issues recur and which are noteworthy. During an audit involving an industry or issue covered by an ATG, the IRS examiner generally attempts to reconcile any discrepancies between the taxpayer's reported income or expenses, or both, and what would typically be expected based on the market segment profile.

Currently, there are more than 50 publicly available ATGs that have been prepared under the MSSP. Examples of the wide range of issues and industries covered by ATGs include:

- The research credit in the aerospace industry;
- Attorneys and law firms;
- Whether the cost of an asset should be capitalized or expensed as a repair deduction;
- When items of executive compensation are taxable fringe benefits;
- How to distinguish between a business activity and a hobby (for which the tax code strictly limits deductions);
- Methods of accounting in veterinary clinics; and
- Winery and vineyard operations.

Because the tax world is not static, new issues crop up frequently. The IRS continually updates its ATGs as needed. Recently the IRS updated ATGs to cover issues including:

- Artists and art galleries (January 2012);
- COBRA cases (Continuation of Employee Health Care Coverage) (March 2012);
- Conservation easements (November 2011);
- Indoor tanning services (September 2011);
- Interest charge domestic international sales corporations (IC-DISCs) (March 2012);
- Shore-based and offshore fishing operations (September 2011); and
- Taxi cabs (December 2011).

APPEALS

If the taxpayer disagrees with the examiner's proposed changes and/or adjustments at the end of an audit, the taxpayer may exercise its appeal rights. These rights include several options:
- The taxpayer may appeal through an informal conference with the examiner's supervisor.
- The taxpayer may also appeal the case administratively
  - Within the IRS Office of Appeals, and/or
  - To the U.S. Tax Court, U.S. Claims Court, or the local U.S. District Court.

The taxpayer also has the right to stop the audit on any particular issue immediately by requesting that the IRS Appeals Office consider the matter.

One of the most significant advantages of filing an appeal with the IRS Office of Appeals first before seeking judicial review is that it gives the taxpayer a chance to resolve the case without the expense of litigation.

If the taxpayer chooses to appeal through a conference with the examiner's supervisor, and this conference does not resolve the dispute, the taxpayer has 30 days to consider its next course of action. This could be, for example, a request for an independent review by the IRS Office of Appeals. However, if the taxpayer does not respond within 30 days, the IRS will issue Letter 3219, a Notice of Deficiency. After the issuance of this notice, the taxpayer can opt to either pay the liability or not pay and file a petition with the U.S. Tax Court within 90 days from the issue date of statutory notice. The Claims Court and District Court will generally hear tax cases only *after* the taxpayer has paid the tax and had its administrative refund claims denied by the IRS.

EXAMPLE

Following the conclusion of an audit of Madison Worthington's returns, the IRS examiner makes a determination that Madison has additional tax liability. She disagrees, but would prefer to take her case directly to court. Madison waits until she receives the IRS's notice of deficiency, which sets forth the amount that the IRS examiner determined Madison owed. She decides not pay the liability, but instead files a timely petition with the Tax Court within the 90 days after she first received the notice of deficiency.

Ex Parte Communications

The taxpayer's right to have the IRS Office of Appeals consider any particular issue is considered a right to a fresh, unbiased "second look" at the merits of an assessment determination without taint from any IRS employee previously involved with the case. The IRS Office of Appeals has encountered criticism in recent years for engaging in *ex parte* communications regarding an issue under audit. (*Ex parte* communications occur when employees of the Appeals Office communicate with other IRS function employees concerning issues subject to the appeals process without the participation of the taxpayer or its representative.) In numerous instances IRS Appeals Office officials have communicated with respect to audit issues with members of the IRS Office of Chief Counsel who had previously provided legal advice on the same issue to the examining agent who made the audit determination. Under current IRS policy, this practice is prohibited because the IRS Office of Appeals is supposed to provide a fair and independent forum for resolving tax controversies.

In response to unfavorable taxpayer perception of the Appeals Office, the IRS recently provided guidance clarifying the rules for *ex parte* communications (Rev. Proc. 2012-18; Chief Counsel Notice 2012-010). The revenue procedure and chief counsel notice both state that an IRS attorney cannot participate in an *ex parte* communications with an official from the IRS Office of Appeals regarding an issue in a pending case, if the IRS attorney personally provided legal advice on the same issue in the same case to the originating function or personally served as an advocate for the originating function regarding the same issue in the same case.

Fast Track Mediation

Requesting mediation from the Fast Track Mediation (FTM) program is another alternative to the traditional appeals process, and it provides a more expedited attempt to find a solution if a taxpayer disagrees with the results of the audit. During FTM a trained mediator facilitates communication between the IRS and taxpayer and tries to help them come to a mutually satisfying result. If, however, an agreement is not made, the taxpayer still retains all of its appeal rights.

Most cases qualify for mediation, making it a viable option for many taxpayers, including those under the purview of Large Business and International (LB&I), Small Business and Self-Employed (SB/SE), and the Tax Exempt and Government Entities (TE/GE) divisions. The TE/GE Fast Track program has experienced great success since its 2008 launch, with tax-exempt cases generally settling within 60 days, according to IRS officials. The IRS announced in December 2011 that the program would become permanent.

STUDY QUESTIONS

3. Formal indirect methods designed to reveal unreported income include:

    a. Ratio analyses and changes in the taxpayer's net worth
    b. Reviewing the taxpayer's books and records for LUQs
    c. Inspecting a business taxpayer's inventory and other assets and touring its business
    d. Minimum income probes

4. After a taxpayer receives a notice of deficiency after an audit that results in adjustments to tax liability, but before the taxpayer has paid the deficiency, the taxpayer may appeal a determination to which of the following courts?

    a. Local U.S. District Court
    b. U.S. Court of Federal Claims
    c. U.S. Tax Court
    d. Small Claims Court

PARALLEL CIVIL AUDITS AND CRIMINAL INVESTIGATIONS

The IRS is increasingly conducting "parallel investigations" of a taxpayer suspected of fraud, in which one division pursues a criminal investigation at the same time that another division is in the process of a civil audit. Whereas in the past civil auditors who discovered evidence of fraud would suspend the audit and report the findings to the Criminal Investigation (CI) Division, now an examiner will usually continue with a civil audit even after a criminal fraud investigation commences. This new policy is largely the result of the growing corporate tax shelter industry and other corporate scandals such as Enron in 2001.

Tax Fraud

The IRM defines *fraud* as deception by misrepresentation of material facts, or silence when good faith requires expression, resulting in material damage to one who has the right to rely on it and does so. *Tax fraud* is defined as an intentional wrongdoing on the part of a taxpayer with the specific purpose of evading a tax which the taxpayer knows or believes to be owed. Tax fraud requires both of the elements of underpayment and fraudulent intent.

Fraud may be either civil or criminal in nature, but the government's burden of proof for civil cases is by clear and convincing evidence. For criminal cases, the government must prove its case beyond a reasonable doubt.

Disclosure. The IRS is not required to disclose to a taxpayer under civil audit that it has discovered evidence of fraud or that a criminal investigation is underway. Meanwhile, the examiner conducting the civil audit may be accumulating evidence of fraud and sharing it with the CI division. The IRM encourages civil and criminal examiners to meet regularly to "coordinate their efforts" and to "facilitate sharing important case developments."

Eggshell audits. During a civil audit of a taxpayer, the taxpayer may fear that the examiner will find evidence indicating a fraudulent return and refer the taxpayer to the IRS CI division. This situation is commonly referred to as an *"eggshell audit."*

By contrast, in a *reverse eggshell audit,* the examiner collects information in a purportedly civil audit, intending to secretly contribute the information to a simultaneous criminal investigation of which the taxpayer is unaware.

Should a taxpayer or its legal representative realize there is a high potential that its civil examination might be referred to CI, it should be careful in all communications with the IRS. For example, a taxpayer should be careful not to provide information or documents to the IRS examiner without first seeking the advice of a qualified tax attorney.

Signs of a referral. Civil agents may engage in telling behavior that can alert taxpayers that they may be undergoing a parallel criminal investigation. These behaviors include:

- Showing an unusually large amount of interest in a particular transaction that might be perceived as aggressive or questionable;
- Questioning taxpayers with a focus on the intent behind, rather than the structure of, a transaction;
- Requesting excessive amounts of copied documents rather than reviewing originals;
- Examining bank records exhaustively, perhaps to corroborate or disprove items reported on the return; and
- Disappearing for an extended period, ostensibly to provide time for the criminal investigation.

STUDY QUESTIONS

5. The audit type generally initiated for questions about small business expenses and deductions is the:

    a. Correspondence audit
    b. Full-scale field audit
    c. Office examination
    d. Coordinated Industry Case audit

6. When tax fraud is suspected, IRS employees may conduct:

    a. Criminal, rather than civil, audits
    b. Parallel investigations
    c. Undisclosed civil audits
    d. Full-scale field audits

CONCLUSION

This chapter outlined the basic steps of the IRS audit process from selection to conclusion and also described the steps a taxpayer may take if it chooses to appeal an examiner's determination. There have been several changes or emerging trends relating to the IRS's audit examination process, some of which reflect the agency's limited budget environment. At present the IRS is trying to generate more revenue with fewer resources, meaning it has increased its focus on high-income taxpayers and automated, "cost-effective" systems, such as batch processing of returns in the correspondence audit program. In some respects this is cause for concern; in others, the consequences of certain IRS resource reallocations from examinations to prefiling compliance improvement are still unknown. IRS audit examinations, however, remain a significant aspect of promoting tax compliance and generating additional tax revenue for the government.

Dealing with IRS Collections

This chapter provides an overview of the IRS collection process, including the tools the IRS uses to collect delinquent tax liabilities and secure delinquent tax returns. This chapter also discusses some of the options that are available to taxpayers who are unable to pay their liabilities and the steps the IRS has taken to help taxpayers facing financial difficulties meet their tax obligations using its Fresh Start Initiative.

LEARNING OBJECTIVES

- Understand the IRS collection process;
- Describe the methods and tools the IRS employs to collect unpaid taxes;
- Identify options that are available to taxpayers with outstanding tax liabilities; and
- Understand the changes the IRS has made in its efforts to assist struggling taxpayers.

INTRODUCTION

The U.S. federal tax system relies on taxpayers to voluntarily comply with their federal tax obligations. In general, taxpayers are responsible for determining their tax liabilities, filing the appropriate returns, and paying the amount due. However, when taxpayers are unwilling or unable to file their required tax returns and pay their taxes owed, the IRS is empowered to take steps to bring them into compliance with federal tax law, using a variety of enforcement tools.

The IRS has collection tools that are not available to most creditors, including the ability to encumber a taxpayer's property with a tax lien and to administratively levy on a taxpayer's assets. However, as Americans continue to face difficult economic conditions, the IRS faces the challenge of collecting delinquent taxes without exacerbating financial hardships. To that end, in 2011 the IRS instituted a "Fresh Start Initiative" offering new policies and procedures to help delinquent taxpayers meet their tax obligations without creating additional burdens.

This chapter provides an overview of the IRS collection process and the options that are available to delinquent taxpayers to meet their tax obligations. This chapter also discusses the recent changes the IRS has implemented to help struggling taxpayers address their tax liabilities.

COLLECTION BASICS

Assessment

The collection process begins with *a tax assessment,* which is a formal recording of a tax liability with the IRS.

Types of assessment. Most assessments are made based on the amount of tax due as reported by a taxpayer on an undisputed return. These amounts are "self-assessed." Other assessments are based on determinations made by the IRS after an examination through the deficiency assessment process. In these cases, the IRS generally must issue a statutory *notice of deficiency,* which allows the taxpayer to challenge the determination of the tax in the U.S. Tax Court.

In certain cases, the IRS may assess a deficiency without following the usual deficiency procedures. These include assessments:

- Permitted to correct mathematical or clerical errors, assessments resulting from tentative carryback adjustments;
- Permitted because the tax has actually been paid; and
- For criminal restitution ordered by a court that are treated as if they were a failure to pay tax.

The IRS may also make a *jeopardy assessment* to immediately assess the tax and immediately levy against the taxpayer's property if it believes that delay puts the collection of tax in jeopardy. Additionally, the IRS may make a *termination assessment* when it finds that the taxpayer intends to suddenly leave the United States, remove or conceal property, or perform any other act that will threaten the normal tax collection process.

Assessment period. Generally, the IRS must assess taxes within three years after the tax return is filed. However, the normal period of limitations is extended to six years if an amount more than 25 percent of the gross income shown on the return is omitted. Additionally, if a taxpayer fails to file a return, or files a false or fraudulent return with the intent to evade tax, there is no statute of limitations on assessment, and the IRS can assess and collect the tax at any time.

> **COMMENT**
>
> In *Home Concrete & Supply, LLC,* (SCt, 2012-1 USTC ¶50,315), the U.S. Supreme Court held that a taxpayer's overstatement of its basis in an asset that resulted in an understatement of gross income from the asset's sale did not trigger the extended limitations period under Code Sec. 6501(e)(1)(A) because a basis overstatement is not an "omission from gross income."

Collection Period

The IRS generally has 10 years from the time an assessment is made to collect the assessed liability, either through its administrative levy power or by initiating a court proceeding (Code Sec. 6502). The 10-year limitation period begins to run from the date of the underlying assessment. However, the statute of limitations on collection can be suspended in a number of ways. For example, the collection period is suspended during the pendency of a taxpayer's bankruptcy case and for six months thereafter (Code Sec. 6503). The collection period is also suspended during the period the IRS is prohibited from levying to collect tax that is the subject of a pending offer in compromise or installment agreement (Code Sec. 6331(k)).

Notice of Tax Due and Demand for Payment

Delivery of the notice. Within 60 days of a tax assessment, the Treasury Secretary must give the taxpayer notice of the assessment, list the amount due, and make a demand for payment. This *notice and demand for payment* can be given to the taxpayer, left at the taxpayer's home or usual place of business, or sent to the taxpayer's last known address (Code Sec. 6303).

Referral to the automated collection system. If the taxpayer does not respond to the initial demand for payment, the IRS will begin sending a series of notices requesting with increasing urgency that the taxpayer pay the amount due or contact the IRS to make payment arrangements. If taxpayers do not respond to these notices, most cases are sent to the IRS's automated collection system (ACS) for action. ACS will attempt to contact the taxpayer by phone and by mail. ACS also has the power to initiate enforced collection actions.

Transfer to a revenue officer and beyond. If the amount due is not collected by ACS, the case may be sent to a field revenue officer, who will contact the taxpayer directly to request payment or work out a payment solution. If the taxpayer is unwilling or unable to pay the tax liability in full, the revenue officer will investigate the taxpayer's income and assets to determine whether to pursue enforced collection actions such as levies and asset sales. The revenue officer can also refer the case for a lawsuit to reduce tax liabilities to judgment and to foreclose on the federal tax liens.

Collection Powers and Tools

The IRS has numerous collection tools at its disposal. The IRS's collection powers include the power to:

- File a *Notice of Federal Tax Lien* to encumber a taxpayer's assets;
- Levy on the taxpayer's assets;

- Offset a taxpayer's overpayment of tax against an unpaid liability;
- Agree to a collection alternative, such as an installment agreement or offer in compromise; and
- Initiate a collection lawsuit against the taxpayer.

The IRS also has powerful resources to support its collection efforts. In addition to the available internal information resources, the IRS can also use its summons power to gather information from taxpayers and third parties, including books, records, papers or other data that may be relevant to the collection of a tax liability, such as bank records, financial statements, property records and records of property transactions.

FRESH START INITIATIVE

In February 2011 the IRS introduced its Fresh Start Initiative to help struggling taxpayers with their tax liabilities. As part of the program, the IRS has made a number of changes to its collection practices, including:

- An increase in the dollar threshold for filing notices of federal tax lien;
- New rules making it easier for taxpayers to obtain a withdrawal of a federal tax lien when a liability is paid or when taxpayers enter into a direct debit installment agreement;
- An increase in the dollar limits for streamlined installment agreements ($50,000) and in-business trust fund express installment agreements ($25,000);
- An expansion of the streamlined offer in compromise program for qualifying taxpayers whose household income is $100,000 or less and whose tax liability is $50,000 or less; and
- More flexibility in the evaluation of offers in compromise and the financial analysis of a taxpayer's ability to pay an outstanding liability. These changes are discussed in greater detail below.

Fresh Start Penalty Relief

As part of the Fresh Start program, the IRS has also announced a penalty relief policy for unemployed taxpayers for failure-to-pay penalties. The Fresh Start Penalty Relief Initiative gave eligible taxpayers a six-month extension to fully pay 2011 taxes. Interest still applies on the 2011 taxes from April 17, 2012, until the tax is paid, but taxpayers would not be liable for failure-to-pay penalties if the total amount owed was paid in full by October 15, 2012. The penalty relief was available to wage earners who had been unemployed at least 30 consecutive days during 2011 or in 2012 up to the April 17th filing tax deadline, and to self-employed individuals who experienced a 25 percent or greater reduction in business income in 2011 due to the economy. The penalty relief is subject to income limits and a cap on the amount owed. Taxpayers who qualify were required to complete a new Form 1127A, *Application for Extension of Time for Payment of Income Tax for 2011 Due to Undue Hardship,* to request the 2011 penalty relief.

STUDY QUESTIONS

---

1. If the taxpayer does not respond to the initial IRS contact regarding a demand for payment, the case is sent to the:

  a. Appeals Office
  b. Revenue officer
  c. Automated collection system
  d. Tax Court or U.S. District Court

2. The Fresh Start Initiative penalty relief policy targeted all of the following taxpayers *except:*

  a. Self-employed individuals whose business income decreased by at least 25 percent in 2011
  b. Taxpayers who were unemployed for at least 30 consecutive days prior to the filing deadline
  c. Higher-income taxpayers
  d. Taxpayers who expected to complete payment of their 2011 tax liability by October 15, 2012

LIENS AND LEVIES

The federal tax lien and the administrative tax levy are the two principal enforced collection tools the IRS uses to collect unpaid tax liabilities. The lien and levy are administrative collection tactics; neither requires any judicial action to become available to the IRS. Although they are closely related, they are used for different purposes and have different effects. A *lien* is a security claim against the taxpayer's property to secure the tax debt, whereas a *levy* is the actual seizure of property to satisfy the debt.

Federal Tax Liens

A federal tax lien arises after the IRS assesses the tax and issues a notice and demand for payment, but the taxpayer fails to pay the full amount demanded. After the IRS makes its demand, the taxpayer has 10 days in which to pay (Code Sec. 6321). If the taxpayer fails to do so, the lien becomes effective as of the date of assessment.

A federal tax lien attaches to all of a taxpayer's property at the time the lien arises and all property acquired after the assessment date (Code Sec. 6321). It does not give the IRS a priority position relative to other creditors unless they have knowledge of the tax lien, which occurs when the IRS provides actual notice or files a *Notice of Federal Tax Lien.* To gain priority over other creditors, the IRS must file a *Notice of Federal Tax Lien* in the recording office designated by the state or government subdivision. The IRS uses Form 668(Y)(c) for this purpose. Until a tax lien is filed, it is not valid against competing claims of purchasers, holders of security interests, mechanic's lienors, and judgment lien creditors. Additionally, the lien does not have priority against certain other "superpriority" claims even if it is recorded.

The IRS must notify the taxpayer in writing of the filing of a lien within five days of the filing. The notice must include;

- The amount of the unpaid tax;
- The right to request a hearing within 30 days after the five-day period;
- Administrative appeals procedures; and
- The provisions and procedures relating to release of liens.

Appeal procedures are discussed in greater detail later.

Until 2011, the IRS's policy was to file a *Notice of Federal Tax Lien* when a tax liability exceeded $5,000. As part of its Fresh Start Initiative, the IRS increased the threshold from $5,000 to $10,000. However, the IRS may still file liens to secure tax liabilities of less than $10,000 when circumstances warrant doing so.

> **COMMENT**
>
> In 2011, the IRS filed 1,042,230 notices of federal tax lien, approximately 5 percent fewer than it filed in 2010 *(2011 IRS Data Book)*.

> **COMMENT**
>
> In her 2011 Annual Report to Congress, Taxpayer Advocate Nina Olson expressed concern that the IRS's tax lien filing practices were inflicting unnecessary harm on struggling taxpayers. She noted that despite Fresh Start, the IRS continued to file most notices of federal tax lien based on a dollar threshold of liability, and without consideration of the facts and circumstances of the taxpayer's case. Olson recommended a number of changes to the IRS's lien filing policies to improve compliance and increase collection of tax, without causing further harm to struggling taxpayers.

Relief from Liens

Once a federal tax lien arises, it continues until the liability is satisfied or becomes unenforceable because the statutory collection period has expired. However, the lien may be released, withdrawn, or subordinated, and property may be discharged from it or certified that the lien does not apply to that property.

Release of a Federal Tax Lien

Once a taxpayer satisfies a tax liability by payment or by posting a bond for payment of the entire amount owed, or the debt becomes legally unenforceable, the IRS is required to release its tax lien within 30 days (Code Sec. 6325). The release of a federal tax lien completely extinguishes the IRS's lien.

Federal tax liens self-release when the statutory collection period expires, in which case the *Notice of Federal Tax Lien* itself is the release document. Taxpayers can also request a certificate of release by following the procedures prescribed in IRS Publication 1450, *Request for Release of Federal Tax Lien.*

Discharge of a Federal Tax Lien

A discharge of a federal tax lien discharges only specific property to which the lien has attached. A discharge does not affect the lien on any other property to which the lien has attached.

The IRS may discharge property from its lien if:

- The taxpayer's property remaining subject to the lien has a fair market value equal to at least twice the unpaid tax liability plus all the encumbrances that have priority over the federal tax lien;
- The taxpayer or another person makes partial payment equal to the value of the government's interest in the property discharged;
- The IRS determines that the government's interest in the property has no value; or
- The property subject to the lien is sold and, by agreement with the IRS, the sale proceeds are held as a fund subject to the liens and claims of the United States (Code Sec. 6325(b)).

Additionally, the IRS is required to issue a discharge if a third-party owner submits a proper request and either deposits money equal to the value of the lien on the property or furnishes a bond acceptable to the IRS (Code Sec. 6325(a)(2)).

Taxpayers can apply for a certificate of discharge by completing Form 14135, *Application for Certificate of Discharge of Federal Tax Lien.* Instructions for making the application can be found in IRS Publication 783.

Subordination of a Federal Tax Lien

In certain circumstances the IRS may agree to subordinate its lien to the interest of another creditor. The IRS has discretion to issue a certificate of subordination if the government is paid an amount equal to the amount by which the tax lien will be subordinated or if the IRS believes that the subordination will ultimately increase the amount realizable from the property in question.

Taxpayers can apply for a certificate of subordination by completing Form 14134, *Application for Certificate of Subordination of Federal Tax Lien.* Instructions for making the application are in IRS Publication 784.

> **COMMENT**
>
> Publications 783 and 784 recommend that the applications for discharge and subordination be submitted to the IRS at least 45 days before the transaction for which the discharge or subordination is needed. In December 2008, the IRS announced that it was expediting the discharge process to make it easier for financially distressed homeowners to avoid having a federal tax lien hinder refinancing of mortgages or the sale of a home (IRS News Release IR-2008-141).

Withdrawal of Notice

In certain circumstances, the IRS has the authority to withdraw a Form 668(Y)(c), *Notice of Federal Tax Lien.* A notice that is withdrawn is treated as if it had not been filed. Therefore, withdrawal of a notice of lien does not affect the underlying tax lien (Reg. § 301.6323(j)-1(a)); rather, it causes the IRS to give up any lien priority that had been obtained when the notice was filed.

The IRS may withdraw a *Notice of Federal Tax Lien* upon a determination that:

- The filing of the notice was premature or otherwise not in accord with administrative procedures;
- The taxpayer has entered an installment agreement to satisfy the liability for which the lien was imposed (and the installment agreement does not preclude the lien withdrawal);
- The withdrawal of the lien will facilitate collection of the liability for which the lien was imposed; or
- Withdrawal would be in the best interests of the taxpayer and of the United States (Code Sec. 6323(j)(1)).

At the written request of the taxpayer, the IRS must also make reasonable efforts to give notice of the withdrawal to credit reporting agencies, financial institutions, and creditors specified by the taxpayer (Code Sec. 6323(j)(2)).

As part of its Fresh Start initiative, the IRS has made a number of changes to make it easier for taxpayers to obtain lien withdrawals. The IRS will withdraw a lien notice at the taxpayer's request once the taxpayer's liability is paid in full on the basis of a withdrawal being in the best interest of the taxpayer and the government (IRS News Release IR-2011-20, February 24, 2011; IRM 5.17.2.8.7.1). A taxpayer may request a tax lien withdrawal by filing Form 12277, *Application for Withdrawal of Filed Form 668(Y), Notice of Federal Tax Lien.*

Additionally, as part of the Fresh Start program, the IRS will allow lien withdrawals for certain taxpayers who enter into a direct debit installment agreement or convert from a regular installment agreement into a direct debit installment agreement. The IRS will also withdraw a lien at the request of a taxpayer who is already in an existing direct debit installment agreement. Requests for lien withdrawals will generally be approved for individual taxpayers, businesses with income tax liabilities, and taxpayers that are no longer in business with any type of tax liability. These taxpayers must meet the following criteria:

- The total amount owed must be $25,000 or less;
- The liability must be paid in full within 60 months or prior to the expiration of the collection statute of limitations, whichever is earlier;
- The taxpayer must be in compliance with all other filing and payment requirements;
- At least three consecutive payments must have been made under the agreement;
- The taxpayer cannot have defaulted on the current direct debit installment agreement or any previous agreement;
- The taxpayer cannot have previously had a lien withdrawn for any tax period included in the agreement, unless it was for the improper filing of a lien (IRS News Release IR-2011-20, February 24, 2011; IRM 5.17.2.8.7.2).

Installment agreements are discussed in greater detail below.

Levies

The IRS is authorized to start procedures to levy on the property of any person liable to pay any tax who fails to do so within 10 days of notice and demand for payment (Code Sec. 6331).

> **COMMENT**
>
> Although the IRS is authorized to begin these procedures after 10 days of making notice and demand for payment, the process typically takes far longer.

Generally, the IRS may levy upon any property or property rights of a delinquent taxpayer other than ones specifically exempted from levy. However, the IRS generally must get a court order to seize a taxpayer's principal residence, and higher-level administrative approval is required before the IRS can seize an individual's business property (Code Sec. 6334(e)).

Certain property is exempt from levy by statute, including:
- Wearing apparel and schoolbooks, to the extent necessary for the taxpayer or members of the taxpayer's family;

- Books and tools necessary for the taxpayer's trade, business, or profession up to an inflation-adjusted amount ($4,290 for 2012);
- Fuel, provisions, furniture, and personal effects in the household, arms for personal use,
- Livestock and poultry, up to an inflation adjusted amount ($8,570 for 2012); and
- Real property used by the taxpayer as a residence (whether or not a principal residence), and any nonrental property owned by the taxpayer but used by another person as a residence, if the amount of the levy does not exceed $5,000 (Code Sec. 6334(a); Rev. Proc. 2011-52).

There are two types of levies: continuous and noncontinuous. As a general rule, levies only attach to property and obligations in existence at the time of the levy. Therefore, most levies are noncontinuous. However, there are two exceptions to that rule:

- A levy on wages is continuous from the date of the levy until the levy is released; and
- The IRS can approve a continuous levy on up to 15 percent of certain specified payments made to or received by a taxpayer that are otherwise exempt.

Before the IRS can actually make a levy, it is required to provide the taxpayer with notice of intent to levy and notice that the taxpayer can appeal the proposed levy under the collection due process (CDP) procedures (discussed later in this chapter). This notice is in addition to the initial notice and demand for payment that the IRS is required to give after making an assessment.

In addition, prior to making a levy on property or rights to property that are to be sold, the IRS is required to make an investigation that includes:

- A verification of the taxpayer's liability;
- An analysis of the costs of levy and sale compared to the value of the property;
- A determination that the equity in the property is sufficient to yield net proceeds from a sale; and
- A thorough consideration of alternative collection methods.

COMMENT

The general levy requirements do not apply if the IRS finds that collection of the tax is in jeopardy. Instead, the IRS is allowed to levy on the taxpayer's property without giving prior notice of its intent to levy and the taxpayer's right to a hearing. Within five days of the jeopardy levy, the IRS must provide the taxpayer with a written statement of the information the IRS relied upon in making the jeopardy levy. The taxpayer may then seek an administrative review of the determination and, if necessary, may file a civil suit to challenge the determination.

Release of Levies

The IRS is required to release a levy if:

- The liability for which the levy was made is satisfied or becomes unenforceable through lapse of time;
- Release of the levy will facilitate collection of the tax liability;
- The taxpayer has entered into an installment agreement (unless the agreement prohibits releasing the levy, or releasing the levy would jeopardize the government's status as a secured creditor);
- The IRS determines that the levy is causing the taxpayer an economic hardship; or
- The fair market value of the property exceeds the tax liability and release of the levy on the property could be made without hindering the collection of the liability (Code Sec. 6343(a)(1); Reg. § 301.6343-1(b)).

As a practical matter, before it will consider releasing a levy, the IRS will require a taxpayer to file any missing tax returns and provide the appropriate collection information statements, Form 433-A, *Collection Information Statement for Wage Earners and Self-Employed Individuals,* and/or Form 433-B, *Collection Information Statement for Businesses.*

The IRS will release a levy based on economic hardship if the levy will cause an individual taxpayer to be unable to pay his or her reasonable basic living expenses. In determining a reasonable amount for basic living expenses, the IRS will consider any information provided by the taxpayer, including:

- The taxpayer's age, employment status and history, ability to earn, number of dependents, and status as a dependent;
- The amount reasonably necessary for food, clothing, housing, medical expenses, transportation, current tax payments, alimony, child support, or other court-ordered payments, and expenses necessary to the taxpayer's production of income;
- The cost of living in the taxpayer's geographic area;
- The amount of exempt property that is available to pay the taxpayer's expenses;
- Any extraordinary circumstances such as special education expenses, a medical catastrophe, or natural disaster; and
- Any other relevant factor that the taxpayer identifies.

Additionally, the taxpayer must act in good faith and not falsify financial information, inflate actual expenses or costs, or fail to make full disclosure of assets.

> **COMMENT**
>
> Because *economic hardship* is defined as the inability to meet reasonable basic living expenses, it applies only to individuals.

> **COMMENT**
>
> Although the taxpayer must provide information proving undue economic hardship, the Tax Court has held that Reg. § 301.6343-1(b)(4) requires the IRS to release a levy that creates an economic hardship, regardless of a taxpayer's noncompliance with filing requirements. Neither case law nor the tax code or regulations condition the release of a levy upon compliance with filing and payment requirements when there is an economic hardship (*K.A. Vinatieri*, 133 TC 392).

As part of its efforts to help struggling taxpayers, the IRS announced that it will speed the delivery of levy releases by easing requirements on taxpayers who request expedited levy releases for hardship reasons. Taxpayers seeking expedited releases for levies to an employer or bank should contact the IRS at the number shown on the notice of levy to discuss available options. Taxpayers should be prepared to provide the IRS with the fax number of the bank or employer processing the levy (IRS News Release IR-2009-2, January 6, 2009).

STUDY QUESTIONS

3. When property subject to a tax lien is sold and the IRS agrees that sale proceeds are held as a fund subject to the government's claim, the lien is:

   a. Discharged
   b. Subordinated
   c. Released
   d. Withdrawn

4. The IRS may *not* levy:

   a. Any real property the taxpayer uses as a residence, provided the levy is for $5,000 or less
   b. Any amount of livestock and poultry
   c. Business or trade books and tools worth any amount
   d. Personal effects of the taxpayer's household

COLLECTION ALTERNATIVES

Installment Agreements

An *installment agreement* is an agreement that allows for a tax liability to be paid over time through scheduled periodic payments. The IRS is authorized to enter into an installment agreement if the IRS determines that the agreement will facilitate full or partial collection of the liability (Code Sec. 6159(a)).

Generally, four types of installment agreements provide for the full payment of taxes over time:

- Guaranteed installment agreements;
- Streamlined installment agreements;
- In-business trust fund express agreements; and
- Installment agreements requiring financial analysis.

Guaranteed installment agreements . A *guaranteed,* or mandatory, *installment agreement* is available for the payment of tax liabilities of $10,000 or less, exclusive of interest, penalties, additions to tax, and any other additional amounts, provided that the liability can be paid within three years and during the preceding five years, the taxpayer (and spouse if filing jointly) has filed all required income tax returns, paid all required taxes as shown on the returns, and has not entered into an installment agreement to pay any income tax. The taxpayer must also agree to comply with the tax laws while the agreement is in effect (Code Sec. 6159(c)). Taxpayers seeking a guaranteed installment agreement are not required to submit a Form 433-A, *Collection Information Statement for Wage Earners and Self-Employed Individuals,* or otherwise disclose information about their ability to pay their outstanding tax liabilities.

> **CAUTION**
>
> Guaranteed installment agreements are only available to individuals. Businesses and other entities are not entitled to a guaranteed installment agreement, regardless of the amount of the liability.

Streamlined installment agreements. Taxpayers who do not qualify for a guaranteed installment agreement, but whose tax liabilities are $50,000 or less, may qualify for a *streamlined installment agreement.* A streamlined installment agreement will generally be granted if a taxpayer's assessed liabilities total $50,000 or less and can be paid within 72 months.

> **COMMENT**
>
> These agreements are "streamlined" because the IRS will grant them without requiring taxpayers to submit Forms 433, *Collection Information Statement,* or otherwise disclose information about their ability to pay their outstanding tax liabilities (IRM 4.20.4.3).

The IRS previously limited the availability of streamlined installment agreements to liabilities of $25,000 or less, and to a maximum term of 60 months. The IRS increased the dollar limit and maximum term for these agreements as part of its Fresh Start Initiative. However, in order to qualify for a streamlined installment agreement under the expanded guidelines, a taxpayer must agree to make payments via direct debit from a bank account (IRS News Release IR-2012-31, March 7, 2012).

> **COMMENT**
>
> A taxpayer with assessed liabilities in excess of $50,000 may still qualify for a streamlined installment agreement if the taxpayer is able to make payments that reduce the balance due to the streamlined range.

Unlike guaranteed installment agreements, streamlined installment agreements are available for both individuals and businesses. However, in-business taxpayers may only seek a streamlined installment agreement for income tax liabilities.

In-business trust fund express agreements. An *in-business trust fund express installment agreement* is available to business taxpayers with trust fund liabilities, such as employment tax liabilities, provided that the total balance due does not exceed $25,000 and can be paid within 24 months, or before the expiration of the collection statute of limitations, whichever is earlier. No financial statement is required, and the IRS does not determine any trust fund recovery penalty.

> **COMMENT**
>
> In-business trust fund express installment agreements were previously available to business taxpayers having tax liabilities of $10,000 or less. The dollar limit was increased to $25,000 in order to make the program available to more taxpayers. However, if the amount owed is between $10,000 and $25,000, the taxpayer must enroll in a *direct debit installment agreement* (IRS News Release IR-2011-20, February 24, 2011).

Installment agreements requiring financial analysis. The last type of agreement is available for taxpayers that do not qualify for a guaranteed, streamlined, or in-business trust fund express installment agreement, typically because their total tax liabilities exceed $50,000. The IRS requires these taxpayers to submit a collection information statement that details their income, expenses, and assets. There are special considerations with this type of agreement for in-business taxpayers that do not qualify for in-business trust fund express agreements.

A Form 433-A, *Collection Information Statement for Wage Earners and Self-Employed Individuals*, and/or Form 433-B, *Collection Information Statement for Businesses.*, is used to determine the taxpayer's ability to pay the liability in full or in part from assets and disposable income (gross income less allowable expenses). The installment agreement must reflect the taxpayer's ability to pay on a monthly basis. This amount is equal to the taxpayer's gross monthly income less allowable monthly expenses, which must be necessary expenses. A *necessary expense* is one that is required to provide for the health, welfare, and/or production of income for a taxpayer and his or her family. Allowable expenses are based on the IRS's Collection Financial Standards, which establish national and local expense standards for housing, household expenses, food, clothing, miscellaneous expenses, transportation, and health care. For purposes of determining an individual's ability to pay, the national and local standards normally represent the maximum amounts that the IRS will allow for living expenses. However, the IRS will allow more than the standard amount if failing to do so will cause the taxpayer economic hardship. For example, a taxpayer with physical disabilities or an unusually large family may have housing costs in excess of the local standard. Additionally, the IRS will in some cases temporarily allow excess necessary expenses in order to give the taxpayer the opportunity to modify or eliminate those expenses. Expenses that are not necessary expenses are considered *conditional expenses* and generally are not allowed unless they meet certain exceptions to Installment agreement limitations.

If a business taxpayer is in compliance with current tax obligations, and has the ability to remain current while paying the delinquent tax liabilities and ongoing operating expenses, the IRS considers an installment agreement based on the taxpayer's ability to pay. If the taxpayer has the ability to pay the balance due from current income and/or assets, the IRS will not grant an installment agreement. If the taxpayer's Form 433 shows that the taxpayer can sell or borrow against equity in assets, the IRS may request that the taxpayer do so.

> **COMMENT**
>
> The IRS does not categorize a business taxpayer's expenses as necessary or conditional, as it does an individual's expenses. Although the IRS may review the business's Form 433-B and determine that a particular expense is not allowable, a business taxpayer has more room than does an individual for negotiation.

Partial payment installment agreements. If a taxpayer is unable to pay an outstanding liability in full under general installment agreement guidelines, the IRS may enter into a *partial payment installment agreement* that does not provide for full payment of the liability within the statutory period for collection.

> **COMMENT**
>
> Although a partial payment installment agreement does not provide for the full payment of a tax liability, it does not reduce the amount of taxes, interest, or penalties owed (Reg. § 301.6159-1(c)(1)(ii). As with any installment agreement, however, the penalties for failure to pay may accrue at a reduced rate.

A taxpayer seeking a partial payment installment agreement must submit a Form 433-A or 433-B detailing the taxpayer's ability to pay. The IRS takes a stricter approach to its analysis of income and expenses in determining the taxpayer's eligibility for a partial payment agreement than for typical installment agreements. Conditional expenses are not allowed for partial payment installment agreements; only necessary expenses are permitted.

Requesting an installment agreement. Taxpayers can request an installment agreement by mailing their request to the IRS. The IRS uses Form 9465, *Installment Agreement Request,* and Form 433-D, *Installment Agreement,* for this purpose.

An Online Payment Agreement application is also available on the IRS website, **http://www.irs.gov.** Eligible taxpayers and their authorized representatives can apply, and if qualified, receive immediate notification that the installment agreement was approved. The application allows users to pay a balance due in full, request an extension of up to 120 days to pay the balance due in full, enter into an installment agreement, or modify an existing agreement.

Generally, a taxpayer who enters into an installment agreement must pay a nonrefundable user fee of $105, payable by check, money order, credit card, or payroll deduction. A reduced fee of $52 applies when a taxpayer enters into a direct debit installment agreement, in which payments are made by electronic funds withdrawal from a checking account (Reg. § 300.1). For an individual whose income is at or below 250 percent of the dollar amount established by U.S. Department of Health and Human Services (HHS) poverty guidelines, the fee is $43, regardless of the method of payment. An additional fee of $45 applies for restructuring or reinstating an installment agreement after a default.

By entering into an installment agreement, taxpayers agree to meet certain terms and conditions. Most importantly, each installment payment must be made in full and on time. All payments must be received by the IRS by the due date each month. Unlike most tax filing and payment requirements, the timely mailing rule does not apply to payments made under an installment agreement. Therefore, taxpayers making payments by check or money order should send their payments well in advance of the due date.

> **COMMENT**
>
> The IRS is allowing more flexibility for missed payments on installment agreements for previously compliant individuals who have difficulty making payments. The IRS may allow a missed payment before placing an installment agreement in default. Although this is not a new policy, the IRS has not openly publicized it in the past (IRS News Release IR-2010-29, March 10, 2010; IRS News Release IR-2009-2, January 6, 2010; IRM 5.19.1.5.5.20).

Extension of time to pay. If a taxpayer is able to pay a tax liability in full but needs some additional time to obtain the funds, a short-term extension of time to pay a tax liability may be available as an alternative to an installment agreement. For taxpayers whose cases are in the notice stage or are being handled by the IRS automated collection system (ACS), the IRS can generally authorize an extension of time to pay delinquent liabilities in full, without requiring taxpayers to submit Forms 433-A or 433-B, *Collection Information Statements*. An extension can be granted on assessed or preassessed balances due for individual and business taxpayers, regardless of the dollar amount. The maximum extension is 120 days, or 60 days if the taxpayer's account is being handled by the ACS (IRM 5.19.1.5.4).

> **PLANNING POINTER**
>
> An extension of time to pay can be a useful tool for a taxpayer who will be able to pay a balance due within a relatively short period of time but is temporarily short of funds. This is particularly true for a taxpayer who is ineligible for a guaranteed or streamlined installment agreement but does not want to provide the IRS with the financial statement that is required for regular installment agreements.

An extension of time to pay is not an installment agreement; therefore, the taxpayer does not have to pay a user fee (IRM 5.19.1.5.3.4(11)). However, it is important to note that interest and penalties for failure to pay will accrue until the tax is paid in full.

Offers in Compromise

A compromise is an agreement between the taxpayer and the IRS that settles a tax liability for payment of less than the full amount owed (Code Sec. 7122). Most *offers in compromise* are submitted during the collection process, by taxpayers who are experiencing financial difficulty. If the IRS accepts the offer, tax liens are removed and enforced collection is avoided.

The IRS will accept an offer in compromise in three situations:

- Doubt as to collectability—if it is unlikely that the IRS can collect the tax liability in full;
- Doubt as to liability—if there is a legitimate dispute as to the amount the taxpayer owes; and

- Effective tax administration—if collection of the full amount of unpaid tax liability would cause the taxpayer economic hardship or if there are other compelling public policy or equity considerations (Reg. § 301.7122-1(b)).

An offer in compromise can be made by almost any taxpayer, including an individual and a taxable entity such as a trust, estate, or corporation. However, nonindividual entities cannot make an offer in compromise based on hardship grounds. Because *economic hardship* is defined as the inability to meet reasonable basic living expenses, it applies only to individuals.

> **COMMENT**
>
> In 2011, the IRS accepted approximately 34 percent of the offers in compromise that were submitted. The prior year, the IRS accepted approximately 27 percent of the offers that were submitted.

Doubt as to collectibility. The IRS generally accepts an offer in compromise based on *doubt as to collectibility* if:
- It is unlikely that the tax liability can be collected in full; and
- The offer reasonably reflects the taxpayer's *reasonable collection potential* (RCP), which is the amount the IRS could collect through all available means.

The IRS determines a taxpayer's RCP based on the information presented in financial statements required to be submitted with the taxpayer's offer, the Form 433-A, *Collection Information Statement for Wage Earners and Self-Employed Individuals,* and/or Form 433-B, *Collection Information Statement for Businesses.* RCP generally has four components:
- The amount collectible from the taxpayer's realizable equity in assets;
- The amount collectible from the taxpayer's future income;
- The amount the IRS could expect to collect from third parties through administrative or judicial action; and
- Assets and/or income that are available to the taxpayer, but are beyond the reach of the government.

For purposes of calculating an offer amount, a taxpayer's income includes gross monthly income, less allowable expenses. For individual taxpayers, expenses are generally only allowable if they are necessary expenses, using the same test discussed above regarding installment agreements. As with installment agreements, allowable expenses for purposes of offers in compromise are based on the IRS's Collection Financial Standards, which establish national and local expense standards for housing, household expenses, food, clothing, other miscellaneous expenses, transportation, and health care. The national and local standards normally represent the maximum amounts that the IRS will allow for living expenses; however, the IRS will allow more than the standard amount if failing to do so will cause the taxpayer economic hardship.

> **COMMENT**
>
> The IRS recently expanded the category of other miscellaneous allowable expenses to include minimum payments on student loans guaranteed by the federal government and payments to state taxing authorities (I.R.M. 5.8.5.20.4).

> **COMMENT**
>
> The Collection Financial Standards are available on the IRS website, at **http://www.irs. gov/individuals/article/0,,id=96543,00.html.**

Expenses that do not meet the necessary expense test are considered conditional expenses, and are generally only allowed in limited cases.

Future income. The determination of a taxpayer's future income is based on an estimate of the taxpayer's ability to make payments for a specific number of months into the future. Generally, the amount is calculated by taking the projected gross monthly income, less allowable expenses, and multiplying the difference by the applicable number of months. The number of months used in the calculation of future income depends on the proposed payment terms of the offer.

As part of its Fresh Start Initiative, the IRS recently revised its formula for calculating future income. For an offer that will be paid in 5 or fewer months, the IRS will now look at only one year of future income, rather than four years. For offers that will be paid in 6 to 24 months, the IRS will now look at two years of future income, rather than five years (IRS News Release IR-2012-53, May 21, 2012; IRM 5.8.5.23). Additionally, the IRS will consider a taxpayer's current income and potential for future income in the evaluation for an offer in compromise. Previously, when the IRS evaluated an offer from an unemployed or underemployed taxpayer, the income calculation was based on an average that included income in prior years. This new policy gives the IRS greater flexibility in evaluating offers from unemployed taxpayers (IRS News Release IR-2010-29, March 10, 2010; IRM 5.8.5.18).

Valuation. For offer purposes, assets are valued at *net realizable equity*, which is generally the quick sale value of the asset less amounts owed to secured lien holders with priority over the IRS's federal tax liens. Quick sale value is an estimate of the price a seller could expect to receive for an asset if forced to sell in a short period of time, usually 90 days or fewer. The IRS generally calculates quick sale value as 80 percent of fair market value. However, a higher or lower percentage may be applied when appropriate, depending on the type of asset and current market conditions. For example, if a taxpayer owns a home in an area where real estate is selling slowly and well below listing prices, the IRS may agree to use a percentage lower than 80 percent.

For real estate, the IRS first establishes the fair market value of the property, using the recent purchase price or an existing contract to sell, recent appraisals, real estate tax assessments, market comparables, or insurance replacement cost. Once fair market value is established, an appropriate reduction of value for offer purposes must be determined. As part of the Fresh Start Initiative, the IRS now provides an additional review of the information used to value real property (IRS News Release IR-2010-29, March 10, 2010; IRM 8.23.3.3.2.4).

Special circumstances. The IRS will also consider an offer based upon doubt as to collectibility with special circumstances, which is something of a hybrid between an offer based upon doubt as to collectibility and an offer based upon effective tax administration due to economic hardship. As with a regular doubt as to collectibility offer, the taxpayer must demonstrate that he or she cannot fully pay the tax due. However, the IRS will accept an amount less than the taxpayer's RCP if paying the full RCP would cause the taxpayer economic hardship.

Offers in compromise based on doubt as to collectibility and effective tax administration must be submitted on Form 656, *Offer in Compromise.* Taxpayers must pay a user fee of $150 for each offer in compromise submitted, unless the offer is filed by a low-income taxpayer. Taxpayers submitting offers based on doubt as to collectibility or effective tax administration must also make partial payments with their offers. For offers in compromise based on doubt as to collectibility or effective tax administration, taxpayers must submit collection information statements with their offers (Form 433-A, *Collection Information Statement for Wage Earners and Self-Employed Individuals,* or Form 433-B, *Collection Information Statement for Businesses*).

For offers in compromise based upon doubt as to collectibility or effective tax administration, taxpayers have two payment options:

- A required 20 percent of the total offer to be paid with the offer and the remaining balance paid in five or fewer payments within 24 months upon acceptance of the offer; or
- Payment of the offer amount in more than five monthly installments over a maximum of 24 months.

Under the latter option, the taxpayer submitting the offer must submit the first payment with the offer and continue making subsequent payments under the terms proposed while the IRS is evaluating the offer.

Doubt as to liability. A taxpayer may make an offer in compromise based on *doubt as to liability,* which exists where there is a genuine dispute as to the existence or amount of the correct tax liability under the law. Doubt as to liability does not exist if the liability has been established by a final court decision or judgment concerning the existence or amount of the liability (Reg. §301.7122-1(b)(1)).

> **COMMENT**
>
> Because doubt as to liability requires a legitimate dispute regarding an assessed tax liability, it is rarely used as a ground for compromise. However, doubt as to liability offers can be used to contest certain liabilities, such as the trust fund recovery penalty under Code Sec. 6672 and matters involving an innocent spouse.\

The taxpayer files a doubt as to liability offer on Form 656-L, *Offer in Compromise (Doubt as to Liability).* In evaluating an offer based on doubt as to liability, the IRS is not concerned with the taxpayer's ability to pay; therefore, the taxpayer does not have to file a *Collection Information Statement.* Instead, the taxpayer must submit documentation and other relevant evidence to support doubt regarding the liability. An offer to compromise based on doubt as to liability is generally acceptable if it reasonably reflects the amount the IRS would expect to collect through litigation (Rev. Proc. 2003-71). For offers in compromise based upon doubt as to liability, taxpayers do not have the option to propose payment terms. The offer amount must be paid within 90 days after the offer has been accepted.

Effective tax administration. If there is no doubt as to liability for a tax or doubt concerning the collectibility of a tax, the IRS may still accept an offer in compromise based upon *effective tax administration.* There are two general types of effective tax administration offers: those based on economic hardship and those based upon equity or public policy (Reg. § 301.7122-1(b)(3)).

Economic hardship. The IRS may compromise a tax liability to promote effective tax administration when it determines that it could collect the full amount of the liability, but doing so would cause the taxpayer economic hardship. The standard for determining economic hardship for this purpose is similar to the standard the IRS uses to determine whether a levy is causing an economic hardship. For this purpose, *economic hardship* exists when collection of the full tax liability would leave the taxpayer unable to pay reasonable basic living expenses (Reg. § 301.7122-1(b)(3)(i); Reg. § 301.6343-1(d)). An offer in compromise based on economic hardship is generally acceptable when the amount offered reflects the amount the IRS can collect without causing the taxpayer economic hardship (Rev. Proc. 2003-71).

EXAMPLE

Larry Hampton has a $100,000 tax liability and a RCP of $125,000. In order to avoid economic hardship, it is determined that Larry will need $75,000 to pay his basic living expenses. The remaining $50,000 will be considered the acceptable offer amount (IRM 5.8.11.4.3).

CAUTION

Because economic hardship is the inability to meet reasonable basic living expenses, it applies only to individuals (including sole proprietorships). Nonindividual entities are not eligible for effective tax administration offers based on economic hardship.

Equity or public policy. If there are no other grounds for compromise, the IRS may compromise a tax liability based on compelling public policy or equity considerations identified by the taxpayer. The IRS may accept an offer on these grounds when, due to exceptional circumstances, collection of the full amount owed would undermine public confidence that the tax laws are being administered in a fair and equitable manner. For instance, a case may be compromised on these grounds if a taxpayer incurred a liability as a result of following erroneous advice or instructions from the IRS, or because of a processing error or delay by the IRS. An acceptable offer would be expected to restore the taxpayer to the same position as if the error or delay had not occurred (IRM 5.8.11.4.3).

COMMENT

The IRS assumes that Congress imposes tax liabilities only when it determines it is fair to do so. Therefore, the IRS rarely accepts compromises on the grounds of equity or public policy. The IRS will not compromise such a tax liability because the imposition of a particular tax law provision is unjust or inequitable. For example, the IRS properly rejected an offer in compromise from married taxpayers who had significant alternative minimum tax (AMT) liability arising from their exercise of an incentive stock option on stock that then fell in value. The fact that their tax bill was much higher than the value of the stock they received was not a reason for the IRS to accept their offers. Whether the AMT is unfair is a question for Congress, not the IRS or the courts (*Speltz v. Commr*, CA-8, 2006-2 USTC ¶50,403).

Streamlined program. In 2010, the IRS implemented a "streamlined" offer in compromise program. Over time, the program has expanded to accommodate the large number of taxpayers that continue to struggle because of the economic downturn. In investigating streamlined offers, the IRS makes fewer requests for additional financial information, relying instead on internal research, and when additional information is needed, it is requested by phone. Further, the IRS is more flexible in allowable expenses and future income calculations in considering taxpayers' ability to pay. The streamlined offer in compromise program is open to taxpayers with annual household incomes up to $100,000 and tax liabilities of less than $50,000 (Interim Guidance Memorandum SBSE-05-0511-026, May 13, 2011).

COMMENT

The streamlined offer in compromise program was previously open only to taxpayers with liabilities of less than $25,000. The program was expanded as part of the IRS's Fresh Start initiative (IRS News Release IR-2011-20, February 24, 2011).

Defaults. If a taxpayer fails to meet the terms and conditions of an accepted offer, the agreement will be considered in default and terminated, and the IRS may attempt to collect the unpaid balance of the offer or the unpaid balance of the original liability. However, as part of its Fresh Start initiative, the IRS has announced that it will be flexible with previously compliant taxpayers that have difficulty meeting the periodic payment terms of an accepted offer.

COLLECTION APPEALS

In many cases, taxpayers have the right to administratively appeal IRS collection actions to the IRS Office of Appeals. The Office of Appeals is an independent division of the IRS and acts as an informal forum for the resolution of tax disputes.

There are three main types of collection appeals:

- Collection due process (CDP) appeals;
- Appeals in an equivalent hearing; and
- Appeals under the IRS Collection Appeals Program (CAP).

Taxpayers also have certain rights to appeal other IRS actions and decisions, including the assessment of the trust fund recovery penalty, the rejection of an offer in compromise, the denial of a request for penalty abatement, and jeopardy levies.

Collection Due Process Hearings

The CDP hearing provisions give taxpayers an opportunity for an independent review by the IRS Appeals Office to ensure that a levy on the taxpayer's property or filing of a Form 668(Y)(c), *Notice of Federal Tax Lien,* is warranted and appropriate.

The IRS generally must notify taxpayers of their rights to CDP hearings when it files a notice of federal lien with respect to an unpaid liability or prior to levying on a taxpayer's property to collect an unpaid liability. The IRS issues either a *Notice of Federal Tax Lien Filing and Your Right to a Hearing Under IRC 6320 (Lien Notice),* or a *Final Notice—Notice of Intent to Levy and Notice of Your Right to Hearing (levy notice)* (Code Secs. 6320 and. 6330). In either case, the taxpayer may appeal the collection action by submitting Form 12153, *Request for a Collection Due Process or Equivalent Hearing,* within 30 days after receiving the notice.

The request for a CDP hearing must state the reason or reasons why the taxpayer disagrees with the IRS's collection action and must identify the taxpayer's proposed collection alternative.

CAUTION

A request for a hearing may be disregarded if the IRS determines that the application is frivolous. The IRS can treat the portion of the application that is considered frivolous as if it were never submitted, and that portion is not subject to any further administrative or judicial review (Code Sec. 6330(g)). Further, a $5,000 penalty can be imposed on taxpayers making frivolous tax submissions (Code Sec. 6702).

The Appeals Office considers the following matters raised by a taxpayer at a CDP hearing:

- The validity, sufficiency, and timeliness of the CDP notice and the request for the CDP hearing;
- Any relevant issue relating to the unpaid tax;
- Appropriate spousal defenses;
- Challenges by the taxpayer to the appropriateness of the collection action;
- Any offers for collection alternatives; and
- Whether the proposed collection action balances the need for the efficient collection of taxes with the taxpayer's legitimate concern that the collection action be no more intrusive than necessary (Code Sec. 6330(c)(2)(A)).

A taxpayer can only dispute the underlying tax liability in a CDP hearing if he or she did not receive a notice of deficiency or otherwise have a prior opportunity to dispute the liability.

Following the hearing, the Appeals Office issues a *Notice of Determination* setting forth its decision and advising the taxpayer of the right to seek judicial review of the determination in the Tax Court.

Equivalent Hearings

A taxpayer that files an untimely request for a CDP hearing nevertheless has the right to request a similar administrative appeals hearing, called an *equivalent hearing*. Appeals considers the same issues that it would have considered at a CDP hearing and follows the same procedures in arriving at its decision. Following the equivalent hearing, Appeals issues a *Decision Letter*, which generally contains the same information as a *Notice of Determination*.

However, unlike that of a CDP hearing determination, the decision of Appeals following an equivalent hearing is final and cannot be appealed to the Tax Court. Additionally, a collection action and the statute of limitations for collection are not automatically suspended during the period of the equivalent hearing, as they are during CDP hearings.

A taxpayer may request an equivalent hearing by submitting Form 12153 to the IRS at the address shown on the lien or levy notice. The taxpayer must check the box indicating an equivalent hearing request on Line 7 of Form 12153.

COMMENT

The Treasury Inspector General for Tax Administration (TIGTA) found in an audit of the Office of Appeals Collection Due Process Program that the Office of Appeals did not always grant taxpayers the correct type of hearing, which could affect the taxpayer's right to seek judicial review and determine whether collection activity was suspended. Appeals Office management agreed with TIGTA's recommendations and agreed to make improvements in the areas identified (TIGTA Report: IRS Needs To Improve Appeals' Collection Due Process Program (Reference Number: 2011-10-062)).

Collection Appeals Program

As an alternative to a collection due process hearing, taxpayers have the option to appeal certain collection actions under the IRS Collection Appeals Program (CAP). The CAP procedure is available under a greater range of circumstances than CDP appeals. Unlike a CDP appeal, which can only be requested after the IRS issues a *Notice of Federal Tax Lien Filing* or a *Final Notice of Intent to Levy*, a taxpayer may request a CAP hearing before or after the IRS files a *Notice of Federal Tax Lien* or levies property, or to protest the rejection of a proposed installment agreement or the termination of an existing installment agreement. However, a CAP appeal offers taxpayers fewer options. Taxpayers cannot challenge the existence or amount of a tax liability in a CAP case. Additionally, Appeals' decisions are final following a CAP conference; taxpayers cannot appeal an adverse decision to the Tax Court.

Prior to initiating a CAP appeal, a taxpayer is generally required to contact an IRS collection manager to discuss the collection action at issue. If the taxpayer is unable to reach a favorable outcome with the manager, the case is forwarded to the Office of Appeals for review. If the taxpayer has been contacted by a revenue officer, the taxpayer must request a conference with a collection manager prior to submitting a CAP request. A taxpayer who is unable to resolve the disagreement with the manager may submit a request for Appeals consideration, preferably by completing Form 9423, *Collection Appeal Request*. A request for an appeal of a lien, levy, or seizure must submitted within two business days after the date of the conference with the collection manager (IRS Publication 1660, *Collection Appeal Rights*).

> **COMMENT**
>
> No conference is required before appealing the termination or rejection of an installment agreement because the right to appeal is established by statute (Code Sec. 7122).

After the taxpayer requests a CAP appeal, the IRS Appeals Office employee holds a conference with the taxpayer and reviews the disputed action based on law, regulations, policy, and procedures, considering all of the relevant facts and circumstances. CAP conferences, like collection due process conferences, are conducted very informally, typically by telephone.

STUDY QUESTIONS

5. A partial payment installment agreement:

  a. Eliminates the penalties for failure to pay

  b. Is an installment agreement under which the underlying liability may not be fully paid

  c. Automatically withdraws the taxpayer's notice of lien

  d. Does not require the taxpayer to submit a Form 433, *Collection Information Statement*

6. Appeals under the Collection Appeals Program (CAP):

  a. May challenge the amount of a tax liability

  b. May be further appealed to the Tax Court if the outcome is unfavorable to the taxpayer

  c. May not protest the rejection of the taxpayer's proposed installment agreement

  d. May be initiated before the taxpayer receives notice of a tax lien filing of intent to levy

CONCLUSION

The IRS's collection powers and resources make it unlike any other creditor. However, the IRS has made a number of changes to its policy and procedures in order to help taxpayers meet their obligations without facing unnecessary burdens. Further, taxpayers have a number of options for resolving their unpaid liabilities and avoiding enforced collection. These options and the new measures adopted by the IRS give delinquent taxpayers opportunities to satisfy their unpaid liabilities, regardless of the taxpayers' financial situations.

CPE NOTE: When you have completed your study and review of chapters 3-5, which comprise Module 2, you may wish to take the Quizzer for this Module.

Go to **CCHGroup.com/PrintCPE** to take this Quizzer online.

New Repair Regulations

This chapter discusses the new tangible property repair regulations that already apply, effective for tax years that begin on or after January 1, 2012. The regulations are temporary and, therefore, subject to change. The IRS expects to issue final regulations, without major revision, well before the official December 24, 2014, expiration date. The repair regulations are comprehensive, often complex, and affect virtually every business taxpayer. This chapter will focus on the portion of the regulations specifically dealing with the repair versus capitalization issue. Other parts of the repair regulations deal with the capitalization of property acquisition costs and special rules that affect modified accelerated cost recovery system (MACRS) property, such as dispositions of MACRS property and accounting for MACRS property in item accounts, mass asset accounts, and general asset accounts.

LEARNING OBJECTIVES

Upon completion of this chapter you will be able to:

- Understand the standards used in distinguishing a repair from an improvement;
- Identify what constitutes a unit of property and why the concept is important;
- Distinguish among improvements that are betterments, restorations, or adaptations to a new or different use;
- Understand how deductions function under the routine maintenance safe harbor rule;
- Identify materials and supplies and the timing of their deduction;
- Apply special rules for rotable spare parts;
- Understand the operation of the *de minimis* expensing rule;
- Become familiar with accounting method change requirements necessary to comply with the temporary regulations.

INTRODUCTION

The temporary tangible property repair regulations basically formalize general principles that have been developed in case law and IRS rulings for distinguishing capital improvements from repairs. In general, the regulations apply these principles using the same "facts and circumstances" approach that led to uncertainty and conflicting results in the first place. The IRS largely rejected the view that the repair versus capitalization controversy could and should be resolved through simple bright line rules and tests.

Nevertheless, the regulations do provide clarity in some areas. For example, the definition of a unit of property is precisely stated and a new safe harbor allows the deduction of routine maintenance costs on property other than buildings. Specific standards are set forth for *de minimis* expensing policies and the treatment of materials and supplies, including rotable spare parts.

The repair regulations are generally effective for tax years beginning on or after January 1, 2012 (Temporary Reg. § 1.263(a)-3T(p)). Therefore, the automatic change of accounting method procedures issued for changing accounting methods to comply with the regulations generally require the computation of a Code Sec. 481(a) adjustment that is taken into account in income over four years. (Rev. Proc. 2012-19).

COMMENT

Those portions of the temporary regulations which are effective for tax years that apply on or after January 1, 2012, require the computation of a Code Sec. 481(a) adjustment because this effective date requires taxpayers to bring the tax treatment of property previously placed in service into current compliance with the regulations. Portions of the regulations that are effective for *amounts paid or incurred* in tax years beginning on or after January 1, 2012 require no adjustments for earlier transactions and, accordingly are applied using a "cutoff method" (i.e., the regulations are applied prospectively with no Code Sec. 481(a) adjustment for preeffective date transactions). Provisions for which no Code Sec. 481(a) adjustment is required will be noted in this discussion.

BASIC RULE: IMPROVEMENTS ARE CAPITALIZED

The basic capitalization rule requires a taxpayer to capitalize amounts paid to "improve" a "unit of property." If an amount does not improve a unit of property, it is generally deductible as a cost of repair or maintenance.

Capitalization is required for all direct costs of an improvement. In addition, all indirect costs (including otherwise deductible repair and removal costs) that directly benefit the improvement or are incurred by reason of the improvement are capitalized as part of the cost of the improvement.

A property is *improved* if the activities performed on the property result in:

- A betterment;
- A restoration; or
- An adaptation to a new or different use.

The regulations explain these three types of capitalized improvements in detail and offer numerous examples of each.

However, before this discussion delves into the definitions of betterments, restorations, and adaptations it is necessary to consider the key "unit of property" concept.

CAUTION

The temporary regulations only apply for purposes of determining whether an amount must be capitalized under Code Sec. 263. Other tax code provisions may require capitalization of an amount that is not capitalized by reason of the temporary regulations. Most notably, the uniform capitalization rules (Code Sec. 263A) require taxpayers to capitalize the direct and allocable indirect costs, including the cost of materials and supplies, to property produced or to property acquired for resale. However, the UNICAP rules do not apply to small resellers with gross receipts of $10 million or less and producers that use the simplified production method and have less than $200,000 in indirect costs.

UNIT OF PROPERTY

Determining the proper unit of property is critical. The larger a unit of property is, the more likely that an activity performed on it is a repair. For example, if the windshield of a car is a separate unit of property, then the replacement of the glass is likely an improvement that must be capitalized. On the other hand, if the entire car is considered a unit of property, the replacement of the windshield is likely a repair. For this reason taxpayers have attempted to use the largest possible unit of property.

Subject to important exceptions for buildings, "plant property," and "network assets," a unit of property comprises all functionally interdependent components (Temp. Reg. § 1.263(a)-3T(e)). Components are functionally interdependent if placing one component in service depends on placing the other component in service. For example, an airplane, including its engines (if not purchased separately as replacement parts) is a single unit of property because all the parts on an airplane are functionally interdependent. Similarly, an entire passenger automobile would be considered one unit of property.

Buildings

Each building and its structural components comprise a unit of property. However, the improvement rules are applied separately to each "building system." In effect, this means that each building system is a separate unit of property and the remaining building structure is a separate unit of property (Temp. Reg. § 1.263(a)-3T(e)(2)). The regulations identify the following building systems:

- *Heating, ventilation, and air conditioning (HVAC) systems* (including motors, compressors, boilers, furnace, chillers, pipes, ducts, radiators);
- *Plumbing systems* (including pipes, drains, valves, sinks, bathtubs, toilets, water and sanitary sewer collection equipment, and site utility equipment used to distribute water and waste to and from the property line and between buildings and other permanent structures);
- *Electrical systems* (including wiring, outlets, junction boxes, lighting fixtures and associated connectors, and site utility equipment used to distribute electricity from property line to and between buildings and other permanent structures);
- All *escalators;*
- All *elevators;*
- *Fire protection and alarm systems* (including sensing devices, computer controls, sprinkler heads, sprinkler mains, associated piping or plumbing, pumps, visual and audible alarms, alarm control panels, heat and smoke detection devices, fire escapes, fire doors, emergency exit lighting and signage, and fire fighting equipment, such as extinguishers, hoses);
- *Security systems* (including window and door locks, security cameras, recorders, monitors, motion detectors, security lighting, alarm systems, entry and access systems, related junction boxes, associated wiring and conduit);
- *Gas distribution systems* (including associated pipes and equipment used to distribute gas to and from property line and between buildings or permanent structures); and
- Any other *structural components* classified by the IRS as a building system.

All elevators in the same building are treated as a single building system or unit of property. In effect, each separate elevator is a component (part) of the elevator building system. A similar rule applies to escalators.

COMMENT

Building systems are depreciated as part of the overall cost of a building when the building is purchased (i.e., the temporary regulations do not reinstate the pre-ACRS (pre-1981) "composite" depreciation rules). However, if a building system is replaced (or capitalized improvements to a system are made), the cost is separately depreciated using the modified accelerated cost recovery system (MACRS) depreciation period that applies to the building.

COMMENT

The standards given in the regulations will often result in a smaller unit of property than many taxpayers have chosen to use. For example, a taxpayer may have treated a building and all of its structural components, including building systems, as one unit of property and deducted the cost of replacing an entire building system (e.g., an HVAC system) or a major structural component, such as a roof, as a repair. Under the new regulations, the replacement of an entire building system (or major components thereof) or an entire roof is capitalized. Under these circumstances taxpayers will need to file accounting method changes to change their definition of unit of property for the building and begin capitalizing the previously deducted repair costs. A Section 481(a) adjustment that takes into account the difference between the repair expenses claimed and the amount of depreciation that would have been allowed if the expenses had been capitalized will need to be reported.

CAUTION

If a taxpayer properly depreciates a component (or group of components) of a unit of property over a different depreciation period than the remainder of the unit of property, then the separately depreciated components are treated as one unit of property. For example, if a taxpayer properly depreciates the tires on a truck as MACRS 3-year property and the truck as MACRS 5-year property, the tires and truck are separate units of property.

Plant Property

Plant property consists of functionally interdependent machinery or equipment used to perform an industrial process within a plant (Temp. Reg. § 1.263(a)-3T(e)(3)).

Examples of an industrial process include:

- Manufacturing;
- Generation (e.g., electrical generation);
- Warehousing;
- Distribution;
- Automated materials handling in service industries; and
- Similar activities.

In the case of plant property, the unit of property consists of each component (or group of components) within a plant that performs a discrete and major function or operation within the plant. Thus, typically, individual machines will be treated as a unit of property even though the entire plant might otherwise be considered a unit of property under the functional interdependence standard.

COMMENT

The unit of property determined under the general functional interdependence test in an industrial plant will generally consist of a group of functionally interdependent machinery and equipment within the plant. Under this standard, it is possible that the entire plant could be considered a unit of property. This "initial" unit of property, however, must be further divided into smaller units of property that consist of each component (or group of components) that performs a discrete and major function or operation within the functionally interdependent machinery or equipment.

EXAMPLE

The NorthwestEd electric power plant consists of a structure that is not a building, four pulverizers that grind coal, one boiler that produces steam, one turbine that converted steam into mechanical energy, and one generator that converts mechanical energy into electricity. The initial unit of property is the entire plant because the components are functionally interdependent. However, because NorthWestEd's power plant is plant property (i.e., property used for electrical generation) and each of these components performs a discrete and major function within the plant, each component (including each pulverizer) is treated as a separate unit of property.

EXAMPLE

Crisp Lines, a uniform and linen rental business has two laundering lines in its plant. One line is used for uniforms and the other line for linen. Each line operates independently and each line consists of sorters, boilers, washers, dryers, ironers, folders, and water treatment systems. The initial unit of Crisp Lines property consists of each line because the components of each line are functionally interdependent. However, because each line is plant property and each component performs a discrete and major function within a line, each sorter, boiler, washer, dryer, ironer, folder, and water treatment system is treated as a separate unit of property.

EXAMPLE

Tortillas Suprema, a retail restaurant, has a large piece of equipment that prepares and cooks tortillas. The unit of property is the entire piece of equipment because the components of the equipment are functionally interdependent. The equipment is not used to perform an industrial process because it performs a small-scale function within the restaurant. Therefore, Tortillas Surprema is not subject to the plant property rules that would require the equipment to be further divided into separate units of property.

Network Assets

Network assets consist of:

- Railroad tracks;
- Oil and gas pipelines;
- Water and sewage pipelines;
- Power transmission and distribution lines; and
- Telephone and cable lines.

In the case of network assets, the unit of property is based on a taxpayer's particular facts and circumstances. The functional interdependence standard is not determinative (Temp. Reg. § 1.263(a)-3T(e)(3)).

COMMENT

Previously published guidance addressing the treatment of network assets for particular industries will remain in effect. This guidance includes:

- Rev. Proc. 2011-43 (2011-37 IRB 326) (safe harbor method for electric utility transmission and distribution property);
- Rev. Proc. 2011-18 (2011-18 IRB 743) (network asset maintenance allowance or units of property method for wireless telecommunication network assets);
- Rev. Proc. 2011-27 (2011-18 IRB 740) (network asset maintenance allowance or units of property method for wireline telecommunication network assets);
- Rev. Proc. 2003-65 (2002-2 CB 700) (track maintenance allowance method for Class II and III railroads); and
- Rev. Proc. 2001-46 (2001-2 CB 263) (track maintenance allowance method for Class I railroads).

The IRS will likely continue issuing industry-specific guidance for network assets.

Effective Date

The temporary regulations dealing with the definition of a unit of property are effective for tax years beginning on or after January 1, 2012 (Temp. Reg. § 1.263(a)-3T(p)).

Change in Accounting Method

An automatic change of accounting method procedure may be used by a taxpayer to change its definition of a unit of property for purposes of determining whether an amount paid or incurred improves a unit of property (Rev. Proc. 2012-19 adding section 3.10 to the Appendix of Rev. Proc. 2011-14).

COMMENT

Presumably the expenditures would not be capitalized if the building had been purchased by Sam James when it was new. In this case, the expenditures would merely return the building to its original state as of the time it was placed in service by Sam. If the building could not be used because of the extent of the necessary repairs, then the expenses would need to be capitalized as a restoration as discussed below.

STUDY QUESTIONS

1. Which of the following is *not* capitalized as an improvement?

    a. Betterment
    b. Repair
    c. Restoration
    d. Adaptation

2. Which of the following is a separate unit of property?

    a. Functionally interdependent components
    b. An automotive engine
    c. An entire plant that performs an industrial process
    d. A structural component of a building

BETTERMENTS AS IMPROVEMENTS

Betterments to a unit of property are the first of three types of capitalized improvements (Temp. Reg. § 1.263(a)-3T(h)). A *betterment* is an expenditure that:

- Ameliorates a material condition or material defect that existed prior to the taxpayer's acquisition of the unit of property (regardless of whether or not the taxpayer was aware of the condition or defect at the time of acquisition);
- Ameliorates a material condition or material defect that arose during the taxpayer's production of the unit of property;
- Results in a material addition to a unit of property, such as a physical enlargement, expansion, or extension; or
- Results in a material increase in the unit of property's capacity, productivity, output, efficiency, strength, or quality.

A *facts and circumstances test* applies t1o find a betterment. Factors taken into consideration include:

- The purpose of the expenditure;
- The physical nature of the work performed;
- The effect of the expenditure on the unit of property; and

- The treatment of the expenditure on the taxpayer's applicable financial statement.

EXAMPLE

Sam James incurs costs on a recently purchased building to repair damaged drywall, repaint, rewallpaper, replace windows, repair and replace doors, replace and regrout tile, repair millwork, and repair and replace roofing materials. The building remains in use while the repairs are made. These costs are capitalized because they ameliorate material conditions or defects that existed prior to acquisition of the property (Temp. Reg. § 1.263(a)-3T(h)(4), Example 5).

COMMENT

Presumably the expenditures would not be capitalized if the building had been purchased by Sam James when it was new. In this case, the expenditures would merely return the building to its original state as of the time it was placed in service by Sam. If the building could not be used because of the extent of the necessary repairs, then the expenses would need to be capitalized as a restoration as discussed below.

EXAMPLE

Ed Campe, a self-employed trucker, purchases a truck and immediately performs a minor tune-up. He may deduct the tune-up costs as a repair expense because the condition of the truck when purchased was not a preexisting material defect and the repairs do not result in a material increase in the truck's capacity, productivity, output, efficiency, strength, or quality (Temp. Reg. § 1.263(a)-3T(h)(4), Examples (3) and (4)).

A particular event may trigger the need for an expenditure. In this situation, for purposes of determining whether there has been (a) a "material addition" to a unit of property, such as a physical enlargement, expansion, or extension or (b) a "material increase" to capacity, productivity, output, efficiency, strength, or quality, a comparison is made to the condition of the property after the expenditures and the condition of the property immediately before the event (Temp. Reg. § 1.263(a)-3T(h)(3)(iii)(C)).

If the expenditures are the result of normal wear and tear, the condition of the property after the last time that the taxpayer corrected the normal effects of the wear and tear is compared to the condition of the property immediately after the expenditures. If the taxpayer has not previously corrected the normal effects of the wear and tear, the condition of the property at the time the taxpayer placed it in service is compared to the condition of the property after the expenditures (Temp. Reg. § 1.263(a)-3T(h)(3)(iii)(B)).

The replacement of a part of a unit of property with an improved but *comparable* part is not evidence of a betterment as long as the same type of part is not practicably available, for example, due to technological advancements or product enhancements (Temp. Reg. § 1.263(a)-3T(h)(3)(ii)).

Additional IRS examples conclude:

- Replacing columns and girders supporting the second floor of a building to permit storage of supplies with a gross weight 50 percent greater than the previous load-carrying capacity of the storage area is a betterment because it results in a material increase in strength (Temp. Reg. § 1.263(a)-3T(h)(4), Example 16);
- Deepening a harbor channel from 10 to 20 feet is a betterment because it results in a material increase in capacity. Costs incurred a few years later to redredge the silted channel to its 20-foot depth is not a betterment (Temp. Reg. § 1.263(a)-3T(h)(4), Examples 17 and 18); and
- Removing a drop-down ceiling and repainting the original ceiling is not a betterment because it does not result in a material addition to the building structure or a material increase in its capacity, productivity, efficiency, strength, or quality.

Environmental Cleanup Costs

Generally, under the regulations, a taxpayer may claim a deduction for remediating property that it contaminated during its business operations because the taxpayer is merely restoring the property to its previous condition. However, if the taxpayer acquires contaminated property (or reacquires property that it previously contaminated), the restoration costs are capitalized as a betterment.

IRS examples conclude:

- Soil remediation costs caused by leaking gas tanks before a taxpayer's purchase of the land (the unit of property) result in a betterment that ameliorates a preexisting material condition or defect (Temp. Reg. § 1.263(a)-3T(h)(4), Example 1); and
- Replacing asbestos insulation that has begun to deteriorate and could eventually pose a health risk is *not* a betterment because it does not ameliorates a preexisting *material* condition or defect and does not result in a material addition to the building structure or a material increase in the structure's capacity, output, efficiency, strength, or quality (Temp. Reg. § 1.263(a)-3T(h)(4), Example 2).

> **COMMENT**
>
> Commentators have argued that it is difficult to reconcile the conclusions in these two examples. Apparently, the primary distinction is that the soil contamination poses an immediate health risk and, therefore, is a material defect.

Retail Building Refresh Examples

The regulations provide "building refresh" examples that are of particular significance to retail store owners because major and minor remodeling projects are quite common. However, commentators have requested additional clarifications in this area because the examples do not adequately illustrate the range of situations taxpayers face in typical store remodeling and refreshing.

The first example provides that periodic cosmetic and layout changes to the interior of a store to make the store more attractive and the merchandise more accessible to customers are not capitalized as a betterment.

> **EXAMPLE**
>
> Josh Madigan, a retail store owner, replaces and reconfigures display tables and racks, relocates lighting, and repairs flooring and moves a single wall to accommodate the reconfigurations in his retail grocery store. In addition, Josh patches holes in walls, repaints the interior of the store, replaces damaged ceiling tiles, repairs vinyl flooring throughout the building, and power washes the exterior. The costs are not capitalized betterments because they do not result in material increases in capacity, productivity, efficiency, strength, or quality of the store's structures or any building systems when compared to the condition of the building after the previous refresh (Temp. Reg. § 1.263(a)-3T(h)(4), Example 6).

In the second example, the store owner also makes an improvement unrelated to the store refresh.

> **EXAMPLE**
>
> Assume the preceding facts except that Josh also upgrades all of the toilets, sinks, and other bathroom fixtures and repairs the damage to floors, ceilings, and walls caused by the replacement. The costs of replacing the toilets, sinks, and fixtures, as well as the indirect repair costs attributable to the replacement, are capitalized betterments because they result in a material increase in the quality of the store's plumbing system. The refresh expenses, however, remain deductible because they are not incurred by reason of the improvements to the building's plumbing system (Temp. Reg. § 1.263(a)-3T(h)(4), Example 7).

The third example, illustrates that building refresh expenses incurred by reason of a related substantial store remodeling project that includes significant upgrades are capitalized as indirect costs of the remodeling project (Temp. Reg. § 1.263(a)-3T(h)(4), Example 8).

EXAMPLE

Now assume that Josh not only makes all of the replacements and updates to his existing grocery store but also alters the appearance and layout of the store by removing and rebuilding walls, replacing ceilings, rebuilding facades, to replacing doors, and replacing flooring. These changes materially increase the productivity, efficiency, and quality of the building structure and must be capitalized. In addition, the amounts paid for the refresh of the store building described above must also be capitalized because these expenditures directly benefitted or were incurred by reason of the improvements to the store structure (Temp. Reg. § 1.263(a)-3T(h)(4), Example 8).

STUDY QUESTION

3. A betterment does *not* include:

   a. The amelioration of a material condition or defect that existed prior to the acquisition of a unit of property
   b. Environmental remediation costs that correct soil contamination caused by the taxpayer while the taxpayer owned the property
   c. A substantial store remodeling project
   d. A material increase in a unit of property's capacity, productivity, output, efficiency, strength, or quality.

RESTORATIONS AS IMPROVEMENTS

Amounts paid to restore a unit of property are capitalized as an improvement (Temporary Reg. § 1.263(a)-3T(i)).

A restoration includes any of the following situations:

- Replacing a major component of a unit of property or a substantial structural part of a unit of property;
- Returning a unit of property to its ordinary operating condition if it has deteriorated to a state of disrepair and is no longer functional;
- The replacement of a component part of a unit of property if the taxpayer has either
  — Properly deducted a loss (other than a casualty loss) for the component or
  — Sold or exchanged the replaced component and realized a gain or loss; and
- Rebuilding a unit of property to a like-new condition (i.e. to the manufacturer's original specifications) after the end of its MACRS class life (i.e., alternative depreciation system (ADS) depreciation period).

COMMENT

As indicated above, the cost of replacing a component of a unit of property cannot be claimed as a repair expense if a taxpayer sells or exchanges the component and realizes a gain or loss or properly deducts a loss. For example, if a loss deduction is claimed by retiring a component, the cost of replacing the component may not be claimed as a repair expense. This rule for retirements is generally unfavorable insofar as the loss deduction is limited to the remaining basis of the component which has not been depreciated and the cost of replacing the component (i.e., the repair cost) will usually far exceed this amount.

The retirement of a component of MACRS property will trigger a loss if the retirement is treated as the disposition of an asset under the MACRS depreciation rules (Temp. Reg. § 1.168(i)-8T). The disposition rules are fairly complex and are not the subject of this chapter. However, in general, a taxpayer may claim a loss on a component of a unit of property that is Section 1245 property if the taxpayer consistently treats the component as a separate asset for MACRS disposition purposes. The temporary regulations create a new rule that treats the retirement of a structural component of a building (Section 1250 property) as a loss equal to the unrecovered basis of the structural component. However, under the temporary regulations, a taxpayer may place depreciable property in a general asset account and elect whether to claim a loss on the retirement of a component of Section 1245 property or a structural component of a building (Temp. Reg. § 1.168(i)-1T). If a loss is not claimed, it is not necessary to compute the remaining basis of the retired component for purposes of computing the loss deduction and a repair deduction will not be disallowed because a loss was claimed. A repair deduction, however, may be disallowed for other reasons even if no loss is deducted. For example, no loss is allowed if the component replaced is a major component or a substantial structural part of a unit of property, as discussed below.

COMMENT

The retirement of a component of a fully depreciated asset will not generate a loss because the asset (including the component) will have no unrecovered basis.

Major Component or Substantial Structural Part Defined

The cost of replacing a major component of a unit of property or a substantial structural part of a unit of property is a capitalized restoration regardless of whether a loss is claimed on the retired component or structural part. All facts and circumstances are considered in determining what constitutes a major component or substantial structural part (Temp. Reg. § 1.263(a)-3T(i)(4)). The term includes a part (or group of parts) that compose a "large portion" of the physical structure of a unit of property or that perform a discrete and critical function in the operation of the unit of property. However, the replacement of a minor component that affects the function of a unit of property is not by itself a capitalized restoration.

EXAMPLE

Francis Hauling Inc. owns a petroleum hauling truck. The truck consists of two units of property: the tractor and a trailer with a petroleum tank. The cost of replacing the engine on the tractor is capitalized as a restoration because it is a major component of the tractor. The cost of replacing the tank on the trailer is capitalized because it is a major component of the trailer. Although the cost of painting a logo on the tank would normally be considered a deductible expense, this cost must also be capitalized because it directly benefits and is incurred by reason of the restoration of the tank. The cost of repairing a tail light, however, is not incurred by reason of the trailer restoration and may be deducted as a repair (Temp. Reg. § 1.263(a)-3T(i)(5), Example 8).

COMMENT

Under proposed regulations, a component or part was major or substantial only if its cost exceeded 50 percent of the original cost of the unit of property. The temporary regulations eliminate this bright line test and rely solely on the facts and circumstances.

Roofs

Several IRS examples consider the treatment of roof expenses by applying the rule requiring capitalization of the replacement of major components or substantial structural parts of a unit of property. For a building, the unit of property is the building structure, which also includes all structural components other than the enumerated building systems. One example makes the obvious conclusion that the cost of replacing all of the components of a roof (i.e. sheathing, rafters, covering) that developed a leak is capitalized. Another example makes a similar conclusion where a major portion of a roof's decking, insulation, and membrane is replaced. However, the replacement of the membrane alone is a deductible repair because the membrane is not a major component or substantial structural part of the building structure (Temp. Reg. § 1.263(a)-3T(i)(5), Examples 12, 13, and 14).

COMMENT

Based on the IRS examples treating the replacement of a roof membrane as a repair, the cost of replacing all of the asphalt shingles on a roof should be deductible as a repair, provided little or no work is done to the sheathing.

Additional IRS examples include:

- Acquisition and installation costs of new components of a walk-in freezer (separately depreciated as an item of Section 1245 property) must be capitalized if the taxpayer discards the components and properly claims a loss or sells the components and realizes a gain or loss even if the replacement would otherwise be considered a deductible repair (Temp. Reg. § 1.263(a)-3T(i)(5), Example 1);

- Amounts paid to rebuild a freight car to a like-new condition in accord with the manufacturer's original specifications by replacing, upgrading, or reconditioning all of its substantial components are currently deducted if the rebuild occurs *before the end* of the freight car's 14 year class life (Temp. Reg. § 1.263(a)-3T(i)(5), Example 6);
- A broken switch on a drill press is not a major component and the cost of replacement is a repair expense assuming no gain or loss claimed on broken switch (Temp. Reg. § 1.263(a)-3T(i)(5), Example 11); and
- The cost of shoring up walls and replacing the siding of a farm building that is no longer structurally sound is a capitalized restoration because it returns a nonfunctional building to its ordinary operating condition (Temp. Reg. § 1.263(a)-3T(i)(5), Example 5).

COMMENT

For the drill press example, even though the machine is nonfunctional due to the broken switch, the machine would need to be in a significant state of disrepair to require capitalization under the rule for nonfunctional property.

Casualty Losses

Under the temporary regulations, if a taxpayer reduces the basis of a property by any amount on account of a casualty loss or the receipt of insurance proceeds then the taxpayer must capitalize all related repairs even if the repair expenses exceed the basis adjustment (Temp. Reg. § 1.263(a)-3T(i)(1)(iii)).

COMMENT

Some taxpayers currently claim both a repair expense deduction and a casualty loss deduction. The temporary regulations now only allow a taxpayer to claim a casualty loss deduction. Moreover, all of the repair expenses must be capitalized regardless of the size of the casualty loss deduction. A taxpayer can work around the rule by placing its property into a general asset account (GAA) and making an election allowed by the new GAA rules (discussed in another chapter) to not recognize the casualty loss.

STUDY QUESTION

4. A restoration does *not* include:

   a. Replacing a major component of a machine that is a unit of property
   b. Rebuilding an item of property to the manufacturer's original specifications before the MACRS ADS period (class life) for the property has expired
   c. Replacing the membrane on a roof so long as no additional components of the roof are replaced
   d. Returning a building to its ordinary operating condition if it has deteriorated to a state of disrepair and is no longer functional

ADAPTATION AS IMPROVEMENT

Amounts paid to adapt a unit of property to a new use or a use that is different than the use of the property when it was placed in service by the taxpayer are capitalized improvements (Temporary Reg. § 1.263(a)-3T(j)).

IRS examples of capitalized adaptation expenses include:

- Costs to convert a building used for manufacturing into a showroom adapt the building to a new or different use (Temporary Reg. § 1.263(a)-3T(j)(3), Example 1);
- Amounts paid to remove walls between three retail spaces in a building with 20 retail spaces that are designed to be reconfigured does not adapt property to new or different use because the combination of retail spaces is consistent with the intended use of the building (Temporary Reg. § 1.263(a)-3T(j)(3), Example 2); and
- Amounts paid to regrade land so that it can be used for residential housing adapts the land to a new or different use if the land was originally used to operate a manufacturing facility (Temporary Reg. § 1.263(a)-3T(j)(3), Example 4).

CHANGE IN ACCOUNTING METHOD

Taxpayers who previously deducted repair or maintenance expenses that should have been capitalized applying the standards of the temporary regulations will need to change their accounting method to comply with the regulations and compute a positive Code Sec. 481(a) adjustment based on the difference between the previously deducted amount and the depreciation (if any) that could have been claimed on that amount if it had originally been capitalized. Conversely, a taxpayer may change its accounting method to deduct (through a negative Code Sec. 481(a) adjustment) amounts that were previously capitalized as improvements but are allowed as a repair or maintenance deduction under the temporary regulations.

Rev. Proc. 2012-19 adds Sections 3.10 and 10.10 to Appendix of the Rev. Proc. 2011-14 (the procedure governing automatic change of accounting methods) for these purposes. Additional automatic change of accounting method procedures are provided in Rev. Proc. 2012-19 for special accounting method changes discussed below. Some of these additional method changes are applied on a cutoff basis, meaning that no Code Sec. 481(a) adjustment is required if the regulations are applied as of their effective date.

COMMENT

A positive Code Sec. 481(a) adjustment is included in income over four tax years. A negative (taxpayer-favorable adjustment) may be deducted in one tax year.

Taxpayers making more than one accounting method change under Rev. Proc. 2012-19 may generally file a single Form 3115, *Application for Change in Accounting Method,* that includes all of the concurrent changes.

Automatic accounting method changes under Rev. Proc. 2012-19 may be filed no later than the due date (including extensions) of the income tax return for the year of change. A signed copy of the completed Form 3115 must be filed with the IRS's Ogden Utah office instead of the IRS's national office as is customary. The signed original Form 3115 is filed with the tax return.

Rev. Proc. 2012-19 also suspends the scope limitations of Section 4.01 of Rev. Proc. 2011-14 for a taxpayer's first and second tax years beginning after December 31, 2011. The scope limitations prevent a taxpayer who is under audit or who has filed an accounting method change in the past five years from using the automatic change of accounting method procedures for the same method change. Thus, a taxpayer may file a change of accounting method for its 2012 tax year and make additional corrections in the subsequent tax year for the same change using the automatic method procedures. Thereafter, the advance consent procedures are required to be followed in order to make additional corrections.

Examination Activity Suspended

Examiners in the IRS's Large Business & Industry (LB&I) Division have been told to stop current exam activity on pre-2012 returns with respect to the issue of whether costs incurred to maintain, replace, or improve tangible property must be capitalized under Code Sec. 263(a). The assumption is that taxpayers under exam who have claimed repair expenses for costs that the temporary regulations require to be capitalized will apply for an accounting method change under Rev. Proc. 2012-19 to comply with the temporary regulations. For tax years beginning in 2012 and 2013 examiners are expected to determine whether a taxpayer applied for an accounting method change and took into account any required Code Sec. 481(a) adjustment into account (LB&I Directive issued on March 15, 2012).

ROUTINE MAINTENANCE SAFE HARBOR

The cost of routine maintenance on a unit of property other than a building is currently deductible if certain safe-harbor requirements are met (Temp. Reg. § 1.263(a)-3T(g)). This is not an elective provision.

> **COMMENT**
>
> The *routine maintenance safe harbor (RMSH)* does not apply to a building or its structural components, including building systems. Taxpayers must apply the general rules for improvements and capitalize costs incurred for a betterment or restoration to the building or the building systems, or to adapt the building or any of its systems to a new or different use.

Routine maintenance is defined as a recurring activity that is necessary to keep a unit of property in its ordinary efficient operating condition as a result of the taxpayer's use of the property. Routine maintenance does not include the cost of returning a nonfunctioning unit of property to a functional state. Nor does it include maintenance performed in conjunction with a betterment. This rule is similar to the building refresh examples in which otherwise-deductible repairs performed in conjunction with a major remodeling are capitalized.

COMMENT

If a taxpayer acquires a unit of property and performs scheduled maintenance, the routine maintenance safe harbor does not apply to the portion of the costs attributable to the prior owner's use. These costs must be analyzed using the general rules applicable to improvements.

A routine maintenance activity is *recurring* only if the taxpayer expects to perform the activity more than once during the class life of the unit of property. The class life is the same as the MACRS ADS period. If the unit of property has more than one component with different depreciation periods, the class life of the unit of property is the same as the class life of the component with the longest class life.

The following nonexclusive factors are considered in determining whether the routine maintenance safe harbor applies:

- The number of times the activity is performed;
- Industry practice;
- Manufacturer's recommendations for scheduled maintenance;
- Taxpayer's experience; and
- Taxpayer's treatment of the activity on its financial statement.

The RMSH does not apply to the cost of replacing a component of property if the taxpayer deducts a loss or reports a gain for the replaced component.

The RMSH does not apply to the cost of repairing or maintaining rotable or temporary spare parts (both of which are defined below) if the taxpayer applies the optional method of accounting for rotable and temporary spare parts (as also described below).

IRS examples conclude:

- Engine shop visits (ESVs) required every four years on commercial aircraft engines consisting of disassembly, cleaning, inspection, repair, replacement, reassembly, and testing of the engine and its component parts qualify for the RMSH. ESVs conducted after the 12-year class life of the aircraft also qualify for the RMSH as long as the ESVs were conducted more than once during the 12-year class life. ESVs performed on engines that are rotable spare parts because acquired separately from the aircraft also qualify for the RMSH as long as the optional method of accounting for rotable and temporary spare parts is not elected (Temp. Reg. § 1.263(a)-3T(g)(5), Examples 1 and 2);

- Maintenance performed every four years to the diesel engine of a towboat (not a rotable spare part) with a class life of 18 years qualifies for the RMSH when the maintenance consists of inspecting and cleaning the engine and replacing or reconditioning worn parts. However, if this maintenance is ever performed in conjunction with an upgrade to the engine to increase its towing capacity, the maintenance does not qualify for the RMSH (Temp. Reg. § 1.263(a)-3T(g)(5), Examples 8 and 9);
- Routine maintenance on a used machine shortly after purchase does not qualify for the RMSH because the maintenance relates to a period when the taxpayer did not own the machine (i.e., did not result from taxpayer's use of the machine). Although the safe harbor does not apply, the expense is likely deductible as a repair if major parts are not replaced (Temp. Reg. § 1.263(a)-3T(g)(5), Example 4);
- The replacement every three years of the lining of a container with a 12-year class life in which chemical reactions convert raw material to a finished product in order to keep the container in efficient operating condition qualifies for the RMSH even though the lining is a substantial structural part of the unit of property (i.e., the container) (Temp. Reg. § 1.263(a)-3T(g)(5), Example 6); and
- Reconditioning a railroad freight car with a 14-year class life every eight years to keep the car in reasonable operating condition does not qualify for the RMSH because the reconditioning activity is only performed once during the class life (Temp. Reg. § 1.263(a)-3T(g)(5), Example 7).

Effective Date

The routine method safe harbor applies to tax years beginning on or after January 1, 2012.

Change in Accounting Method

An automatic accounting method change is provided to change to the routine safe-harbor method if the taxpayer has been capitalizing as an improvement amounts that otherwise qualify for the safe harbor. A Code Sec. 481(a) computation is required (i.e., the change is not applied on a cutoff basis) (Rev. Proc. 2012-19, adding Section 3.19 to the Appendix of Rev. Proc. 2011-14).

STUDY QUESTION

5. The routine maintenance safe harbor applies to:

   a. The cost of maintenance that is performed more than once during an asset's MACRS alternative depreciation system (ADS) period (class life)
   b. The cost of returning a nonfunctioning unit of property to a functional state
   c. The portion of a maintenance cost attributable to a prior owner's use
   d. Routine maintenance performed on a building

OPTIONAL SIMPLIFIED METHOD FOR CERTAIN REGULATED TAXPAYERS

A taxpayer that is subject to the regulatory accounting rules of the Federal Energy Regulatory Commission (FERC), the Federal Communications Commission (FCC), or the Surface Transportation Board (STB) may use the regulatory rules to determine whether an amount is capitalized for federal income tax purposes. The temporary regulations continue to apply to any property that is not subject to the regulatory accounting method (Temp. Reg. § 1.263(a)-3T(k)).

COMMENT

Regulated taxpayers who choose to use the optional simplified method will not need to concern themselves with the federal tax capitalization rules of the temporary regulations unless they also own property that is not subject to the regulatory rules.

Effective Date

The optional method for regulated taxpayers is effective for tax years beginning on or after January 1, 2012.

Change in Accounting Method

An automatic accounting method change is provided to change to the optional simplified method for a regulated taxpayer. A Code Sec. 481(a) adjustment is required (i.e., the change is not applied on a cutoff basis) (Rev. Proc. 2012-19, adding Section 3.11 to the Appendix of Rev. Proc. 2011-14).

MATERIALS AND SUPPLIES

When used to improve a unit of property, the cost of materials and supplies is capitalized unless an exception to capitalization such as the *de minimis* expensing rule (described below) or the routine maintenance safe harbor applies (Temp. Reg. § 1.263(a)-3T(c)(2)).

The cost of materials and supplies that do not improve a unit of property is generally deducted in the tax year the materials or supplies are used or consumed. However, the cost of incidental materials and supplies is deducted in the tax year the cost is paid or incurred (Temp. Reg. § 1.162-3T(a)).

> **COMMENT**
>
> *Incidental materials and supplies* are materials and supplies for which a beginning and year-end inventory or record of consumption is not kept.

> **CAUTION**
>
> Under the uniform capitalization rules of Code Sec. 263A, the cost of materials and supplies is considered an indirect material cost subject to capitalization in the case of property produced or acquired for resale, regardless of the treatment otherwise provided by the temporary regulations. The UNICAP rules do not apply to small resellers having gross receipts of $10 million or less and producers who use the simplified production method and have less than $200,000 in indirect costs.

Definition of Materials and Supplies

The temporary regulations now provide a definition of materials and supplies (Temp. Reg. § 1.162-3T(c)). Specifically, *materials and supplies* are:

- A component (whether or not the component is a unit of property) that is acquired to maintain, repair, or improve a unit of tangible property owned, leased, or serviced by the taxpayer. This category does not include components that are acquired as part of a unit of property (e.g., the original aircraft engines on an aircraft);
- A unit of property that has an acquisition or production cost of $100 or less;
- Fuel, lubricants, water, and similar items, that are reasonably expected to be consumed in 12 months or less, beginning when used in taxpayer's operations;
- A unit of property that has an economic useful life of 12 months or less, beginning when the property is used or consumed in the taxpayer's operations, such as stationary and cleaning supplies; and
- Any property identified in IRS guidance as a material and supply.

> **COMMENT**
>
> The IRS has the authority to increase the $100 cap for the acquisition or production cost. This definition only encompasses articles that are separate units of property (e.g., low-cost tools, cheap furniture). More expensive items that are a unit of property (or are a component of a unit of property) are materials and supplies only if used to maintain, repair, or improve another unit of tangible property. However, if used to improve a unit of property, the cost of the material or supply is capitalized unless the cost is deductible under the *de minimis* expensing rule described later.

EXAMPLE

Subsonic Air, a commercial airline, purchases a stock of spare parts that are not rotable spare parts to maintain and repair its aircraft. The spare parts are materials and supplies that are deducted in the year the spare parts are used to repair or maintain aircraft. However, if the parts improve, rather than repair or maintain the aircraft, Subsonic capitalizes the cost unless an exception to capitalization, such as the *de minimis* expensing rule, applies (Temp. Reg. § 1.162-3T(h), Example 1).

EXAMPLE

Levon Landlord pays for the acquisition, delivery, and installation of a new window to replace a broken window in an apartment building he owns. In the same tax year, the new window is installed. The replacement of the window does not improve the property. The new window is a material or supply because it is a component acquired and used to repair or improve a unit of property (that is., the building and its structural components other than the enumerated building systems). The amounts paid for the acquisition and delivery of the window are deductible as a material and supply in the tax year in which the window is installed in the apartment building assuming no gain or loss is recognized on the broken window (Temp. Reg. § 1.162-3T(h), Example 5).

COMMENT

The deduction for materials and supplies that are not used to improve a unit of property only applies to the amount paid or incurred to acquire or produce the materials and supplies. Delivery costs are treated as part of the acquisition cost. Installation costs are not treated as part of the cost of the materials and supplies. Installation costs (if any) of a material or supply that does not improve property will generally be deductible as a repair expense.

Election to Capitalize Materials and Supplies

A taxpayer may elect to capitalize the cost of materials and supplies purchased or produced during the tax year. The election is made by capitalizing the amounts paid or incurred to acquire or produce the material or supply in the tax year the amounts are paid or incurred and by beginning to depreciate the materials and supplies in the tax year placed in service (Temp. Reg. § 1.162-3T(d)).

Election to Expense Materials and Supplies
Under *De Minimis* Expensing Rule

An affirmative election may be made to apply a *de minimis* expensing rule to any material and supply that is not used as an improvement if the taxpayer otherwise qualifies to use the *de minimis* rule. If the election is made, the taxpayer deducts the cost of the material or supply under the *de minimis* rule in the tax year the cost is paid or incurred. The election may be made for any portion of materials and supplies acquired during the tax year (Temp. Reg. § 1.162-3T(f)). Materials and supplies used in an improvement may qualify for the *de minimis* rule without making an affirmative election, as explained below (Temp. Reg. 1.263(a)-3T(c)(2)).

> **COMMENT**
>
> It is unnecessary to make the election for incidental material and supplies because they are already deductible in the tax year their cost is paid or incurred.

Effective Date

The temporary regulations relating to materials and supplies apply to amounts paid or incurred (to acquire or produce property) in tax years beginning on or after January 1, 2012 (Temp. Reg. § 1.162-3T(k)).

Change in Accounting Method

An automatic consent procedure allows a taxpayer that wants to change its accounting method to comply with the definition *nonincidental* materials and supplies and deduct such amounts in the tax year in which they are actually used or consumed (Rev. Proc. 2012-19 adding Section 3.12 to the Appendix of Rev. Proc. 2011-14). This change is applied on a cutoff basis (i.e. does not require a Code Sec. 481(a) adjustment).

An automatic consent procedure allows a taxpayer that wants to change its accounting method for *incidental* materials and supplies to comply with the definition materials and supplies and deduct such amounts in the tax year in which they are paid or incurred (Rev. Proc. 2012-19 adding Section 3.13 is added to the Appendix of Rev. Proc. 2011-14). This change is also applied on a cutoff basis.

STUDY QUESTIONS

---

6. The cost of materials and supplies:

   a. May not exceed in the aggregate $5,000
   b. May be deducted if they are used to improve a unit of property
   c. Are capitalized if the materials and supplies are incidental
   d. Are deducted in the tax year used or consumed, if the materials and supplies are nonincidental

7. The temporary regulations relating to materials and supplies:

   a. Are applied on a cutoff basis without a Code Sec. 481(a) adjustment
   b. Are adopted using a nonautomatic accounting method change procedure
   c. Are effective for tax years beginning on or after January 1, 2012
   d. Do not include a specific definition of materials and supplies

---

DE MINIMIS EXPENSING RULE

One of the most important parts of the repair regulations is a *de minimis* expensing rule that allows a qualifying taxpayer to deduct the cost of acquiring or producing a unit of low-cost property or the cost of acquiring or producing materials and supplies, in the tax year paid or incurred (Temp. Reg. § 1.263(a)-2T(g)).

The cost of acquiring property includes transaction costs that facilitate the acquisition, most commonly transportation costs. Labor (e.g., installation costs) and overhead are not included in transaction costs.

The *de minimis* rule may be used if the following three requirements are satisfied:

- The taxpayer must have an "applicable financial statement";
- *At the beginning of the tax year*, the taxpayer must have written accounting procedures that treat amounts costing less than a certain dollar amount as an expense for nontax purposes; and
- The taxpayer must treat these amounts as expenses on its applicable financial statement.

> **COMMENT**
>
> Many taxpayers, particularly calendar year taxpayers, did not have the required written accounting procedures in effect as of the beginning of their 2012 tax year due to the late year-end (2011) issuance of the temporary regulations. Practitioners have requested that the final regulations provide needed relief.

A consolidated group member may rely on the written accounting procedures of the consolidated group if its financial results are reported on the applicable financial statement of the group.

Applicable Financial Statement Defined

Any of the following is considered an applicable financial statement (Temp. Reg. § 1.263(a)-2T(g)(6)):

- Financial statement required to be filed with the SEC (e.g. an annual Form 10-K statement); or
- Certified audited financial statement accompanied by the report of an independent CPA that is used for
  - Credit purposes,
  - Reporting to shareholders, partners, or similar persons, or
  - Any other substantial nontax purpose; or
- A financial statement other than a tax return that must be provided to the federal or a state government, or their agencies (other than the SEC or the IRS).

> **COMMENT**
>
> A financial statement submitted to and reviewed by a bank in connection with a credit application is not an AFS. A financial statement used for credit purposes is an AFS only if it is a certified audited financial statement that is accompanied by the report of an independent CPA (or in the case of a foreign entity, by the report of a similarly qualified independent professional).

> **COMMENT**
>
> Many small businesses do not have applicable financial statements and will not be able to qualify for the *de minimis* rule. Unless the rule is relaxed, those businesses will need to rely on the Section 179 expensing election, which is limited to $139,000 in a tax year that begins in 2012 and to $25,000 thereafter.

De minimis Expensing Cap

There is no specific cap on the dollar amount per item that may be expensed under a taxpayer's expensing policy. However, the total amount that may be expensed is limited to the greater of:

- 0.1 percent of gross receipts reported for Federal income tax purposes for the tax year; or
- 2 percent of total depreciation and amortization reported on the applicable financial statement for the tax year (Temp. Reg. § 1.263(a)-2T(g)(1)(iv)).

> **COMMENT**
>
> A taxpayer must elect to capitalize amounts in excess of the 0.1 percent gross receipts/2 percent depreciation limit that otherwise qualify for the *de minimis* rule. However, the preamble to the temporary regulations indicates that if an examining agent and taxpayer agree that certain amounts in excess of the *de minimis* rule ceiling are immaterial, the agreement should be respected and the *de minimis* rule will also apply to these excess amounts. A taxpayer may also elect to capitalize amounts that are not in excess of the ceiling if it does not wish to expense those amounts.

The regulations treat the capitalization of excess amounts as an "election." The election is made by capitalizing the excess amount in the tax year paid or incurred and by depreciating the costs in the year the related property is placed in service. The election must be made on a timely filed original income tax return (including extensions) for the tax year the property is placed in service (Temp. Reg. § 1.263(a)-2T(g)(4)).

Types of Property Covered

The *de minimis* expensing rule applies to:

- Amounts paid for the acquisition or production of unit of property; and
- Amounts paid for the acquisition or production of a material or supply (Temp. Reg. § 1.263(a)-2T(g)(1).

However, the *de minimis* rule does not apply to materials and supplies except to the extent a special election is made to treat the materials and supplies as subject to the expensing rule (Temp. Reg. § 1.162-3T(f)).

> **COMMENT**
>
> The election to apply the *de minimis* rule to materials and supplies can apply to any type of material and supply. Therefore, the election can apply to components acquired to maintain, repair, or improve a unit of tangible property and fuel, lubricants, water, and similar items reasonably expected to be consumed in 12 or fewer months. All other categories of materials and supplies consist of units of property (i.e., units of property costing less than $100 to acquire or produce or units of property have an useful life of less than 12 months).

The cost of acquiring land and the cost of inventory (or property that is intended to be used in inventory) may not be expensed under the *de minimis* rule.

Generally, materials and supplies not used for improvements are deducted in the year used or consumed. Electing the *de minimis* rule for those materials and supplies not used or consumed in the tax year of purchase will accelerate the deduction to the year of purchase.

> **EXAMPLE**
>
> Frank Johnson has a written policy that expenses for nontax purposes property that costs less than $500. Johnson purchases 100 suitcases that cost $90 each and 200 chairs that cost $150 each. The chairs are expensed under the *de minimis* rule (assuming all requirements are otherwise satisfied) because they are units of property acquired for less than $500 each. The suitcases are materials and supplies because each has a cost of less than $100. The chairs, therefore, will qualify for immediate expensing only if the taxpayer makes an election to subject the chairs to the de minimis rule.

> **COMMENT**
>
> The *de minimis* expensing rule is one of the most notable aspects of the temporary regulations. The IRS has long allowed taxpayers to deduct *de minimis* amounts that have no material impact on tax liability. The temporary regulations now provide specific

standards for deducting *de minimis* amounts. Taxpayers who currently have a *de minimis* expensing policy will need to comply with these standards in order to continue expensing low-cost items. However, as noted above, an IRS examining agent may reach a separate agreement with a taxpayer to increase the expensing cap.

Effective Date

The *de minimis* rule is effective for amounts paid or incurred (to acquire or produce property) in tax years beginning on or after January 1, 2012.

Change in Accounting Method

An automatic change in accounting method procedure allows a taxpayer to apply the *de minimis* rule on a cutoff basis. Therefore, no Code Sec. 481 adjustment is necessary if a taxpayer changes its accounting method to comply with the *de minimis* rule effective for the taxpayer's first tax year beginning on or after January 1, 2012 (Rev. Proc. 2012-19 adding Section 3.17 to the Appendix of Rev. Proc. 2011-14).

STUDY QUESTIONS

8. The cost of eligible property is deducted under the *de minimis* expensing rule:

   a. In the tax year the eligible property is placed in service
   b. In the tax year the cost of the eligible property is paid or incurred
   c. In the tax year the eligible property is used or consumed
   d. In the tax year the eligible property is delivered

9. Under the *de minimis* expensing rule:

   a. There is no specific cap on the dollar amount per item that may be expensed under a taxpayer's expensing policy
   b. There is no dollar limit on the aggregate amount that may be expensed
   c. Materials and supplies may not be expensed
   d. The cost of inventory may be expensed

OPTIONAL METHOD FOR ROTABLE SPARE PARTS

Rotable spare parts are components of a unit of property that are acquired for installation on a unit of property and then removed from that unit of property, generally repaired or improved, and either reinstalled on the same or other unit of property or stored for later installation.

Rotable spare parts do not include components that are acquired as part of a unit of property (e.g., the original engines on an aircraft).

COMMENT

Temporary spare parts are components of a unit of property that are used temporarily until a new or repaired part can be installed and then are removed and stored for later (emergency or temporary) installation. Temporary spare parts are subject to the same rules as rotable spare parts (Temp. Reg. § 1.162-3T(c)(2)).

Rotable (including temporary) spare parts are treated as a material and supply. Consequently, their cost is usually deducted in the tax year "used or consumed" (unless the rotable is considered an incidental material or supply, in which case the cost is deducted in the year of purchase). Because rotable spare parts are typically removed, repaired, and reused over a period of years, rotables are treated as used or consumed (and, therefore, deductible) in the tax year in which the taxpayer disposes of the parts (Temp. Reg. § 1.162-3T(a)(3)).

A taxpayer, however, may use an optional method of accounting for rotable spare parts and deduct the acquisition and installation cost in the tax year of the first installation. If the optional method is used, it applies to all rotable parts used in the same trade or business. Use of the optional method does not require a formal election (Temp. Reg. § 1.162-3T(e)).

Rotable spare parts do not include components that are acquired as part of a unit of property (e.g., the original engines on an aircraft) Under the optional method, in each tax year that a rotable is removed:

- The fair market value of the removed rotable is included in gross income;
- The basis of the removed rotable is increased by the fair market value; and
- The basis of the removed rotable is increased by the amount paid to remove the rotable.

The basis is also increased by any amount paid or incurred to maintain, repair, or improve the rotable after it is removed in the tax year paid or incurred.

In the tax year the removed rotable is reinstalled, the basis increases described above are deducted along with the reinstallation costs.

This cycle continues with each reinstallation and removal until the tax year of disposition when the basis is deducted.

EXAMPLE

John MacKinley uses the optional method for rotable spare parts for his aircraft. In Year 1, John installs a new rotable part that cost of $1,000. Installation costs are $300. In Year 1 John may deduct the $1,000 purchase price plus $300 in installation costs. If the removed part is also a rotable, he must include the fair market value of the removed part in income and increase the basis of the removed part by its fair market value, the removal costs, and any subsequent repair costs.

In Year 2, John removes the rotable part installed in Year 1 at a cost of $200. At that time he includes the fair market value of the removed part in income and increases the basis of the removed part by its fair market value plus any removal and repair costs. However, he may deduct the basis the rotable that was removed in Year 1 plus installation costs if it is reinstalled in Year 2.

COMMENT

The optional method provided in the temporary regulations corresponds to a method currently used by many taxpayers for their rotables.

The election to capitalize materials and supplies may not be elected for rotable spare parts if the optional method is used (Temp. Reg. § 1.162-3T(d)(2)).

Effective Date

The optional method applies to amounts paid or incurred (to acquire or produce property) in tax years beginning on or after January 1, 2012. However, a taxpayer may apply the optional method to tax years beginning on or after January 1, 2012 (Temp. Reg. § 1.162-3T(j))

Change in Accounting Method

An automatic consent procedure is provided to change to the optional method for accounting for rotable and temporary spare parts (Rev. Proc. 2012-19, adding Section 3.15 to the Appendix of Rev. Proc. 2011-14). Adoption of the optional method requires the computation of a Code Sec. 481(a) adjustment (i.e., the change does not apply on a cutoff basis) if the taxpayer chooses to apply the method to tax years beginning on or after January 1, 2012. Statistical sampling techniques are allowed to make the Section 481 computation.

A separate automatic consent procedure for persons who do not want to use the optional method allows a taxpayer to change its method of accounting for costs to acquire or produce nonincidental rotable and temporary spare parts to the method of deducting the costs in the tax year of disposition (Rev. Proc. 2012-19 adding Section 3.14 to the Appendix of Rev. Proc. 2011-14). The change is made on a cutoff basis.

STUDY QUESTIONS

10. If the optional method for rotable spare parts is used, the fair market value of a rotable is included in gross income in the year of:

a. Purchase
b. Installation
c. Disposition
d. Removal

---

11. If a taxpayer uses the optional method for rotable spare parts:

    a. The method applies to tax years beginning on or after January 1, 2010

    b. The election to capitalize materials and supplies does not apply to the rotable spare parts

    c. A formal election must be filed to adopt the method

    d. The method can apply to a component originally acquired as part of a unit of property

---

CONCLUSION

The temporary repair regulations are the result of years of IRS effort to make logical sense of a patchwork of legal principles that have been difficult to apply and that have often produced conflicting results. Practitioners have complimented the IRS's efforts but on average are far from completely satisfied.

The major disappointment for some practitioners is the failure of the regulations to articulate expansive bright line tests that replace general principles that are applied on a facts and circumstances basis. Many commentators, especially those who represent small businesses with limited resources, feel that the ease of complying with bright line tests outweighs the need to reach conclusions that are "theoretically pure."

Another area of considerable concern is that application of most parts of the regulations on a retroactive basis will require most taxpayers to file accounting method changes and report complicated Code Sec. 481(a) adjustments based on transactions that occurred years ago and for which adequate records may not be available. To mitigate this problem—at least in the case large businesses—commentators have requested that the IRS approve extrapolation techniques in addition to the statistical sampling techniques already permitted by Rev. Proc. 2012-19 to compute the adjustments.

The IRS has stated that final regulations will refine rather than significantly revise the temporary regulations. Nevertheless, even minor changes and clarifications could makes big differences in particular cases. Accordingly, it will be necessary for all practitioners to review the final regulations in detail when they are issued.

MACRS Asset Dispositions and General Asset Accounts Rules

The IRS surprised taxpayers by including several important sections dealing with the modified accelerated cost recovery system (MACRS) in the temporary "repair" regulations issued in December 2011 (T.D. 9564). Neither of the two versions of the previously issued proposed repair regulations contained any provisions relating to MACRS.

The MACRS portion of the temporary regulations provides rules for dispositions of MACRS property (Temp. Reg. § 1.168(i)-8T) and modifies the rules for MACRS general asset accounts (GAAs) (Temp. Reg. § 1.168(i)-1T). Rules for accounting for MACRS property in item and multiple asset accounts are also formalized (Temp. Reg. § 1.168(i)-7T). These sections are generally effective for tax years beginning on or after January 1, 2012. Many taxpayers will need to change accounting methods to bring the treatment of property previously placed into service into compliance with the new rules.

The regulations reflect a fundamental shift in IRS policy. Namely, they now permit (or more accurately, now require) a taxpayer to claim a loss deduction on a retired structural component of a MACRS building if the building has not been fully depreciated. Previously, a taxpayer continued to depreciate a retired structural component (e.g., a roof) as part of the cost of the building and separately depreciated the replacement as new property beginning in the tax year it was placed in service. However, under the temporary regulations, if a building is placed in a GAA, no loss must be recognized upon the retirement of a structural component unless the taxpayer elects to recognize it. The flexibility offered by a GAA to either recognize or not recognize a retirement loss means that newly acquired and previously acquired buildings should be placed into a GAA in most cases. A retroactive GAA election allows a taxpayer to place existing buildings in a GAA. The election is only available for a taxpayer's first or second tax year beginning after December 31, 2011.

The temporary regulations also confirm that a taxpayer must claim a deduction on a retired component of most types of Section 1245 property if the taxpayer treats the component as an "asset" under the MACRS disposition rules. Section 1245 property may also be placed into a GAA in order to give a taxpayer the choice of whether to recognize the loss. A retroactive GAA election can also be made for Section 1245 property.

LEARNING OBJECTIVES

Upon completion of this chapter, the reader should be able to:

- Delineate what types of transactions are considered "dispositions" of MACRS assets;
- Identify MACRS assets that may be disposed of;
- Determine the amount of gain upon a disposition of an asset outside of a GAA;
- Understand which assets may be placed in the same GAA;
- Compute deprecation, gain, and loss on assets in a GAA; and
- Understand accounting method changes that may be used to comply with the regulations.

MACRS DISPOSITIONS

The temporary regulations define the term *disposition,* provide rules for determining the asset disposed of, and describe how to compute the amount of gain or loss on the disposition (Temp. Reg. § 1.168(i)-8T(b)).

Disposition Defined

A *disposition* of MACRS property occurs when ownership of an "asset" is transferred or when an asset is permanently withdrawn from business use. For example, a disposition includes the sale, exchange, retirement, physical abandonment, or destruction of an asset or the transfer of the asset to a supplies, scrap, or similar account. A disposition also includes the retirement of a structural component of a building (Temp. Reg. § 1.168(i)-8T(b)(1)).

The manner of the disposition (i.e., normal retirement, abnormal retirement, ordinary retirement, or extraordinary retirement) is not taken into account to determine whether a disposition has occurred or gain or loss is recognized (Temp. Reg. § 1.168(i)-8T(c)).

COMMENT

This definition of a disposition is substantially identical to the one that applied under accelerated cost recovery system proposed regulations and that practitioners and the IRS have been using for MACRS property. However, a critical difference is that a disposition now includes the retirement of a structural component of a building. As a result, taxpayers must claim a loss deduction equal to the adjusted depreciable basis of a retired structural component at the time of disposition (unless the building has been placed in an MACRS general asset account (GAA), as discussed in detail later in this chapter). The adjusted depreciable basis of an asset is generally equal to its cost less amounts previously claimed as depreciation, including the Code Sec. 179 deduction and Code Sec. 168(k) bonus depreciation.

COMMENT

The preamble to the temporary regulations indicates that the regulations "clarify" that the retirement of a component of a unit of Section 1245 property may generate a loss deduction equal to the adjusted depreciable basis of the component at the time of disposition. However, in actual practice, few if any taxpayers have been claiming loss deductions on components of Section 1245 property except when the taxpayer treats the component as a separate asset.

EXAMPLE

John Green, a calendar-year taxpayer, places a commercial building, MACRS 39-year property, in service on January 1, 2000. In January 2012 John Green replaces the property's entire roof. Under the temporary regulations, the 2012 retirement of the roof is a disposition that triggers a retirement loss equal to the adjusted depreciable basis of the retired roof at the time of disposition (i.e., the cost allocable to the replaced roof that is undepreciated at the time of retirement). The new roof is depreciated over 39 years beginning in January 2012. If the roof had been replaced in 2010, Green would need to file an accounting method change and compute a Code Sec. 481(a) adjustment equal to the adjusted depreciable basis of the retired roof as of the beginning of the year of change (unless a retroactive GAA election is made). This process is explained later.

COMMENT

The regulations allow a taxpayer to use any reasonable method to determine the adjusted depreciable basis of a replaced structural component if a taxpayer does not have actual records from which to make the determination. *Reasonable methods* are not specifically defined but clearly include valuations based on information obtained from a valid cost segregation study. The IRS has also unofficially suggested that it may also be reasonable to use the cost of the new structural component to derive a reasonable cost for the replaced component by applying an inflation adjustment factor to the cost of the new structural component.

Amount of Gain or Loss upon Disposition of a MACRS "Asset"

The temporary regulations provide the following basic rules for determining the amount of gain or loss upon the disposition of a MACRS asset (Temp. Reg. § 1.168(i)-8T(d)):

- When an MACRS asset is disposed of during a tax year by sale, exchange, or involuntary conversion, a taxpayer is required to recognize gain or loss as computed under applicable provisions of the tax code;
- A physical abandonment (including retirement or destruction of the asset) loss is recognized in the amount of the asset's adjusted depreciable basis. However, if the asset is subject to nonrecourse debt, gain or loss is

computed under the rules applicable to sales, exchanges, and involuntary conversions;

- If an asset is disposed of other than by sale, exchange, involuntary conversion, physical abandonment, or conversion to personal use (for example, when an asset is transferred to a supplies or scrap account), gain is not recognized but loss is recognized in the amount of the excess of the asset's adjusted depreciable basis over its fair market value at the time of disposition; and
- If an asset is disposed of by conversion to personal use, no gain or loss is recognized (Temp. Reg. § 1.168(i)-4(c)).

What Constitutes an Asset?

The recognition of gain or loss is only required upon the dispositions of an "asset" (Temp. Reg. § 1.168(i)-1T(d)).

The first principle in determining the appropriate asset disposed of is that the facts and circumstances of each disposition must be considered. In addition, the asset, subject to certain minor exceptions, cannot be larger than a unit of property.

A *unit of property* generally consists of a group of all functionally interdependent components. Components are functionally interdependent if placing one component in service depends on placing the other component in service (Temp. Reg. § 1.263(a)-3T(e)). For example, an entire machine, car, desk, or airplane is a unit of property and is generally also considered an asset.

Each structural component of a building is treated as a separate asset. Thus, the retirement of a structural component is treated as the disposition of an asset that gives rise to a loss deduction. The building excluding its structural components (i.e., the "shell") is also a separate asset (Temp. Reg. § 1.168(i)-8T(c)(2)(A) and (B)).

Examples of structural components of a building include walls, partitions, floors, and ceilings, as well as any permanent coverings such as:

- Paneling or tiling; windows and doors;
- All components (whether in, on, or adjacent to the building) of a central air conditioning or heating system, including motors, compressors, pipes and ducts;
- Plumbing and plumbing fixtures, such as sinks and bathtubs;
- Electric wiring and lighting fixtures;
- Chimneys;
- Stairs, escalators, and elevators, including all components thereof;
- Sprinkler systems;
- Fire escapes; and
- Other components relating to the operation or maintenance of a building (Reg. § 1.48-1(e)(2)).

NOTE

Under the regulations, the building *shell* (i.e., the building without structural components) is treated as an asset and each structural component are treated as separate assets. Thus, a taxpayer who retires only a portion of a specific structural component—for example, the shingles or rubber membrane of an entire roof (the structural component)—is not allowed to recognize a loss because there has been no disposition of an entire asset. However, the regulations allow a taxpayer to adopt any reasonable, consistent method to treat the component parts of a structural component of a building as an "asset" (Temp. 1.168(i)-8T(c)(2)(E)). Thus, although the default rule requires a taxpayer to treat the retirement of an entire structural component as the disposition of an asset that generates a loss, the taxpayer is *permitted* under the reasonable and consistent standard to adopt a method of accounting that divides a building's structural components into smaller component assets. For a roof, a taxpayer could adopt a method that treats the shingles or rubber membrane as the asset. Thus, a loss deduction could be claimed if the shingles or membrane were replaced.

CAUTION

When the taxpayer chooses a level of granularity for defining an asset, it is critical to keep in mind that the temporary regulations provide that a taxpayer may not claim a repair deduction with respect to the replacement of a component of a unit of property if a loss deduction is claimed for the retired component, or if the retired component is sold or exchanged (Temp. Reg. § 1.263(a) 3T(i)(1)). Because a current repair deduction is almost always preferable to a retirement loss deduction that is limited to the adjusted depreciable basis of the replaced component, a taxpayer ideally will choose a level of granularity in the definition of an asset that does not result in a loss deduction when a repair deduction may be claimed. For example, generally, the replacement of the shingles on a roof or a rubber roof membrane is treated as a repair expense. However, if a taxpayer treated the shingles and membrane as separate assets, the repair costs would have to be capitalized even though the loss deduction is limited to the adjusted depreciable basis of the replaced shingles or membrane.

PLANNING POINTER

As explained below, under the default rule for general asset accounts the disposition of an asset does not result in a loss deduction unless a taxpayer makes an affirmative election to recognize the loss. Thus, a taxpayer could place a building in a GAA and selectively decide whether to recognize a loss on a retired asset. The taxpayer could apply the default no-loss rule each time a repair deduction is available and elect to recognize a loss when the repair activities are so extensive that they must be capitalized regardless of whether a loss is claimed on the retired component assets.

COMMENT

Apparently, when defining an asset, taxpayers have a wide leeway in choosing a level of granularity. For example, an IRS spokesperson at a meeting held by the American Bar Association's tax section on May 11, 2012, in Washington, D.C., indicated a taxpayer could treat each linear foot of concrete (e.g., from a building foundation) as an asset for disposition purposes. Similarly, each shingle on a roof or each square foot of roof membrane could be treated as an asset. Previously, the IRS informally took a similar position on the definition of a component in applying the special 100-percent bonus depreciation election for components of a larger self-constructed asset that was not eligible for the 100 percent rate (Rev. Proc. 2011-42, Sec. 3.03(2)).

COMMENT

In addition to the rule that denies a repair expense if a taxpayer claims a loss on a retired component or sells the component at a gain or loss, it is important to be aware that no repair expense can be claimed when a major component or a substantial structural part of a unit of property is replaced (Temp. Reg. § 1.263(a)-3T(i)(1)). Accordingly, when a major component or substantial structural part is replaced, a taxpayer will not be adversely impacted by treating the retired major component or substantial structural part as a disposed-of asset and claiming a loss deduction. A *major component* or *substantial structural part* includes a part or combination of parts that comprise a large portion of the physical structure of the unit of property or that performs a discrete and critical function in the operation of the unit of property. However, the replacement of a minor component of the unit of property, even though such component may affect the function of the unit of property, generally will not,, by itself, constitute a major component or substantial structural part.

Certain Commonly Used Business Property Is the Asset

Asset Classes 00.11 through 00.4 of Rev. Proc. 87-56 provide the MACRS depreciation period for certain assets commonly used in all businesses. These commonly used assets are each treated as a separate asset for disposition purposes (Temp. 1.168(i)-8T(c)(2)(D)).

COMMENT

In contrast to the rule that applies to the component parts of a structural component of a building (e.g., the membrane of a roof), a taxpayer may not treat the disposition of a component part of an asset described in Asset Classes 00.11 through 00.4 as a separate asset for disposition purposes under the "reasonable and consistent" standard (Temp. 1.168(i)-8T(c)(2)(E)).

The following items of property are described in Asset Classes 00.11 through 00.4 and each is treated as a separate asset for disposition purposes:

- Office furniture fixtures, and equipment;
- Computers and peripheral equipment;
- Noncommercial airplanes;
- Automobiles, taxis, buses, and trucks (light and heavy);
- Railroad cars and locomotives;
- Trailers and trailer-mounted containers;
- Vessels, barges, and tugs;
- Land improvements; and
- Industrial steam and electric generation/distribution systems

---

EXAMPLE

Stan Dalton, a taxpayer, owns a light-duty truck (the unit of property). Stan replaces the engine with a new one. Even though the new engine is a major component and must be capitalized and separately depreciated, the replacement of the engine is not a disposition because the truck is described in Asset Class 00.241. Depreciation continues for the cost of the truck (including the replaced engine) and no loss is recognized. Stan separately depreciates the new engine beginning in the year it is placed in service (Temp. Reg. § 1.168(i)-8T(h), Example 2).

EXAMPLE

Assume that Jet Red, a taxpayer, replaces the engine on a *commercial* aircraft (the unit of property). A commercial aircraft is *not* described in Asset Classes 00.11 through 00.4 or in Code Sec. 168(e). If Jet Red consistently treats each major component of the aircraft, including its engines, as an asset for disposition purposes, the company may claim a loss on the retired engine and cease claiming depreciation on the retired engine. On the other hand, if Jet Red treats the entire aircraft as the "asset," the replacement of the engine is not a disposition. Depreciation continues on the aircraft (including the replaced engine) and the new engine (a major component) is separately depreciated (Temp. Reg. § 1.168(i)-8T(h), Examples 2 and 3).

EXAMPLE

George Johnson replaces several components of a walk-in freezer that is Section 1245 property. If George treats the components as assets and claims a loss upon their retirement (i.e., abandonment) or sells the components at a gain or loss, he must capitalize the cost of the replacement parts, including the installation costs (Temp. Reg. § 1.263(a)-3T(i)(5), Examples (1) and (2)).

If the walk-in freezer were placed in a GAA, George would recognize no loss and could claim a repair deduction if the repairs do not otherwise rise to the level of a capitalized improvement. If the repairs rise to the level of a capitalized improvement, George would want to make the GAA election to recognize the loss on the adjusted depreciable basis of the replaced components.

STUDY QUESTIONS

1. Under the temporary regulations, when a MACRS asset such as a structural component is retired through destruction:

   a. No gain or loss is recognized because the retirement is not a disposition
   b. Loss is recognized in the amount of excess of the adjusted depreciable basis over the asset's fair market value
   c. Depreciation continues on the retired asset
   d. Loss is recognized equal to the asset's adjusted depreciable basis

2. In determining the definition of an asset, which of the following statements is correct?

   a. Components of commonly used assets described in Asset Class 00.11 through 00.4 of Rev. Proc. 87-56 may not be treated as assets
   b. An entire building including its structural components is a single asset
   c. Components of a structural component may not be treated as separate assets
   d. The asset may be larger than a unit of property

Property Described in Code Sec. 168(e)(3) Is a Separate Asset

Property described in Code Sec. 168(e)(3), except for buildings and structural components, is also treated as a separate asset for disposition purposes and component parts of such property may not be treated as a separate asset under the "reasonable and consistent" standard. Property described in Code Sec. 168(e)(3) includes:

- Rent-to-own property;
- Semiconductor manufacturing equipment;
- Computer-based telephone central office switching equipment;
- Qualified technological equipment;
- Section 1245 property used in connection with research and experimentation;
- Certain types of energy producing property (e.g., solar and wind) specified in Code Sec. 168(e)(3)(B)(vi);
- Railroad track;
- Motorsports entertainment complexes;
- Alaska natural gas pipelines;

- Certain natural gas gathering lines;
- Single-purpose agricultural or horticultural structures;
- Qualified smart electric meters;
- Qualified smart electric grid systems;
- Municipal wastewater treatment plants;
- Telephone distribution plants and comparable equipment used for the two-way exchange of voice and data communications;
- Section 1245 property used in the transmission at 69 or more kilovolts of electricity for sale; and
- Certain natural gas distribution lines.

COMMENT

The rule that allows a taxpayer to use a reasonable and consistent standard to treat smaller components of a larger asset as assets applies to any Section 1245 or Section 1250 property that is not described in Asset Classes 00.11 through 00.4 of Rev. Proc. 87-56 and Code Sec. 168(e)(3). Thus, most assets can be "componentized" if a taxpayer wishes. The IRS has been criticized for excluding Asset Classes 00.11 through 00.4 and Code Sec. 168(e)(3) from the "reasonable and consistent" rule. It is unclear why the IRS made this decision other than perhaps to simplify their tax treatment.

COMMENT

It may be particularly difficult to determine the adjusted depreciable basis of a disposed of component for industries in which a taxpayer has capitalized a number of improvements as part of cyclical remodels or renovations. The final regulations will probably contain computational methodologies or safe harbors that a taxpayer may use to simplify this determination.

PLANNING POINTER

The cost of replacing a major component of Section 1245 property must be capitalized under the temporary regulations and, accordingly, there is no downside to treating major components as assets and claiming a loss deduction on each retired major component, except for the potential burden of calculating its adjusted depreciable basis. If this burden is too great under a taxpayer's circumstances, then a taxpayer may simply choose to treat the entire unit of property as the asset. Alternatively, a taxpayer could place the unit of Section 1245 property in a GAA account, treat major components as separate assets, and decide whether to recognize a loss whenever a major component is replaced.

Effective Date of Asset Disposition Regulations

The asset disposition regulations apply to tax years beginning on or after January 1, 2012 (Temp. Reg. § 1.168(i)-8T(i)(1)).

Accounting Method Changes

A change to comply with the disposition regulations is a change in accounting method (Temp. Reg. § 1.168(i)-8T(i)(2)). Thus, taxpayers that failed to claim a loss deduction on a retired structural component of a building and are currently depreciating the retired component (in accordance with the former rules) need to change their accounting method and claim a Code Sec. 481(a) adjustment in the amount of the adjusted depreciable basis of the retired component. Alternatively, as explained below, a taxpayer may make a late GAA election for the building and either not recognize the loss (i.e. confirm the present tax treatment) or make a late election to recognize the loss through a Code Sec. 481(a) adjustment.

STUDY QUESTION

> **3.** Under the temporary regulations, when a major component is replaced:
>
>   **a.** The cost of replacing the component must be capitalized
>
>   **b.** Depreciation continues on the replaced major component if it is treated as a separate asset
>
>   **c.** A loss deduction may be claimed on the retired major component if the component is not treated as an asset
>
>   **d.** The cost of the replacement may be capitalized or deducted as a repair

MACRS GENERAL ASSET ACCOUNTS

Prior to issuance of the temporary regulations, MACRS GAA elections were rarely on the radar of most practitioners and were seldom, if ever, used as a vehicle to depreciate buildings. To the extent previously used, GAAs were viewed as a method to simplify depreciation and loss computations on a large group of similar assets by treating the group as a single asset with a combined depreciable basis. Due to the new rule that requires a taxpayer to recognize a loss on the disposition of a structural component of a building, the GAA election will provide the only mechanism by which a taxpayer can avoid making a potentially complicated adjusted depreciable basis calculation in order to compute the loss deduction on a retired structural component. By placing a building in a GAA a taxpayer also will have the flexibility to either elect to recognize the loss on the disposition of a particular structural component or to follow the default rule that no loss is recognized upon the disposition of an asset from a GAA. Similar considerations apply to a unit of Section 1245 property if a taxpayer chooses a method of accounting that treats components of the property as an asset for disposition purposes.

> ### PLANNING POINTER
>
> The cost of replacing a major component of Section 1245 property must be capitalized under the temporary regulations and, accordingly, there is no downside to treating major components as assets and claiming a loss deduction on each retired major component, except for the potential burden of calculating its adjusted depreciable basis. If this burden is too great under a taxpayer's circumstances, then a taxpayer may simply choose to treat the entire unit of property as the asset. Alternatively, a taxpayer could place the unit of Section 1245 property in a GAA account, treat major components as separate assets, and decide whether to recognize a loss whenever a major component is replaced.

Grouping Assets in a General Asset Account

Each GAA may include one or more assets. Thus, for example, it is permissible for a taxpayer to create a separate general asset account for each depreciable MACRS asset owned by the taxpayer, regardless of whether it is Section 1245 property or real property. However, if more than one asset is placed in the same GAA, each asset in that account must be have been placed in service in the same tax year (Temp. Reg. § 1.168(i)-1T(c)(2)). In addition, each asset in the same GAA must have the same:

- MACRS depreciation method;
- MACRS depreciation period; and
- MACRS convention.

If the taxpayer uses the mid-quarter MACRS convention, then only assets with the same depreciation method and period that were placed in service in the same quarter of the same tax year may be grouped in the same GAA.

MACRS residential rental property may only be placed in service with other MACRS residential property that was placed in service in the same month of the same tax year. Similarly, MACRS nonresidential real property is subject to the same rule.

> ### COMMENT
>
> Assets can only be placed in the same GAA if depreciation is computed the same way for each asset throughout its recovery period. For this reason, only assets with identical MACRS depreciation methods, periods, and conventions that are placed in service in the same tax year can be placed in the same GAA.

> **EXAMPLE**
>
> George Anderson places two desks (MACRS 7-year property depreciated using the 200 percent declining-balance method) in service in the same tax year. The MACRS mid-quarter convention applies because George placed more than 40 percent of the basis of all MACRS Section 1245 property in service in the last quarter of his tax year. The first desk was placed in service in the first quarter of the tax year and the second desk was placed in service in the fourth quarter. Although both desks are subject to the mid-quarter convention, they may not be placed in the same GAA even though the same depreciation method and period apply because George placed them in service in different quarters.

The following grouping rules also ensure that only assets for which depreciation calculations are identical are placed in the same GAA (Temp. Reg. § 1.168(i)-1T(c)(2)(ii)).

The same GAA may not include assets for which bonus depreciation (Code Sec. 168(k)) was claimed and assets for which bonus depreciation was not claimed. Furthermore, if bonus depreciation is claimed, the same GAA may only include assets that are subject to the same bonus depreciation rate.

Passenger automobiles (MACRS 5-year property) that are subject to the luxury car depreciation caps of Code Sec. 280F may only be grouped with other passenger automobiles subject to the caps, and the same caps must apply to each vehicle in the same account.

> **COMMENT**
>
> Trucks (including SUVs) and cars have different annual depreciation caps. Thus, a truck and car cannot be placed in the same GAA even though they are placed in service in the same year and have the same depreciation period (5 years), method, and convention.

Listed property (as defined in Code Sec. 280F(d)(4)) may not be placed in a GAA with nonlisted property.

An asset used for both business and personal purposes may not be placed in a GAA. If an asset is used 100 percent for business purposes in the year it was placed in service but is later used for personal purposes, it must be removed from the GAA.

Key Terms for Computing Depreciation in a GAA

The following key terms are commonly used to compute MACRS depreciation on assets in a GAA.

The "unadjusted depreciable basis" of a GAA is the sum of the unadjusted depreciable bases of all assets included in the GAA.

Unadjusted depreciable basis of each asset included in the GAA is the basis of that property for purposes of determining gain or loss without any adjustments for depreciation. This basis is reduced by any amount that the taxpayer elects to expense under Code Sec. 179. Unadjusted depreciable basis also reflects any reductions to basis required on account of claiming certain tax credits and deductions. Unadjusted depreciable basis is not decreased by any amount claimed as a bonus depreciation deduction (Temp. Reg. § 1.168(i)-1T(b)).

COMMENT

Generally, the unadjusted depreciable basis of an asset is its cost less any amount expensed under Code Sec. 179.

The *adjusted depreciable basis* of a GAA is the unadjusted depreciable basis of the GAA (cost minus Section 179 deduction) reduced by the depreciation deductions (including bonus allowance) claimed on the assets in the GAA. The adjusted depreciable basis of a GAA will decrease each year until it reaches $0 when the assets in the GAA are fully depreciated.

The *remaining adjusted depreciable basis* of a GAA is the unadjusted depreciable basis of the GAA less the amount of bonus depreciation claimed (if any) for the GAA. Thus, remaining adjusted depreciable basis is generally equal to the aggregate cost of GAA assets minus any Section 179 deduction minus any bonus deduction.

COMMENT

The remaining adjusted depreciable basis is the amount to which the MACRS table percentages are applied throughout the depreciation period of the GAA. However, this amount needs to be adjusted in any tax year that an asset is removed from the GAA (for example, because an election is made to recognize gain or loss upon its disposition) if the taxpayer wants to continue using the table percentages to compute depreciation on the remaining assets.

Depreciation on all assets in a GAA must be computed the same way—either using the table percentages or not using them.

Each GAA must maintain a *depreciation reserve* account in which cumulative depreciation allowances are recorded (Temp. Reg. § 1.168(i)-1T(d)(1)).

EXAMPLE

Kim McHenry, a taxpayer, places seven machines in service in Year 1. Each machine is 5-year MACRS property, depreciated using the 200 percent declining-balance method, and is subject to the half-year convention. Assume the machines cost $100, $200, $300, $400, $500, $600, and $700 (or $2,800 in total). No amount is expensed under Code Sec. 179 and an election out of bonus depreciation is made. Kim's adjusted depreciable basis of the GAA at the beginning of the tax year is $2,800 because no Section 179 deduction or bonus allowance is claimed. This is the amount to which the table percentages are applied during each year of the 5-year recovery period until $2,800 is deducted.

If the assets in a GAA are eligible for bonus depreciation, the bonus depreciation deduction for the account is the product of the bonus depreciation rate and the unadjusted depreciable basis of the account (generally, aggregate cost of assets in the GAA less any amount expensed under Section 179). The remaining adjusted depreciable basis of the account (i.e., unadjusted depreciable basis less bonus allowance) is then depreciated over the applicable recovery period of the account (Temp. Reg. § 1.168(i)-1T(d)(2)).

EXAMPLE

Alternatively, Kim decides to claim the 50 percent bonus deduction on the machines in the GAA. The total bonus deduction claimed is $1,400 ($2,800 unadjusted depreciable basis × 50% rate). The table percentages are applied during the 5-year recovery period to the remaining adjusted depreciable basis, which is computed as $1,400—the unadjusted depreciable basis of the GAA at the beginning of the tax year ($2,800 – $0 Section 179 deduction) minus the machines' bonus depreciation ($1,400).

Dispositions of Assets from GAA

A disposition of an asset from a GAA is defined in the same way as a disposition of an asset outside of a GAA and, therefore, includes the sale, exchange, retirement, physical abandonment, or destruction of an asset, including the retirement of a structural component of a building. (Temp. § 1.168(i)-1T(e)(1)).

Subject to the exceptions described below, the disposition of an asset from a GAA has the following effects (Temp. § 1.168(i)-1T(e)(2)):

- The adjusted depreciable basis of the asset is treated as $0 and no loss is realized;
- If the asset is disposed of by the transfer to a supplies, scrap, or similar account, the basis of the asset in the account is $0 and no loss is realized;
- Any gain realized is recognized as ordinary income to the extent that the sum of the unadjusted depreciable basis of the GAA plus any amount

expensed under Code Sec. 179 for all assets in the GAA, exceeds any previously recognized ordinary income from prior dispositions;

- The recognition and character of any excess gain realized are determined under applicable provisions of the Internal Revenue Code other than the recapture provisions of Code Sec. 1245 and Code Sec. 1250; and
- The unadjusted depreciable basis and the depreciation reserve of the GAA are unaffected by the disposition.

COMMENT

A special election discussed later allows a taxpayer to elect to recognize a gain or loss on an asset disposed of from a GAA determined by reference to the disposed asset's adjusted depreciable basis. This election was available for a few types of dispositions under the former GAA rules but is allowed for almost any disposition under the new GAA rules. This election does not apply to the disposition of the last asset in a GAA or to dispositions that involve all of the assets in a GAA. A similar but separate election, however, applies to such dispositions, as discussed below.

EXAMPLE

Pizza Pizzazz maintains a GAA for 10 assets that are MACRS 5-year property. One pizza oven cost $8,200 and the remaining 9 machines, automated pizza rollers, cost a total of $1,800 ($200 per machine). No amount was expensed under Code Sec. 179 or claimed as a bonus deduction. The unadjusted depreciable basis of the GAA is $10,000. In Year 1 Pizza Pizzazz claims a $2,000 depreciation deduction ($10,000 × 20% first-year table percentage).

In Year 2 Pizza Pizzazz sells the $8,200 oven for $9,000. The oven is treated as having an adjusted depreciable basis of $0 and Pizza Pizzazz must recognize $9,000 as ordinary income because $9,000 does not exceed the unadjusted depreciable basis of the GAA account plus expensed amounts less previously recognized ordinary income, as shown:

($10,000) + $0 Section 179 deductions claimed on account assets − $0 previously recognized ordinary income from prior dispositions.

The depreciation calculation for the GAA in Year 2 is unaffected by the disposition and is equal to $3,200 ($10,000 × 32% second-year table percentage).

In Year 3 Pizza Pizzazz sells 7 of the pizza rollers for $1,100. The adjusted depreciable basis of the machines is treated as $0 and ABC must recognize $1,000 as ordinary income, as shown:

$10,000 unadjusted depreciable basis of GAA account + $0 Section 179 deductions − $9,000 previously recognized gain).

The remaining $100 is Section 1231 gain. The depreciation deduction for Year 3 is unaffected and is equal to $1,920 ($10,000 × 19.2% third-year table percentage).

COMMENT

Assuming the special election to recognize loss is not made, no loss is recognized when·an asset is disposed of from a GAA. The entire amount received is recognized as ordinary income unless the amount received exceeds the original cost of all of the assets placed in the GAA (plus any amount expensed under Section 179) less any amount previously recognized as ordinary income. Any excess is generally treated as Section 1231 gain. The amount recognized as ordinary income is in effect ordinary income depreciation recapture. The adjusted depreciable basis of the disposed-of asset is recovered during the remaining recovery period of the GAA. When an asset is not in a GAA, gain is only recognized to the extent that the amount realized exceeds the adjusted depreciable basis of the asset. However, depreciation on the asset ceases. The gain from a non-GAA asset is ordinary income under the Section 1245 recapture rules to the extent of depreciation claimed on the asset (but not in excess of the gain). Any excess gain is Section 1231 gain.

Determining Asset Disposed of from GAA

The rules for determining the asset that is disposed of from a GAA are identical to those described previously for property not in a GAA. Thus, the following property is considered an asset for GAA disposition purposes (Temp. Reg. § 1.168(i)-1T(e)(2)(viii)):

- Each building other than its structural components;
- Each structural component of a building;
- Each item described in Asset Classes 00.11 through 00.4 of Rev. Proc. 87-56 (certain commonly used business property); and
- Each item described in Code Sec. 168(e)(3) that is not a building or structural component.

For other property, a facts and circumstances test is applied to determine the proper asset. Generally, this means that the asset will be a unit of property. The same rule applies to property that is not in a GAA.

As in the case of an asset not placed in a GAA, a taxpayer may use any reasonable and consistent method to treat components of an item of property placed in a GAA as an asset except that components of property described in Asset Classes 00.11 through 00.4 and Code Sec. 168(e)(3) may not be treated as assets. Thus, for example, components of structural components of a building and components of Section 1245 and Section 1250 property that is not described in Asset Classes 00.11 through 00.4 or Code Sec. 168(e)(3) can be treated an "asset" disposed of if a taxpayer chooses a consistent and reasonable method of accounting for making this determination.

PLANNING POINTER

As previously explained, when a taxpayer claims a loss on any component of an asset, such as a component of a structural component of a building or a component of an item of Section 1245 property (e.g., a machine), the cost of the replacement must be capitalized even though the cost is otherwise deductible as a repair. Because a repair deduction provides a greater immediate tax benefit than a loss deduction limited to the adjusted depreciable basis of a retired asset, the ideal method of identifying the asset disposed of is to adopt a method that allows a taxpayer to claim a loss deduction whenever the costs incurred with respect to the replaced components are treated as a capitalized improvement and, conversely, to capitalize the costs with respect to the replaced asset whenever the costs of replacement are a repair. It is possible for a taxpayer to accomplish this feat but only by placing the asset in a GAA. By choosing a minimal asset size (i.e., a minimal level of asset granularity) for property placed in a GAA, a taxpayer may in each instance that components are replaced either defer recognition of loss (the default GAA rule) or elect to recognize the loss. Whenever the election to recognize a loss is made, however, the taxpayer must be able to compute the adjusted depreciable basis of the disposed-of asset. The IRS will allow any reasonable method in making the computation, including statistical sampling methods.

COMMENT

For purposes of the GAA rules, the building structure and each structural component of the building are separate assets. (As previously indicated, a taxpayer may also choose to treat components of structural components as separate assets). However, a GAA for a building will only list the building as an asset. If a structural component (such as an entire roof) is retired and a loss deduction is elected, the retired structural component is treated as a separate asset and removed from the GAA by making appropriate adjustments to the balances in the GAA. The new roof (because it is not deductible as a repair expense) is also treated as a separate depreciable asset and may be placed in its own GAA. The new roof cannot be placed in the GAA for the building because it is not placed in service in the same month or same tax year as the building.

Election to Recognize Gain or Loss on a Qualifying Disposition

When an asset in a GAA is disposed of and the disposition does not involve all of the assets in the GAA or the last asset in the GAA, a taxpayer may elect to recognize gain or loss on the disposed-of asset by taking into account the asset's adjusted depreciable basis at the time of the disposition (Temp. Reg. § 1.168(i)-1T(e)(3)(iii)(A)).

> **COMMENT**
>
> This election does not apply to the disposition of the sole asset from a GAA because it is also the last asset in the GAA. However, the election can apply where a component of a sole asset in a GAA is properly treated as a separate asset for disposition purposes. For example, an election can be made to recognize a loss on the retirement of a structural component of a building or a component of a structural component even though the building is the sole asset in a GAA.

Such a disposition is referred to as a "qualifying disposition." In addition to a disposition involving all of the assets or the last asset in a GAA, a qualifying disposition does not include dispositions in transactions pertaining to:

- The treatment of transferees in certain nonrecognition transactions (Code Sec. 168(i)(7));
- Like-kind exchanges (Code Sec. 1031);
- Involuntary conversions (Code Sec. 1033);
- Technical terminations of partnerships (Code Sec. 708(b)(1)(b)); or
- Certain abusive transactions involving the shifting of income or deductions among taxpayers to take advantage of their differing tax rates or the use of net operating losses.

> **COMMENT**
>
> The prior GAA rules had a similar provision for qualifying dispositions. However, a qualifying disposition was very narrowly defined to include only dispositions attributable to casualty or theft losses, deductible charitable contributions, business terminations, and nonrecognition transactions. The new rules essentially expand the scope of a qualifying disposition to include any disposition that does not involve the disposition of the last asset or all of the assets of the GAA.

For purposes of computing gain or loss, the adjusted depreciable basis of a GAA asset at the time of its disposition is the unadjusted depreciable basis of the asset (cost less any Section 179 deduction claimed on the asset) less the aggregate depreciation claimed on the asset (taking into account the applicable convention in the year of disposition), including any bonus depreciation attributable to the asset.

If a taxpayer elects to recognize gain or loss and disposes of an asset at a gain, the amount of gain that is subject to depreciation recapture under Code Sec. 1245 (personal property) or Code Sec. 1250 (real property) is limited to the lesser of (Temp. Reg. § 1.168(i)-1T(e)(3)(iii)(A)):

- The depreciation allowed or allowable for the asset (including any Section 179 deduction and bonus allowance); or
- The excess of

— The original unadjusted depreciable basis of the GAA plus any amount expensed under Code Sec. 179 on all assets in the GAA, over

— The cumulative amounts of gain previously recognized as ordinary income under the rules applicable for disposed assets for which this election was not made or as ordinary recapture income under Code Sec. 1245 or Code Sec. 1250.

A qualifying disposition has the following additional effects on the GAA (Temp. Reg. § 1.168(i)-1T(e)(3)(iii)(B)):

■ The asset is removed from the GAA as of the first day of the tax year of disposition and depreciated separately;

■ The unadjusted depreciable basis of the GAA as of the first day of the tax year of disposition is reduced by the unadjusted depreciable basis of the disposed asset as of the first day of the tax year of disposition;

■ The depreciation reserve of the GAA as of the first day of the tax year of disposition is reduced by the depreciation claimed on the disposed of asset (including any bonus depreciation attributable to the disposed asset) prior to the tax year of disposition; and

■ For purposes of determining the amount of gain that is recognized on subsequent dispositions of other assets in the GAA that is treated as ordinary income under the rules that apply when the qualifying disposition election is not made, the amount of the disposed of asset that was expensed under Code Sec. 179 is ignored.

EXAMPLE

Bread N' Bake Inc., (B&B) purchases a mixing machine and an oven in Year 1. Both assets are MACRS 5-year property, depreciated using the 200 percent declining-balance method and the half-year convention. The mixing machine cost $1,000 and the oven cost $2,000. No amount is expensed under Section 179. However, a 50 percent bonus depreciation allowance is claimed on each machine. B&B places the machines in the same GAA.

The unadjusted depreciable basis of the GAA is $3,000 ($1,000 + $2,000 – $0 expensed under Section 179).

In Year 2 B&B sells the mixing machine for $400 and elects to compute gain or loss by taking into account the mixing machine's adjusted depreciable basis at the time of disposition.

As of the beginning of Year 2, the depreciation claimed on the mixing machine was $600 ($500 bonus depreciation ($1,000 × 50%) + $100 first year regular depreciation ($1,000 – $500) × 20%)). In the disposition year (Year 2), an additional $160 depreciation is allowed (($1,000 – $500) × 32% second-year table percentage × 50% to reflect half-year convention).

The mixing machine's adjusted depreciable basis for purposes of determining gain or loss is $240 ($1,000 – $500 – $100 – $160)). Accordingly, ABC reports a $160 gain on the machine ($400 – $240). The entire gain is ordinary income depreciation recapture.

Election to Terminate GAA upon Disposition of All or Last Asset in GAA

Upon the disposition of all remaining assets in a GAA or the last asset in a GAA, a taxpayer may elect to terminate the GAA and determine gain or loss by reference to the adjusted depreciable basis of the GAA at the time of the disposition (Temp. Reg. § 1.168(i)-1T(e)(3)(ii)).

PLANNING POINTER

If this election is not made the remaining adjusted depreciable basis of the GAA is recovered through annual depreciation deductions claimed on the disposed-of assets over their remaining depreciation period. No loss will be recognized and any gain will be computed as if the adjusted depreciable basis of the disposed-of assets is $0 under the rules previously described.

If the election is made, the amount of gain subject to depreciation recapture as ordinary income under Code Sec. 1245 (or Code Sec. 1250) is limited to the aggregate depreciation claimed on the assets in the GAA (including the Section 179 allowance and bonus depreciation) over amounts previously recognized as ordinary income as the result of prior dispositions.

EXAMPLE

SmallCo purchases 1,000 calculators for $60,000 in Year 1. The company claims no Section 179 deduction or bonus deduction. The calculators are MACRS 5-year property subject to the half-year convention.

Year 1 depreciation is $12,000 ($60,000 × 20% first-year table percentage).

In Year 2, SmallCo sells 200 of the calculators for $10,000.

SmallCo does not make the election to treat the sale as a qualifying disposition. Thus, SmallCo is required to recognize $10,000 of ordinary income because the amount realized ($10,000) does not exceed the unadjusted depreciable basis of the account ($60,000) reduced by amounts previously recognized as ordinary income upon earlier dispositions ($0).

Year 2 depreciation is $19,200 ($60,000 × 32% second-year table percentage).

In Year 3 SmallCo sells all of the remaining calculators for $35,000 and makes the election to terminate the GAA.

Year 3 depreciation is $5,760 ($60,000 × 19.20% third-year table percentage × 50% to reflect half-year convention).

Total depreciation claimed on the GAA at the time of disposition is $36,960 ($12,000 + $19,200 + $5,760).

On the date of disposition the adjusted depreciable basis of the account is $23,040 ($60,000 − $36,960).

Recognized gain is $11,960 ($35,000 − $23,040).

The entire amount is recaptured as ordinary income under Section 1245 because the $26,960 difference between the $36,960 total depreciation claimed and $10,000 ordinary income previously recognized exceeds $11,960.

How to Make the General Asset Account Election

The GAA election is made on a timely filed (including extensions) income tax return for the tax year in which the assets included in the general asset account are placed in service. Alternatively, the election may be made by filing an amended return within six months of the due date of the return (excluding extensions). The taxpayer attaches the election to the amended return and writes "Filed pursuant to Section 301.9100-2" on the election statement.

Form 4562, *Depreciation and Amortization,* provides that the election is made by checking box 18, which simply indicates that the taxpayer is making an election to establish at least one GAA for assets placed in service during the tax year. The taxpayer should maintain records that:

- Identify the assets placed in each GAA;
- Establish the unadjusted depreciable basis and depreciation reserve of the GAA; and
- Reflect the amount realized from dispositions.

It is not necessary to make a GAA election for all assets placed in service during the tax year.

An election to place an asset in a GAA is irrevocable (Temp. Reg. § 1.168(i)-1T(l)(1)).

A retroactive GAA election described below may be made for a taxpayer's first two tax years beginning after December 31, 2011. This election applies to assets placed in service in tax years that began before January 1, 2012.

Effective Date of GAA Rules

The new GAA rules are effective for tax years beginning on or after January 1, 2012 (Temp. Reg. § 1.168(i)-1T(m)(1)).

STUDY QUESTIONS

4. Multiple assets within the same GAA:

    a. May use both the mid-quarter and half-year conventions
    b. Must use the same depreciation method
    c. May be added to the account during different tax years
    d. Are limited to being Section 1245 property

5. The new rules for qualifying dispositions from a GAA expand the definition of their scope from the prior rules to include:

   a. Dispositions of nearly any kind except the last asset or all assets of the GAA

   b. Disposition of assets attributable to business terminations

   c. Like-kind exchanges of assets

   d. Involuntary conversions of assets

ACCOUNTING METHOD CHANGES

A change to comply with the MACRS disposition and GAA regulations (i.e., Temp. Reg. § 1.168(i)-8T and Temp. Reg. § 1.168(i)-1T) is a change in accounting method (Temp. Reg. § 1.168(i)-1T(m)(2) and Temp. Reg. § 1.168(i)-8T(i)(2)). Automatic accounting method change procedures to be used to come into compliance with the temporary regulations were issued by the IRS in Rev. Proc. 2012-20. Rev. Proc. 2012-20 adds various new sections to the Appendix of Rev. Proc. 2011-14, the governing procedure for all automatic accounting method changes.

COMMENT

Generally, a late depreciation tax "election" (or revocation of an election) is not treated as a change in accounting method (Reg. § 1.446-1(e)(2)(ii)(d)(3)) and is only granted if permission can be received through a letter ruling. However, as a result of the change to the disposition rules, the IRS will treat the three types of late GAA elections described next as a change in accounting method—but only for a taxpayer's first and second tax year beginning after December 31, 2011 (Rev. Proc. 2012-20).

Late Election to Place Assets in GAA Permitted for 2012 and 2013

Taxpayers may make late GAA elections for assets placed in service prior to tax years beginning on January 1, 2012 (Rev. Proc. 2012-20, adding Section 6.32 to the Appendix of Rev. Proc. 2011-14). The late election (i.e., a retroactive election) may only be made for a taxpayer's first or second tax year beginning after December 31, 2011.

A late GAA election is applied on a on a modified cutoff basis. That is, the beginning balance for the unadjusted depreciable basis of the GAA is equal to the unadjusted depreciable basis of the asset(s) placed in the GAA as of the beginning of the tax year of change, and the depreciation reserve is equal to the depreciation previously allowed or allowable as of the beginning of the year of change. If a taxpayer makes the late election described next to recognize a loss in a qualifying disposition of an asset, these amounts are adjusted to reflect the required removal of the retired asset from the GAA.

> **COMMENT**
>
> The late GAA election will be particularly useful for existing buildings. By placing an existing building in a GAA account a taxpayer will be able to choose whether to recognize a loss on past and future retirements of the building's structural components (or components of structural components that are treated as assets).

Late GAA Election to Recognize Gain or Loss in a Qualifying Disposition

A taxpayer may make a late election to recognize gain or loss upon the disposition of an asset in a GAA (whether the GAA was previously set up or set up under the preceding late election procedure) in a qualifying disposition (Rev. Proc. 2012-20, adding Section 6.32 to the Appendix of Rev. Proc. 2011-14). This election also only applies to a taxpayer's first or second tax year beginning on or after January 1, 2012.

> **COMMENT**
>
> The election for qualifying dispositions was previously described and allows a taxpayer to recognize a gain or loss upon the disposition of a GAA account asset by reference to the asset's adjusted depreciable basis at the time of the disposition.

The late GAA election to recognize gain or loss requires a Code Sec. 481(a) adjustment.

Late Election to Recognize Gain or Loss
Upon Disposition of All Assets or Last Asset in GAA

A taxpayer may make a late election to recognize gain or loss upon the disposition of all of the assets, or the last asset, in a general asset account. This election also only applies to a taxpayer's first or second tax year beginning on or after January 1, 2012, and requires a Code Sec. 481(a) adjustment.

> **NOTE**
>
> The most common situation addressed by Rev. Proc. 2012-20 involves taxpayers who previously retired a structural component of a building and are currently depreciating the retired component.

EXAMPLE

Sam Watson placed a building in service in 2005 and replaced the roof in 2007. He did not claim a loss deduction on the basis of the building allocable to the retired roof and continued to claim a depreciation deduction attributable to that basis. To bring his accounting method into compliance with the temporary regulations, which now treat the retirement of a structural component as a disposition that generates a loss, Sam may change his accounting method by:

- Changing from depreciating the retired roof to recognizing a loss on the retired roof by means of a Code Sec. 481(a) adjustment equal to the adjusted depreciable basis of the roof as of the first day of the year of change (Rev. Proc. 2012-20, adding Section 6.29 to the APPENDIX of Rev. Proc. 2011-14). If this option is chosen, Sam must continue to recognize a loss whenever it retires a structural component.
- Making a late GAA election for the building and following the GAA default no loss recognition rule (Rev. Proc. 2012-20, adding Section 6.32 to the Appendix of Rev. Proc. 2011-14)). If Sam makes this election, his current method of accounting for the roof (recognizing no loss and depreciating the retired roof) is correct and no Code Sec. 481(a) adjustment is needed to account for an unclaimed loss; or
- Making a late GAA election for the building and a late election to treat the retirement of the roof as a qualifying GAA disposition that generates a loss (Rev. Proc. 2012-20, adding Section 6.32 to the Appendix of Rev. Proc. 2011-14). Sam claims a Code Sec. 481(a) adjustment equal to the adjusted depreciable basis of the roof as of the first day of the year of change.

If a late GAA election is made, Sam may decide whether to recognize a loss on previously retired structural components and on structural components that are retired in the future. If the late GAA election is not made, Sam is required to recognize a loss on future retirements of structural components.

Optional Rule for Assets Placed in Service in Tax Years Ending Before December 30, 2003

If a taxpayer placed MACRS assets in service in a tax year ending before December 30, 2003 (pre-2003 assets), the taxpayer may treat the change to comply with the temporary MACRS regulations for all, or some, of the pre-2003 assets as a change that is not considered a change in method of accounting. In this situation, the taxpayer should file amended federal tax returns for tax years that remain open under the statute of limitation for assessment to implement the change to comply with the regulations for these pre-2003 assets. If the taxpayer chooses this option, however, a Code Sec. 481(a) adjustment or a similar cumulative depreciation adjustment is not required or permitted (Rev. Proc. 2012-20, Section 5.01;). Consequently, use of this optional rule can have adverse consequences.

EXAMPLE

John James, a calendar year taxpayer, placed a building in service in 2002 and retired the roof in 2005. John may comply with the rule that treats the retirement of the roof as a disposition that generates a loss by amending his returns for open years to remove the depreciation deduction attributable to the retired roof. However, the basis of the building must be reduced by the adjusted depreciable basis of the roof, no loss deduction through a Code Sec. 481(a) adjustment may be claimed, and no depreciation on the retired roof may be claimed for returns filed in 2012 and later tax years.

COMMENT

This special rule allowing amended returns can be traced to IRS Chief Counsel Notice 2004-007, in which the IRS announced that it will not treat a change in computing depreciation on an asset placed in service in a tax year ending before December 30, 2003, as a change in accounting method.

STUDY QUESTION

6. If a taxpayer makes a late election to place an existing building in a GAA account, the benefit is:

   a. Flexibility of whether to recognize losses on past and future retirements of the building's structural components
   b. No requirement to maintain a depreciation reserve account for the GAA
   c. The unadjusted depreciable basis may be depreciated in a shorter period
   d. The taxpayer may revoke the election after the first two tax years

CONCLUSION

The new temporary regulations affect every taxpayer that owns a building by requiring a loss computation on the retirement of a structural component unless the building is placed in a GAA. For buildings currently in service, taxpayers may make a late GAA election but only for their first or second tax year beginning after December 31, 2011. Taxpayers who fail to make the late election must stop depreciating previously retired components and compute a Section 481 adjustment that takes into account the loss deduction that could have been claimed. Going forward, a loss deduction computation will be required on any additional retirements of structural components.

In a comment letter submitted on July 16, 2012, the American Institute of Certified Public Accountants (AICPA) requested that the IRS make the loss recognition rule for retired structural components elective for buildings that are not placed in a GAA. Alternatively, the AICPA requested that the GAA rules be amended to provide that a taxpayer is deemed to make a GAA election for each building that it places in service unless an affirmative election out of GAA treatment is made. Either of these changes would eliminate the administrative burden of mandatory loss computations and avoid the adverse consequence of failing to claim a timely loss deduction (viz., the reduction in the basis of the building by the amount of the unclaimed loss). Hopefully, the IRS will adopt one of these approaches. Until and unless it does, taxpayers must make an affirmative GAA election in order to obtain the unique flexibility to either recognize or not recognize a loss on the retirement of a structural component.

Net Operating Losses

Any individual or entity may suffer a loss during the tax year. The loss may be economic, tax-related, or both. These types may not be the same. For example, stock may decline in value, generating an economic loss, but until the stock is sold, the taxpayer usually declares no tax loss. Or a business may be able to take a depreciation deduction on an asset, even though the asset's value increases or decreases more slowly than it depreciates. Although economic losses are never desirable, a tax loss can be valuable. It can be used to offset other tax gains and provide a tax benefit. One type of tax loss is a net operating loss (NOL). To maximize tax savings, taxpayers need to understand NOLs and how to use them.

LEARNING OBJECTIVES

Upon completion of this course, you will be able to:

- Define net operating losses;
- Determine the application of NOLs to individuals and different types of entities;
- Calculate NOL carrybacks and carryforwards;
- Describe the concept of trafficking in NOLs; and
- Understand how to apply for refunds using NOLs.

INTRODUCTION

NOLs are an important and useful tax benefit for any trade or business. A taxpayer that determines its net income for the year may discover it has a net loss. This loss may be a net operating loss that can be carried over to a past or future tax year. This chapter explores the rules for net operating losses: how to determine NOLs, how to use NOLs, and how to apply potential limits on their use. The chapter also notes recent developments involving NOLs, such as the expiration of the special five-year carryback period for business losses and the issuance of IRS guidance involving transfers of NOLs to another corporation.

NOL DEDUCTIONS DEFINED

Code Sec. 172 describes the net operating loss deduction. Under Code Sec. 172(c), an *NOL* is the excess of the deductions allowed by the tax code, less gross income computed under the law in effect for the year of the loss (the "loss year"). This excess must be computed with certain modifications described in Code Sec. 172(d). For example, an NOL does not include capital losses.

Generally, the NOL is generated from a trade or business, but it is possible for individual taxpayers to have an NOL based on certain tax deductions, even if the individual is not engaged in a trade or business or is not a separate entity from the trade or business. Still, an NOL usually results from the operations of a business activity. The business may be operated as a corporation, a partnership, or a noncorporate entity, including a disregarded entity or an unincorporated sole proprietorship taxed at the individual level. The treatment of the NOL depends on the form of the entity's business ownership.

In most cases, the taxpayer can carry back the NOL 2 years, and carry it forward up to 20 years. The applicable carryback periods may be longer for certain taxpayers, certain types of losses, or certain loss years. The carryforward is deducted and reduces taxable income for the year to which it is carried.

> **COMMENT**
>
> For both corporations and individuals, the NOL carryback or carryforward is that part of the NOL that has not previously been applied against income for other carryforward or carryback years. The NOL that has not been applied is determined by taking into account only carrybacks and carryforwards from tax years preceding the loss year.
>
> The NOL computation is determined by the law for the year in which the NOL arose. The amount of the NOL is not determined by the law for the year to which the loss is carried.

WHY ALLOW OFFSETS FOR NOLS?

There are several justifications for the NOL deduction. One is to offset the timing consequences of the annual tax accounting period. A year may be a relatively short time span in the operation of a business. Because there is no negative income tax, a year with losses would be equivalent to a year with zero income. If the losses did not carry over to a year with positive income, then taxable income would be exaggerated on average.

> **COMMENT**
>
> The ability to carry losses forward to a future year or back to a previous year thus allows companies with fluctuating income to be taxed more equally with businesses that have stable income from year to year.

Businesses may also have other options for "smoothing out" deductions and other tax benefits. For example, the election of a slower method of depreciation or the postponement of certain expenses is another consideration in lieu of carryforward losses generated by these items. Passthrough businesses also raise special situations, as discussed later.

The NOL deduction allows a business to fully deduct its expenses and offset income in another year. Without loss offsets, a company with losses in some years would not be able to deduct all the expenses of earning income. Furthermore, the allowance of loss carryforwards may stimulate investment by a new business or venture, which is more likely to generate a loss in its early years. The NOL rules allow losses from early years to be carried forward to future years when the business has income.

Taxpayers are able to spread their NOLs across tax years and decrease their tax liabilities (perhaps significantly) in years that they had net income. Thus, a taxpayer that had income in years when the economy was growing, and paid substantial taxes, may be able to allocate the NOL to those years and reduce reported income for the year. If this is performed for a past (carryback) year, the taxpayer will be entitled to a refund.

Tax deductions reduce gross income. Unlike refundable tax credits, deductions do not provide a refund to taxpayers in the loss year (the year that the NOL arises) if the taxpayer has no income tax liability. To provide a tax benefit, the tax code allows taxpayers with excess deductions to carry over the benefit to another year.

STEPS IN FIGURING AN NOL

Determining and applying an NOL is a multistep process. For individuals, the process can involve the following steps:

1. Filling out the Form 1040 income tax return. If taxable income (before personal exemptions) is a negative number, the taxpayer may have an NOL. If the amount is not negative, the taxpayer does not have an NOL.
2. Determining whether the taxpayer has an NOL and the amount of the NOL.
3. Deciding whether to carry back the NOL to a past year or to waive the carryback period and instead carrying over the NOL to a future year.
4. Deducting the NOL in the carryback or carryforward year. If the NOL deduction is less than or equal to taxable income in that year, the taxpayer has used up its NOL.
5. Determining the unused NOL if the NOL exceeds taxable income for the carryback/carryforward year, then carrying over the unused NOL to the next succeeding carryforward year.
6. If the NOL deduction includes more than one NOL amount, the taxpayer applies the NOL by starting with the amount from the earliest year.

For corporations, the determination of net income and the calculation of the NOL are different, but the steps are essentially the same.

> **NOTE**
>
> Code Sec. 172(b) refers to carrybacks for carrying an NOL to a prior year, and carry*overs* for carrying an NOL to a future year. However, to emphasize the difference, this chapter refers to carry*forwards* for carrying an NOL to a future year.

USES BY INDIVIDUALS

An individual's NOL is usually primarily the result of his or her net business losses, although certain specified personal expenses and losses are allowed to be included in the NOL computation. Nevertheless, if a taxpayer's overall income exceeds deductions for the year, no NOL is possible irrespective of NOL exclusions and inclusions. Tax credits, however, are not considered either in this initial evaluation or in determining the size of an NOL. Any excess NOL can be carried over to another year to offset business income. Business losses generally arise in a sole proprietorship or through a passthrough entity such as an S corporation, partnership, or a limited liability company (LLC) that elects to be treated as a partnership.

The NOL deduction is generally determined by subtracting deductions from gross income, but with a number of modifications. Income from separate businesses is aggregated. Items that are excludable from gross income are generally excluded from the calculation of the NOL.

In addition to including trade or business losses, an individual computes an NOL by treating certain items as if they were direct business deductions. These deductions that add to the size of an NOL include:

- Employee business expenses;
- Casualty and theft losses;
- Job relocation moving expenses; and
- Expenses of rental property that is held for the production of income.

In determining the amount of an NOL, a number of subtraction rules also apply:

- No deduction is allowed for personal exemptions;
- No deduction is allowed for the excess of capital losses over capital gains;
- Nonbusiness deductions are allowed only to the extent of nonbusiness income;
- No exclusion is allowed for the gain on the sale of qualified small business stock;
- No Code Sec. 199 manufacturing deduction is allowed; and
- NOL deduction carrybacks and carryforwards from preceding or following tax years must be excluded.

> **COMMENT**
>
> Thus, net capital losses can never increase the amount of an NOL.

As explained, an individual can also take nonbusiness deductions in calculating an NOL, but only to the extent of nonbusiness income. Nonbusiness income and losses include those from activities that the taxpayer does not regularly engage in, or from sources that do not require the taxpayer's substantial active participation. Salary, however, is considered business income for this purpose. A self-employed individual's contributions to a retirement plan on his or her own behalf are considered nonbusiness deductions. Other nonbusiness deductions include contributions to an individual retirement account (IRA) and to a health savings account.

> **COMMENT**
>
> Generally, nonbusiness income is passive income. It includes dividends, interest, annuities, and the excess of nonbusiness capital gains over nonbusiness capital losses.

Bankruptcy

The bankruptcy estate of an individual debtor succeeds to certain tax attributes of the debtor, including any NOL carryforward. If a carryback year (a year to which the NOL can be carried) of the estate is a year before the estate's first year, the debtor can take the NOL into account for the year that corresponds to the carryback year. Thus, the NOL can offset prebankruptcy income of the debtor. When the bankruptcy estate terminates, any unused carryforward of the estate can be used and deducted by the debtor.

Marriage and Divorce

A married couple can apply an NOL incurred during a year they are married against their joint income, just as if applied to an individual who has an NOL and carries it back. The loss is treated as a joint NOL. If a married couple files separate returns, the spouse who sustained the loss may take the NOL deduction on the separate return.

If a husband and wife file a joint return for a carryback or carryforward year, and are married but file a separate return for the year of the NOL, the couple can treat the separate NOL as a joint carryback or carryforward.

If an individual has an NOL and then marries, courts have indicated that the NOL deduction can only be applied to the separate income of the spouse who had the loss. Similarly, if an individual incurs an NOL after a divorce and carries the NOL back to a year during which the individual was married, the individual must use the NOL to offset his or her separate income, as if the couple had filed separate returns. The NOL cannot offset the spouse's income, and the joint rates will apply to the resulting taxable income.

EXAMPLE

Jeff and Sabrina MacPhearson have net income for 2011. They divorce in 2012. Jeff experienced an NOL for 2012. When carrying back the NOL to the 2011 return, Jeff must calculate his individual portion of the couple's net income for 2011.

COMMENT

The rules are the same if the change in marital status results from the death of a spouse.

Cancellation of Debt

Borrowing money is not a taxable event because there is an offsetting obligation to repay the debt. However, if the debtor does not repay the debt and the lender cancels the obligation, the cancellation generates taxable income under Code Sec. 108 unless certain exclusions apply.

In some situations, cancellation of debt (COD) is excluded from income, for example, if the debtor is in bankruptcy or is insolvent. The amount of income that is cancelled must be applied to reduce tax attributes. The first attribute that generally has to be reduced is the amount of an NOL. However, taxpayers can elect, alternatively, to reduce the basis of property instead.

COMMENT

NOLs generally have more immediate tax value than reductions in the basis of an asset, so it often is useful to reduce the basis attribute instead when the taxpayer excludes COD income, so that the full NOL remains to be carried over to another year. However, if a taxpayer has NOLs that are approaching the end of their 20-year carryforward period, it makes sense to reduce NOLs that would otherwise expire unused.

EXAMPLE

East Corporation has an NOL from 2011 of $20,000. It holds depreciable property with a basis of $10,000. In 2012, East has $5,000 of COD income, which it excludes from taxable income. East must reduce its NOL to $15,000 to reflect the excluded income. Alternatively, it can elect to reduce the basis of its depreciable property to $5,000.

Tax liability for the year of the cancellation is calculated taking full advantage of available NOLs, before the NOLs are reduced. If the NOL is not fully absorbed by taxable income, the balance may be reduced as a tax attribute. As an attribute, NOLs are reduced in the following order:

1. Any NOL for the year the debt is discharged;
2. The next oldest year that would otherwise be carried forward to the discharge year; and
3. The following year in the sequence.

USES BY ESTATES AND TRUSTS

An estate or trust is allowed an NOL deduction. In computing its NOL, an estate or trust cannot take the deduction for the personal exemption that is available to it under Code Sec. 642(b).

An estate cannot deduct a capital loss or NOL incurred by the decedent in his or her final year. These losses must be deducted on the decedent's final return. In calculating an NOL, a trust cannot claim deductions for charitable contributions and for distributions to beneficiaries. A trust also cannot take into account any income or deductions attributed to another taxpayer under the grantor trust rules. An NOL, as well as other losses and deductions, for the year in which the estate or trust terminates can be deducted by a beneficiary who succeeds to the property of the estate or trust.

USES BY PARTNERSHIPS

A partnership cannot itself use NOL deductions. The partnership's losses flow through to the partners and can be used to offset other income of the partners (subject to at-risk and passive activity loss requirements). If the losses exceed the partner's basis, the excess losses can be carried forward and claimed in a subsequent year when the partner has additional basis.

> **EXAMPLE**
>
> Abel Watson owns 50 percent of a partnership and has a $5,000 basis in a partnership. The partnership incurs a $15,000 loss for the year. Abel's share of the loss is $7,500. He can claim $5,000 of the loss, which is the amount of his basis. Abel can carry over the remaining $2,500 of partnership loss to the following tax year and can claim the loss if he increases his basis sufficiently.

USES BY CORPORATIONS

C Corporations

A C corporation (organized under Subchapter C of the tax code and taxable as a separate entity) is entitled to deduct an NOL from corporate income at the entity level. The corporate NOL is derived from the normal income tax deductions that a corporate takes in determining taxable income. It is not a freestanding deduction, like the capital loss deduction, for example. The eligibility to deduct an NOL cannot be used to take a deduction that is not allowed by a specific provision of the tax code and cannot overturn the disallowance of a deduction.

> **EXAMPLE**
>
> Thomas Corporation has $300,000 of gross income for 2012. Thomas has ordinary business expenses of $200,000; $60,000 of interest expense; and $80,000 for contributions to a qualified retirement plan. Thomas has an NOL of $40,000, equal to total expenses of $340,000 minus gross income of $300,000.

A C corporation is a distinct entity from its shareholders, even if it has only one shareholder. A corporation may not deduct its shareholders' NOLs, and its shareholders similarly may not deduct the corporation's NOLs.

> **COMMENT**
>
> Because a corporation is a separate and distinct entity, its NOLs do not automatically carry over to a successor entity. See the discussion of the Code Sec. 382 limits on NOL carryforwards, in case of a change of corporate ownership.

S Corporations

An S corporation, which is generally taxed as a passthrough entity, is treated differently from a C corporation. As is the case for partnerships, an S corporation is not itself eligible to take an NOL deduction. Instead, the corporation's losses "pass through" to the shareholders and are reflected on the shareholder's returns. Each shareholder may take its share of an S corporation's operating loss and use it to offset other income of the shareholder. However, NOLs from a C corporation do not carry over to an S corporation that used to be a C corporation. This prevents C corporations from passing on their NOLs to their shareholders for the individuals' use.

An S corporation may not carry back NOLs or carry them forward to a tax year when it was a C corporation. However, the carryforward period does not change when a C corporation changes its status. If a C corporation becomes an S corporation and then converts back to C corp status, the C corp's NOLs are preserved and can again be used when it reverts to being a C corporation. The effect is to treat the C corp's income as zero during the years it was an S corp.

> **EXAMPLE**
>
> West Corporation was a C corporation in 2010. It converted to an S corporation in 2011, then converted back to a C corporation in 2012. In 2010, West had earnings of $100,000. The corporation had an NOL of $40,000 in 2011, and an NOL of $60,000 in 2012. West cannot carry back the 2011 NOL, when it was a S corporation, to 2010, when it was a C corporation. However, West can carry back the 2012 NOL, when it again was a C corporation, to 2010, offset $60,000 of income for 2010, and claim a refund for the tax paid on $60,000. If West had had income of $40,000 in 2011, when it was an S corporation, it would have treated its taxable income as zero for carrying back the C corporation's NOL.

Corporate Modifications

To compute a corporation's NOL, certain modifications apply—some unfavorable, others favorable. Corporations can take the full dividends-received deduction and do not have to reduce the deduction (and thus increase income) for the overall limitations that normally apply. Thus, the NOL can be larger than it would be with the normal dividends-received deduction. On the other hand, corporations are not allowed to take the domestic production activities deduction under Code Sec. 199 and thus must add back the deduction into income.

The most important modification for corporate and individual taxpayers alike is that the NOL deduction itself is not allowed in computing an NOL. Otherwise, the NOL would be counted twice, and the number of years for carrying over the NOL would be extended.

Other Corporate Entities

A life insurance company cannot take an NOL deduction. However, it can take an "operations loss deduction" that is similar to an NOL deduction. Nonlife insurance companies may be allowed to take an NOL deduction, depending on their size:

- A very small nonlife company is not taxed at all;
- A small nonlife company is taxed only on its taxable investment income; and
- An "ordinary" nonlife company is permitted to take the NOL deduction.

> **COMMENT**
>
> NOLs cannot be carried over to or from a company's tax year when the firm was an ordinary nonlife insurance company.

A mutual fund or regulated investment company is not permitted to claim any NOL deductions. A cooperative organization can take an NOL deduction to determine its corporate income tax. An exempt organization, which is taxable on unrelated business taxable income, can claim an NOL in computing unrelated business taxable income.

A real estate investment trust (REIT) can claim an NOL carryforward deduction for the 20 years following the REIT's loss. However, there are modifications to a REIT's taxable income when computing NOLs. As a result, a REIT can have positive income and an NOL in the same year, or can have negative income and no NOL in the same year.

However, an NOL from a REIT's tax year (a year when the corporation is a REIT) cannot be carried back to any prior year (generally the same as other NOLs). Furthermore, an NOL from a non-REIT year cannot be carried back to any year that is a REIT year. However, that prior REIT year counts as a carryback year; there is no extension of the carryback period so that the taxpayer can reach counting an earlier non-REIT year. However, the NOL is not reduced by the amount of income in a REIT year, since an NOL deduction is not available.

STUDY QUESTIONS

1. When a decedent has incurred an NOL in his or her final year, the loss is deducted:

   a. On the decedent's final year's tax return
   b. In lieu of the decedent's personal exemption
   c. By allocating the deduction evenly for all beneficiaries in the first year's return by the estate or trust
   d. On the estate or trust's return for that tax year

2. An NOL deduction may be claimed at the entity level by:

   a. A partnership
   b. A C corporation
   c. An S corporation
   d. A life insurance company

NOL CARRYBACKS/CARRYFORWARDS

Code Sec. 172(b)(2) requires that taxpayers carry the entire amount of an NOL to the earliest carryback year for which the NOL is allowed, absent waiver of the entire carryback period, discussed below. Taxpayers must apply the NOL to the income earned in that year to the full extent of that year's tax liability. If the NOL exceeds the income for the carryback year, the remaining NOL is carried over to the next succeeding year.

When an NOL is carried back to a particular year, any income, deductions, or credits based on or limited by the percentage of AGI must be recomputed, after applying the NOL to the carryback year. For example, an individual taxpayer must recompute the amount of:

- Taxable Social Security benefits;
- IRA deductions (which may produce nondeductible IRA contributions);
- Excludable savings bond interest;
- The student loan interest deduction; and
- Itemized deductions, such as medical expenses, casualty losses, and miscellaneous itemized deductions.

However, the taxpayer does not have to recompute the charitable deduction. Based upon these AGI adjustments, the taxpayer then must recompute his or her income tax, alternative minimum tax (AMT), and nonrefundable credits.

If the NOL is not used up in the carryback period, the taxpayer can carry forward the remaining NOL during the 20 years following the NOL loss year. A taxpayer generally cannot extend the carryback and carryforward periods unless the tax code specifically permits it. Thus, the taxpayer will lose any portion of an NOL remaining after the 20-year period for carryforwards. The taxpayer can attempt to accelerate income into the last year of the carryforward to use an expiring NOL.

COMMENT

A short tax year is treated as a full year for applying the NOL carryback and carryforward periods.

For any tax year, the NOL deduction is the total of carry backs and carryforwards of NOLs carried over from other tax years. When more than one carryback or carryforward applies to a tax year, the carrybacks and carryforwards must be applied in the order in which they arose.

Waiver of Carryback

Under Code Sec. 172(b)(3), the taxpayer can waive the entire carryback period for any NOL. A taxpayer that makes this election can immediately start to carry forward the NOL and can only carry forward the NOL. Once made, the election is irrevocable.

EXAMPLE

North Corporation had net income of $40,000 in 2010 and net income of $15,000 in 2011. North had an NOL of $25,000 in 2012. If North chooses to carry back the NOL, North must carry back the NOL to 2010 to offset $25,000 of income. However, North can elect to waive the two-year carryback period and carry the NOL over to a future year, beginning in 2013.

COMMENT

When the law was changed on a temporary basis to provide an extended five-year carryback period for 2008 and 2009 NOLs, the law allowed taxpayers to revoke their prior election to waive the two-year period. This gave taxpayers a chance to take advantage of the longer carryback period.

COMMENT

The election applies for all purposes, including the AMT. Thus, either the NOL is carried back for both normal taxes and the AMT, or it is carried back for neither.

The IRS does not have a particular form for making the election. However, it has prescribed the requirements for making an election, and these procedures are interpreted strictly. A technical failure can invalidate the election.

The taxpayer attaches a statement to its return and must make the election by the due date of the return for the loss year (the year that the NOL arose), including extensions. A taxpayer can also make the election on an amended return filed within six months of the due date of an original timely filed return, excluding extensions. The IRS has the discretion to grant a reasonable extension of time beyond the ordinary deadline.

COMMENT

A taxpayer that chooses to waive the carryback period for more than one NOL must attach a separate statement for each NOL.

For a consolidated group of corporations, the waiver must be made by the common parent. The election must be filed with the group's income tax return for the consolidated return year in which the loss arose. If a member of a consolidated group joins another consolidated group, the acquiring group must make the carryback waiver for the new member.

COMMENT

A corporate taxpayer may waive a carryback in a consolidated setting if it would create a refund for years in which the corporation was not a member of the group.

Intervening Years

The NOL deduction subtracted from gross income is the sum of the carrybacks and carryforwards to the particular tax year. No adjustments are necessary. The NOL carryback or carryforward generally is that part of the NOL that has not been previously applied against income for another carryback or carryforward year. A taxpayer must recompute its taxable income of an intervening year. This recomputed or modified income is the amount that will be subtracted from the NOL and used to determine the remaining portion of the NOL for a subsequent year. In making this computation, the taxpayer must make certain adjustments to taxable income. This modified taxable income cannot be less than zero:

- The NOL deduction for the intervening year is computed using only carrybacks and carryforwards from tax years preceding the loss year;
- If the taxpayer is not a corporation, nonbusiness capital losses are deductible only up to the amount of capital gains (thus, no excess capital losses are deductible);
- Personal and dependency exemptions are not allowed; and
- The domestic activities production deduction is not allowed.

Extended Carryback

There are exceptions to the two-year carryback period. In these circumstances, a portion of a taxpayer's NOL is treated as a separate NOL with a separate carryback/carryforward period. The first and subsequent years to which to carry these amounts must be determined separately. When both NOLs are used, the amount attributable to a special rule is used after the normal amount. Thus, the special NOL is used in those years only to the extent that the ordinary NOL does not fully eliminate taxable income.

Three-year period. The carryback period for individuals is three years for any part of an NOL from a casualty or theft loss (also including fire, storm, shipwreck, or other casualty), regardless of whether there is a disaster. It is also three years for an NOL from a federally declared disaster (formerly known as a presidentially declared disaster) that affects a qualified small business or a business engaged in the trade or business of farming. A farm loss from a disaster must be distinguished from a farming loss related to the ordinary operation of a farming business, which qualifies for a five-year carryback.

> **EXAMPLE**
>
> Jack has an NOL of $42,000 in 2012. $4,000 of the NOL is attributable to a casualty loss and qualifies for a three-year carryback period. Jack applies $3,000 of the casualty loss to 2009 income and carries the remaining $1,000 to 2010. Jack also carries back the remaining $38,000 NOL ($42,000 – $4,000) for two years, to 2010.

A *qualified small business* is a corporation or partnership that meets a gross receipts test, based on gross receipts for the year of the loss and the previous two years. If the average of those numbers is no more than $5 million, the gross receipts test is met for the year. Corporations that are members of the same controlled group are treated as a single corporation.

> **COMMENT**
>
> If the existing entity had a predecessor during the three years, the predecessor is considered the same as the existing entity. If the entity was not in existence for three years, the average is taken for the period it was in existence. If any of the years is a short year, the gross receipts need to be annualized.

A farming business is any trade or business of farming, including a nursery, sod farm, and raising or harvesting ornamental trees or trees that bear fruit, nuts, or other crops. An evergreen tree that is more than six years old when cut down is not considered an ornamental tree.

> **COMMENT**
>
> This may eliminate some Christmas tree businesses from being a farming business.

Five-year period. A "farming loss" can be carried back five years. A farming loss does not include a loss from a federally declared disaster that is eligible for the limited five-year carryback period for qualified disaster losses. A qualified disaster loss, for purposes of the five-year carryback, applied to losses arising in tax years beginning after 2007, which were attributable to a federally declared disaster that occurred before January 1, 2010. The five-year carryback also would have applied to an eligible loss of a small business occurring in 2008 or 2009 that met the definition of a qualified disaster loss. A taxpayer can elect out of the five-year period.

Farming and Disaster Losses

A *farming loss* is the smaller of:

- The NOL amount for the year if only income and deductions attributable to farming businesses were taken into account; or
- The NOL for the tax year.

A taxpayer can elect to waive the five-year carryback period and apply the two-year carryback period. The farming loss is taken into account after the remaining portion of the NOL for the year. Farm losses can be attributable to any losses, not just disaster losses. A farming loss does not include a federal disaster loss.

A five-year NOL carryback period is available for "qualified Disaster Recovery Assistance Losses" from severe storms, tornados, and flooding that occurred in the summer of 2008 in the Midwestern disaster area (as designated by the IRS in Publication 4492-B). The carryback applies to expenses for repairs, housing, and moving, incurred after the event occurred and before January 1, 2011.

Ten-year period. A 10-year period carryback period is available for a "specified liability loss." Such a loss includes losses from product liabilities, workplace liabilities, and environmental remediation.

Specified Liability Losses

A *specified liability loss* relates to amounts imposed by statute, generally relating to environmental and workplace liabilities. A loss includes payment of a liability under a federal or state law that requires land reclamation, nuclear power plant decommissioning, drilling platform dismantling, environmental remediation, or payment under a workers' compensation act. Potentially, nuclear decommissioning losses can be carried back even further than 10 years.

> **COMMENT**
>
> A corporation can waive the carryback period for specified liability losses. Generally, the carryback period reverts to the ordinary two-year period.

Additional conditions are applicable to such significant losses. The act, or failure to act, that resulted in liability must have occurred at least three years prior to the tax year in which the expenses occur. The corporation must have been on the accrual method throughout the period during which the act (or nonact) occurred.

Product liability losses are the actual product liability incurred by the taxpayer corporation or expenses incurred by the corporation in investigating, settling, or opposing product liability claims. Amounts paid for insurance against product liability risks are not paid on account of product liability.

The specified liability loss is treated as a separate NOL that is taken into account after the remaining portion of the NOL for the year. However, the amount of the specified liability loss cannot exceed the NOL amount for the year.

> **EXAMPLE**
>
> Southworth Corporation has an NOL of $1 million for 2012. Of that amount, $700,000 is attributable to a specified liability loss and has a 10-year carryback period. The other $300,000 has a two-year carryback period. The NOL is treated as two NOLs: $700,000 that can be carried back to the years 2002–2011, and $300,000 that can be carried back to 2010 and 2011.

STUDY QUESTIONS

3. If a taxpayer elects to waive the carryback period for an NOL:
   a. The NOL may be carried forward to up to 20 future tax years in which the taxpayer has income
   b. The election may be reversed after 10 tax years if the taxpayer does not generate income in that timeframe
   c. The waiver is conditional based on whether the taxpayer has income in the current tax year
   d. The taxpayer can still claim the loss for AMT purposes

4. Which of the following allows the longest carryback period for deducting NOLs?
   a. A federally declared disaster affecting a qualified small business
   b. A farming loss
   c. A specified liability loss
   d. Theft loss

Previous Extended Carryback Periods

Congress periodically extends the carryback period for certain taxpayers or for certain years. For example, for years ending in 2001 and 2002, as part of the September 11 recovery program, the carryback period was set as five years. Losses attributable to qualified timber property located in the Gulf Opportunity (GO) Zone was eligible for a five-year carryback as a farming loss. Covered losses must have occurred after the GO Zone's applicable date (usually 2005) and before January 1, 2007.

For commercial bank bad-debt losses, special rules applied during the period 1987–1993. The carryback period was 10 years, while the carryforward period was only five years.

An electric utility could make an election, in tax years ending after 2005 and before 2009, to apply a five-year carryback period to NOLs that arose in 2003, 2004 or 2005. The election could only be made for one of the three years. The NOL was limited to 20 percent of the taxpayer's capital expenditures for electric transmission property and pollution control facilities, for the tax year preceding the year for which the election was made.

Under the *Emergency Economic Stabilization Act of 2008* (EESA), a five-year carryback period was available for qualified disaster losses attributable to a federally declared disaster occurring after December 31, 2007 and before January 1, 2010.

Disasters. As discussed above, a five-year carryback period also applied for federally declared disasters occurring after 2007 and before 2010. Such losses were treated as a separate NOL to be taken into effect after the remaining portion of the NOL for the tax year. They included the 2007 Kansas disaster area loss from a May 4, 2007, storm, but did not apply to types of property for which Midwestern disaster loss treatment was not allowed. Eligible expenses included depreciation or amortization of certain Kansas disaster area property for the year the property was placed in service. A taxpayer could waive the five-year carryback period.

Congress amended Code Sec. 172 twice to allow both individuals and businesses to carry back an NOL for three, four, or five years. For eligible small businesses, Congress provided an election to carry back 2008 NOLs for three to five years. An eligible small business had to have average gross receipts of $15 million or less for the year in which the loss arose and the previous two years.

Business carryback. With the popularity of the elective three- to five-year carryback for small businesses, Congress temporarily decided to provide the same benefits to all businesses for an NOL incurred in any tax year ending after December 31, 2007, and beginning before January 1, 2010. Most taxpayers could only make the election for one year, but eligible small businesses that had made the election for 2008 could make a similar election for 2009. For the period this election was available, the three-year carry back for eligible losses was not available.

The law had a special limit on NOLs carried back five years. The NOL used in the fifth year could not exceed 50 percent of the business's taxable income for that year. An NOL carried back three or four years was not limited and could be fully used to reduce taxable income.

CORPORATE EQUITY REDUCTION LIMIT ON NOLS

Some corporations may incur substantial debt in transactions that reduce their outstanding equity. They reduce equity in their capital structure in favor of debt to take advantage of the deduction for interest expenses compared to the nondeductibility of dividends.

If a corporation has an equity-reduction transaction, Code Sec. 172(h) limits the corporation's ability to carry back a corporate equity reduction interest loss (CERIL). The CERIL cannot be carried back to any tax year before the one in which the corporate equity reduction transaction (CERT) occurred. This restriction applies to a "loss limitation year," which is the year in which the CERIL occurs and the two tax years that immediately follow.

> **COMMENT**
>
> The idea is that the CERT generates excessive interest deductions in future years that also generate "excess" NOLs. The provision prevents the excess NOL from being carried back over the normal two-year carryback period.

A CERT can be either a major stock acquisition or an excess distribution. A CERT is an acquisition of stock by another corporation. The acquired stock must represent at least 50 percent of the first corporation's stock. The stock must be acquired in a plan of the acquiring corporation (or a group of persons acting in concert with the corporation). All acquisitions in any 24-month period are aggregated.

An excess distribution is determined by comparison to past distributions and stock prices. Distribution amounts are reduced by the amount of stock the corporation issued in exchange for money or property other than stock, during the same period in which distributions are measured. "Plain vanilla" preferred stock is disregarded.

The CERIL equals the excess of the NOL for the year over the NOL for the same year determined without regard to any "allocable interest deduction." This is the interest deduction on the portion of debt allocable to a CERT. The deduction is the amount allowable as a deduction for interest paid or accrued by the corporation during the loss limitation year, reduced by the average of the interest paid or accrued for the three tax years preceding the year in which the CERT occurred.

In computing taxable income, the allocable interest deduction is taken into account after all other deductions. The result is that the NOL is allocated to the CERIL, but only up to the amount of the allocable interest deduction for the year.

EXAMPLE

PETRA Corporation has a CERT in 2011; 2012 is a loss limitation year. In 2012, its NOL is $2 million. Its allocable interest deduction is $1.8 million. Without the allocable interest deduction, PETRA's NOL would be $200,000. Therefore, the CERIL is $1.8 million.

REFUND PROCEDURES

Taxpayers claiming an NOL must file statements to substantiate the amount of the deduction. Taxpayers may claim a refund by filing an amended return for the year to which the loss is carried to—Form 1120X, *Amended U.S. Corporation Income Tax Return,* or Form 1040X (for individuals). Taxpayers can instead file for a tentative carryback adjustment, also called a quick carryback claim, on Form 1139, *Corporate Application for Tentative Refund,* or Form 1045, *Application for Tentative Refund,* for individuals, estates, or trusts.

Corporations Expecting a Refund

If a corporation expects to have an NOL in its current year, it can extend the time for paying part or all of its income tax for the immediately preceding year, by filing Form 1138, *Extension of Time for Payment of Taxes by a Corporation Expecting a Net Operating Loss Carryback.* The extension continues until the end of the month in which the return for the NOL year is due (including extensions). If the corporation files Form 1139 before this date, the extension will continue until the date that the IRS notifies the corporation that its Form 1139 is allowed or disallowed in whole or in part.

The corporation must explain on Form 1138 why it expects the loss. The payment of tax that may be postponed cannot exceed the expected overpayment from the NOL carryback.

Corporation filings. A corporation can get a faster refund by filing Form 1139, so corporations generally apply for a refund using Form 1139 instead of Form 1120X. A corporation cannot file Form 1139 before filing its income tax return for the NOL year. It must file Form 1139 no later than one year after the year it sustains the NOL. These procedural requirements may discourage the use of Form 1139. If the corporation does not file Form 1139, it must file Form 1120X within three years of the due date, plus extensions, for filing the Form 1120 for the year in which it sustains the NOL.

When filing an amended return to carry back an NOL, a corporation must include the following:

- Copies for the loss year and the carry back year of Form 1120, pages one and three;
- A statement providing the details regarding the calculation and facts relating to the NOL; and
- Any other forms needed to support the claim.

Corporate waivers. If a corporation carries forward an NOL, it enters the carryforward on Schedule K, Form 1120. It also enters the deduction for the carryforward on Form 1120 or the applicable income tax return.

For corporations, an election to waive the two-year carryback period is made on Schedule K, Form 1120. Consolidated tax return filers must attach a statement to their original return, filed by the due date (including extensions) for the NOL year.

Individuals, Estates, and Trusts

An individual can get a faster refund using Form 1045 than by filing Form 1040X but has a shorter time to file Form 1045. Individuals can use Form 1045 to apply an NOL to all carryback years. Form 1045 is processed within the later of 90 days after being filed or 90 days after the last day of the month that includes the due date for filing Form 1040 (or 1041) for the loss year. Individuals will generally prefer a faster refund but may not satisfy the procedures for Form 1045. If the taxpayer uses Form 1040X, he or she must use a separate Form 1040X for each carryback year to which an NOL is applied.

Estates and trusts that do not file Form 1045 must file an amended Form 1041, *U.S. Income Tax Return for Estates and Trusts*, instead of Form 1040X, for each carryback year. There is no amended Form 1041X. If the taxpayer files an amended return, it must still attach the NOL computation using the Form 1045 schedules. The IRS generally processes an amended return within six months after filing.

Like corporations filing Form 1139, individuals can apply for a quick refund using Form 1045, which results in a tentative adjustment of tax in the carryback year. If the IRS makes the refund and later determines that the refund is too much, the IRS may assess and collect the excess immediately. Form 1045 is due on or after the date the taxpayer files Form 1040 and Form 1041, but no later than one year after the end of the NOL year.

A taxpayer filing Form 1040X or an amended Form 1041 has three years, after the due date, including extensions, for filing the return for the NOL year. Taxpayers must attach a computation of their NOL to Form 1045, Schedule A, and should figure their NOL carryforward on Form 1045, Schedule B.

EXAMPLE

PETRA Corporation has a CERT in 2011; 2012 is a loss limitation year. In 2012, its NOL is $2 million. Its allocable interest deduction is $1.8 million. Without the allocable interest deduction, PETRA's NOL would be $200,000. Therefore, the CERIL is $1.8 million.

ASSESSMENTS

Normally, the IRS has three years after a return is filed to make an assessment. In the case of an NOL carryback, the assessment period is extended to include the loss year (the year of the NOL). Thus, the IRS can assess a deficiency for a carryback year based on the three-year period that applies to the loss year. However, the additional assessment period applies only to deficiencies related to the NOL carryforward.

EXAMPLE

Lane Corp has an NOL in 2010 and carries it back to 2009. The IRS can assess a deficiency through September 2014 for Lane's 2010 tax year. In addition, the IRS can assess a deficiency against Lane for 2009 through September 2014. However, a deficiency that is not assessed until 2014 for the 2009 tax year can only involve a deficiency related to the NOL carryforward from 2010.

Unlike the example above, if a corporation files a refund claim on Form 1139, the IRS may assess a deficiency that is related or unrelated to the NOL carryback in the additional year. However, the total deficiency that may be assessed in the final year is limited to the amount credited or refunded.

TRANSFERS OF NOLS

Special rules apply to limit the use of NOLs in a variety of situations. Code Sec. 381, Carryovers in Certain Corporate Acquisitions, provides operating rules for the use of NOL carryforwards but does not provide limits. If an acquiring corporation receives assets of another corporation (the target) in a qualifying transaction, such as a liquidation, the acquiring corporation succeeds to all of the NOLs of the target corporation. This can be true even if the acquiring corporation does not receive all of the target corporation's assets.

The target corporation's NOLs may not be carried back to tax years of the acquiring corporation that occurred before the acquisition. Similarly, the acquiring corporation's NOLs may not be carried back to a preacquisition year of the target. Of course, the acquiring corporation can continue to carry its own NOLs back to a preacquisition year of its own, or forward after the acquisition.

Corporate tax attributes, such as NOLs, that can have the effect of reducing tax liability are valuable assets. It is tempting for the corporation with the NOL to try to find a way to transfer or "sell" its unused NOL deductions. A corporation with large NOLs is an attractive target for a profitable corporation, because those NOLs could be used to soak up future profits of the acquiring corporation and produce a tax savings. However, Code Sec. 382 may limit the NOL amount that can be used by the acquiring corporation after the acquisition.

Loss Trafficking

Congress and the IRS are opposed to loss trafficking. *Loss trafficking* can occur if a corporation has more NOLs than it can use and transfers the NOLs to a profitable corporation in a reorganization or other ownership change. NOLs are intended to benefit the corporation that suffers the losses. The theory is that transactions that are motivated by NOL trafficking would distort the economic benefits of acquiring a business. Secondly, NOLs are meant only to offset the income of the same economic person. Congress has enacted Code Sec. 382 to prevent trafficking in NOLs by corporations, which could otherwise acquire another corporation to use its NOLs.

The target corporation's NOLs may be carried to the postacquisition period in the year of acquisition. The short year of the target corporation counts as a carryforward year. The permissible carryforward amount is based on the pro-rata portion of the days remaining in the acquisition year.

Under Code Sec. 382, Limitations on Net Operating Loss Carryforwards and Certain Built-in Losses Following Ownership Change, the amount of income that, after an ownership change, a corporation may offset each year by preacquisition NOL carryforwards is limited. The permissible amount is determined by multiplying the value of the corporation's equity just prior to the ownership change by the federal long-term tax-exempt rate in effect on the date of the change. The long-term tax-exempt rate is published each month by the IRS. Any unused limitation may be carried forward to the succeeding year.

Ownership Change

The loss limitation rules apply to a loss corporation when shareholders who bore the economic burden of a corporation's prechange loss no longer control the corporation. The term *loss corporation* refers to a corporation that has NOLs or a corporation with assets that have an aggregate basis greater than their aggregate fair market value. A corporation must determine whether it has had an ownership change if it experiences a testing date. A testing date occurs when:

- A loss corporation has an owner shift involving a 5-percent owner;
- A loss corporation has an equity structure shift; or

- When there has been a transfer of an option to acquire or dispose of loss corporation stock.

The transfer must be to or by a person who would be a 5-percent owner if the option were exercised.

An owner shift occurs when there is a change in the stock ownership of a corporation, and the change affects a shareholder who is a 5-percent owner before or after the change. An equity structure shift occurs when a loss corporation is a party to a tax-free reorganization other than certain "D" reorganizations or an "F" reorganization.

An ownership change occurs if the aggregate owner shifts over a three-year testing period exceed 50 percentage points. The date on which the ownership change occurs is called the *change date*. The three-year testing period ends on the most recent testing date.

Regulatory Changes

The IRS has provided some guidance to ease the impact of these rules. Proposed regulations issued at the end of 2011 focus on stock ownership changes involving small shareholders that own less than 5 percent of the loss corporation's stock. Small shareholders are generally aggregated in a "public group" and treated as a single 5-percent shareholder.

The prior approach usually resulted in the creation of new 5-percent shareholders, increasing the number of owner shifts and ownership changes. The new approach makes it unnecessary to track small shareholders, reducing the number of owner shifts, because they generally cannot acquire loss corporation stock and cannot take greater advantage of the existing NOLs. The IRS also issued a notice that disregards a change in proportionate ownership that results solely from fluctuations in the relative fair market value of different classes of stock.

BUILT-IN GAINS AND LOSSES

A built-in gain or loss may exist when a loss corporation owns an asset with a basis that is different from the asset's fair market value. These built-in gains and losses may affect the loss corporation's ability to use NOLs after an ownership change. A net unrealized built-in gain (NUBIG) exists on a change date, when the aggregate value of the loss corporation's assets exceeds the aggregate adjusted basis of the assets. The Code Sec. 382 limit will be increased by any recognized built-in gain if a NUBIG exists and one of the assets with a built-in gain that is held by the loss corporation is disposed of in the five-year period following the change date.

Conversely, if the loss corporation has a net unrealized built-in loss (NUBIL), and one of the assets with a built-in loss is disposed of by the loss corporation in the same five-year period, the recognized built-in loss will be treated as a prechange loss that is subject to the Code Sec. 382 limit.

CONTINUITY OF BUSINESS

If a loss corporation fails to meet continuity-of-business-enterprise (COBE) standards, the Code Sec. 382 limit will be zero. The COBE standard must be met for at least two years after the ownership change. The loss corporation must continue a significant historic business or must use a significant amount of historic assets in a business. Using cash proceeds from the sale of historic business assets does not meet the COBE standard.

STUDY QUESTIONS

5. Form 1045, *Application for Tentative Refund*, helps individuals with NOLs obtain a quick refund in no longer than _____ after the last day of the month that includes the due date for their annual federal income tax return.

   a. 30 days
   b. 60 days
   c. 90 days
   d. 120 days

6. The Code Sec. 382 limit for continuity-of-business-enterprise standards must be met for at least _____ after an ownership change.

   a. One tax year
   b. Two tax years
   c. Three tax years
   d. Five tax years

CONCLUSION

NOLs are a valuable tax benefit that, if carried back properly, can be used to obtain a refund, providing additional funds that can be used for operating expenses, investments, or any other purpose. NOLs can benefit an individual, an unincorporated business, or an incorporated business. NOLs that may be carried forward may also add value to the business, especially if viewed as an asset that will reduce future tax liability as business conditions improve. Taxpayers will need to follow the appropriate steps to determine whether they may claim an NOL, calculate the NOL amount, and apply the carryover rules (both carryback and carryforward) to take the NOL in another year (generally 2 to 10 years before the loss year; up to 20 years after the loss year), so that they can claim a refund.

Proper accounting becomes crucial to determine the NOL amount. Taxpayers must distinguish between financial accounting and tax accounting and take advantage of the differences. Regardless of whether the taxpayer has suffered an economic loss, proper tax accounting may generate a tax loss. Businesses (as well as other taxpayers) who understand the benefits of NOLs are in a good position to make the most of their tax deductions and losses.

CPE NOTE: When you have completed your study and review of chapters 6-8, which comprise Module 3, you may wish to take the Quizzer for this Module.

Go to **CCHGroup.com/PrintCPE** to take this Quizzer online.

MODULE 4 — CHANGING LEGISLATIVE LANDSCAPE — CHAPTER 9

Health Care Reform Moves Forward

Since enactment of the *Patient Protection and Affordable Care Act* (PPACA) and its companion law, the *Health Care and Education Reconciliation Act of 2010* (both referred to as the Affordable Care Act in this chapter), health care policy has featured prominently, both at a national level and around kitchen tables. In June 2012, the United States Supreme Court upheld the Affordable Care Act, which allows the law to move forward. Individuals, employers, and taxpayers of all types must prepare for implementation of the act. This chapter explores some of the tax provisions in the Affordable Care Act that impact individuals and businesses.

LEARNING OBJECTIVES

Upon completion of this chapter, you will be able to:

- Understand the tax basics of the U.S. Supreme Court's decision in *National Federation of Independent Business, et al. v. Sebelius* (2012-2 USTC 50,423), which upheld the Affordable Care Act (except for certain provisions related to the expansion of Medicaid);
- Describe the individual shared responsibility provisions (individual mandate) in the Affordable Care Act;
- Understand the employer shared responsibility provisions (employer mandate) in the Affordable Care Act;
- Describe the Code Sec. 36B premium assistance tax credit;
- Determine qualifications for the Code Sec. 45R small employer health insurance tax credit
- Identify certain changes made to health flexible spending arrangements (health FSAs) by the Affordable Care Act;
- List provisions, exemptions, and safe harbor terms of the medical device excise tax imposed by the Affordable Care Act;
- Delineate types of drugs subject to and exempted from the Affordable Care Act's branded prescription drug fee; and
- Identify new reporting requirements for certain employers and plan sponsors under the Affordable Care Act.

INTRODUCTION

In 2010, Congress passed and President Obama signed a sweeping overhaul of the nation's health care system: the *Patient Protection and Affordable Care Act* and its companion law, the *Health Care and Education Reconciliation Act of 2010* (commonly referred to as the Affordable

Care Act). Contributing to the complexity of the Affordable Care Act are the various effective dates for many of its provisions, especially tax provisions. In some cases, the changes in the Affordable Care Act took place immediately; in many other cases, the changes in the Affordable Care Act are scheduled to take effect after 2012.

> **NOTE**
>
> The Affordable Care Act comprises more than 1,900 pages. This chapter is not intended to address every change made by the Affordable Care Act to the Internal Revenue Code or the nation's health care laws. Nor does it anticipate what Congress may change in future years. Rather, this chapter highlights some of the key tax-related provisions in the Affordable Care Act, as this law now stands, and how those provisions impact individuals and businesses.

COURT CHALLENGES TO THE AFFORDABLE CARE ACT

Almost immediately after President Obama signed the Affordable Care Act, legal challenges to the new law began. A number of states filed suit to overturn the act. Those states were later joined by the National Federation of Independent Business and other groups. In 2011, a federal district court in Florida ruled that the Affordable Care Act's individual mandate was unconstitutional. According to the district court, the individual mandate could not be severed from the Affordable Care Act, and therefore, the entire law had to be struck down. The Court of Appeals for the Eleventh Circuit subsequently upheld the district court's decision but found that that the individual mandate could be severed from the Affordable Care Act. The Eleventh Circuit struck down the individual mandate but left intact the other provisions of the Affordable Care Act. The U.S. Supreme Court agreed to hear an appeal of the Eleventh Circuit case.

Supreme Court's Decision

In March 2012, the U.S. Supreme Court heard three days of oral arguments about the Affordable Care Act. The Supreme Court asked the lawyers for the plaintiffs and the government to address several issues, namely:

- Whether the *Anti-Injunction Act* (Code Sec. 7421) applies;
- Whether the individual responsibility payment (individual mandate under Code Sec. 5000A) is a proper exercise of Congress' taxing power or its power under the Constitution's Commerce or Necessary and Proper Clauses; and
- Whether the Affordable Care Act's expansion of Medicaid exceeds the government's spending authority.

The Court also heard arguments about the viability of the Affordable Care Act without the individual mandate.

Majority opinion. On June 28, 2012, Chief Justice John Roberts announced the Supreme Court's decision (*National Federation of Independent Business, et al. v. Sebelius,* 2012-2 USTC ¶50,423). The Supreme Court, in a 5–4 ruling, upheld the Affordable Care Act (except for certain provisions affecting the expansion of Medicaid, discussed below). Justices Stephen Breyer, Ruth Bader Ginsburg, Elena Kagan, and Sonia Sotomayor joined Chief Justice Roberts in the majority opinion.

Writing for the majority, Justice Roberts explained:

> The most straightforward reading of the (individual) mandate is that it commands individuals to purchase insurance. If an individual does not maintain health insurance, the only consequence is that he must make an additional payment to the IRS when he pays his taxes. That, according to the government, means the mandate can be regarded as establishing a condition—not owning health insurance—that triggers a tax—the required payment to the IRS. Under that theory, the mandate is not a legal command to buy insurance. Rather, it makes going without insurance just another thing the Government taxes, like buying gasoline or earning income. And if the mandate is in effect just a tax hike on certain taxpayers who do not have health insurance, it may be within Congress's constitutional power to tax.

Justice Roberts further explained that the penalty that the Affordable Care Act imposes on those without health insurance "looks like a tax in many respects." The penalty would be paid when individuals file their federal income tax returns. He stated, "The requirement to pay is found in the Internal Revenue Code and enforced by the IRS."

COMMENT

Justice Roberts acknowledged that the penalty is intended to influence conduct. "Taxes that seek to influence conduct are nothing new. Today, federal and state taxes can compose more than half the retail price of cigarettes, not just to raise more money, but to encourage people to quit smoking."

Justice Roberts concluded:

> [The[Affordable Care Act's requirement that certain individuals pay a financial penalty for not obtaining health insurance may

reasonably be characterized as a tax. Because the Constitution permits such a tax, it is not our role to forbid it, or to pass upon its wisdom or fairness.

Dissent. Four justices—Justices Samuel Alito, Anthony Kennedy, Antonin Scalia, and Clarence Thomas—dissented from the majority's decision. The minority opinion stated:

> Our cases establish a clear line between a tax and a penalty: A tax is an enforced contribution to provide for the support of government; a penalty is an exaction imposed by statute as punishment for an unlawful act. In a few cases, this Court has held that a "tax" imposed upon private conduct was so onerous as to be in effect a penalty. But we have never held that a penalty imposed for violation of the law was so trivial as to be in effect a tax. We have never held that any exaction imposed for violation of the law is an exercise of Congress' taxing power—even when the statute calls it a tax, much less when (as here) the statute repeatedly calls it a penalty. When an act adopts the criteria of wrongdoing and then imposes a monetary penalty as the principal consequence on those who transgress its standard, it creates a regulatory penalty, not a tax, the dissenting justices would have found.

Medicaid. The U.S. Supreme Court also issued an important ruling on Medicaid in *National Federation of Independent Business et. al. v. Sebelius.* The Affordable Care Act generally requires states to expand Medicaid coverage to qualified individuals who are younger than age 65 with incomes up to 133 percent of the federal poverty level (FPL). The Affordable Care Act also requires states to maintain current Medicaid coverage levels through 2013 for adults and 2019 for children. Additionally, the Affordable Care Act requires that for states to obtain Medicaid matching funds, the states cannot make Medicaid eligibility standards, methodologies, or procedures more restrictive than those in effect on March 23, 2010 (the date of enactment of the Affordable Care Act).

The Supreme Court held that the federal government could not withhold existing federal Medicaid funding to force a state to extend Medicaid coverage to individuals whose income was less than 133 percent of the applicable federal poverty levels. The extension so exceeded the original parameters of the Medicaid program that states could not be considered to have voluntarily agreed to it at the time they agreed to participate in the Medicaid program. However, this provision could simply be severed from the remainder of Affordable Care Act, the Supreme Court held.

> **COMMENT**
>
> The Supreme Court's health care decision restrains the federal government's imposition of Medicaid expansion on the states. Although states are free to adopt the expanded requirements (and to accept some federal funding), the Supreme Court held that the federal government cannot punish recalcitrant states by eliminating existing Medicaid funding benefits to states that choose not to expand their program.

SHARED RESPONSIBILITY FOR INDIVIDUALS

The individual mandate in the Affordable Care Act was at the center of the litigation over the act's provisions. The words *individual mandate* do not appear in the Affordable Care Act. The law refers to a "shared responsibility payment" to be imposed on a monthly basis on applicable individuals who do not carry minimum essential health coverage for themselves and their dependents. The shared responsibility payment is effective for each month beginning after 2013. The payment also is subject to phase-in rules. Before a description of who is covered by the shared responsibility payment, it is necessary to convey what constitutes minimum essential coverage under the Affordable Care Act, as detailed in Figure 1's reprint of the definition under Code Sec. 5000A(f).

Figure 1. Affordable Care Act Description of Minimum Essential Coverage Under Code Sec. 5000A(f)
Code Sec. 5000A(f) as enacted by the Affordable Care Act defines minimum essential coverage as meaning any of the following:
(A) Coverage under—
(i)   the Medicare program under part A of title XVIII of the Social Security Act,
(ii) the Medicaid program under title XIX of the Social Security Act,
(iii) the CHIP program under title XXI of the Social Security Act,
(iv) medical coverage under chapter 55 of title 10, United States Code, including coverage under the TRICARE program;
(v)   a health care program under chapter 17 or 18 of title 38, United States Code, as determined by the Secretary of Veterans Affairs
(vi) a health plan under section 2504(e) of title 22, United States Code (relating to Peace Corps volunteers); or
(vii) the Nonappropriated Fund Health Benefits Program of the Department of Defense,
(B) Employer-sponsored plan: Coverage under an eligible employer-sponsored plan.
(C) Plans in the individual market: Coverage under a health plan offered in the individual market within a State.
(D) Grandfathered health plan: Coverage under a grandfathered health plan.
(E) Other coverage: Such other health benefits coverage, such as a State health benefits risk pool, as the Secretary of Health and Human Services, recognizes for purposes of Code Sec. 5000A(f).

> **COMMENT**
>
> Certain plans or coverage existing as of March 23, 2010 (the date of enactment of the Affordable Care Act), are subject to only some provisions of the PPACA. These plans are known as "grandfathered plans." The IRS, Department of Health and Human Services (HHS) and Department of Labor (DOL) issued regulations in 2010 and subsequently amended the regulations (TD 9506). The agencies explained that a group health plan or group or individual health insurance coverage is a grandfathered health plan with respect to individuals enrolled on March 23, 2010, regardless of whether an individual later renews the coverage. Additionally, a group health plan that provided coverage on March 23, 2010, generally is also a grandfathered health plan with respect to new employees (whether newly hired or newly enrolled) and their families that enroll in the grandfathered health plan after March 23, 2010.

Exempt Individuals

The Affordable Care Act's shared responsibility payment applies to applicable individuals. The term *applicable individual* is best understood first by referring to which taxpayers are excluded from the definition. The Affordable Care Act exempts the following certain individuals from the shared responsibility payment:

- Individuals who qualify for a religious conscience exemption;
- Individuals who are members of a health care sharing ministry;
- Individuals not lawfully present in the United States; and
- Incarcerated individuals.

In addition, the following persons who are applicable individuals are nevertheless exempt from the penalty for not having health insurance, or are deemed otherwise to have minimum essential coverage:

- Individuals who cannot afford coverage (subsidies may be available);
- Individuals covered by Medicaid, Medicare and certain other federal programs;
- Individuals who would suffer a hardship;
- Individuals who are members of a Native American tribe; and
- Individuals covered by qualified employer-sponsored plans.

Calculating the Payment

The taxpayer shared responsibility payment is calculated on a monthly basis. The payment is generally calculated by taking the greater of a flat dollar amount and a calculation based on a percentage of the taxpayer's household income, and is imposed on a monthly basis (one-twelfth per month of this "greater of" amount). The annual flat dollar amount is assessed per individual or dependent without coverage and is scheduled to be phased in over three years ($95 for 2014; $325 for 2015; and $695 in

2016 and subsequent years, indexed for inflation after 2016; one-half of these amounts for individuals under the age of 18). The flat dollar amount is compared to a percentage of the extent to which the taxpayer's household income exceeds the income tax filing threshold. The applicable percentage is 1 percent for 2014, 2 percent for 2015, and 2.5 percent for 2016 and subsequent years. The taxpayer's penalty is equal to the greater of the flat dollar amount or the percentage of household income. The amount cannot exceed the national average of the annual premiums of a "bronze level" health insurance plan offered through a health exchange.

COMMENT

The Affordable Care Act requires each state to establish an American Health Benefit Exchange and Small Business Health Options Program (SHOP Exchange) to provide qualified individuals and qualified small business employers access to health plans. Exchanges will have four levels of coverage: bronze, silver, gold, or platinum. In early 2012, the Department of Health and Human Services (HHS) reported that 34 states and the District of Columbia have received grants to fund their progress toward building exchanges. HHS also provided an exchange blueprint that states may use. If a state decides not to operate an exchange for its residents, HHS will operate a federally facilitated exchange (FFE).

Guidance Expected

As of the publication date of this course, the IRS has not issued guidance on the shared responsibility payment. The IRS announced in 2011 that it was deliberately refraining from issuing guidance until the Supreme Court decided the fate of the Affordable Care Act. Now that the Supreme Court has upheld the Affordable Care Act, the IRS is expected to issue guidance about the shared responsibility payment.

COMMENT

The Affordable Care Act would generally have required employers offering qualified health insurance to provide a free choice voucher to employees with incomes of less than 400 percent of federal poverty guidelines whose share of the premium exceeded 8 percent but was less than 9.8 percent of their income, and who chose to enroll in a plan in an exchange beginning in 2014. The amount of the free choice voucher generally would have been excluded from the employee's gross income. However, the *Department of Defense and Full-Year Continuing Appropriations Act, 2011,* repealed the free choice voucher provisions in the Affordable Care Act.

SHARED RESPONSIBILITY FOR EMPLOYERS

The Affordable Care Act also provides for shared responsibility for employers (Code Sec. 4980H)—the employer mandate—that is effective for months beginning after December 31, 2013.

Under Code Sec. 4980H, an applicable large employer is subject to a shared responsibility payment (an *assessable payment*) if any full-time or full-time-equivalent employee (FTE) is certified to receive an applicable premium tax credit or cost-sharing reduction payment, and:

- The employer does not offer to its FTEs and their dependents the opportunity to enroll in minimum essential coverage under an eligible employer-sponsored plan (Code Sec. 4980H(a)); or
- The employer offers its FTEs and their dependents the opportunity to enroll in minimum essential coverage under an eligible employer-sponsored plan that either is unaffordable relative to an employee's household income or does not provide minimum value (that is, that pays at least 60 percent of benefits) (Code Sec. 4980H(b)).

Applicable Large Employer

Under the Affordable Care Act, for purposes of the employer shared responsibility payment, an applicable large employer is an employer that on average employed 50 or more FTEs on business days during the preceding calendar year.

Calculating the Payment

Code Sec. 4980H(a). The applicable employer's assessable payment for failing to offer its full-term employees the opportunity to enroll in minimum essential coverage under an employer-sponsored health plan is equal to the product of the applicable payment amount, which is 1/12 of $2,000 for any month (that is, $166.67 per month) times the number of FTEs for the month. In computing the assessable payment, however, the number of the employer's FTEs for any month is reduced by 30. After 2014, the $2,000 amount will be adjusted for inflation.

Code Sec. 4980H(b). A large employer that does offer its employees a health plan providing minimum essential coverage but has one or more employees certified in a qualified health plan offered through a health insurance exchange with respect to which a premium tax credit or cost-sharing subsidy is allowed or paid for the employee is also subject to an assessable payment. In this case, the assessable payment is equal to the product of the number of the FTEs receiving the premium tax credit or cost-sharing subsidy for the month times an amount equal to 1/12 of $3,000 for any month (that is, $250 per month). After 2014, the $3,000 amount will be adjusted for inflation. However, the Affordable Care Act further provides that the aggregate amount of the assessable payment imposed in this case be capped. For any month, it is limited to the product of the "applicable payment amount" in this case (1/12 of $2,000 per month) and the number of all FTEs during that month. After 2014, the $2,000 amount will be adjusted for inflation. For purposes of this calculation, the number of FTEs for any month is reduced by 30.

Affordable Coverage

In Notice 2011-73, the IRS described what affordable coverage is for purposes of Code Sec. 4980H's shared responsibility for employers. Coverage under an employer-sponsored plan is affordable to an employee if the employee's required contribution to the plan does not exceed 9.5 percent of the employee's household income for the tax year. The percentage may be adjusted for inflation after 2014. An employee's household income is generally the employee's modified adjusted gross income (MAGI) and the MAGI(s) of his or her spouse and/or dependents who are required to file a federal income tax return.

Safe Harbor

An employer may not know the amount of an employee's household income. In this case, the IRS has indicated that it intends to develop a safe harbor whereby affordability for purposes of Code Sec. 4980H(b) would be measured by reference to an employee's wages from that employer. Wages would be the amount reported in Box 1 (wages, tips, and other compensation) of the employee's Form W-2.

Under Notice 2011-73, a couple of requirements must be satisfied for the proposed safe harbor:

- The employer must offer its FTEs and their dependents the opportunity to enroll in minimum essential coverage under an eligible employer-sponsored plan; and
- The employee portion of the self-only premium for the employer's lowest cost coverage that provides minimum value (the employee contribution) must not exceed 9.5 percent of the employee's W-2 wages.

In Notice 2011-73, the IRS explained that if an employer satisfies both of these requirements for a particular employee (as well as any other yet to be determined conditions for the safe harbor), the employer would not be subject to an assessable payment under Code Sec. 4890H(b) with respect to that particular employee. The safe harbor would be determined after the end of the calendar year. However, the IRS indicated that an applicable employer could use the safe harbor prospectively. Thus, an employer could structure its coverage plan so that the contribution from each employee would not exceed 9.5 percent for 2014 (adjusted for inflation after 2014) of the employee's W-2 wages.

CAUTION

The proposed safe harbor for Code Sec. 4980H(b) would only apply to Code Sec. 4980H(b) and not to the Code Sec. 36B premium assistance tax credit (discussed below), per IRS Notice 2011-73.

COMMENT

The IRS followed up Notice 2011-73 with Notice 2012-17. In Notice 2012-17, the IRS indicated:

Future guidance is expected to provide that, at least for the first three months following an employee's date of hire, an employer that sponsors a group health plan will not, by reason of failing to offer coverage to the employee under its plan during that three-month period, be subject to the employer shared responsibility. The guidance is also expected to provide that, in certain circumstances, employers have six months to determine whether a newly hired employee is an FTE and will not be subject to a shared responsibility payment during that six-month period with respect to that employee.

STUDY QUESTIONS

1. An employer's assessable payment under Code Sec. 4980H(a) applies to:

   a. Small employers that lack an employer-sponsored health plan
   b. Large employers that do not offer FTEs and dependents an opportunity to enroll in a plan with minimum essential coverage
   c. Large employers that offer plans unaffordable relative to employees' household income
   d. Large employers that offer plans that do not provide minimum value

2. The proposed safe harbor to avoid Code Sec. 4890H(b) assessable payments requires a large employer to:

   a. Offer FTEs and their dependents minimum essential coverage under an eligible employer-sponsored plan
   b. Offer free choice vouchers for employees and their dependents younger than age 26
   c. Offer bronze, silver, gold, and platinum levels of coverage
   d. Offer part-time employees the opportunity for coverage under the employer-sponsored health plan

CODE SEC. 36B PREMIUM ASSISTANCE TAX CREDIT

The Affordable Care Act provides a refundable tax credit (the Code Sec. 36B credit) to lower-income individuals to help them cover the cost of health insurance for themselves and their dependents. Beginning in 2014, eligible lower-income individuals who obtain coverage under a qualified health plan through an insurance exchange may qualify for the Code Sec. 36B premium assistance tax credit. However, lower-income individuals will not qualify for the Code Sec. 36B credit if they are eligible for other minimum essential coverage, including employer-sponsored coverage that is affordable and provides minimum value.

Eligibility for the Credit

The IRS issued regulations (TD 9590) on the Code Sec. 36B premium assistance tax credit in 2012. The IRS explained that:

> Eligibility for the Code Sec. 36B premium assistance tax credit is determined by the relationship of the taxpayer's household income to the federal poverty level (FPL). A taxpayer's household income for the tax year must be at least 100 percent but not more than 400 percent of the FPL for the taxpayer's family size. A taxpayer's family includes the individuals for whom the taxpayer claims a deduction for a personal exemption under Code Sec. 151 for the tax year.

Employer-Sponsored Coverage

The IRS regulations treat an employer-sponsored plan as affordable for an employee and related individuals if the portion of the annual premium the employee must pay for self-coverage does not exceed the required contribution percentage (9.5 percent for tax years beginning before January 1, 2015) of the taxpayer's household income.

EXAMPLE

In 2014, Renaldo Cruz has household income of $35,000. His employer, Marketo Salinas, offers its employees a health insurance plan that requires Renaldo to contribute $2,100 for self-only coverage for 2014 (which represents 6.0 percent of Renaldo's household income). Because Renaldo's required contribution for self-only coverage does not exceed 9.5 percent of household income for 2014, Marketo's plan is affordable for him and is deemed to provide minimum essential coverage. Therefore, Renaldo is not eligible for the Code Sec. 36B premium assistance tax credit.

> **COMMENT**
>
> In certain cases, an applicable large employer may be liable for an assessable payment if any FTE receives a Code Sec. 36B premium assistance tax credit. The assessable payment for applicable large employers is discussed later.

Advance Payment

The Code Sec. 36B premium assistance income tax credit is fully refundable (that is, it is payable irrespective of whether any tax is otherwise due for the year). Additionally, a taxpayer may qualify for an advance payment of the credit. The Treasury Department has indicated that it intends to transmit the advance payment directly to the insurer. The IRS is expected to issue guidance on advance payment of the Code Sec. 36B credit before 2014.

> **COMMENT**
>
> Because the PPACA is being implemented by multiple federal agencies, the statute authorizes the IRS to disclose return information to HHS and other agencies. Return information is scheduled to be disclosed for, among other purposes, eligibility for the Code Sec. 36B premium assistance tax credit. In NPRM REG-119632-11, the IRS explained that it will disclose taxpayer identity information, filing status, the number of individuals for which a deduction under Code Sec. 151 was allowed ("family size"), MAGI, and the tax year to which the information relates or, alternatively, that the information is not available. Where modified adjusted gross income is not available, the IRS will disclose adjusted gross income.

CODE SEC. 45R SMALL EMPLOYER HEALTH CARE CREDIT

The Affordable Care Act created the temporary Code Sec. 45R small employer health care credit. To be an eligible small employer for purposes of the credit:

- The employer must have fewer than 25 FTEs for the tax year;
- The average annual wages of its employees for the year must be less than $50,000 per FTE; and
- The employer must maintain a qualifying arrangement.

Small Employers

Employers with 10 or fewer FTEs paying average annual wages of not more than $25,000 may be eligible for a maximum credit of 35 percent for tax years beginning in 2010 through 2013. The maximum credit for tax-exempt employers is 25 percent for tax years beginning in 2010 through 2013. For tax years beginning in 2014 through 2015, the maximum credit climbs to 50 percent of qualified premium costs paid by for-profit employers (35 percent for tax-exempt employers). However, an employer may claim the credit after 2013 only if it offers one or more qualified health plans through a state insurance exchange.

> **EXAMPLE**
>
> ABC Co. (a for-profit employer) has 10 FTEs and pays average annual wages of $250,000 in tax year 2012. ABC's qualified employee health care costs for tax year 2012 are $70,000. ABC's Code Sec. 45R credit is $24,500 ($70,000 × 35 percent). If ABC was a tax-exempt employer with the same number of FTEs and the same amount of qualified employee health care costs, its Code Sec. 45R credit for tax year 2012 would be $17,500 ($70,000 ×25 percent)

Phaseout

The Code Sec. 45R credit is subject to phaseout rules. The credit is reduced by 6.667 percent for each FTE in excess of 10 employees. The credit is also reduced by 4 percent for each $1,000 that average annual compensation paid to the employees exceeds $25,000. This means that the credit completely phases out if an employer has 25 or more FTEs and pays $50,000 or more in average annual wages.

Full-time Equivalent Employees

To determine eligibility for the credit, employers have to calculate their number of FTEs. The number of an employer's FTEs is determined by dividing the total hours of service (but not more than 2,080 hours for any employee) by 2,080. The result, if not a whole number, is rounded to the next lowest whole number.

> **COMMENT**
>
> Congress selected 2,080 hours because 2,080 hours compose the number of hours in a 52-week assuming a 40-hour work week. Any hours beyond 2,080, such as overtime hours, are not taken into account when calculating FTEs.

Average Annual Wages

Employers also need to calculate average annual wages. The amount of average annual wages is determined by first dividing the total wages paid by the employer to employees during the employer's tax year by the number of the employer's FTEs for the year. The result is then rounded down to the nearest $1,000 (if not otherwise a multiple of $1,000).

Hours of Service

In Notice 2010-44, the IRS provided three methods that employers are permitted to use for calculating employees' hours of service for the tax year:

- Counting actual hours worked;
- Using a days-worked equivalency; or
- Using a weeks-worked equivalency.

In Notice 2010-82, the IRS explained that employers do not need to use the same method for all employees. Employers may apply different methods for different classifications of employees, if the classifications are reasonable and consistently applied. The IRS further clarified that an employer may change the method for calculating employees' hours of service for each tax year.

> **EXAMPLE**
>
> Serena worked 48 weeks, took 3 weeks of vacation, and 1 week of unpaid leave in tax year 2012. Serena's employer uses the weeks-worked equivalency method to calculate the total number of hours of service. Using this method, Serena would be credited with 2,040 hours of service (51 weeks × 40 hours per week).

> **COMMENT**
>
> The Affordable Care Act imposes some important limitations on the Code Sec. 45R credit. Employers must exclude certain individuals, including family members, from the calculation of FTEs and average annual wages.

Qualifying Arrangement

The Code Sec. 45R credit applies only to premiums paid by the employer under a qualifying arrangement. In Notice 2010-80, the IRS explained that a qualifying arrangement is an arrangement under which the employer pays premiums for each employee enrolled in health insurance coverage offered by the employer in an amount equal to a uniform percentage (not less than 50 percent) of the premium cost of the coverage. The cost of coverage also must exceed the cost of the average premium for the small group market in the employer's state.

> **COMMENT**
>
> A qualifying arrangement does not include plans that provide accident or disability income benefits, liability insurance, workers' compensation, automobile medical payments, on-site medical clinics, or credit-only insurance. A qualifying arrangement also excludes benefits provided by flexible spending accounts (FSAs), health savings accounts (HSAs), or health reimbursement accounts (HRAs).

Claiming the Credit

To calculate the credit:

- Small employers, whether for-profit or tax-exempt, use Form 8941, *Credit for Small Employer Health Insurance Premiums*;
- Businesses use Form 3800, *General Business Credit;* and
- Tax-exempt organizations use revised Form 990-T, *Exempt Organization Business Income Tax Return.*

Fiscal Year Taxpayers

The Code Sec. 45R credit is effective for tax years beginning after December 31, 2009. In Notice 2010-80, the IRS explained that if a taxpayer is a calendar year taxpayer, the credit first applies for the tax year beginning on January 1, 2010, and ending on December 31, 2010. If the taxpayer is a fiscal year taxpayer with a tax year beginning, for example, on July 1, 2010, the credit first applies for the tax year beginning on July 1, 2010, and ending on June 30, 2011.

HEALTH FLEXIBLE SPENDING ACCOUNTS

Health FSAs are popular savings vehicles for medical expenses. These are arrangements in which an amount is credited to an account from which an employee may be reimbursed for health care, dependent care, or other expenses that are excludable from gross income if paid by an employer. The account may be funded by employer contributions or by a salary reduction agreement.

New Contribution Limit

Effective for tax years beginning after December 31, 2012, the Affordable Care Act limits salary reduction contributions to health FSAs to $2,500, down from an overall $5,000 FSA limit available before 2013. The $2,500 limitation is adjusted annually for inflation for tax years beginning after December 31, 2013. In Notice 2012-40, the IRS provided guidance on the $2,500 limit on salary reduction contributions to health FSAs.

Plan years. The IRS explained that the $2,500 limit does not apply for plan years that begin before 2013. *Taxable year* in Code Sec. 125(i), the IRS further explained, refers to the plan year of the cafeteria plan. Accordingly, the $2,500 limit on health FSA salary reduction contributions applies on a plan year basis and is effective for plan years beginning after December 31, 2012.

> **COMMENT**
>
> A plan year may be changed only for a valid business purpose. A change from a calendar year to a fiscal year to delay application of the $2,500 cap is not a change for a valid business purpose, the IRS cautioned. If a cafeteria plan has a short plan year (of fewer than 12 months) that begins after 2012, the $2,500 limit must be prorated based on the number of months in that short plan year.

Amendment. A plan must be amended to reflect the $2,500 limit. A plan amendment may be adopted on or before December 31, 2014, with retroactive effect, as long as the plan has operated in accordance with the new limit, the IRS explained.

Flex credits. The $2,500 limit applies only to salary reduction contributions and not to employer nonelective contributions, or *flex credits*, which are subject to certain limitations. Generally, an employer may make flex credits available to an employee who is eligible to participate in the employer's cafeteria plan, to be used (at the employee's election) only for one or more qualified benefits.

Grace period. Some plans provide for a 2½-month grace period. Unused salary reduction contributions to a health FSA for the plan year that are carried over into the grace period do not count against the $2,500 limit applicable for the subsequent plan year, the IRS explained.

> **COMMENT**
>
> The $2,500 limit on salary reduction contributions to a health FSA applies on an employee-by-employee basis. The IRS explained that $2,500 (as indexed for inflation) is the maximum salary reduction contribution each employee may make for a plan year, regardless of the number of other individuals (for example, a spouse, dependents, or adult children whose medical expenses are reimbursable under the employee's health FSA.

Excess contributions. A plan may comply with the written plan requirements set forth under Notice 2012-40 that limit health FSA salary reduction contributions, but one or more employees nevertheless may erroneously be allowed to elect a salary reduction of more than $2,500 for a plan year. A plan will continue to be a Code Sec. 125 plan if, among other requirements, the error results from a reasonable mistake by the employer and is not due to willful neglect by the employer. Salary reduction contributions in excess of $2,500 must be paid to the employee and reported as wages.

Use-or-lose rule. Unused amounts in the health FSA are subject to a "use-or-lose" rule. The IRS reported it is revisiting the use-it-or-lose-it rule in light of the $2,500 limitation and requested comments on alternative approaches.

Over-the-Counter Medicines

The Affordable Care Act revised the scope of medical expenses covered by health FSAs. After December 31, 2010, expenses incurred for a medicine or drug are treated as a reimbursement for a medical expense only if the medicine or drug is a prescribed drug or insulin.

Exceptions. The limitation does not apply to items for medical care that are not medicines or drugs. Items such as crutches, supplies such as bandages, and diagnostic devices, such as blood sugar test kits, qualify for reimbursement by a health FSA if purchased after December 31, 2010.

> **EXAMPLE**
>
> Carla Sanchez contributes to a salary reduction health FSA maintained by her employer. In 2010, Carla used her health FSA dollars to purchase chlorpheniramine maleate (an allergy medication), which is available over-the-counter at her local drug store. After December 31, 2010, Carla cannot use her health FSA dollars to purchase chlorpheniramine maleate as an over-the-counter medication. However, Carla could use her health FSA dollars to purchase chlorpheniramine maleate if she obtained a prescription for the medicine.

> **COMMENT**
>
> The Affordable Care Act also increases the threshold to claim an itemized deduction for unreimbursed medical expenses from 7.5 percent of adjusted gross income (AGI) to 10 percent of AGI for tax years beginning after December 31, 2012. However, individuals (or their spouses) age 65 and older before the close of the tax year are exempt from the increased threshold, and the 7.5 percent threshold continues to apply until after 2016. As of the time this chapter was prepared, the IRS had not issued formal guidance on changes made to the medical deduction threshold by the Affordable Care Act.

> **COMMENT**
>
> The Affordable Care Act also made changes to HSAs, Archer medical savings accounts (Archer MSAs), and HRAs. The provisions of these changes are beyond the scope of this chapter.

INDOOR TANNING EXCISE TAX

The Affordable Care Act imposes an excise tax on indoor tanning services (Code Sec. 5000B). The 10 percent excise tax applies to indoor tanning services performed after June 30, 2010. Tanning salons are responsible for collecting the excise tax and paying over the tax on a quarterly basis. Tanning salons that fail to collect the tax from patrons are liable for the excise tax. In 2010, the IRS issued regulations (TD 9486) to implement the new 10 percent Code Sec. 5000B indoor tanning excise tax.

Indoor Tanning Service

An *indoor tanning service,* the IRS explained, is a "service employing any electronic product designed to incorporate one or more ultraviolet lamps and intended for the irradiation of an individual by ultraviolet radiation, with wavelengths in air between 200 and 400 nanometers, to induce skin tanning."

Phototherapy

The excise tax does not apply to phototherapy performed by a licensed medical professional. On its website, the IRS has explained that a *phototherapy service* is a "service which exposes an individual to specific wavelengths of light for the treatment of dermatological conditions, sleep disorders, seasonal affective disorder, or other psychiatric disorder, neonatal jaundice, wound healing, or other medical condition determined by a licensed medical professional to be treatable by exposing the individual to specific wavelengths of light."

Who Must Pay the Tax?

Liability for the Code Sec. 5000B excise tax is imposed at the time of payment for any indoor tanning service. Generally, the individual who pays for the indoor tanning service is deemed to be the person on whom the service is performed for purposes of collecting the tax. The provider of the indoor tanning service receiving a payment for such a service must collect and pay the tax. If the recipient of the indoor tanning service fails to pay the tax or the provider fails to collect the tax, the provider of the indoor tanning service must pay the tax. Full payment is due at the time the provider timely files Form 720, *Quarterly Federal Excise Tax Return.*

Other Services

A provider may offer indoor tanning services as part of a bundle of other services. In this case, the Code Sec. 5000B excise tax applies to that portion of the amount paid to the provider that is reasonably attributed to indoor tanning services. Additionally, other goods may be provided, such as protective eyewear, footwear, and towels. The cost of other goods may be excluded from the Code Sec. 5000B excise tax if they are separable, do not exceed the fair market value of such other goods and are shown in the exact amounts in the records pertaining to the indoor tanning service charge.

BRANDED PRESCRIPTION DRUG FEE

The Affordable Care Act imposes an annual fee on each covered entity engaged in the business of manufacturing or importing certain branded prescription drugs or biologics.

Branded Prescription Drugs

A *branded prescription drug* is any prescription drug whose application was submitted under Section 505 of the *Federal Food, Drug, and Cosmetic Act* (FD&C Act) or any biological product the license for which was submitted under Section 351(a) of the *Public Health Service Act.* Therefore, generic drugs are generally excluded.

Covered Entity

The Affordable Care Act provides that *covered entity* means any manufacturer or importer with gross receipts from branded prescription drug sales. In regulations (TD 9544), the IRS defined a *manufacturer or importer of a branded prescription drug* as "the person identified in the Labeler Code of the National Drug Code (NDC) for such a drug. The NDC is an identifier assigned by the FDA to a prescription drug. The Labeler Code is the first five numeric characters of the NDC or the first six numeric characters when the available five-character code combinations are exhausted."

Orphan Drug Sales

The Affordable Care Act excludes orphan drug sales from the definition of branded prescription drug sales. In regulations (TD 9544), the IRS defined *orphan drug*, subject to certain exceptions, as "any branded prescription drug for which any person claimed a Code Sec. 45C credit and that credit was allowed for any taxable year." An orphan drug also does not include any drug for which there has been a final assessment or court order disallowing the full Code Sec. 45C credit taken for the drug. "Additionally, an orphan drug does not include any drug for any sales year after the calendar year in which the FDA approved the drug for marketing for any indication other than the treatment of a rare disease or condition for which a Code Sec. 45C credit was allowed, regardless of whether a Code Sec. 45C credit was allowed for the drug either before, at the same time, or after this FDA approval," the IRS explained.

Annual Fee

Under the IRS regulations, each covered entity's *allocated fee* for any fee year "is equal to an amount that bears the same ratio to the applicable amount as the covered entity's branded prescription drug sales taken into account during the sales year bears to the aggregate branded prescription drug sales of all covered entities taken into account during the sales year." The applicable amounts for fee years are listed in Table 1.

Table 1. Amounts for Branded Prescription Drug Fee (by Year)

Fee Year	Applicable Amount
2011	$2.5 billion
2012	$2.8 billion
2013	$2.8 billion
2014	$3.0 billion
2015	$3.0 billion
2016	$3.0 billion
2017	$4.0 billion
2018	$4.1 billion
2019 and thereafter	$2.8 billion
Source: TD 9544, IRS	

A covered entity's branded prescription drug sales taken into account during any calendar year are given in Table 2.

Table 2. Percentage of Branded Prescription Drug Sales Considered for Annual Fee

Covered Entity's Branded Prescription Drug Sales During the Calendar Year	Percentage of Branded Prescription Drug Sales Taken into Account
Not more than $5 million	0%
More than $5 million but not more than $125 million	10%
More than $125 million but not more than $225 million	40%
More than $225 million but not more than $400 million	75%
More than $400 million	100%
Source: TD 9544, IRS.	

In Notice 2011-92, the IRS reported that for the 2012 fee year, the IRS plans to mail each covered entity a paper notice of its preliminary fee calculation by April 2, 2012. There is no tax return to be filed for the fee.

Refunds

The Affordable Care Act treats the branded prescription drug fee as an excise tax so that only civil actions for refund may be pursued under the procedures of Subtitle F. The fee may be assessed and collected without regard to the deficiency procedures of Code Secs. 6211-6216. The regulations provide that the IRS must assess the amount of the fee for any fee year within three years of September 30th of that fee year.

STUDY QUESTIONS

3. The Code Sec. 5000B indoor tanning excise tax:
   a. Is payable on the service's annual tax return
   b. Bundles the cost of tanning services with provision of any other goods or services
   c. Does not include phototherapy services performed by a licensed medical professional
   d. Is imposed at a rate of 25 percent of the cost of tanning services

4. The Affordable Care Act treats the branded prescription drug fee as a(n):
   a. Addition to tax
   b. Excise tax
   c. Penalty
   d. Discretionary payment

MEDICAL DEVICE EXCISE TAX

The Affordable Care Act imposes an excise tax under Code Sec. 4191 on the sale of certain medical devices by the manufacturer, producer, or importer of the device in an amount equal to 2.3 percent of the sale price. Generally, the manufacturer, producer, or importer is liable for the excise tax. The excise tax applies to sales of taxable medical devices after December 31, 2012.

Taxable Medical Device

In NPRM REG-113770-10, the IRS issued proposed regulations on the medical device excise tax, explaining that the Affordable Care Act links the definition of *taxable medical device* to the definition of *device* in the *Federal Food, Drug, and Cosmetic Act*. If a medical device is not listed with the Federal Drug Administration (FDA) but the FDA subsequently determines that the device should have been listed, the device will be deemed to be listed as of the date the FDA notifies the manufacturer or importer.

> **COMMENT**
>
> The FDA has issued classification regulations for more than 1,700 types of medical devices.

Retail exemption. Certain medical devices are exempted from the excise tax. These items include eyeglasses, contact lenses, and hearing aids. In the proposed regulations, the IRS provided a facts and circumstances approach to evaluating whether a taxable medical device is of a type that is generally purchased by the general public at retail for individual use. A device is considered to be of a type generally purchased by the general public at retail for individual use if:

- The device is regularly available for purchase and use by individual consumers who are not medical professionals; and
- The device's design demonstrates that it is not primarily intended for use in a medical institution or office, or by medical professionals.

Additionally, the IRS identified nonexclusive factors to help determine whether a device is regularly available for purchase by individuals who are not medical professionals. These factors include (not an exhaustive list) whether nonmedical professionals can purchase the device through retail businesses that sell items other than medical devices (such as supermarkets and drug stores) and whether the device can be used safely by a nonmedical professional.

Safe harbor. The IRS also provided a safe harbor in the proposed regulations, identifying certain categories of taxable medical devices that fall within the retail exemption.

EXAMPLE

Bandease manufactures adhesive bandages. Costsless sells the Bandease adhesive bandages to distributors Marketwise and NewMed, which, in turn, sell the bandages to medical institutions and offices, medical professionals, and retail establishments. The FDA requires manufacturers and importers of adhesive bandages to list the bandages as a device with the FDA. As a result, the IRS explained that the determination of whether Bandease adhesive bandages are devices of a type generally purchased by the general public at retail for individual use must be made on a facts and circumstances basis. Individual consumers who are not medical professionals can regularly purchase the adhesive bandages at drug stores, supermarkets, and other similar establishments, and can use the adhesive bandages safely and effectively for their intended medical purpose without training from a medical professional. Based on the totality of the facts and circumstances, the Bandease adhesive bandages are devices that are of a type that are generally purchased by the general public at retail for individual use, the IRS concluded in its regulations.

Taxable Event

In the proposed regulations, the IRS explained that the "excise tax attaches when the title to the taxable article passes from the manufacturer to the purchaser." The time at which title passes is "dependent upon the intention of the parties as gathered from the contract of sale and the attendant circumstances."

COMMENT

Under the proposed regulations, devices intended for use exclusively in veterinary medicine are not taxable medical devices for purposes of Code Sec. 4191.

NEW REPORTING REQUIREMENTS

The Affordable Care Act imposes new reporting requirements on employers and on sponsors of health insurance coverage. Small employers may qualify for a temporary abatement of reporting.

Form W-2 Reporting of Employer-Sponsored Health Coverage

Under the Affordable Care Act, employers are generally required to disclose the aggregate cost of applicable employer-sponsored coverage on an employee's Form W-2 for tax years beginning on or after January 1, 2011. Reporting is for informational purposes only. In Notice 2010-69, the IRS made reporting optional for all employers for 2011. In Notice 2012-9, the IRS provided transition relief for small employers.

Transition relief for small employers. In the case of the 2012 Forms W-2 (and Forms W-2 for later years unless and until further guidance is issued), an employer is not subject to the reporting requirement for any calendar year if the employer was required to file fewer than 250 Forms W-2 for the preceding calendar year, the IRS explained in Notice 2012-9:

> For this purpose, whether an employer is required to file fewer than 250 Forms W-2 for a calendar year is determined based on the Forms W-2 that employer would be required to file if it filed Forms W-2 to report all wages paid by that employer and without regard to the use of an agent under Section 3504.

The IRS has explained on its website that the transition relief also applies to:
- Multiemployer plans;
- Health reimbursement arrangements;
- Dental and vision plans that either are not integrated into another group health plan or give participants the choice of declining the coverage or electing it and paying an additional premium;
- Self-insured plans of employers not subject to COBRA continuation coverage or similar requirements;
- Employee assistance programs, on-site medical clinics, or wellness programs for which the employer does not charge a premium under COBRA continuation coverage or similar requirements; and
- Employers furnishing forms W-2 to employees who terminate before the end of a calendar year and request a form W-2 before the end of that year.

Applicable employer-sponsored coverage. *Applicable employer-sponsored coverage* for purposes of reporting of costs on Form W-2, the IRS explained in Notice 2012-9, applies with respect to any employee, coverage under any group health plan made available to the employee by an employer that is excludable from the employee's gross income under Code Sec. 106, or plan that would be so excludable if it were employer-provided coverage (within the meaning of Code Sec. 106). Coverage is treated as applicable employer-sponsored coverage regardless of whether the employer or employee pays for the coverage.

Applicable employer-sponsored coverage does *not* include:
- Coverage for long-term care;
- Coverage (whether through insurance or otherwise) described in Code Sec. 9832(c)(1) (other than subparagraph (g) thereof (coverage for on-site medical clinics));
- Coverage under a separate policy, certificate, or contract of insurance that provides benefits substantially all of which are for treatment of

the mouth (including any organ or structure within the mouth) or for treatment of the eye; and
- Coverage described in Code Sec. 9832(c)(3) the payment for which is not excludable from gross income and for which a deduction under code sec.162(l) is not allowable.

Form W-2. The aggregate reportable cost of employer-sponsored coverage to the employee is reported on Form W-2 in box 12 (deferred compensation and other compensation), using code DD.

Health Care Coverage Reporting

The Affordable Care Act requires every health insurance issuer, sponsor of a self-insured health plan, government agency that administers government-sponsored health insurance programs, and other entity that provides minimum essential coverage to file with the IRS annual return reporting information for each individual for whom minimum essential coverage is provided (known as Code Sec. 6055 reporting). Additionally, every applicable large employer within the meaning of Code Sec. 4980H (discussed above) that is required to meet the shared employer responsibility requirements of the Affordable Care Act during a calendar year must file a return with the IRS reporting the terms and conditions of the health care coverage provided to the employer's FTEs for the year (known as Code Sec. 6056 reporting).

Section 6055 reporting. Code Sec. 6055 generally requires that all information returns reporting minimum essential coverage must include:
- Name, address, and taxpayer identification number of the primary insured and each other individual covered under the policy or plan;
- Dates each individual was covered under minimum essential coverage during the calendar year;
- Whether the coverage is a qualified health plan offered through an exchange; and
- When the coverage is offered through an exchange, the amount (if any) of any advance payment of the Code Sec. 36B premium assistance tax credit.

Section 6056 reporting. An *applicable large employer* for purposes of Code Sec. 6056 is, with respect to a calendar year, an employer that employed an average of at least 50 FTEs on business days during the preceding calendar year. An exemption applies to employers whose workforce exceeds this 50-or-more FTE limit for 120 or fewer days during the calendar year, provided the employees in excess of 50 for the 120-day period are seasonal workers.

In Notice 2012-33, the IRS described the information that an applicable large employer must furnish to the agency. This includes:

- Name and employer identification number (EIN);
- Number of FTEs for each month of the calendar year; and
- Name, address, and taxpayer identification number of each employee and the months during which the FTE was covered under the employer's plan.

Plan years. The reporting requirements apply to calendar years beginning on or after January 1, 2014. The IRS issued guidance in 2012 in Notices 2012-32 and 2012-33, and reported that it intends to issue regulations about the reporting requirements and how sponsors and applicable large employers will file information returns.

> **COMMENT**
>
> Reporting under Code Sec. 6055 and Code Sec. 6056 is separate from reporting of health care coverage on an employee's Form W-2.

STUDY QUESTIONS

5. The medical device excise tax under Code Sec. 4191 will be applied to:

   a. Items regularly purchased by the general public
   b. Imported medical products
   c. Devices used in medical facilities or by medical professionals
   d. Devices used in veterinary medicine

6. *Applicable employer-sponsored coverage* reported on Form W-2 for employees includes:

   a. The aggregate cost of employer-sponsored health care plans
   b. Costs of providing long-term care plans
   c. Health plans provided by federally recognized Indian tribal governments
   d. Employers required to file fewer than 250 Forms *W-2 for the preceding year*

CONCLUSION

The Affordable Care Act represents a sea-change in the delivery of health care in the United States. After withstanding a constitutional challenge, the Affordable Care Act is on track to maintain its scheduled implementation. Some of the most controversial provisions, such as the individual mandate, will not be fully implemented until a future date. Nonetheless, taxpayers of all types must prepare for them.

Tax Reform: Policy and Proposals

It has been 26 years since President Ronald Reagan and the 99th Congress last reformed the U.S. tax code through the *Tax Reform Act of 1986* (P.L. 99-514). Subsequently, the U.S. tax code has slowly but surely acquired new layers of complexity as Congress inserts provisions, one after another, designed to benefit myriad special interests, social goals, or certain economic behavior. Although interest in tax reform has never abated, the 2012 election year has made it a rallying point for lawmakers from both parties. Lawmakers and taxpayers are also aware of the mounting series of challenges ranging from a growing federal deficit, decreasing tax revenues, and heated economic competition from the international business sector. Numerous proposals have emerged for addressing these issues through fundamental tax reform, and in many cases they involve a complete overhaul of the existing tax code. The enormity of such a task, however, means that final tax reform legislation may not be an effort that U.S. lawmakers will complete before debating a bit longer. This chapter presents some of the important issues relating to tax reform that are currently under consideration.

LEARNING OBJECTIVES

Upon completion of this course you will be able to:

- Name many possible reforms for corporate, small business, and individual taxation;
- Understand the obstacles and concerns facing policymakers and lawmakers in addressing tax reform;
- List the proposals currently under debate in Congressional committee as a possible framework for tax reform in 2013 and beyond; and
- Project certain "winners and losers," depending upon which reforms are approved.

INTRODUCTION

In the decades since the U.S. tax code was last comprehensively reformed in 1986, more than 15,000 changes have been made. The result is a tax law comprising so many tax deductions, credits, exemptions, and exclusions that compliance has become too burdensome for many taxpayers to achieve on their own. "A simpler, more transparent tax code will substantially reduce the estimated 6.1 billion hours and $163 billion that taxpayers spend on return preparation," said Nina Olson, national taxpayer advocate, during the January 20, 2011, House Ways and Means Committee Hearing that kicked off a series of similar hearings exploring fundamental tax reform. Her statement also highlighted the difficulty for the IRS of enforcing the complex tax code.

Reformers have also stated repeatedly that the U.S. tax system stifles businesses and job growth, and have pushed for an overhaul of the current system under which businesses are taxed. Many lawmakers, including House Ways and Committee Chair Dave Camp, R-Mich., warn that the high corporate tax rates and the tax on foreign income of American businesses deter profitable multinational corporations from setting up shop within our borders. Existing U.S. corporations that pay higher taxes are left with less capital to reinvest, innovate, and create jobs.

Both Democratic and Republican lawmakers are unified in the idea that the patchwork tax code is broken, but when it comes to deciding how reform should occur, bipartisan agreement has not yet been reached. Proposals have been advanced recently, however, that go far and beyond the habitual creation, extension, or elimination of tax preferences to effect change. Due to the budget deficit crisis, proposals that would have been considered "extreme" only a few years ago are encountering a legislative environment more receptive to significant tax reform. Many observers anticipate sweeping tax reform legislation will take place in 2013 or 2014.

Some plans for tax reform, such as that currently advocated by Congressman Dave Camp, include increasing revenue through government spending cuts and across-the-board tax cuts, which ideally would stimulate economic growth (and as a result increase income and tax revenue). The Obama Administration has also put forth its plan for business and individual tax reform in several published proposals including *The President's Framework for Business Tax Reform* (herein called the President's Framework), and indirectly through the National Commission on Fiscal Responsibility and Reform's (Deficit Commission's) ambitious December 2010 report, *The Moment of Truth: Report of the National Commission on Fiscal Responsibility and Reform.* Clearly, certain proposals are the result of political posturing that is expected to lessen following the November 2012 elections, after which common ground will be found to be in the interests of both parties.

Republican lawmakers have also presented reports on how to reduce the budget deficit and implement tax reform. An example would be the House Budget Committee's Fiscal Year 2012 report, *The Path to Prosperity,* which calls for two marginal tax rates, a top corporate basic rate of 25 percent, and rejection of President Obama's tax increase proposals.

The Senate Finance Committee, controlled by Democrats, and the House Ways and Means Committee, controlled by Republicans, explored a variety of issues related to fundamental tax reform during 2012. Both the committees have held a series of hearings on corporate, international, small business, and individual tax reform. Thus far the hearings have generated volumes of insightful testimony concerning what should be done, what should not be done, and what might happen with or without tax reform. The road ahead will not be a straight one, but tax reform is on everyone's mind, and the gathering consensus among experts is that reform is coming soon.

FUNDAMENTAL TAX REFORM: THE BUILDING BLOCKS

According to the Congressional Research Service Report, *Tax Reform: An Overview of Proposals in the 112th Congress* (December 9, 2011), there are two main routes for addressing the federal budget deficit through tax reform:

- Base-broadening; and
- Levying a new tax.

The idea is that these two methods will provide the government with new revenue that could allow Congress to reduce marginal tax rates. Effective and responsible tax reform requires that changes to the U.S. tax code be *revenue neutral.*) In other words, change that decreases tax revenue through lower tax rates, addition of tax expenditures, or other means must be accompanied by offsets for those revenue losses. Proposals should be structured so that the government will receive no fewer tax dollars than before the reforms. Once again, base-broadening and new taxes are suggested with this revenue neutrality in view.

Base-Broadening

Base-broadening, when used within the context of tax reform proposals, in essence means that the government would expand the number of taxpayers subject to tax on what income they make by eliminating or lowering many of the costly tax expenditures (deductions and credits) currently available. Examples of expensive tax expenditures that could be targeted during base-broadening tax reform include the deduction for home mortgage interest on owner-occupied residences and the deduction for property taxes on residences. Although these and other incentives are often popular among taxpayers, reformers argue that Congress should consider whether the costs exceed the benefits.

New Taxes

Some lawmakers have argued that revenue generated through a new tax, such as a consumption tax or environmental tax, could allow the retention of more tax expenditures and lower reductions in other tax expenditures. Three alternative new taxes that have been recently proposed are discussed here.

Value-added tax. A *value-added tax* (VAT) is a consumption tax on the value that a company adds to a product at each stage of production. The VAT is collected by each firm at every stage of production.

> **COMMENT**
>
> In 2010, most members of the U.S. Senate opposed a VAT. Republicans feared it would provide more revenue for the government to spend; Democrats viewed the VAT as a regressive tax. However, Robert Carroll, former U.S. Treasury deputy assistant secretary for tax analysis (Treasury's top economist), said a VAT would be a potential source of new revenue, and many countries have devised one. The issue is also whether a VAT would replace the income tax or only supplement it, albeit allowing for a reduction in income tax rates.

Retail sales tax. A *retail sales tax* is a consumption tax levied only at the retail stage. A federal retail tax would operate much the same way as a state sales tax. The retailer would collect and remit a specific percentage of the retail price of a good or service.

> **EXAMPLE**
>
> A few senators and representatives have tried over the years to enact a national sales tax in lieu of a federal income tax. The Fair Tax Act of 2011 (H.R. 25/Sen. 13) is the most recent incarnation and is currently before the 112th Congress. The Fair Tax Act would abolish the IRS, repeal the federal income tax and other taxes, and replace them with a 23-percent rate national sales tax to be administered primarily by the states. Although not viewed as having much traction in the extreme, the plan of pairing a national sales tax with a lower, more streamlined income tax system may attract a broader audience.

Environmental tax. *Environmental taxes* arguably provide the dual benefit of discouraging pollution and raising revenue. The most frequently discussed energy tax is a carbon tax that would be levied on the volume of carbon emitted pollutants. The Obama Administration is attempting to implement a cap and trade system, one in which large pollutant emitters could purchase "emissions permits" from other companies that use less than the cap amount.

Another alternative energy tax would be higher gasoline taxes, an increase which the Deficit Commission has supported.

Tax Committees and Proposals

The Deficit Commission's report. President Obama created the bipartisan National Commission on Fiscal Responsibility and Reform in 2010, chaired by Sen. Alan Simpson, R-Co., and Erskine Bowles, former chief of staff under President William Clinton. The Deficit Commission's December 2010 report, *The Moment of Truth*, outlined a six-part plan designed to reduce the federal deficit by almost $4 trillion by 2020. Tax reform as envisioned by the Deficit Commission would account for at least 20 percent of the $4 trillion reduction. The Deficit Commission plan aims to reduce, if not eliminate, $1.1 trillion in tax expenditures in the current tax code for individuals and businesses.

Congressman Dave Camp. In October 2011, the House Ways and Means Committee, and its chairman Dave Camp, R-Mich., released a discussion draft based on committee hearing testimony received up until that point. The draft outlined a territorial tax plan for international taxation and invited additional input from employers, workers, tax practitioners and other tax experts.

The President's Framework. Published in February 2012, *The President's Framework for Business Tax Reform* (President's Framework) contains a large number of general proposals that, according to the Obama administration, would make the tax code less complicated for businesses and increase the nation's competitiveness in the global economy. The resident's overall proposal included elimination of certain tax expenditures and subsidies, expansion of the corporate tax base, reduction of the corporate and small business tax rates, and a strengthened international tax system. According to the President's Framework, a reduction in the corporate tax rate would be fully paid for by repeal of business tax preferences.

> **COMMENT**
>
> Congressional reaction to the President's Framework was mixed. Democrats in Congress generally applauded it for laying out a plan to reduce the corporate tax rate, a proposal that enjoys bipartisan support in Congress. Republicans were less enthusiastic, although some GOP lawmakers said that the President's Framework could serve as a starting point for comprehensive tax reform.

Other plans. Other proposals for tax reform include presidential candidate Gov. Mitt Romney's tax plan, the House Budget Committee's Fiscal Year 2012 report, *The Path to Prosperity*, released in conjunction with its House Report 112-421, several legislative bills, and other plans formulated by academics. Most of these proposals, such as the flat-tax plan put forward by Hoover Institute economists Robert Hall and Alvin Rabushka, are unlikely to make it past both the House and Senate.

CORPORATE TAXATION

To many economists, corporate tax reform is necessary—regardless of whatever individual tax reforms follow suit—for several reasons. First, some supporters argue that a reduction in the corporate tax rate would increase after-tax corporate profits and therefore raise stock value, which would induce greater capital investment and job growth. Second, the developing international business community has produced a number of serious competitors for American businesses. All the member nations of the Organisation for Economic Cooperation and Development (OECD) have corporate tax rates that are lower than the U.S. rate. Thus, when companies are looking for a home in which to do business, they are ostensibly less likely to select the United States.

> **COMMENT**
>
> Japan's corporate tax rate was higher than the U.S. corporate rate until April 1, 2012, when Japan dropped its effective rate of 39.5 percent to an effective rate of 38.01 percent. The U.S. corporate rate of 35 percent, when combined with state and local taxes, results in an effective rate of 39.2 percent. Nevertheless, corporations in certain industries pay far less when measured by the effective tax rate (see below).

Comparing Corporate Tax Reform Proposals

Lowering the corporate tax rate. At the center of the President's Framework is the reduction in the top U.S. corporate tax rate (not including additions for state and local taxes) from 35 percent to 28 percent. The rate cut would be funded by repealing many business tax preferences and tax extenders, which could potentially include popular tax expenditures for accelerated depreciation, deductions for domestic production activities, research and development (R&D) credits and expensing, renewable energy incentives, the low-income housing tax credit, charitable deductions for corporations, and the LIFO inventory method.

Many Republican lawmakers support a lower corporate tax rate of 25 percent. Both Congressman Dave Camp and the *Path to Prosperity* proposal adopted by the House Budget Committee call for a maximum corporate rate of 25 percent. The Deficit Commission recommended a single corporate tax rate of between 23 and 29 percent.

A lower corporate tax rate arguably would place the United States on an equal (or better) footing with other OECD members throughout Europe and Asia. According to the OECD, the average 2012 corporate tax rate for the 34 developed countries is 25.4 percent. The OECD listed the current combined corporate tax rates (including state and local and/or excise taxes) for OECD members, shown in Table 1.

Table 1. Corporate Tax Rates of OECD Member Nations

Country	Tax Rate
Australia	30.0
Belgium	34.0
Canada	26.1
France	34.4
Korea	24.2
Germany	30.2
Israel	25.0
Mexico	30.0
Norway	28.0
United Kingdom	24.0
United States	39.2

Table 2 compares the tax rates according to industry types.

Table 2. Effective Actual Corporate Tax Rates by Selected Industry, 2007–2008*

Industry	Tax Rate
Construction	31%
Wholesale and Retail Trade	31%
Manufacturing	26%
Real Estate	23%
Transportation and Warehousing	19%
Mining	18%
Leasing	18%
Utilities	14%
*Source: U.S. Treasury, Office of Tax Analysis.	

Manufacturing. Proponents of tax reform are also concerned with promoting U.S. manufacturing. During a March 6, 2012, Senate Finance Committee hearing on tax reform and manufacturing, Sen. Orrin Hatch, R-UT., stated:

> For the year 2010, the manufacturing sector generated about $1.8 trillion in gross domestic product. The United States still has the world's largest manufacturing sector. If it were a separate economy, with its own GDP, the U.S. manufacturing sector would be the world's ninth largest economy.

The Deficit Commission and Republican proposals would simply lower the corporate tax rates in order to stimulate domestic manufacturing. The President's Framework, on the other hand, would expand the Code Sec. 199 deduction for domestic production activities to 10.7 percent. This would cut the tax rate for domestic manufacturers to an effective rate of 25 percent. Additionally, the Preisdent's Framework would increase the Code Sec. 199 deduction to an even higher level for "advanced manufacturing."

COMMENT

The president's FY 2013 budget proposes to exclude oil and gas taxpayers from the Code Sec. 199 deduction.

Business Tax Expenditures

In exchange for a lower corporate tax rate, businesses likely would have to give up many tax preferences. Treasury officials have indicated that for every tax preference retained, revenue would have to be raised elsewhere. Provisions that could face repeal in the face of business tax reform include ones described here.

LIFO. Under the last-in, first-out (LIFO) pricing method, inventory is taken at cost, but the items contained in the inventory are treated as being, first, those contained in the opening inventory, to the extent thereof, and second, those acquired during the tax year. The items deemed to be in the opening inventory are taken in order of acquisition, except for the first year in which the method is used. The President's Framework, among other reform and revenue raising proposals, would repeal the use of LIFO, which the administration noted would bring the U.S. in line with international financial reporting standards. Manufacturers holding inventory would be especially hurt by this rule.

Oil and gas tax preferences. Current tax preferences in this "fossil fuel" category, as listed in the president's FY 2013 budget, include:
- The enhanced oil recovery credit for eligible costs attributable to a qualified oil recovery project;
- Tax credit for oil and gas produced from marginal wells;
- Expensing of intangible drilling costs;
- Deduction for costs paid or incurred for any tertiary injectant used as part of a tertiary recovery method;
- Exception to passive loss limitations provided to working interests in oil and natural gas properties;
- The use of percentage depletion with respect to oil and gas wells; and
- Two-year amortization of independent producers' geological and geophysical expenditures (which would be increased to seven years).

Carried Interest. *Carried interest* is generally the share of any profits that the general partners of private equity and hedge funds receive as compensation or quasicompensation. Certain legislators consider this treatment to be a tax loophole and would tax carried interest as ordinary income. The President's Framework carries few details of the proposal to tax carried interest as ordinary income. For example, President Obama's FY 2013 budget includes a proposal to tax as ordinary income a partner's share of income on an investment services partnership interest (ISPI) in an investment partnership, regardless of the character of the income at the partnership level. Such income would not be eligible for tax rates that apply to long-term capital gains. The partner would be required to pay self-employment taxes on such income. Although the President's Framework does not provide for any exceptions for small partnerships, others would carve out such exceptions.

Life insurance. A number of reform proposals over the past years have targeted life insurance companies and products. One proposal would not allow interest deductions allocable to life insurance policies unless the contract is on an officer, director or employee who is at least a 20-percent owner of the business. The President's Framework would make other unspecified reforms to the treatment of insurance companies and products. The president's FY 2013 budget explains that purchases of life insurance by small businesses that depend heavily on the services of a 20 percent or more owner would be unaffected, but the funding of deductible interest expenses with tax-exempt or tax-deferred inside buildup would be curtailed.

Business Tax Extenders

A large number of business tax extenders expired after December 31, 2011, or (at press time) are scheduled to expire after December 31, 2012. Under the President's Framework and other proposals, apparently all of the business tax extenders would be allowed to expire except for the research tax credit. The extenders, by virtue of their temporary nature, are considered by many as the easiest hurdle that lawmakers could surmount on the way to tax reform. Eliminating some of these temporary tax preferences would enable lawmakers to enter into a more serious discussion of lowering tax rates. In addition, the act of lawmakers from both parties laying down certain special interest extenders may also foster a cooperative bipartisan dialogue leading to fundamental tax reform.

Research tax credit. The research tax credit provides a 20-percent credit for qualified research and experimentation expenditures above a base amount. An alternative simplified credit of 14 percent is also available to eligible taxpayers. The research credit expired after December 31, 2011, having been extended numerous times since its creation in 1981. The President's Framework would revive the research tax credit and make it permanent in order to give businesses a long-term incentive to reinvest in research and, as a consequence, increase the strength of the U.S. economy. The President's Framework would also increase the rate of the alternative simplified credit to 17 percent, thereby making the alternative form of the credit more attractive as well as providing a simpler method of filing for the credit.

> **COMMENT**
>
> The bipartisan Senate Greater Research Opportunities with Tax Help (GROWTH) Act (Sen. 1577) would also increase the research tax credit rate from 14 to 20 percent and make it permanent. Although introduced by Democratic Senator Baucus, the bill has seven Republican cosponsors.

International Tax System

As discussions have heated up over international tax reform, commentators have debated whether the United States should have a territorial tax system, a worldwide tax system or a combination of the two. The current system is a combination that theoretically taxes worldwide income, but defers (sometimes permanently) foreign-earned income that is not repatriated to the United States.

Congressman Dave Camp, the Deficit Commission report, and the Republican party leadership in general all support a move to a territorial tax system. A territorial system would tax U.S.-source profits of multinational corporations but would exempt profits earned abroad, whereas a worldwide system would tax all income, wherever derived. President Obama, in contrast, has come out strongly in favor of a worldwide tax system in which U.S. companies generally pay taxes on their worldwide income, but with certain deferment of foreign-source income. Changing from a worldwide to a territorial tax system would also create "winners and losers," even if a transition period accompanied the change. Concern over use of current foreign tax credit carryovers, for example, has been raised as a major issue if the international system changes too abruptly.

COMMENT

According to the Treasury Department, a purely territorial system would aggravate many of the problems of the current tax code. If foreign earnings of U.S. multinational companies are not taxed at all, for instance, these firms would have greater incentive to locate operations overseas or use accounting mechanisms to shift profits out of the United States. Shifting profits abroad would also erode the U.S. tax base, requiring that more taxes be collected from U.S. taxpayers, according to the Treasury Department.

Minimum tax on overseas profits. The President's Framework describes subjecting income earned by foreign subsidiaries of U.S. corporations to an unspecified minimum tax. Foreign income deferred in a low-tax jurisdiction would be subject to immediate U.S. taxation up to the minimum tax rate. To avoid double taxation, a U.S. corporation would be entitled to a foreign tax credit for income taxes paid to the host country.

COMMENT

Congressman Camp's plan would exempt 95 percent of certain foreign-source income from U.S. tax. The exemption applies to dividends paid by foreign companies to U.S. corporate shareholders owning at least 10 percent of the shares. It also would apply to capital gains from sales of shares in foreign companies by 10-percent U.S. corporate shareholders. Thus, the effective U.S. tax rate on most foreign dividends would be 1.25 percent.

Incentives for returning/retaining U.S. jobs. There is a large consensus among lawmakers that the U.S. tax code, with its higher corporate tax rates, complexity of business provisions, and its worldwide tax on U.S. profits, has deterred U.S. business growth. It has created a disincentive for U.S. companies to repatriate foreign-source income and an incentive for U.S. companies to transfer intangible assets (patents, for example) to low-tax foreign jurisdictions such as Ireland or the Netherlands.

Several tax reform proposals include possible means of ameliorating this lockout effect, whether through implementing a territorial tax system, simplifying the tax code, and lowering rates, or in a less sweeping way through a tax credit. For example, the President's Framework proposed to give qualified taxpayers a 20 percent tax credit for the expense of moving operations back to the United States and also to deny a tax deduction for any business expenses incurred in moving operations overseas. The President's Framework would also add a disincentive to U.S. companies for transferring intangible assets to low-tax jurisdictions. It would tax the excess profits associated with this type of shifting and collaterally reduce the benefits from certain transfer-pricing rules that U.S. businesses have traditionally used to transfer profits overseas.

COMMENT

In summer 2012 the Senate introduced the Bring Jobs Home Bill (Sen. 3364), which provided for the tax credit and elimination of the business expense deduction for overseas relocation costs. However, on July 19, the bill failed to advance after a 56 to 42 procedural test vote essentially killed the measure.

STUDY QUESTION

1. All of the following are disincentives for companies to locate in the United States *except:*

   a. Tax on the worldwide income of U.S. companies
   b. Transfer-pricing rules for transferring profits overseas
   c. The complexity of business tax provisions
   d. The high corporate tax rate

SMALL BUSINESS TAXATION

Small businesses, like corporations, want lower tax rates. At an August 2, 2012 House Ways and Means Committee hearing, several experts testified that small business profits were overwhelmingly reinvested in the business. As such, they supported lower tax rates that would increase profit margins, and—in the short term—an extension of all the Bush-era tax cuts. A simpler tax code, they added, would reduce resources expended on tax planning and result in greater investment.

The desire to lower tax rates for all business entities, not just those taxable as regular C corporations raises the issue of whether corporate tax reform can move forward without simultaneously coordinating with individual tax reform. Many businesses operate as passthrough entities—S corporations, partnerships, LLCs, or sole proprietorships—under which business owners are taxed as individuals under their own individual tax rates.

Proposed Tax Reforms

Apart from proposals to lower the tax rates for small businesses, some of the more frequently appearing proposals for reform of small business taxation include ones described here.

Extending 100 percent expensing. Businesses are generally required to divide certain business expenses (such as those for capital equipment) and deduct them over a set period. For investments placed in service between September 9, 2010 and December 31, 2011, however, Congress temporarily increased the amount of expensing to 100 percent. If tax reform made 100 percent expensing permanent, small businesses could immediately recover all costs and reinvest in their businesses.

Lowering of the income tax rate for passthrough income. Small business taxpayers, like their corporate counterparts, want lower tax rates. Ostensibly this would allow businesses to pay a lower portion of their profits to the government and allow organizations to reinvest that money in the company. This reform might also, however, come at the expense of many popular tax expenditures.

Eliminating estate taxes. Many small businesses are owned by families or closely held among a small number of people. Thus, the death of one owner may significantly impact business operations and/or division of assets. Consequently, small businesses must plan for the estate tax if they want to keep the business operating after the death or retirement of their owner. Elimination of the estate tax would protect the future of small businesses and their assets.

Issuing definitive rules on independent contractor status. Misclassifying a worker's status has serious consequences for employers including severe penalties. Some employers may misclassify their workers on purpose in order to avoid the employment taxes associated with employees. However, many small businesses that misclassified workers have done so because of uncertainty about the workers' true status. The IRS relies on 20 factors in a common law test to determine whether a worker is an employee or an independent contractor. Small businesses have supported a clarification of the worker classification rules to improve tax planning.

Repealing the alternative minimum tax. Business profits may become subject to the alternative minimum tax (AMT). The Deficit Commission and the House Budget Committee Report all support the repeal of the AMT, which requires a patch every year so that the exemptions for individual taxpayers do not fall drastically. Because noncorporate business income is taxed at the individual's rate, a proposed AMT repeal would arguably benefit small businesses by eliminating both an unnecessary level of complexity from their tax planning and compliance attempts as well as a potential tax increase.

> **COMMENT**
>
> When enacted more than three decades ago, the AMT parallel tax system was intended to affect only a small number of high-income taxpayers who had previously been able to reduce their taxable income by claiming large itemized deductions and other tax preferences. Inflation, however, has increased taxpayer incomes, so that contrary to its original purpose, the AMT is capable of capturing middle-income taxpayers.

> **COMMENT**
>
> The corporate AMT, on the other hand, affects few corporations and brings in relatively little revenue when compared to the regular corporate tax. Proponents of a repeal of the corporate AMT argue that it is an inefficient means of generating revenue and that the compliance burden on corporate taxpayers far outweighs its benefits.

Establishing Parity Among Business Forms

Whereas the primary vehicle for business was once the corporate entity, U.S. businesses regardless of size have increasingly taken advantage of alternate business forms: partnerships, limited liability firms, sole proprietorships, and S corporations. Such structures are *passthrough entities* that today they make up 95 percent of all U.S. businesses. Passthrough entities offer greater legal protection to officers and directors without subjecting the company to a double taxation of corporate profits and dividends (taxed to shareholders after being distributed). Passthroughs are also taxed at individual income tax rates, meaning they are often taxed far below the corporate rate. Some lawmakers have stated the tax benefits discourage U.S. businesses from going public.

Proposals have been introduced to achieve at least some degree of parity between corporate business forms and noncorporate ones to discourage businesses from using non-corporate forms merely to avoid the corporate income. So far, these proposals for the most part have been thin on details. The President's Framework, for example, does not describe how parity would be accomplished (for example, by eliminating the double tax on corporate income), but specifies in a broad statement that any negative changes should not affect small businesses.

STUDY QUESTION

> **2.** Small businesses favor tax reforms that would:
>
> **a.** Raise the alternative minimum tax applied to corporations
> **b.** Increase the number of factors that may be used to classify workers as employees versus independent contractors
> **c.** Make 100-percent expensing of business equipment permanent
> **d.** Raise the maximum estate value for triggering the estate tax

INDIVIDUAL TAXATION

Individuals as well as businesses are increasingly affected by the impermanent nature of the tax provisions enacted for their benefit. Tax uncertainty and complexity means that most individuals must hire a tax professional in order to complete their income taxes and plan for the next tax year. Douglas Shulman, the IRS Commissioner, said during a speech at the National Press Club in Washington in April 2012 that 9 out of 10 taxpayers hire a tax professional or purchase software to aid them in their tax return preparation. Complexity has a negative effect on compliance and the IRS's ability to enforce the tax code, which has contributed to the estimated $385 billion net tax gap reported between what taxpayers may owe and what is collected.

Lowering Income Tax Rates

Some urge lawmakers to simplify the tax code and ease taxpayer burden by lowering the marginal tax rate and eliminating many of the current deductions and credits in return. For example, on May 17, 2012, Congressman Dave Camp addressed a legislative policy seminar on tax and budget issues held by the Washington-based Federal Policy Group. Camp urged that tax reform should collapse the six individual tax rates—now 10, 15, 25, 28, 33, and 35 percent—to just two rates—10 percent and 25 percent. This proposal somewhat mirrors the proposal put forward in July 2011 by the so-called Gang of Six.

COMMENT

In July 11 the Gang of Six, or the bipartisan group of senators led most recently by Sen. Mark Warner, D-Va., and Sen. Saxby Chambliss, R-Ga., proposed a solution to the U.S. debt ceiling crisis that included tax reform. The senators would have replaced the current individual marginal income tax rate schedule with three new tax brackets, with the ranges 8–12 percent, 14–22 percent, and 23–29 percent. The group also would have abolished the AMT. In return for lower tax rates and no AMT, the Gang of Six would have reduced an unspecified number of tax expenditures, possibly including the home mortgage interest deduction, the deduction for charitable contributions, and the deduction for certain medical expenses.

Under another, similar scenario, the Deficit Commission's plan would impose three ordinary income tax rates as low as 8, 14, and 23 percent. The plan would treat capital gains and dividends as ordinary income, but ordinary income rates would be lower.

Alternative Minimum Tax

Many have complained that the AMT represents an ineffectual means of curtailing the use of certain tax preferences and that the purpose of the AMT can be fulfilled within the regular tax system. As such, many proposals for tax reform, including those put forward by the Deficit Commission and Congressman Dave Camp, call for the elimination of this parallel system for individuals as well as small businesses with taxes paid at the individuals' rate.

Tax Expenditures

There are more than 200 tax expenditures according to the Joint Committee on Taxation's January 2012 list (JCS-1-12), and the sum of the estimated revenue loss due to tax expenditures was over $1 trillion in 2010. Tax expenditures are often aimed at policy goals similar to those of federal spending programs. Existing tax expenditures, for example, help students and families finance higher education and provide incentives for people to save for retirement. Because tax expenditures result in forgone revenue for the government, they have a significant effect on overall tax rates—all else being equal, for any given level of revenue, tax expenditures mean that overall tax rates must be higher than a tax system with no tax expenditures.

The largest 20 tax expenditures, listed in the March 22, 2012 report by the Congressional Research Service (CRS Report, March 22, 2012, "The Challenge of Individual Income Tax Reform"), include:

- Exclusion of employer health insurance;
- Exclusion of employer pensions;
- Mortgage interest deduction;

- Exclusion of Medicare;
- Capital gains rates;
- Earned income credit;
- Deduction of income taxes;
- Exclusion at death/gift carryover;
- Deduction of charitable contributions;
- Employer cafeteria plans;
- Tax-exempt/tax-credit bonds;
- Exclusion of Social Security benefits;
- Exclusion of capital gains on housing;
- Deduction of property taxes;
- Deduction of medical expenditures;
- Individual retirement accounts (IRAs);
- Child credit;
- Accelerated depreciation; and
- Exclusion of foreign earned income.

COMMENT

Some have also argued that tax expenditures are regressive, meaning they benefit higher-income taxpayers more than lower-income taxpayers. This is because taxpayers in the 35 percent bracket would receive a 35 cent tax reduction if they used a deduction or credit to reduce their taxable income by $1. Lower-income taxpayers in the 15 percent bracket would only reduce their tax by 15 cents per $1 deducted from their taxable income.

The Deficit Commission's proposal has included limiting the charitable deduction for individuals to a 12-percent tax credit for amounts over 2 percent of adjusted gross income; repealing the state and local tax deduction for individuals; repealing all miscellaneous itemized deductions for individuals, and capping the income tax exclusion for employer-provided health insurance.

Others argue that tax revenues would be raised as the result of the economic prosperity that would come with lower tax rates, therefore eliminating the need for making significant reductions in tax expenditures. Many, however, have opposed this strategy of lowering the individual marginal rates and eliminating popular tax expenditures. Some express concern that an across-the-board reduction in the marginal rate for individuals would eliminate many tax expenditures that currently benefit lower and middle-income taxpayers. They argue that lower rates would create a more regressive tax system under which wealthy taxpayers with greater income (and thus greater ability to pay a larger percentage to the federal government) would derive more benefit than lower and middle-class taxpayers.

Although the Deficit Commission's proposal calls for a dramatic reduction in the number of tax expenditures, it also recognized that some tax expenditures serve important functions that should be preserved, and that elimination or reforms of other tax expenditures should be phased in gradually to avoid adverse consequences or an overly progressive tax system. In fact, the commission called for tax reform to include provisions providing support for low income workers and families, mortgage interest for principal residences, employer-provided health insurance, charitable giving, and retirement savings in a manner that is better targeted and less expensive than the provisions in the current code.

Specifically, the Deficit Commission proposal warned against eliminating all tax expenditures. It stated that a new tax code should still include provisions (in some cases permanent, in others temporary) including:

- Support for low-income workers and families (e.g., the child credit and earned income tax credit);
- Mortgage interest for principal residences;
- Employer-provided health insurance;
- Charitable giving; and
- Retirement savings and pensions.

Charitable deductions. The Senate Finance Committee in October 2011 turned to potential reform of charitable giving tax incentives as lawmakers began to weigh budget pressures against the current charitable contributions deduction. Although there is no clear consensus at this point, proposals generally fall into four categories:

- Capping the amount of the deduction;
- Establishing a floor underneath the deduction;
- Converting the deduction to a credit; and
- Replacing the deduction with matching grants paid directly by the government to the Code Sec. 501(c)(3) organization.

The Obama Administration proposes to cap the itemized deduction for contributions at 28 percent under the current rate structure, but some studies indicate that the cap would lead to a drop in total charitable giving of $6 billion. In addition to curbing the deduction, proposals have been made to convert it to a nonrefundable tax credit.

> **COMMENT**
>
> The Deficit Commission proposed a 12 percent nonrefundable tax credit for all taxpayers on contributions that exceed 2 percent of AGI in lieu of the current itemized deduction for charitable contributions.

Retirement planning. At an April 18, 2012, the House Ways and Means Committee hearing experts testified that the current system in place for incentivizing retirement savings through tax expenditures was working. They cautioned lawmakers against altering the deductions currently available to employers and workers who can claim deductions for wages set aside in retirement accounts through means including 401(k) plans and IRAs.

> **COMMENT**
>
> The Deficit Commission had proposed to consolidate all retirement accounts, cap tax-preferred contributions to the lower of $20,000 or 20 percent of a taxpayer's income, and to expand the availability of the saver's credit.

Home mortgage interest deduction. The Deficit Commission would repeal the mortgage interest deduction and replace it with a nonrefundable tax credit for all taxpayers of 12 percent of the interest paid on a mortgage of up to $500,000 in value. The proposal would not provide a credit for home equity loans or a mortgage that is not on a principal residence.

> **COMMENT**
>
> The home mortgage interest deduction is an example of how the federal government can use a tax expenditure to promote a social goal, namely home ownership. However, it is available only to taxpayers who elect to itemize their miscellaneous deductions rather than take the standard deduction. This is only 30 percent of taxpayers, whereas more than two-thirds of taxpayers own homes. Further, because wealthier taxpayers have more expensive homes and therefore may pay more interest on their mortgages, the value of the deduction generally increases alongside the taxpayer's income. This is arguably a regressive policy because it disproportionately promotes home ownership for the wealthy.

STUDY QUESTION

> **3.** Experts, lawmakers, and policy makers have argued that negative outcomes of an across-the-board reduction in the individual tax rates could include all *except*:
>
> **a.** Creation of a more regressive tax system with fewer tax deductions and credits
> **b.** The need to create even more tax deductions and credits
> **c.** Disincentives for higher-income individuals to make charitable contributions
> **d.** Disincentives for retirement saving

CONCLUSION

There is a growing momentum for U.S. tax reform, although it has been slow-going given the 2012 political environment that featured both a presidential and congressional election year. Nevertheless, 2012 saw numerous congressional hearings on the important issues of tax rate reform: corporate and international, business, individual. The president and other lawmakers have put forth their suggestions, with varying specificity. An encouraging thought is that many of the proposals share similar features; for example, they all agree that the current corporate tax rate must be reduced. In the near future, lawmakers must move beyond proposals and begin working toward a real consensus on what the corporate rate should be, how to offset the revenue loss, and whether reform can be accomplished through base broadening or if discussions must also include a new consumption tax such as a VAT. But lawmakers should also look beyond balancing the budget in reforming the tax code and consider important aspects such as equity of tax burden and simplification of compliance.

The shape and scale of the coming tax reform will largely depend on whether the November elections bring one party into firm control of the White House and Congress or if they maintain the current political stalemate. But although tax reform may not arrive by the end of 2012, it is on everyone's agenda. It is only a matter of time.

CPE NOTE: When you have completed your study and review of chapters 9–10, which comprise Module 4, you may wish to take the Quizzer for this Module.

Go to **CCHGroup.com/PrintCPE** to take this Quizzer online.

TOP FEDERAL TAX ISSUES FOR 2013 CPE COURSE

Answers to Study Questions

MODULE 1 — CHAPTER 1

1. a. *Incorrect.* A four-year period was the former requirement, before regulations were issued.

b. *Correct.* The final regulations provide a five-year test ending with the tax year tested.

c. *Incorrect.* The final regulations, which became effective on September 8, 2011, provide a different requirement for testing, with some transition relief.

d. *Incorrect.* The redesigned Form 990 and tax code continue the requirement that a Code Sec. 501(c)(3) organization pass the public support test.

2. a. *Correct.* A small exempt organization must provide a summary of its mission or most significant activities on a Form 990, not the Form 990-N.

b. *Incorrect.* The e-postcard requires an organization to provide its website address.

c. *Incorrect.* The name and address of an organization's principal officer must be disclosed on the Form 990-N.

d. *Incorrect.* Form 990-N requires organizations to report any other names by which they are known or that they use.

3. a. *Incorrect.* The Auto-Revocation list is one of three search sites consolidated in the Exempt Organizations Select Check.

b. *Incorrect.* Searching for Forms 990-N can be done on the search tool.

c. *Correct.* The online tool does not provide information if an organization has applied for exempt status.

d. *Incorrect.* The effective revocation date is included in the lists by Select Check.

4. a. *Correct.* Certain kinds of income from the ACO, including dividends, interest, and royalties, may be excluded from UBI under one of the modifications described in Code Sec. 512(b).

b. *Incorrect.* Dividends and interest are not taxable UBI under one of the modifications described in Code Sec. 512(b), so no comparable tax rate applies to royalties.

c. *Incorrect.* Charitable organizations may hold assets for use of which royalties may be paid.

d. *Incorrect.* The royalties need not be linked to the exempt organization's charitable purpose.

5. a. *Incorrect.* The new examples illustrate the breadth and flexibility of PRIs in current situations.

b. *Incorrect.* The regulation added new examples to, and do not replace, the standing examples from 1972.

c. *Correct.* The likelihood of a high rate of return does not prevent an investment from being a PRI.

d. *Incorrect.* A PRI is an investment whose primary purpose is to accomplish a charitable, religious, scientific, or other qualified purpose; thus, it is not considered a jeopardy investment.

6. a. *Correct.* Membership in AAA, an association of personal property appraisers, is not required.

b. *Incorrect.* The appraiser must be paid for appraisals, and he or she must do so regularly.

c. *Incorrect.* During the three-year period before the date of the appraisal, the appraiser must be allowed to practice before the IRS.

d. *Incorrect.* Pertinent education and experience in valuing the specific type of property are requirements for qualified appraisers.

MODULE 1 — CHAPTER 2

1. a. *Incorrect.* Any such annuity payment is a withholdable payment if its source is within the United States.

b. *Incorrect.* Interest and dividends from sources within the United States are withholdable payments triggering FATCA requirements.

c. *Incorrect.* Premiums paid from sources within the United States trigger FATCA requirements.

d. *Correct.* Such proceeds are an exception to the triggers of FATCA requirements.

2. a. *Correct.* Unless the FFI participates in an FFI agreement or is deemed compliant with the law, FATCA withholding rules apply.

b. *Incorrect.* Foreign government payments are exempt from the withholding requirements because the secretary of the U.S. Treasury has identified them as posing a low risk of tax evasion.

c. *Incorrect.* No withholding amount must be deducted from payments made on obligations existing on January 1, 2013.

d. *Incorrect.* The withholding rules do not apply when the withholding agent has no possibility of deducting the tax.

3. a. *Correct.* The IRS decided to require only an account's balance at year's end, not month's end.

b. Incorrect. Participating FFIs must report the TIN of each specified U.S. person or, for a U.S.-owned foreign entity, the TIN of U.S. persons who are substantial U.S. owners of the entity.

c. Incorrect. The IRS requires the participating FFI to report an account's year-end balance.

d. Incorrect. All payments made during the calendar year regarding the account must be reported by March 31 of the year following the reporting year.

4. a. Incorrect. Participating FFIs must report dormant accounts (those inactive under applicable laws, regulations or normal operating procedures) for recalcitrant account holders.

b. Correct. Corporate accounts are not considered one of the categories for separate reporting about recalcitrant account holders.

c. Incorrect. Accounts of other recalcitrant account holders must be reported by participating FFIs.

d. Incorrect. Accounts having indicators associated with United States persons are reportable to the IRS.

5. a. Incorrect. A local FFI is considered one of the categories of registered deemed-compliant FFIs.

b. Correct. The fixed place of business of a local FFI must be within its country of organization.

c. Incorrect. A registered deemed-compliant local FFI has no solicit account holders outside of its national borders.

d. Incorrect. A registered deemed-compliant local FFI must have 98 percent of its maintained accounts held by residents of its country of organization.

6. a. Correct. Each financial account (or expanded affiliate group member's account) must have a balance not exceeding $50,000.

b. Incorrect. The FFI's balance sheet may have up to $50 million in assets on its balance sheet.

c. Incorrect. The certified deemed-compliant FFI must accept deposits or hold financial assets for the accounts of others.

d. Incorrect. If an owner-documented FFI meets eligibility requirements regarding deposits, account maintenance, and a withholding agent, it may obtain deemed-compliant status.

MODULE 2 — CHAPTER 3

1. a. Incorrect. Although Code Sec. 6694(a) imposes higher standards for undisclosed tax positions of this type, the penalties apply if the return reflects an understatement of a client's tax liability that results from an undisclosed, nonabusive position for which the tax return preparer did not have substantial authority.

b. *Correct.* **Previously, the definition applied only to preparers of income tax returns.**

c. *Incorrect.* The traditional "one preparer per firm" changed under the act, which enables the IRS to advise multiple individuals that they may be primarily responsible. The Code Sec. 6694(b) penalty, however, is assessed against only against the primarily responsible tax return preparer.

d. *Incorrect.* The RTRP designation was not created until after the 2009 IRS study of preparer types.

2. a. *Correct.* **The reasonable basis standard applied by the IRS to disclosed tax positions is higher than the not frivolous or not patently improper standard but less stringent than the substantial authority standard or more likely than not standard.**

b. *Incorrect.* The more likely than not standard is more stringent than the standard applied under Code Sec. 6694(a) for disclosed tax positions. To avoid the penalty for an undisclosed position related to items such as tax shelters, the more likely than not standards apply to the position.

c. *Incorrect.* Adequate disclosure of a position disclosed on the taxpayer's return requires meeting a different standard under Code Sec. 6694(a).

d. *Incorrect.* Good faith is intent used to determine whether the reasonable cause exception applies. Good faith is not itself a standard.

3. a. *Correct.* **These factors are described in Notice 2009-5.**

b. *Incorrect.* The tax return preparer may not substantiate a tax position for a tax shelter merely because it has no prior precedent.

c. *Incorrect.* Merely advising the taxpayer of the standards is insufficient substantiation to avoid preparer penalty for holding a deemed an unreasonable tax position.

d. *Incorrect.* The absence of accuracy-related errors does not mean that the tax position is reasonable.

4. a. *Correct.* **The IRS must prove a preparer willfully attempted to understate the taxpayer's tax liability.**

b. *Incorrect.* The return preparer does not bear responsibility to prove that he or she did not willfully intend to understate the taxpayer's tax liability.

c. *Incorrect.* The return preparer's firm is not responsible for proving that the preparer's understatement of tax liability was willful.

d. *Incorrect.* The taxpayer is not responsible for proving that the return preparer made a willful attempt to understate the taxpayer's tax liability.

5. a. *Incorrect.* In the absence of willful neglect, the $50 per-failure penalty is not applied if the preparer substantiates the reasonable cause claim in writing.

b. Incorrect. Although a preparer's employer must retain records for each return preparer employed to comply with Code Sec. 6060, the $50 per-failure is not imposed if the failure was due to reasonable cause.

c. Incorrect. A tax return preparer's failure to retain a completed copy of returns or claims for refund (on paper or electronically) may not incur the Code Sec. 6695(d) penalty if the failure was not due to willful neglect.

d. Correct. The $500 per-check penalty has no reasonable cause exception.

6. a. Incorrect. The new requirements increase, not decrease, the due diligence measures that the return preparer performs in compliance with Code Sec. 6695(g).

b. Correct. The return preparer may not ignore the implications of information furnished to him or her and must make reasonable inquiries if the information appears to be incorrect, inconsistent, or incomplete.

c. Incorrect. Both the prior and new compliance requirements of Code Sec. 6695(g) involve completing the EIC worksheet in the Form 1040 instructions and Form 8867, *Paid Preparer's Earned Income Credit Checklist.*

d. Incorrect. The tax return preparer is not required to withhold his or her signature on the tax return if EIC eligibility concerns are raised under the Code Sec. 6695(g) due diligence requirements.

7. a. Incorrect. Registered tax return preparers may prepare and sign tax returns and claims for refund but do not have unlimited practice rights before the IRS.

b. Correct. Registered tax return preparers have limited practice rights before the IRS. RTRPs have the right to prepare and sign tax returns and claims for refund. RTRPs also may represent clients before revenue agents, customer service representatives, or similar officers and employees of the IRS (including the Taxpayer Advocate Service) during an examination if they signed the tax return or claim for refund for the tax period under examination.

c. Incorrect. Registered tax return preparers do not require assistance of these tax professionals when the preparers prepare and sign tax returns and claims for refund. RTRPs also may represent clients before revenue agents, customer service representatives, or similar officers and employees of the IRS (including the Taxpayer Advocate Service) during an examination if they signed the tax return or claim for refund for the tax period under examination.

d. Incorrect. The RTRP is not required to surrender taxpayer representation efforts to a CPA, attorney, or enrolled agent whenever a return is subject to examination by the IRS.

8. a. Incorrect. This supervision requirement applies to supervised preparer individuals, not RTRPs.

b. Incorrect. The RTRP must obtain a passing score on the RTRP examination.

c. Correct. RTRPs must complete a minimum of 15 hours of continuing education per year.

d. Incorrect. All preparers of federal tax returns must have a current PTIN.

9. a. Correct. Under Circular 230, the IRS can initiate disciplinary proceedings against practitioners who engage in disreputable conduct. Circular 230 includes willfully failing to e-file in the definition of disreputable conduct for which a person can be sanctioned.

b. Incorrect. Willful failure to adhere to the mandatory e-filing rules does not necessarily pertain to improper conduct under international rules of tax return practice.

c. Incorrect. Willful failure to adhere to the mandatory e-filing rules does not trigger a $1,000 fine under the federal rules of criminal procedure.

d. Incorrect. Willful failure to adhere to the mandatory e-filing rule does not trigger an automatic $100 per violation fine under IRS rules.

10. a. Incorrect. The IRS has instructed that referrals of asserted Code Sec. 6694(a) penalties to OPR should be based on a pattern of failing to meet the required penalty standards.

b. Correct. Code Sec. 6694(b) penalties trigger mandatory referrals to the OPR.

c. Incorrect. Absent evidence of willful neglect, employees of the IRS have discretion in referring violations of Code Sec. 6695(c) to the OPR.

d. Incorrect. When there is willful neglect by preparers, examiners should consider making a referral for noncompliance with Code Sec. 6695(d); absent such neglect, IRS employees are instructed to use their discretion in referring preparers to the OPR.

MODULE 2 — CHAPTER 4

1. a. Incorrect. Significant transactions between the taxpayer and other taxpayers reveal differences between reported income, called a lateral entry selection technique.

b. Incorrect. Document matching helps to reveal discrepancies between the taxpayer's declared income and information from third parties showing income sources such as interest.

c. Correct. Requests for filing extensions will not flag of returns for audit selection.

d. Incorrect. Both the DIF and UI DIF computer scoring systems select returns to audit by assessing the taxpayer's potential for additional tax liabilities.

2. a. Incorrect. The preselection process occurs before, not following, the initial review by the examiner.

b. Correct. During this analysis before notifying the taxpayer about the impending audit, the examiner reviews the case file, sets the scope of the audit, identifies any LUQs, and conducts preliminary research.

c. Incorrect. An interview or conference is not held with the taxpayer or its representative after an initial review and before disqualifying factors are considered.

d. Incorrect. After the return is initially selected, the role of the group manager is to evaluate whether the audit can be completed within the statute of limitations period and respond to any reported possibility of conflict of interest for the examiner. The group manager does not reach a determination of the audit before the examination begins.

3. a. Correct. Using these methods and others, such as tracking bank deposits, enable the examiner to develop circumstantial proof of income once the examiner has established the likelihood of unreported income.

b. Incorrect. Large, unusual, or questionable income items are revealed directly through reviewing the taxpayer's documentation.

c. Incorrect. Inspections of assets and tours of the business are direct examination techniques, and the business taxpayer is aware of the examiner's analysis.

d. Incorrect. Minimum income probes are a direct method of analyzing the accuracy of reported income.

4. a. Incorrect. A taxpayer generally may choose to pursue an appeal with its local U.S. District Court only after it has paid the tax and filed a refund claim with the IRS.

b. Incorrect. A taxpayer generally may choose to pursue an appeal with its local U.S. Court of Federal Claims only after it has paid the tax and filed a refund claim with the IRS.

c. Correct. Appealing a determination to the U.S. Tax Court is one alternative for taxpayers disputing an assessment and/or penalties prior to payment. The taxpayer may also appeal to the examiner's supervisor.

d. Incorrect. Appeals to IRS assessment and penalty decisions are not pursued in Small Claims Court.

5. a. Incorrect. Correspondence audits typically focus on questionable EITC claims or inconsistencies in line item amounts rather than business income and expenses.

b. Incorrect. Field examinations are conducted by more experienced examiners who consider significant or complex tax issues.

c. *Correct.* **Examinations at an IRS district office include analysis of the taxpayer's financial books and records not easily performed in a correspondence audit, but not complex enough to warrant the time and expense of a full-scale field audit.**
d. *Incorrect.* CIC audits are conducted for the complex tax issues of large business taxpayers at the site of their business.

6. a. *Incorrect.* The civil audit may continue to gather evidence of tax understatement but report findings to the CI division for fraud investigation.
b. *Correct.* **A growing trend in cases of suspected tax fraud is to continue a civil audit while a criminal investigation is launched.**
c. *Incorrect.* The taxpayer is always made aware of a civil audit and given the opportunity to substantiate items in question.
d. *Incorrect.* Tax fraud cases go beyond field audits, with evidence provided to the IRS CI Division to prepare substantiation of criminal intent.

MODULE 2 — CHAPTER 5

1. a. *Incorrect.* The Appeals Office does not get involved at this early stage of collection efforts.
b. *Incorrect.* A revenue officer generally does not become involved just after the IRS makes an assessment.
c. *Correct.* **Most cases are sent to the ACS, which attempts to contact the taxpayer by phone and mail.**
d. *Incorrect.* The courts become involved in collecting assessments only after a determination or decision has been made regarding the taxpayer's liability.

2. a. *Incorrect.* Self-employed taxpayers whose income suffered such a reduction due to the economy were eligible for relief from penalties that would have accrued on the April 17, 2012 filing deadline.
b. *Incorrect.* If taxpayers were unemployed for at least 30 consecutive days during 2011 or before April 17, 2012 were targeted by the relief policy.
c. *Correct.* **The penalty relief is subject to income limits (as well as a maximum amount owed).**
d. *Incorrect.* Taxpayers benefited if they pay the total amount owed for 2011 taxes by October 15, 2012.

3. a. *Correct.* **The IRS may agree to discharge the lien when the property is sold and funds are held to fund the liens and claims. Other payments on the property under lien may also cause the lien to be discharged.**
b. *Incorrect.* A lien is subordinated when another creditor pays the government an amount equal to the amount by which the lien will be subordinated.

c. *Incorrect.* A lien is released when the taxpayer completes all payment on the property under lien, a bond is posted for the entire payment, or the debt becomes legally uncollectible.

d. *Incorrect.* When the *Notice of Federal Tax Lien* is withdrawn, the underlying tax lien remains but the IRS gives up priority it obtained when the notice was filed.

4. a. *Correct.* Also restricted from levy is the taxpayer's nonrental property used by another person as a residence if the levy is for $5,000 or less. A judge's approval is required for a principal residence.

b. *Incorrect.* The cap for the levy restriction is $8,370 for 2011.

c. *Incorrect.* The restriction allows only $4,120 in trade, business, or professional books and tools in 2011 for exclusion from levy.

d. *Incorrect.* Exempted from levy are fuel, provisions, furniture, and other personal effects, including arms for personal use.

5. a. *Incorrect.* Installment agreements do not eliminate the failure to pay penalties, but this type of agreement may reduce the rate of the penalty's accrual.

b. *Correct.* This type of agreement may be appropriate when a taxpayer has some ability to pay, but cannot pay the full amount owed within the remaining collection period.

c. *Incorrect.* The IRS may, but is not required to, withdraw the notice of lien when an installment agreement is in effect.

d. *Incorrect.* The taxpayer must submit the statement, and the IRS is strict in analyzing income and expenses disclosed to determine eligibility for the partial payment installment agreement.

6. a. *Incorrect.* The taxpayer cannot challenge the existence or amount of the tax liability in a CAP appeal.

b. *Incorrect.* The decision of the Appeals Office for CAP appeals is final.

c. *Incorrect.* The CAP appeal may be used to protest the taxpayer's proposed installment agreement.

d. *Correct.* A CAP appeal can be requested before or after the IRS files notices or levies.

MODULE 3 — CHAPTER 6

1. a. *Incorrect.* Betterments are one type of capitalized improvement. In general, betterments ameliorate material defects that existed prior a taxpayer's acquisition of a property, or increase a unit of property's capacity, productivity, output, efficiency, strength, or quality. A betterment also includes the enlargement or expansion of a unit of property.

b. *Correct.* **The cost of repairs are currently deducted and not capitalized. Repairs are costs that maintain a property in its ordinarily efficient operating condition.**

c. *Incorrect.* Restorations are capitalized as improvements. Restorations include replacing a major component of a unit of property, returning a nonfunctioning unit of property to an operating condition, and rebuilding a property to a like-new condition that meets a manufacturer's original specifications.

d. *Incorrect.* Adaptations must be capitalized as an improvement. An adaptation relates to costs that adapt a unit of property to use that is different than the use of the property before the expenditures.

2. a. *Correct.* **Under the general definition, a unit of property consists of all functionally interdependent components. If placing one component in service depends on placing another component in service, then the components are functionally interdependent and are part of a unit of property.**

b. *Incorrect.* An automobile engine is not a separate unit of property. An automobile cannot function as an automobile with an engine alone. Therefore, the engine and all other parts of the car are functionally interdependent and will compose the unit of property.

c. *Incorrect.* Under a special rule for plant property, each machine (or group of machines) that performs a discrete and major function within an industrial process is treated as a separate unit of property. If this special rule did not apply, a group of machines that performed all of the operations in the same industrial process could be aggregated into a single unit of property under the functional interdependence test. This could result in an entire industrial plant being categorized as a unit of property and make it too likely that expenditures would be categorized as repairs.

d. *Incorrect.* A structural component of a building (e.g., a roof, floor, walls) is not a separate unit of property. The entire building including its structural components is a unit of property. However, the improvement standards are applied separately to certain enumerated building systems, such as the HVAC system.

3. a. *Incorrect.* The amelioration of a material condition or defect that exists prior to the acquisition of a unit of property is one type of capitalized betterment. It does not matter whether the purchaser was aware of the condition or defect at the time of the acquisition.

b. *Correct.* **Environmental remediation costs are currently deductible so long as the environmental damage is attributable to the taxpayer's own activities. If a taxpayer purchases environmentally damaged land, the costs would be for the amelioration of an existing material condition**

or defect and, therefore, capitalized as a betterment unless deductible under some other provision of the tax code, such as Code Sec. 198 dealing with environmental remediation costs.

c. *Incorrect.* Substantial store remodeling costs are capitalized as betterments. Basic refresh projects, however, may be currently deducted.

d. *Incorrect.* Costs that result in material increases in capacity, productivity, output, efficiency, strength, or quality of a unit of property are capitalized as betterments. In making this determination, the condition of the property immediately after the costs are incurred is compared to the condition of the property when it was last repaired or placed in service if not previously repaired. However, if a specific event, such as a casualty, necessitated the expenditures, the condition of the property immediately before the event is the point of reference.

4. a. *Incorrect.* A capitalized restoration includes the cost of replacing a major component of a unit of property (or a substantial structural part of a unit of property). Thus, the cost of replacing a major component of a machine (a unit of property) is capitalized.

b. *Incorrect.* Rebuilding an item of property to a manufacturer's original specifications is a capitalized restoration only if the MACRS ADS period (i.e., the class life) of the property has already ended at the time of the rebuilding. These costs may be deducted if the ADS period has not ended.

c. *Correct.* Per a specific IRS example, replacement of a roof membrane that has fallen into a state of disrepair is not a capitalized restoration and is not considered the replacement of a major component of the building structure. The entire building structure is the unit of property. The building structure includes all structural components other than enumerated building systems.

d. *Incorrect.* The definition of a capitalized restoration includes the cost of returning a unit of property to its ordinary operating condition if it has deteriorated to a state of disrepair and is no longer functional. For example, the cost of restoring a deteriorated farm building to a condition of functionality is a capitalized restoration.

5. a. *Correct.* The RMSH may only apply if a taxpayer reasonably expects the maintenance activity to be performed at least twice during the asset's class life, which is the same as an asset's MACRS alternative depreciation system period.

b. *Incorrect.* The cost of returning a nonfunctioning unit of property to a functional state does not qualify for the RMSH. Such costs are considered capitalized restorations.

c. *Incorrect.* The routine maintenance safe harbor only applies to routine maintenance costs attributable to the period that a taxpayer owns a property. Accordingly, if a taxpayer purchases a used unit of property, the cost of repairs attributable to the period that the prior owner held the property cannot be deducted under the RMSH but may be deductible if the maintenance does not otherwise result in an improvement.

d. Incorrect. The RMSH does not apply to buildings. The general rules for improvements—including the rules for determining whether the costs are incurred for a betterment or restoration to the building or the building systems, or to adapt the building or any of its systems to a new or different use—are applied to determine whether a cost results in a repair or improvement to a building.

6. a. Incorrect. There is no aggregate dollar limit on the amount that may be deducted as a material or supply. There is, however, a $100 per unit acquisition cost limit for materials and supplies other than those used as components to repair, maintain, or improve property, or ones that have a useful life of 12 months of less.

b. Incorrect. Material and supplies that are used to improve a unit of property are capitalized just like any other improvement.

c. Incorrect. Incidental materials and supplies are deducted in the tax year that their cost is paid or incurred.

d. Correct. Nonincidental material and supplies are deducted in the tax year that they are used or consumed. Incidental material and supplies are deducted in the year of purchase.

7. a. Correct. No Code Sec. 481(a) adjustment is required if a taxpayer adopts the temporary regulations relating to materials and supplies as of their effective date.

b. Incorrect. The IRS has provided an automatic accounting method procedure (Rev. Proc. 2012-19) to comply with the temporary regulations relating to materials and supplies.

c. Incorrect. Although the repair regulations generally apply to tax years beginning on or after January 1, 2012, the temporary regulations dealing with materials and supplies apply to amounts paid or incurred (to acquire or produce property) in tax years beginning on or after January 1, 2012.

d. Incorrect. Although the former regulations did not specifically define materials and supplies, the temporary regulations provide very specific definitions and requirements to qualify as a material and supply.

8. a. Incorrect. Depreciation on an *asset* begins in the year it is placed in service. *Property* is expensed under the *de minimis* rule and not depreciated.

b. Correct. The cost of eligible property may be deducted under the *de minimis* rule in the year its cost is paid (cash basis taxpayers) or incurred (accrual basis taxpayers).

c. Incorrect. The cost of materials and supplies is generally deducted in the year the materials or supplies are used or consumed.

d. Incorrect. The time for expensing eligible property under the *de minimis* rule is unrelated to the delivery date.

9. a. Correct. A taxpayer's expensing policy may set any dollar limit on the per-item cost of items to be expensed.

b. Incorrect. There is a dollar amount cap on the aggregate expense amount in each tax year. Regardless of the limit chosen, the taxpayer may expense in each tax year no more than the greater of 0.1 percent of gross receipts reported for federal income tax purposes or 2 percent of depreciation reported on the applicable financial statement. Any amount in excess of this aggregate cap must be capitalized.

c. Incorrect. An election may be made to take into account under the *de minimis* rule any amount of materials and supplies that are otherwise deductible in the year paid or incurred (incidental materials and supplies) or deducted in the year used or consumed (nonincidental materials and supplies).

d. Incorrect. Items of inventory may not be expensed under the *de minimis* rule. The expensing rule, however, does apply to materials and supplies (if a special election is made) and to units of property acquired or produced by a taxpayer.

10. a. Incorrect. The purchase of a rotable part does not result in any tax consequence. However, specific consequences flow from the installation, removal, and disposition of a rotable.

b. Incorrect. In the year of installation, the cost of the rotable is deducted.

c. Incorrect. In the year of disposition the basis of the rotable part is deducted as a loss.

d. Correct. In each year that a rotable part is removed the fair market value is included in gross income, and the basis is increased by the fair market value and the removal costs.

11. a. Incorrect. The optional method for rotable spare parts applies to amounts paid or incurred (to acquire or produce property) in tax years beginning on or after January 1, 2012. However, a taxpayer may apply the optional method to tax years beginning on or after January 1, 2012.

b. Correct. A taxpayer that elects the optional method for rotable spare parts may not elect to capitalize the cost of the rotable as is the case with other types of materials and supplies. The cost of the rotables for which the optional election is made may only be deducted for tax purposes in the tax year of first installation as required by the optional method for rotables.

c. Incorrect. No formal election is required to adopt the optional method for rotables. A taxpayer adopts the method by complying with the reporting requirements on its return. However, a taxpayer adopting the method for the first time is adopting an accounting method and will need to comply with the automatic change of accounting method procedures of Rev. Proc. 2012-19.

d. Incorrect. An original component of a unit of property, such as the original engines on an aircraft or car, is depreciated as part of the cost of the unit of property and does not qualify as a rotable even if it is removed and repaired.

MODULE 3 — CHAPTER 7

1. a. Incorrect. Although the retirement of a structural component of a building was previously not considered a disposition, the temporary regulations have changed this rule effective for tax years beginning on or after January 1, 2012.

b. Incorrect. Loss is recognized on the retirement of a structural component but the fair market value of the retired component is not taken into account in determining the amount of the loss.

c. Incorrect. When an asset such as a structural component is retired, a taxpayer must cease depreciating the asset.

d. Correct. The retirement of a structural component triggers recognition of a loss in the amount of the component's adjusted depreciable basis. Adjusted depreciable basis is the amount of the building's original cost that is allocable to the component that has not been depreciated prior to the retirement.

2. a. Correct. Although a taxpayer may treat component parts of most units of Section 1245 property as separate assets under the "reasonable and consistent" standard, a special rule prohibits a taxpayer from treating components of commonly used assets described in asset classes 00.11 through 00.4 as separate assets on which a loss may be claimed upon retirement.

b. Incorrect. Each structural component of a building is a separate asset on which a loss may be claimed upon retirement.

c. Incorrect. A taxpayer may adopt an accounting method that treats components of structural components as separate assets provided the definition used is reasonable and consistently applied.

d. Incorrect. A unit of property may generally be divided into multiple assets. However, multiple units of property may not be combined into one asset.

3. a. *Correct.* **The cost of replacing a major component must be capitalized as an improvement. However, because the replacement's cost is capitalized, the taxpayer may benefit from claiming a loss deduction on the retired major component if it is treated as a separate asset.**

b. *Incorrect.* If a major component is treated as a separate asset, it is considered disposed of when retired. Therefore, a taxpayer may not continue to claim depreciation on the major component in this situation.

c. *Incorrect.* The taxpayer may claim a loss deduction on a retired major component only if the major component is treated as an asset. This rule also applies to retired minor components. Unless a component is treated as an asset, there is no disposition of an "asset" that can trigger a loss.

d. *Incorrect.* The taxpayer may not choose the tax treatment of the major component's cost.

4. a. *Incorrect.* Both conventions may not be used for different assets within a single GAA.

b. *Correct.* **The same MACRS depreciation method, period, and convention must be used for all of the assets in one GAA.**

c. *Incorrect.* All the assets within one GAA must be placed in service during the same tax year.

d. *Incorrect.* The assets may be Section 1245 property or real property.

5. a. *Correct.* **The scope of qualifying dispositions has widened to apply to most transactions that do not involve all of the assets or the last (sole) asset in the account.**

b. *Incorrect.* The prior rules also considered dispositions resulting from terminating a business to be qualifying dispositions.

c. *Incorrect.* The temporary regulations do not allow like-kind exchanges to be treated as qualifying dispositions from a GAA.

d. *Incorrect.* The GAA disposition rules do not allow assets undergoing involuntary conversions to be included in qualifying dispositions.

6. a. *Correct.* **Using the late GAA election the taxpayer is granted the choice of whether to recognize a loss on any past or future retirements of the building's structural components.**

b. *Incorrect.* A reserve account must be maintained for a GAA, regardless of when the asset is placed in the account.

c. *Incorrect.* The recovery period is neither lengthened nor shortened by late GAA election.

d. *Incorrect.* Under the temporary regulations, the election to place an asset in a GAA is irrevocable.

MODULE 3 — CHAPTER 8

1. a. *Correct.* **The NOL and any capital losses are deducted on the decedent's final year tax return.**
b. *Incorrect.* The estate or trust may not substitute the NOL amount for the personal exemption of the decedent.
c. *Incorrect.* A deduction may not be claimed on the estate or trust's return for the first year of existence of the trust or estate. For the tax year in which the trust or estate terminates, the NOL may be deducted by the beneficiary on his or her return.
d. *Incorrect.* An NOL may not be deducted on the estate or trust's return for the decedent's final year.

2. a. *Incorrect.* Losses of a partnership flow through to the partners, who claim their proportionate share of the NOLs on their individual tax returns.
b. *Correct.* **A C corporation may deduct an NOL at the entity level and arises from normal income tax deductions claimed by the corporation.**
c. *Incorrect.* An S corporation is a flow-through entity. Thus, their proportionate losses are claimed by individual S corporation shareholders.
d. *Incorrect.* Life insurance companies are ineligible to deduct NOLs but may claim an operations loss deduction that is similar to an NOL.

3. a. *Correct.* **The irrevocable election enables the taxpayer to only carry the loss forward to future tax years rather than applying it to up to two prior tax years.**
b. *Incorrect.* The waiver is irrevocable.
c. *Incorrect.* The waiver is not conditioned on the taxpayer's level of income in the current tax year.
d. *Incorrect.* The taxpayer loses the option of deducting an NOL by waiving the carryback period.

4. a. *Incorrect.* An NOL from a federally declared disaster may be deducted only within 3 years of the loss.
b. *Incorrect.* A farming loss may be carried back up to 5 years, and the taxpayer can elect out of that period.
c. *Correct.* **A specified liability loss arising from product liabilities, workplace liabilities, or environmental remediation may be deducted up to 10 years prior to the year of the loss.**
d. *Incorrect.* A casualty or theft loss has only a 3-year carryback period.

5. a. *Incorrect.* Processing the application takes more than 30 days but is faster than filing an amended return on Form 1040X.
b. *Incorrect.* The application is subject to a different processing time and must be filed within one year after the end of the NOL year.

c. *Correct.* **Form 1045 is processed within the later of 90 days after being filed or 90 days after the last day of the month that includes the due date for filing Form 1040 (or 1041) for the loss year. It is generally processed faster than an amended return on Form 1040X.**
d. *Incorrect.* The application is processed in less than 120 days and must be filed within one year following the end of the NOL year.

6. a. *Incorrect.* A significant amount of historic assets must be used for a period longer than one year to meet the COBE standards.
b. *Correct.* **COBE standards require a significant amount of the loss corporation's historic assets to be used for at least two years after the ownership change.**
c. *Incorrect.* A different period is used for COBE standards. A three-year testing period is used to determine an ownership change.
d. *Incorrect.* The COBE standards must be met for a period shorter than five years to avoid the Code Sec. 382 limit of zero. A five-year period applies to the trigger of a build-in gain or loss limiting NOL use.

MODULE 4 — CHAPTER 9

1. a. *Incorrect.* The Code Sec. 4980H(a) provisions do not apply to small employers that currently do not offer employer-sponsored plans.
b. *Correct.* **The Code Sec. 4980H(a) provisions impose assessment payments on large employers that do not offer plans with the opportunity for minimum essential coverage to FTEs and their dependents.**
c. *Incorrect.* Assessable payments under Code Sec. 4980H(a) do not apply in the case of plans that may be unaffordable. Payments are imposed under Code Sec. 4980H(b) for employers that do not offer FTEs and dependents minimum coverage that is affordable relative to the employees' household income.
d. *Incorrect.* The Code Sec. 4980H(a) rules do not apply to plans that do not provide minimum value (that is, pay at least 60 percent of benefits). Such plans are subject to assessable payments under Code Sec. 4980H(b).

2. a. *Correct.* **In addition to making minimum essential coverage available, eligibility for the safe harbor would require self-only premiums not to exceed 9.5 percent of an employee's W-2 wages.**
b. *Incorrect.* Free choice voucher provisions were repealed under the *Department of Defense and Full-Year Continuing Appropriations Act, 2011.*
c. *Incorrect.* These coverage levels apply to SHOP Exchange requirements for small business employers and qualified individuals.
d. *Incorrect.* Employer safe harbor requirements apply to employees who work an average of at least 30 hours per week.

3. a. *Incorrect.* The tax must be reported and paid quarterly by providers using Form 720.

b. *Incorrect.* The tax is imposed on that portion of the goods and service attributable to tanning services, excluding the cost for separable goods and services.

c. *Correct.* Such treatment for medical or psychiatric conditions is not subject to the excise tax.

d. *Incorrect.* The excise tax rate is 10 percent.

4. a. *Incorrect.* The Affordable Care Act does not treat the branded prescription drug fee as an addition to tax.

b. *Correct.* The branded prescription drug fee is treated by the Affordable Care Act as an excise tax, so that only civil actions for refunds may be pursued.

c. *Incorrect.* The Affordable Care Act does not treat the branded prescription drug fee as a penalty.

d. *Incorrect.* The Affordable Care Act does not treat the branded prescription drug fee as a type of discretionary payment.

5. a. *Incorrect.* The retail exemption excludes devices generally purchased by the public such as eyeglasses, contact lenses, hearing aids, and adhesive bandages.

b. *Incorrect.* The tax attaches when the title to the taxable article passes from the manufacturer to the purchaser, regardless of where the article is manufactured or produced.

c. *Correct.* The tax applies to devices sold for use by medical professionals, although the tax attaches when the taxable article passes from its manufacturer to the purchaser.

d. *Incorrect.* The proposed regulations for the tax exclude devices intended for use only in veterinary medicine. ·

6. a. *Correct.* The cost is reported on the employee's W-2 for tax years beginning after January 1, 2011.

b. *Incorrect.* Long-term care coverage is not considered applicable employer-sponsored coverage as described in Notice 2012-9.

c. *Incorrect.* Notice 2012-9 exempts tribally chartered corporations from the reporting requirements.

d. *Incorrect.* Notice 2012-9 provides transition relief for small employers that filed fewer than 250 W-2s for the preceding calendar year.

MODULE 4 — CHAPTER 10

1. a. Incorrect. The U.S. tax code imposes tax on profits that U.S. companies earn anywhere in the world.
b. Correct. Favorable transfer-pricing rules currently enable companies in the United States to easily shift business profits to low-tax jurisdictions.
c. Incorrect. Businesses are calling for simplification of business tax provisions.
d. Incorrect. The average U.S. effective corporate tax rate of 39.2 percent crates incentives for companies to locate elsewhere in developed OECD member nations,.

2. a. Incorrect. Small businesses advocate elimination of the AMT, not raising the tax rate.
b. Incorrect. Small businesses want simpler rules for worker classification than the 20 factors that the IRS uses currently.
c. Correct. Small businesses advocate making the temporary 100-percent expensing rate permanent to enable them to immediately recover the costs of capital equipment.
d. Incorrect. Small businesses favor elimination of the estate tax altogether so that assets of closely held and family businesses would not be subject to high taxes upon the death of individual owners.

3. a. Incorrect. Lower overall tax rates could only maintain current federal tax revenue levels if many of the deductions and credits used by lower- and middle-income taxpayers were curbed.
b. Correct. Lower tax rates would not force the addition of new deductions and tax credits into the already complex tax code. Most tax reform proposals support elimination or reduction of many of these tax expenditures in exchange for lower rates and a simplified tax system.
c. Incorrect. Lower tax rates could potentially affect the deduction for charitable contributions and create a disincentive for higher-income taxpayers to donate to charities.
d. Incorrect. Lowering tax rates could potentially affect the incentives for making contributions to retirement accounts, although experts have cautioned the House Ways and Means Committee not to alter deductions now used by employers and individuals to save for retirement.

TOP FEDERAL TAX ISSUES FOR 2013 CPE COURSE

Index

A

Accountable care organizations (ACOs)
dividends and interest income of ... 1.18
fact sheet and guidance for ... 1.15
furthering charitable purpose ... 1.17, 1.18
participation in MSSP by ... 1.16–1.17
as partnership ... 1.16, 1.18
structure of ... 1.16
tax status of ... 1.18
unrelated business income of ... 1.17–1.18

Accounting method
of exempt organizations ... 1.3
unusual, as factor triggering field
examination ... 4.10

**Accounting method, change in, under
temporary repair regulations**
for de minimis expensing rule 6.27
for definition of unit of property ... 6.7–6.8
for MACRS asset disposition ... 7.10
for materials and supplies ... 6.23
for optional method for rotable and
temporary spare parts ... 6.29
for previously deducted repair or
maintenance expenses ... 6.16–6.17
for routine maintenance safe harbor ... 6.19

ACOs. See **Accountable care organizations
(ACOs)**

Adaptations of unit of property ... 6.2, 6.16

Affordable Care Act ... 9.1–9.26
affordable coverage under ... 9.9, 9.11
branded prescription drug
fee under ... 9.18–9.20
court challenges to ... 9.2–9.4
effective dates staggered for
provisions of ... 9.2
employer-sponsored coverage under ... 9.11,
9.23–9.24
enactment of two laws composing ... 9.1
excise taxes under ... 9.17–9.18, 9.20,
9.21–9.23
exemptions of ... 9.6
guidance for ... 9.7, 9.10
health FSA changes under ... 9.15–9.17
indoor tanning services taxed under ...
9.17–9.18
Medicaid expanded by ... 9.2, 9.4
medical device excise tax under ... 9.21–9.23
minimum essential coverage under ... 9.5–9.7,
9.8, 9.24–9.25
reporting requirements of ... 9.23–9.25
safe harbor for large
employers under ... 9.9–9.10
shared responsibility payments for
employers under ... 9.8–9.10
shared responsibility payments for
individuals under ... 9.5, 9.6–9.7
tax credit for individuals for health insurance
costs under ... 9.10–9.12
tax credit for small employer health plan
costs under ... 9.12–9.15
tax on uninsured under ... 9.3

Agent, IRS. See **Examiner, IRS**

**Allocable interest deduction
of corporation ... 8.18**

Alternative minimum tax (AMT)
corporate ... 10.14
effects of NOL deduction on ... 8.11, 8.12
repeal of ... 10.14, 10.16

American Health Benefit Exchange ... 9.7

Anti-Injunction Act ... 9.2

Appeals Office, IRS. See **IRS Office of Appeals**

**Applicable employer-sponsored coverage
under Affordable Care Act ... 9.24**

**Applicable large employer under
Affordable Care Act ... 9.8, 9.25**

Audit examination
definition of ... 4.1
process of ... 4.14–4.20
return selection as beginning of ... 4.2

Audit potential, assessment of
items considered in, LUQ ... 4.13
process of ... 4.12–4.13

**Audit Technique Guides (ATGs) ... 4.13,
4.20–4.22**
examiner review of ... 4.21
focus of ... 4.20
industries covered by ... 4.21
IRS updates to ... 4.20, 4.22

Audits, IRS ... 4.1–4.26. See also
individual types
agreed to adjustments outcome of ... 4.20
appeals for decision of ... 4.22–4.24

conclusion of, audit determination as ... 4.20
definition of audits for ... 4.1–4.2
disagreement of adjustments
outcome of ... 4.20
evidence for ... 4.16–4.19
goal of taxpayers for ... 4.2
initial contact by taxpayer during ... 4.15
no-change outcome of ... 4.2, 4.20
notification of ... 4.14–4.15
representation of taxpayer during ... 4.15–4.16
return selection process for ... 4.2–4.5
scope of ... 4.3
selection of taxpayers interacting with
ones under ... 4.5
statistics for frequency of ... 4.2
statute of limitations for ... 4.11–4.12
stopping ... 4.22
taxpayer rights regarding ... 4.15
types of ... 4.5–4.11

Automated collection system (ACS) ... 5.3

B

Bad-debt losses of commercial banks ... 8.17

Bankruptcy estate, NOL carryforward by ... 8.5

Batch processing for
correspondence audits ... 4.5–4.6

Beneficial owner of payment for FATCA
requirements ... 2.6

Betterments to unit of property ... 6.2, 6.8–6.12

Bonus depreciation, claims of ... 7.12, 7.14

Branch of FFI
definition of ... 2.16
limited ... 2.16–2.17

Branded prescription drug fee for
manufacturers and importers ... 9.18–9.20

"Bronze level" health insurance plan ... 9.7

Building refresh ... 6.11–6.12

Building systems as units of property under
temporary repair regulations ... 6.3, 6.5
list of ... 6.4
routine maintenance safe harbor not
applicable to ... 6.17

Buildings as unit of property under
temporary repair regulations ... 6.3

Buildings, structural components of
examples of ... 7.4
loss claimed on ... 7.17
retired ... 7.1
as separate assets ... 7.4, 7.5

Built-in gains and losses for
NOL use ... 8.23–8.24

Business expenses, 100 percent
expensing of ... 10.13

Business property as separate asset ... 7.6–7.8

Business tax preferences and extenders,
repeal of ... 10.5, 10.6, 10.8–10.12

C

C corporation, NOL of ... 8.8–8.9

Cancellation of debt (COD), NOL reduction
as attribute in cases of ... 8.6–8.7

Cap and trade system for
pollutant emissions ... 10.4

Capitalization requirements of temporary
repair regulations ... 6.1
for cost of replacement
of component ... 7.11, 7.17
for excess amounts ... 6.25
for improvement of unit of property ...
6.2–6.3
for major components of Section 1245
property ... 7.9, 7.11
for materials and supplies ... 6.20, 6.21–6.23
types of improvements under ... 6.3

Carried interest, taxation of ... 10.9

Casualty losses
NOL for loss from ... 8.13
under temporary repair regulations ... 6.15

Centers for Medicare and
Medicaid Services (CMS) ... 1.14

Change in accounting method. See
Accounting method, change in, under
temporary repair regulations

Charitable conservation
easements ... 1.21–1.26
background of ... 1.21–1.22
for land used as golf course ... 1.23–1.24
policy debate regarding ... 1.22–1.23
substantiation requirements for ... 1.24–1.25
Tax Court cases regarding ... 1.21–1.22,
1.23–1.25
valuation of property for ... 1.25–126

Charitable contributions
cap proposed for itemizing ... 10.18
deductibility of ... 1.5, 10.18
NOLs not affecting deduction for ... 8.11

Circular 230, Rules of Practice Before the
IRS, sanctions under ... 3.10, 3.11, 3.18,
3.19–3.20, 3.22

Civil cases of fraud, government's burden of
proof for ... 4.25

Claims court. *See* United States Claims Court

Closely held C corporations, wages from ... 4.10

Code Sec. 36B tax credit for individuals for health insurance costs ... 9.10–9.11

Code Sec. 45R small employer health care tax credit
average annual wages for employees for ... 9.12, 9.13
claiming ... 9.14–9.15
effective date of ... 9.15
employers eligible for ... 9.12–9.13
hours of service for ... 9.12,3–9.14
phaseout rules for ... 9.13
qualifying arrangement for ... 9.12, 9.14

Code Sec. 168(a)(3) property ... 7.8–7.9

Code Sec. 199 deduction for "advanced manufacturing" ... 10.8

Code Sec. 501(c)(3) organizations. *See* Exempt organizations

Code Sec. 4091 medical device excise tax ... 9.21–9.23

Code Sec. 4980H(a) payment by employers ... 9.8

Code Sec. 4980H(b) payments by larger employers ... 9.8–9.10

Code Sec. 5000B indoor tanning excise tax ... 9.17–9.18

Code Sec. 6055 minimum essential coverage reporting ... 9.25

Code Sec. 6056 applicable large employer reporting ... 9.25

Code Sec. 6694(a) penalty
firm liability for ... 3.4
reasonable basis standard applied for ... 3.3
reasonable cause exception to ... 3.3–3.4
referrals to IRS OPR of ... 3.23

Code Sec. 6694(b) penalty
burden of proof on IRS for ... 3.6–3.7
referrals to IRS OPR of ... 3.23
for willful or reckless conduct of return preparer ... 3.6

Code Sec. 6695(a), Failure to Furnish Completed Copy of Return or Claim for Refund to Taxpayer penalty ... 3.7
medium used for copy of returns to avoid ... 3.8
reasonable cause exception to ... 3.9
referrals to IRS OPR of ... 3.23

Code Sec. 6695(b), Failure to Sign Return or Claim for Refund penalty ... 3.7

Circular 230 censure, suspension, or disbarment for disreputable conduct in ... 3.10
electronically signed tax returns subject to ... 3.9
referrals to IRS OPR of ... 3.23

Code Sec. 6695(c), Failure to Furnish Identifying Number penalty ... 3.7
Circular 230 censure, suspension, or disbarment for disreputable conduct in ... 3.11
preparers subject to ... 3.10
reasonable cause exception to ... 3.11–3.12
referrals to IRS OPR of ... 3.23

Code Sec. 6695(d), Failure to Retain Copy or List penalty ... 3.7
reasonable cause exception to ... 3.12
referrals to IRS OPR of ... 3.23
taxpayer records subject to ... 3.12

Code Sec. 6695(e), Failure of Preparer Employer to File Information Returns penalty ... 3.7
employers of preparers subject to ... 3.12
reasonable cause exception to ... 3.13
referrals to IRS OPR of ... 3.23

Code Sec. 6695(f), Negotiation of a Taxpayer's Refund Check penalty ... 3.8
exceptions to ... 3.13
reasonable cause exception not applicable to ... 3.13
referrals to IRS OPR of ... 3.23

Code Sec. 6695(g), EIC Due Diligence penalty ... 3.8
compliance date differences for ... 3.14–3.15
lack of preparer compliance in determining EIC eligibility triggering ... 3.13
referrals to IRS OPR of ... 3.23

Code Sec. 7216 criminal penalties, return preparers subject to ... 3.16–3.18

Collection Appeals Program (CAP) ... 5.23, 5.25–5.26

Collection due process (CDP) appeals for collection actions ... 5.23, 5.24–5.25

Collection Financial Standards, IRS ... 5.18–5.19

Collection Information Statement ... 5.21

Collection period for assessed tax liability ... 5.3

Collection tools of IRS ... 5.3–5.4

Collections, IRS ... 5.1–5.27
alternatives to ... 5.12–5.23
appeals of ... 5.23–5.26
basics of ... 5.2–5.4
changes to practices for ... 5.4
introduction to ... 5.1

Compliance Assurance Process (CAP)
program ... 4.10

Conditional expenses for installment
agreements ... 5.15

Conflict of interest of IRS examiner ... 4.12

Congressional Research Service report on
individual tax expenditures ... 10.16–10.17

Consolidated group
accounting procedures of ... 6.24
applicable financial statement of ... 6.24–6.25
waiver of NOL carryback by ... 8.12

Consumer-operated and oriented plan
(CO-OP) Program ... 1.14–1.15

Continuing education requirements
for RTRPs ... 3.19

Cooperative organization, NOL
deduction of ... 8.10

Coordinated Industry Case (CIC)
Program ... 4.4, 4.10–4.11

Coordinated Issue Papers (ISPs) ... 4.13

Corporate equity reduction interest loss
(CERIL) ... 8.18, 8.19

Corporate equity reduction transaction
(CERT) ... 8.18, 8.19, 8.21

Corporate tax rate ... 10.5–10.12
costs of reducing ... 10.6
effective ... 10.7, 10.8
to encourage manufacturing, changing ... 10.8
industries' comparative ... 10.8
OECD member ... 10.6, 10.7
President's Framework proposals for ... 10.6
reasons to reduce ... 10.2, 10.5–10.6, 10.7
Republican lawmakers'
proposals for ... 10.6, 10.8

Corporation, NOL of
for C corporation ... 8.8–8.9
computing, modifications for ... 8.9
expected ... 8.19–8.20
for S corporation as former
C corporation ... 8.8–8.9
transfer of ... 8.21–8.23
waiver of carryback period for ... 8.20

Correspondence audits (examinations)
batch processing for ... 4.5–4.6
combo letter for ... 4.6
as conducted through U.S. mail ... 4.2, 4.5
failure to respond by deadlines for ... 4.6–4.7
increasing use of, statistics showing ... 4.7
initial contact letter for ... 4.6
notification of ... 4.14
use of office examinations versus ... 4.8

Criminal investigation, alerts of IRS ... 4.25

Criminal Investigation (CI) division of IRS
civil audit findings reported to ... 4.24
referral to ... 4.18

Criminal penalties for unauthorized
disclosure of income tax return
information ... 3.1, 3.16–3.18

Cumulative depreciation adjustment,
Code Sec. 481(a) ... 7.24–7.25

D

De minimis expensing rule under temporary
repair regulations ... 6.2, 6.20, 6.22,
6.24–6.27
change in accounting method for ... 6/27
effective date for ... 6.27

Deemed-compliant FFIs ... 2.18–2.21
certified ... 2.18, 2.20–2.21
registered ... 2.18, 2.19
restricted funds for ... 2.19

Deficiency determination for
tax liability ... 4.7, 4.16

Deficit Commission tax plan. *See* National
Commission on Fiscal Responsibility
and Reform

Deficit, growing federal ... 10.1
base-broadening to address ... 10.3, 10.6
new taxes to address ... 10.3–10.4

*Department of Defense and Full-Year
Continuing Appropriations Act, 2011* ... 9.7

Disasters, NOL carryback
period for ... 8.13, 8.17

Discriminant Index Function (DIF) system
for returns selected for auditing ... 4.3

Dispositions of MACRS property
definition of ... 7.2–7.3
property constituting ... 7.4–7.6
rules for determining gain or loss upon ... 7.3–7.4

District Court, U.S. *See* United States
District Court

Dividends-received deduction of
corporations ... 8.9

Divorced taxpayers, use of NOL by ... 8.5–8.6

Document matching to select returns for
IRS audit ... 4.4

Documentation of rationale for formal indirect
method of determining income ... 4.18

Due diligence requirements for preparers of
clients filing for EIC ... 3.8, 3.13–3.15

E

e-filing of tax returns
administrative exceptions from required ... 3.21
client choice for filing paper versus ... 3.21–3.22
compliance for ... 3.22
covered returns for ... 3.20–3.21
penalties for failure to use ... 3.22
signature authorization for ... 3.9
waivers from mandatory ... 3.21

Earned income tax credit (EIC)
audits of taxpayers claiming ... 4.2–4.3
due diligence required of return
preparers for ... 3.8, 3.13–3.15
reasonable inquiries by return preparers
about information for ... 3.15

Economic hardship
as considerations in tax levies ... 5.11–5.12
definition of, for offers
in compromise ... 5.18, 5.21–5.22

Eggshell audits ... 4.25

**Electric utility, NOL carryback period
election by** ... 8.17

**Electronic filing identification number
(EFIN)** ... 3.11

Electronic health records (EHRs) ... 1.19

Electronically signed tax returns ... 3.9

**Emergency Economic Stabilization Act of
2008 (EESA)** ... 8.17

Employee business expenses, claiming ... 4.10

Employer identification number (EIN)
of QNHII ... 1.15
searching exempt organization
information by ... 1.12

Employer-sponsored health coverage ...
9.11, 9.23–9.25

**Employment tax returns, understatement
of tax liability on** ... 3.2

Environmental cleanup costs ... 6.10

Environmental tax ... 10.4

**Equity or public policy, tax liability
based on** ... 5.22

**Equivalent hearing for
collection appeals** ... 5.23, 5.25

Estate tax, call for eliminating ... 10.13

Estate tax returns
understatement of tax liability on ... 3.2
uses of NOLs for ... 8.7, 8.20

Estimated tax understatement ... 4.19

Evidence for audit
gathered from third parties ... 4.17
methods of acquiring ... 4.16–4.19

Examination techniques ... **4.16–4.19**

Examiner, IRS
appeal of decision of ... 4.22–4.24
approval of penalties approved by
supervisor of ... 4.19
ATG review responsibility of ... 4.21
decision to proceed with examination by ... 4.11
documentation of rationale by ... 4.18
evidence for audit gathered by ... 4.16
for field examinations, experience level of ... 4.9
imposition of taxpayer penalties by ... 4.19
initial taxpayer contact with ... 4.15
items considered in audit
potential by ... 4.12–4.13
recusal from audit of ... 4.12
taxpayer delay tactics determined by ... 4.16

**Excise tax returns, understatement of
tax liability on** ... 3.2

**Exempt Organization Business Master File
(EO BMF)** ... 1.13–1.14

**Exempt Organization
Select Check** ... 1.12–1.13, 1.14

Exempt organization status
application for ... 1.2–1.4
reinstatement of ... 1.13–1.14
revocation of, automatic ... 1.9–1.11, 1.12

Exempt organizations ... **1.1–1.26**
accounting method of ... 1.3
certified deemed-compliant status of ... 2.21
gross receipts of ... 1.9
hospitals as. *See* Hospitals
information returns of ... 1.1. *See also*
individual tax return forms
oversight of ... 1.4
public support test of ... 1.3

Expanded affiliate group
FFI agreement involving ... 2.16–2.17
nonregistering local bank for ... 2.20

**Expensing rules of temporary repair
regulations** ... 6.2, 6.24–6.27

F

Fair market value of real estate ... 5.20

Farming loss, NOL carryback for ... 8.13–8.15

Fast Track Mediation (FTM) Program, IRS ...
4.23–4.24

FATCA. *See Foreign Account Tax Compliance
Act* (FATCA)

Federal Communications Commission (FCC)
accounting rules ... 6.20

Federal Energy Regulatory Commission
(FERC) accounting rules ... 6.20

Federal Food, Drug, and Cosmetic Act
(FD&C Act) ... 9.19, 9.21

Federally declared disaster,
NOL from ... 8.13, 8.17

Federally facilitated exchange (FFE) of HHS
for health insurance ... 9.7

FFI agreement ... 2.9–2.17
account identification requirements in ... 2.3
to become participating FFI ... 2.9, 2.11
deadline for entering into ... 2.22
due diligence compliance
requirements for ... 2.11–2.13
effective date of ... 2.22
for entity accounts ... 2.12
for individual accounts ... 2.11–2.12
reporting requirements under ... 2.13–2.15
verification procedures under ... 2.12–2.13

Field examinations (audits)
factors commonly triggering ... 4.9–4.10
Letter 2205 or Letter 3572
to initiate ... 4.9, 4.14
of small businesses ... 4.3
TIGTA review of fraud revealed by ... 4.10

Field examiners, IRS ... 4.9. *See also*
Examiner, IRS

Field revenue officer, referral to ... 5.3

Final Notice of Intent to Levy ... 5.25

Financial account, scope of,
under FATCA ... 2.9–2.11

Fiscal year (FY) 2013 budget of Obama
Administration ... 1.23

Fixed, determinable, annual, or periodical
(FDAP) income ... 2.4, 2.5
withholding on U.S. source ... 2.6

Flex credits for health FSAs ... 9.16

Foreign Account Tax Compliance Act
(FATCA) ... 2.1–2.24
designed to prevent tax evasion ... 2.1, 2.2
effective date for withholding
requirements under ... 2.5
enactment of ... 2.1
grandfathered obligations for ... 2.7
implementation on government-to-
government basis of ... 2.24
obligations subject to ... 2.7
status of payee under ... 2.7–2.8
statutory framework of ... 2.3–2.9

Foreign financial asset, information
disclosures for ... 2.2

Foreign financial institution (FFI) groups,
nonreporting members of
participating ... 2.18–2.19

Foreign financial institutions (FFIs)
deemed ... 2.19
deemed-compliant ... 2.18–2.21
due diligence
requirements for ... 2.11–2.12, 2.22
FATCA to address offshore tax evasion
facilitated by ... 2.2
intergovernmental agreements for ... 2.24
internal reviews by ... 2.13
limited ... 2.17
local ... 2.18
low-value accounts of ... 2.21
nonparticipating ... 2.3, 2.15, 2.16, 2.19
owner-documented ... 2.21
participating ... 2.3, 2.6, 2.9, 2.11, 2.13–2.16, 2.19
reporting requirements for
accounts of ... 2.22–2.23
registration of ... 2.22
withholding tax by ... 2.2

Foreign passthrough payments
to limited FFI ... 2.17
withholding on ... 2.16

Foreign tax credit ... 10.11

Form 433-A, *Collection Information Statement
for Wage Earners and Self-Employed
Individuals* ... 5.11, 5.13, 5.16, 5.20

Form 433-B, *Collection Information Statement
for Businesses* ... 5.11, 5.16, 5.20

Form 656-L, *Offer in Compromise
(Doubt as to Liability)* ... 5.21

Form 668(Y)(c), *Notice of Federal
Tax Lien* ... 5.3, 5.6, 5.8

Form 970, *Quarterly Federal Excise
Tax Return* ... 9.18

Form 990, *Return of Organization Exempt
from Income Tax* ... 1.2
complexity of ... 1.4–1.5
electively filing ... 1.8
joint venture and investment partnership
reporting on ... 1.5–1.6
redesign of ... 1.2
public inspection of ... 1.6
public support and accounting information
on ... 1.3
use of Schedule K-1 optional for ... 1.5–1.6

Form 990-EZ, *Short Form Return of Organization
Exempt From Income Tax* ... 1.2
electively filing ... 1.8

use of Schedule K-1 optional for ... 1.5–1.6

Form 990-N, *Electronic Notice (E-Postcard) for Tax-Exempt Organizations Not Required to File Form 990 or Form 990-EZ* ... 1.7–1.10
annual filing requirement for ... 1.8
filing relief program for ... 1.9–1.10
gross receipts maximum for using ... 1.8, 1.9
information required for ... 1.7–1.8

Form 990-T, *Exempt Organization Business Income Tax Return* ... 9.15

Form TD F 90-221, *Report of Foreign Bank and Financial Accounts* (the FBAR), information reporting on ... 2.3

Form 1040A, *U.S. Individual Income Tax Return*, EIC worksheet in ... 3.14

Form 1040EZ, *Income Tax Return for Single and Joint Filers With No Dependents*, EIC worksheet in ... 3.14

Form 1040X, *Amended U.S. Individual Income Tax Return* ... 8.19, 8.20

Form 1041, *U.S. Income Tax Return for Estates and Trusts* ... 8.20

Form 1045, *Application for Tentative Refund* ... 8.19, 8.20

Form 1065, *U.S. Return of Partnership Income*, Schedule K-1 information for ... 1.5

Form 1120X, *Amended U.S. Corporation Income Tax Return* ... 8.19

Form 1127A, *Application for Extension of time for Payment of Income Tax for 2011 Due to Undue Hardship* ... 5.5

Form 1138, *Extension of Time for Payment of Taxes by a Corporation Expecting a Net Operating Loss Carryback* ... 8.19

Form 1139, *Corporate Application for Tentative Refund* ... 8.19, 8.21

Form 2848, *Power of Attorney and Declaration of Representative* ... 3.13, 4.16

Form 3115, *Application for Change in Accounting Method* ... 6.17

Form 3800, *General Business Credit* ... 9.15

Form 4562, *Depreciation and Amortization* ... 7.21

Form 4564, *Information Document Request* ... 4.9, 4.15

Form 8718, *User Fee for Exempt Organization Determination Letter Request* ... 1.15

Form 8734, *Support Schedule for Advance Ruling Period* ... 1.2

Form 8821, *Tax Information Authorization (TIA)* ... 4.16

Form 8867, *Paid Preparers Earned Income Credit Checklist* ... 3.14

Form 8879, *IRS e-file Signature Authorization* ... 3.9

Form 8938, *Statement of Specified Foreign Financial Assets* ... 2.2

Form 8941, *Credit for Small Employer Health Insurance Premiums* ... 9.14

Form 12153, *Request for a Collection Due Process of Equivalent Hearing* ... 5.24

Form 12277, *Application for Withdrawal of Filed Form 668(Y), Notice of Federal Tax Lien* ... 5.8

Form 14134, *Application for Certificate of Subordination of Federal Tax Lien* ... 5.8

Form 14135, *Application for Certificate of Discharge of Federal Tax Lien* ... 5.7

Form 14157, *Complaint: Tax Return Preparer* ... 3.8

Form W-2, *Wage and Tax Statement* ... 9.23–9.24, 9.25

Form W-12, *IRS Paid Preparer Tax Identification Number (PTIN) Application* ... 3.11

Formal indirect methods used in examination of income ... 4.19–4.19

Fraud
definition of ... 4.24
disclosures by IRS of evidence of ... 4.25
imposition of penalties for ... 4.19
parallel investigations of taxpayer in civil audit suspected of ... 4.24
revealed by audits ... 4.10, 4.18

Fresh Start Initiative, IRS ... 5.1
formula for calculating future income for ... 5.19
introduction of ... 5.4
lien withdrawals under ... 5.8, 5.9
penalty relief in ... 5.4–5.5

G

GAA rules. *See* General asset account (GAA)

Gang of Six tax reform proposal ... 10.15–10.16

Gasoline taxes ... 10.4

General asset account (GAA) ... 7.1–7.26
adjusted depreciable basis of ... 7.13, 7.15, 7.18
change in accounting
    method for ... 7.22–7.25
computing depreciation in ... 7.12–7.14
default rule for ... 7.5
depreciation reserve of ... 7.15
determining asset disposed of from ... 7.16–7.17
disposition of assets from ... 7.14–7.21, 7.23–7.24
effective date for new rules for ... 7.21
grouping assets in ... 7.11–7.12
remaining adjusted depreciable basis of ... 7.13
temporary repair regulations modification of
    rules for ... 7.1
termination of ... 7.20–7.21
unadjusted depreciable
    basis of ... 7.13, 7.15, 7.18
use of ... 7.10

General asset account (GAA) election
filing ... 7.21
for gain or loss on
    qualifying disposition ... 7.17–7.19
late ... 7.22–7.23
retroactive, for existing buildings ... 7.1

**Gift tax returns, understatement of tax
    liability on ... 3.2**

**Government Accountability Office
    (GAO) ... 3.22**

Gulf Opportunity (GO) Zone ... 8.16

H

*Health Care and Education Reconciliation Act
    of 2010,* **enactment in 2010 of ... 9.1**

**Health care coverage reporting under
    Affordable Care Act ... 9.24–9.25**

Health care reform. *See* **Affordable Care Act**

Health flexible spending accounts (FSAs)
Affordable Care Act changes to ... 9.15–9.17
contribution limit for, new ... 9.15–9.16
funding ... 9.15–9.16
scope of medical expenses
    covered by ... 9.16–9.17
use-of-lose rule for ... 9.16

**Health insurance issuer, reporting
    requirements for ... 9.24–9.25**

Health IT Items and Services ... 1.19

**Hiring Incentives to Restore Employment
    Act of 2010 (HIRE Act), FATCA enacted
    as part of ... 2.1**

Home mortgage interest deduction ... 10.19

Hospitals participating in ACO ... 1.19

House Budget Committee
AMT repeal supported by ... 10.14
corporate tax rate reduction
    proposed by ... 10.6
Fiscal Year 2012 report of ... 10.2
tax reform report of ... 10.2, 10.5, 10.6

I

**Improvements to property under temporary
    repair regulations**
adaptations as ... 6.2, 6.16
betterments as ... 6.2, 6.8–6.12
capitalization rule of ... 6.2–6.8
restorations as ... 6.2, 6.12–6.15

**In-business trust fund express installment
    agreements ... 5.4, 5.13, 5.14**

**Income examination during
    IRS audit ... 4.17–4.18**

Income tax returns. *See also* **Tax return;
    Tax return information**
mandatory e-filing for covered ... 3.20–3.21
understatement of tax liability on ... 3.2

**Independent contractors,
    classification of ... 10.13–10.14**

**Indoor tanning services, excise
    tax on ... 9.17–9.18**

**Industry Issue Resolution (IRR)
    program ... 4.10**

Installment agreement, debit ... 5.9
definition of ... 5.12
extension of time to pay for ... 5.17
guaranteed ... 5.13
missed payment for ... 5.17
requesting ... 5.16–5.17
requiring financial analysis ... 5.13, 5.14–5.15
types of, list of ... 5.13
user fee for ... 5.16

Insurance companies
health ... 9.24–9.25
life ... 8.9, 10.10
NOLs of ... 8.9

**Intergovernmental agreement for FATCA
    implementation, model ... 2.24**

International tax system
for foreign-source income ... 10.12
incentives for locating in United
    States in ... 10.12
minimum tax on overseas profit in ... 10.11
territorial ... 10.11
worldwide ... 10.11

Inventory costs ... 6.26

Investment partnership assets,
reporting ... 1.5–1.6

Investment services partnership interest
(ISPI) ... 10.9

IRS audits. *See* Audits, IRS

IRS collections. *See* Collections, IRS

IRS Office of Appeals
for collection appeals ... 5.23–5.26
ex parte communications of ... 4.23
taxpayer appeal of deficiency
assessment through ... 4.22–4.24

IRS Office of Professional Responsibility (OPR)
Circular 230 rules enforced by ... 3.23
interviews by personnel of ... 3.23–3.24

J

Joint Committee on Taxation (JCT)
corporate tax reform report ... 10.6
individual tax preferences analyzed by ... 10.16

Joint venture assets, reporting ... 1.5–1.6

Judicial review of IRS
examination decision ... 4.22

L

Labeler Code of National Drug Code ... 9.19

Land, cost of acquiring ... 6.26

Large Business and International (LB&I)
Division of IRS, audits by ... 4.10–4.11,
4.24, 6.17

Large, unusual, or questionable item (LUQ)
in analyzing audit potential ... 4.13, 4.17

Last-in, first-out (LIFO) inventory
method repeal under President's
Framework ... 10.6, 10.9

Levies, tax ... 5.9–5.12
continuous versus noncontinuous ... 5.10
investigation prior to issuance of ... 5.10
issuance of ... 5.9
property exempt from ... 5.9–5.10
release of ... 5.11–5.12

Life insurance company ... 8.9, 10.10

Limited liability firms, parity of other
business forms with ... 10.14–10.15

Loss corporation
built-in gains and losses ... 8.23–8.24
continuity-of-business-enterprise (COBE)
standards for ... 8.24
in ownership change ... 8.22–8.23

Loss trafficking of NOLs ... 8.22

M

MACRS asset dispositions. *See* Modified
accelerated cost recovery system
(MACRS) asset

Maintenance activity
recurring ... 6.18
routine ... 6.18

Manufacturing, encouraging U.S. ... 10.8

Market Segment Specialization Program
(MSSP), IRS ... 4.21–4.22

Married taxpayers, use of NOL by ... 8.5–8.6

Materials and supplies under temporary
repair regulations
capitalization and deduction
rules for ... 6.20–6.23
change in accounting method for ... 6.23
de minimis expensing rule for ... 6.26
definition of ... 6.21–6.22
effective date for ... 6.23
election to expense ... 6.22–6.23
incidental ... 6.21, 6.23
rotable and temporary spare parts
treated as ... 6.28

Medicaid, Affordable Care Act
expansion of ... 9.2, 9.4

Medical device excise tax
safe harbor for ... 9.22
taxable event for ... 9.22–9.23
taxable medical device under ... 9.21

Medicare Shared Savings Program
(MSSP) ... 1.15–1.19. *See also*
Accountable care organizations (ACOs)
ACO engaged exclusively in activities of ... 1.18
activities unrelated to ... 1.17
design of ... 1.16
guidance for ... 1.15

Minimum essential coverage under
Affordable Care Act ... 9.5–9.7, 9.8,
9.24–9.25

Minimum income probes ... 4.17, 4.18

Modified accelerated cost recovery system
(MACRS) asset ... 7.1–7.26
certain commonly used business
property as ... 7.6–7.8
change in accounting method for ... 7.10,
7.22–7.25
Code Sec. 168(e)(3) property as ... 7.8–7.9
depreciation period for ... 7.6, 7.11
dispositions of ... 7.2–7.10
effective date of disposition
regulations of ... 7.10
GAA for. *See* General asset account (GAA)
granularity of ... 7.5, 7.6

placed in service before
December 30, 2003 ... 7.24–7.25
residential rental property as ... 7.11

Modified taxable income in computing NOL deduction ... 8.13

Mortgage interest deduction versus tax credit ... 10.19

Mutual fund, NOL deductions prohibited for ... 8.10

N

National Commission on Fiscal Responsibility and Reform
creation in 2010 of ... 10.4
home mortgage interest deduction proposal of ... 10.19
reduction of individual tax preferences proposed by ... 10.17–10.18
repeal of AMT supported by ... 10.14, 10.16
report of ... 10.2
retirement account recommendations of ... 10.19
tax plan recommended by ... 10.4–10.5, 10.6

Net operating loss (NOL) ... 8.1–8.25
carryback of ... 8.2, 8.5–8.6, 8.11–8.17, 8.21
carryforward of ... 8.2, 8.3, 8.5–8.6, 8.10, 8.11, 8.13, 8.21
of C corporation ... 8.8–8.9
in corporate acquisitions, treatment of ... 8.21–8.23
corporate equity reduction limit on ... 8.18–8.19
deficiency assessment related or unrelated to ... 8.21
definition of ... 8.1–8.2
of estate ... 8.7, 8.20
excess ... 8.18
generation of ... 8.2
of individuals ... 8.4–8.5, 8.20
not increased by net capital losses ... 8.5
loss trafficking of ... 8.22
of partnership ... 8.7
of S corporation ... 8.8–8.9
tentative carryback adjustment (quick carryback claim) for ... 8.19
transfer of ... 8.21–8.23
of trust ... 8.7, 8.20
usefulness of ... 8.1, 8.3

Net operating loss (NOL) deduction ... 8.1
addback by corporation of ... 8.9
disallowance of, situations for ... 8.4–8.5
reasons for allowing ... 8.2–8.3
smoothing out ... 8.3
steps in figuring ... 8.3–8.4
substantiation for ... 8.19
subtraction from gross income of ... 8.13

Net realizable equity for valuation of assets ... 5.19

Net unrealized built-in gain (NUBIG) and net unrealized built-in loss (NUBIL) ... 8.23–8.24

Network assets under temporary repair regulations ... 6.7

NOL. *See* Net operating loss (NOL)

Nonbusiness income ... 8.5

Nonfinancial foreign entities (NFFEs)
definition of ... 2.4
disclosure requirements for ... 2.2
withholding tax by ... 2.2, 2.4

Nonprofit organizations. *See* Exempt organizations

Notice and demand for payment, delivery of ... 5.3

Notice of Deficiency (IRS Letter 3219), issuance of ... 4.7, 4.22

Notice of Determination following due process hearing ... 5.25

Notice of Federal Tax Lien ... 5.3, 5.6
issuance of ... 5.24, 5.25
withdrawal of ... 5.8

O

Offers in compromise ... 5.17–5.23
defaults on ... 5.23
doubt as to collectibility ... 5.17, 5.18–5.21
doubt as to liability ... 5.17, 5.21
economic hardship considered for. *See* Economic hardship
effective tax administration ... 5.18, 5.21
flexibility increased for ... 5.4
special circumstances for ... 5.20–5.21
submission of ... 5.17

Office examinations ... 4.5
initial contact by IRS for ... 4.8
interview method used for ... 4.8–4.9
Letter 3572 to initiate ... 4.14
limiting scope of ... 4.9
location used for ... 4.8
for small businesses and sole proprietorships ... 4.7
taxpayer request for ... 4.7–4.8
use of correspondence audits versus ... 4.8

Oil and gas tax taxpayers
Code Sec. 199 deduction for ... 10.8
preferences for ... 10.9

Online Payment Agreement application ... 5.16

Optional simplified method for regulated taxpayers
change in accounting method for ... 6.20
effective date for ... 6.20

Organisation for Economic Cooperation and Development (OECD) member tax rates ... 10.6, 10.7

Orphan drug sales exempted from branded prescription drug fee ... 9.19

Over-the-counter medicines under Affordable Care Act ... 9.16–9.17

Overseas profits, minimum tax on ... 10.11

Ownership change of corporations ... 8.21–8.23

P

Partial payment installment agreements ... 5.15–5.16

Partial property interests, restrictions on contributions of ... 1.21–1.22

Partnership
NOL use by ... 8.7
parity of other business forms with ... 10.14–10.15
treatment of ACO as ... 1.16, 1.18

Passthrough businesses
NOLs of ... 8.3, 8.4, 8.8–8.9
parity of other business forms with ... 10.14–10.15
tax rates for ... 10.13

***Patient Protection and Affordable Care Act* (PPACA).** *See also* **Affordable Care Act**
CO-OP Program created by ... 1.15
enactment in 2010 of ... 9.1
Supreme Court as upholding ... 9.1

Penalties, taxpayer ... 4.15, 4.19, 5.4, 5.24. *See also* **Tax return preparer penalties**

***Pension Protection Act of 2006,* conservation deduction enacted under ... 1.22**

Plan year for health FSAs ... 9.15–9.16

Plant property under temporary repair regulations ... 6.4–6.6

Preparer tax return identification number (PTIN) ... 1.6
application for ... 3.11
for e-filing returns ... 3.9
mandatory ... 3.18
online registration system for ... 3.11
penalty for failure to use ... 3.1, 3.7, 3.10–3.12
types of preparers required to use ... 3.10

Prescription drug manufacturers and importers, annual fee on ... 9.18–9.20

Presidentially declared disaster, NOL from ... 8.13, 8.17

President's Framework for Business Tax Reform (President's Framework)
business entity parity in ... 10.15
carried interest in ... 10.9
Code Sec. 199 deduction in ... 10.8
corporate tax rate reduction in ... 10.6
expiration of business tax extenders in ... 10.10
income of foreign subsidiaries of U.S. corporations in ... 10.11
life insurance companies' tax treatment in ... 10.10
LIFO inventory method in ... 10.6, 10.9
overall plan of ... 10.5
as plan for business and individual tax reform ... 10.2
tax credit for moving operations back to United States in ... 10.12
transferring intangible assets to low-tax jurisdictions in ... 10.12
worldwide tax system in ... 10.11

Private foundation
excise tax on ... 1.20
program-related investments of ... 1.20–1.21
status as, terminating ... 1.4
treatment as ... 1.3

Product liability losses for NOL carryback ... 8.16

Program-related investments (PRIs) of private foundations
background of ... 1.20
charitable purposes served by ... 1.20, 1.21
proposed regulations for ... 1.20–1.21

***Public Health Service Act* ... 9.19**

Q

Qualified appraisal, requirements for ... 1.25

Qualified appraiser, requirements for ... 1.25–1.26

Qualified collective investment vehicles ... 2.19

Qualified conservation contribution. *See also* **Charitable conservation easements**
conservation purposes of, list of ... 1.22
definition of ... 1.21–1.22
of partial property interest ... 1.22

Qualified disaster recovery assistance losses ... 8.15

Qualified nonprofit health insurance issuer (QNHII) ... 1.14–1.15

Qualified real property interest for charitable conservation easements ... 1.22

Qualified small business, NOL carryback for ... 8.13–8.14

Qualifying disposition of GAA asset ... 7.17–7.19, 7.23

Quick sale value ... 5.19–5.20

R

Real estate investment trust (REIT), NOL of ... 8.10

Recalcitrant account holders under FATCA ... 2.8–2.9
  passthrough payments allocable to ... 2.15
  reporting requirements for ... 2.15
  withholding for ... 2.16

Reconstruction of income of taxpayer, IRS authority for ... 4.18

Refund check
  exceptions applied to preparer-bank for cashing or endorsing ... 3.13
  negotiation of taxpayer's ... 3.8, 3.13

Refund claim
  due diligence requirements regarding EIC on ... 3.8, 3.13–3.15
  failure of preparer to retain completed copy or list of ... 3.7, 312

Refund claim, failure of preparer to sign ... 3.7, 3.9
  reasonable cause exception to ... 3.10
  willful, Circular 230 conduct rules prohibiting ... 3.10

Registered tax return preparer (RTRP)
  continuing education for ... 3.19
  examination of ... 3.19
  practice rights before IRS of, limited ... 3.19
  requirements for ... 3.18
  sanctions of Circular 230 applicable to ... 3.19–3.20

Regulated investment company, NOL deductions prohibited for ... 8.10

Repair regulations, new temporary ... 6.1–6.30
  adaptations as improvements under ... 6.16
  basic rule for improvements under ... 6.2–6.3
  betterments as improvements under ... 6.8–6.12
  change in accounting method to comply with ... 6.16–6.17, 6.19, 6.20, 6.23, 6.27, 6.29

de minimis expensing rule under ... 6.2, 6.20, 6.22, 6.24–6.27
effective dates for various provisions of ... 6.7, 6.19, 6.20, 6.23, 6.27, 6.29
issuance of ... 6.24, 7.1
MACRS assets under ... 7.1
materials and supplies under, capitalization versus expensing of ... 6.20–6.23
optional method for rotable spare parts under ... 6.27–6.29
preamble to ... 7.3
restorations as improvements under ... 6.12–6.15
routine maintenance safe harbor of ... 6.17–
unit of property under, determining ... 6.3–6.8

Reportable transactions ... 3.5

Representatives for IRS audit, types of ... 4.16

Research tax credit ... 10.10–10.11

Restorations of unit of property ... 6.2, 6.12–6.15

Retail sales tax ... 10.4

Retirement of component of property ... 6.13, 7.10

Retirement accounts, calls to maintain incentives for ... 10.18–10.19

Retirement plan
  certified deemed-compliant status as ... 2.20
  contributions to, as nonbusiness deductions ... 8.5

Return preparer penalties. *See* Tax return preparer penalties

Roofs under temporary repair regulations ... 6.14–6.15, 7.6

Rotable spare parts
  change in accounting method for treatment of ... 6.29
  definition of ... 6.27
  effective date for treatment of ... 6.29
  optional method of accounting for ... 6.18, 6.27–6.29
  repairing or maintaining ... 6.18–6.19

Routine maintenance safe harbor (RMSH) under temporary repair regulations
  change in accounting method for ... 6.19
  definitions of maintenance activities for ... 6.18
  effective date for ... 6.19
  exclusions from ... 6.17, 6.18

S

S corporation
  NOL of ... 8.3, 8.4, 8.8–8.9
  parity of other business forms with ... 10.14–10.15

Schedule C expenses, claiming ... 4.10

Schedule UTP, Uncertain Tax Positions,
program ... 4.10

Section 1245 property
components as assets for ... 7.9
retirement of component of unit of ... 7.3

Section 1245 property in GAA ... 7.1
depreciation recapture for ... 7.18
disposition of ... 7.16
retroactive election for ... 7.1

Section 1250 property ... 7.9, 7.16
depreciation recapture for ... 7.18

Self-employment income, reported ... 4.2

Senate Greater Research Opportunities
with Tax Help (GROWTH) Act ... 10.10

September 11 recovery program, NOL
carryback period for ... 8.16

Shared Savings Program. See Medicare
Shared Savings Program (MSSP)

Simpson-Bowles recommendations.
See National Commission on Fiscal
Responsibility and Reform

Small Business and Self-Employed (SB/SE)
Division, audits by ... 4.24

Small Business Health Options Program
(SHOP Exchange) ... 9.7

Small businesses
NOL carryback for ... 8.17
office examinations of ... 4.7
tax reform proposals for ... 10.12–10.15

Small employers, health coverage
reporting by ... 9.23–9.24

Sole proprietorships
NOLs of ... 8.4
office examinations of ... 4.7
parity of other business forms with ...
10.14–10.15

Specified liability loss, NOL
carryback for ... 8.15–8.16

Specified tax return preparer ... 3.20,
3.21–3.22

Specified U.S. persons
exceptions for entities not considered ... 2.10
reporting requirements of participating
FFIs regarding ... 2.15
United States account held by ... 2.9

Statute of limitations for assessing
deficiency of tax liability ... 4.11–4.12
extensions to ... 4.12, 5.2

Streamlined installment
agreements ... 5.4, 5.13–5.14

Streamlined offer in compromise program
expansion of ... 5.4
household income restriction for ... 5.23
implementation of ... 5.23
liabilities restriction for ... 5.23

Substantial United States owner under
FATCA FFI agreement ... 2.4, 2.10

Surface Transportation Board (STB)
accounting rules ... 6.20

T

Tangible property repair regulations. See
Repair regulations

Tanning services, excise tax on ... 9.17–9.18

Tax assessment
definition of ... 5.2
statute of limitations for ... 5.2
types of ... 5.2

Tax code revisions. See Tax reform

Tax evasion
class of payment posing low risk of ... 2.6
preventing ... 2.1, 2.2
reportable transaction with purpose of ... 3.5

Tax Exempt and Government Entities
(TE/GE) Division, IRS audits by ... 4.24

Tax-exempt organizations. See Exempt
organizations

Tax exemption, general
requirements for ... 1.18

Tax expenditures
Deficit Commission plan to reduce or
eliminate ... 10.4–10.5, 10.17–10.18
Gang of Six proposal to reduce ... 10.16
largest 20 individual ... 10.16–10.17

Tax fraud, definition of ... 4.24–4.25

Tax gap ... 2.1

Tax identification number (TIN)
of substantial United States owners ... 2.4
of U.S. person account holder ... 2.15

Tax levy, administrative ... 5.5

Tax liability, understatement of ... 3.1, 3.2–3.4

Tax lien
as administrative collection tactic ... 5.5
discharge of ... 5.7
encumbrance of taxpayer property in ... 5.1
notice of filing of ... 5.6, 5.24
relationship of IRS to other
creditors under ... 5.5–5.6
release of ... 5.6, 5.7
subordination of ... 5.6, 5.7–5.8
withdrawal of ... 5.6

Tax rates
corporate ... 10.2, 10.5–10.12, 10.13
Deficit Commission's
recommendations for ... 10.16
on foreign income of
American businesses ... 10.2
House Budget Committee recommendations
for ... 10.2, 10.5
individual ... 10.13, 10.15–10.16
President's Framework
recommendations for ... 10.6

Tax reform ... 10.1–10.20
Camp plan for ... 10.2, 10.5, 10.6, 10.11,
10.15, 10.16
Congressional Research Service
Report on ... 10.3
of corporate tax rate. *See* Corporate tax rate
Deficit Commission's report on. *See* National
Commission on Fiscal Responsibility and
Reform
flat-tax plan for ... 10.5
fundamental ... 10.10
Gang of Six proposal for ... 10.15–10.16
House Budget Committee
report on ... 10.2, 10.5, 10.6
individual ... 10.13, 10.15–10.19
international ... 10.11–10.12
lawmaker interest in, increased ... 10.1, 10.2
legislative push for ... 1.5
President's Framework for ... 10.2, 10.5,
10.8. *See also* President's Framework
for Business Tax Reform (President's
Framework)
Romney's plan for ... 10.5
Senate Financial Committee
hearings on ... 10.2–10.3, 10.8, 10.18
small business ... 10.12–10.15

Tax Reform Act of 1986 ... 10.1

Tax return
analyzing calculation of income
reported on ... 4.17
audits of. *See* Audits, IRS
correction of minor errors on ... 4.1
definition of ... 3.17
due diligence requirements of preparer for
claiming EIC on ... 3.8, 3.13–3.15
electronically signed ... 3.9
failure of preparer to provide taxpayer with
completed copy of ... 3.1, 3.7, 3.8–3.9
failure of preparer to retain copy
or list of ... 3.7, 3.12
failure of preparer to sign ... 3.7, 3.9–3.10
failure to file, fraudulent ... 4.19
frivolous ... 4.19
spending on preparation of ... 10.1
unauthorized disclosure of
information from ... 3.1

Tax return information
missing ... 4.13
permissible disclosures and uses by
preparer of ... 3.17–3.18
unauthorized disclosure of ... 3.1, 3.16–3.17, 3.18
written consent for disclosure of ... 3.18

Tax return preparer. *See also*
individual types
background checks for ... 3.12
criminal sanctions for unauthorized return
information disclosed by ... 3.1, 3.16–3.18
definition of ... 3.15
employer of, penalty to file information returns
regarding preparers by ... 3.7, 3.12–3.13
oversight by IRS of ... 3.18
Social Security number of, in applying for
PTIN ... 3.11
Social Security number of, on Form 990 ... 1.6

Tax return preparer penalties ... 3.1–3.24
Code Sec. 6694 ... 3.2–3.4
Code Sec. 6695 ... 3.7–3.15
reasonable cause exception to ... 3.1, 3.3–3.4,
3.9, 3.11–3.12, 3.13
for tax shelters and
reportable transactions ... 3.5
types of offenses triggering ... 3.1, 4.19

Tax shelters ... 3.5, 4.19

Taxes, types of new ... 10.3–10.4

**Taxpayer Bill of Rights 2 applicable during
IRS audit ... 4.15**

Temporary repair regulations. *See* **Repair
regulations, new temporary**

Temporary spare parts, definition of ... 6.28

Territory financial institutions ... 2.7

Theft loss, NOL carryback period for ... 8.13

**Treasury Inspector General for Tax
Administration (TIGTA) ... 1.6, 1.10, 1.11,
4.10, 5.25**

Trusts, use of NOLs by ... 8.7, 8.20

U

**Understatement of income,
substantial ... 4.19**

Understatement of tax liability
accuracy-related penalty for ... 4.19
explanation of ... 4.18

**Understatement of tax liability, preparer
penalty for ... 3.1, 3.2–3.4**
categories of returns subject to ... 3.2
definition of tax return preparer for ... 3.2

**Unit of property under temporary repair
regulations ... 6.2–6.8**

acquisition or production
cost of ... 6.21, 6.26
adaptations of ... 6.2, 6.16
betterments to ... 6.2, 6.8–6.12
change of accounting method for ... 6.7–6.8
definition of ... 7.4
depreciation of ... 6.5
economic useful life of ... 6.21
effective date of provisions for ... 6.7
major component or substantial structural
part of ... 6.13–6.14
repair deductions for ... 7.5
restorations of ... 6.2, 6.12–6.15
routine maintenance safe harbor for ... 6.17–6.19

**United States account held by
participating FFI ... 2.9**
for members of expanded
affiliate group ... 2.16
reporting requirements for ... 2.13–2.15

United States Claims Court ... 4.22

United States District Court ... 4.22

**United States-owned
foreign entities ... 2.9, 2.10**

*United States-Republic of Korea Free Trade
Agreement Implementation Act
of 2011* ... 3.15

**United States Supreme Court, Affordable
Care Act upheld in 2012 by ... 9.1–9.4**

**Unrelated business income (UBI)
of ACO ... 1.17–1.18**

**Unreported Income DIF (UI DIF) system for
returns selected for auditing ... 4.4**

V

Valuation overstatement ... 4.19

Value-added tax (VAT) ... 10.3–10.4

**Voluntary compliance program (VCP) for
Form 990-N filers ... 1.10**

W

Waiver of NOL carryback ... 8.11–8.13, 8.15

Waiver of taxpayer penalties ... 4.19

Withholdable payments ... 2.3
dates for withholding ... 2.23
payments associated by withholding
agents with ... 2.8
payments excluded from ... 2.5
payments includible as 2.4–2.5
proposed regulations addressing
exclusions from ... 2.7

Withholding agents
acting as intermediaries ... 2.6
exceptions to withholding
requirements for ... 2.5–2.7
grantor trusts as ... 2.3
participating FFIs as ... 2.3
reporting of owner-documented, certified
deemed-compliant FFIs by ... 2.21
requirement to determine FFI's
status for ... 2.8

Withholding certificates ... 2.8

Withholding, tax
exceptions to requirements for
withholding agents for ... 2.5–2.7
by FFIs and NFFEs ... 2.2–2.4, 2.6, 2.15–2.16
for passthrough payments ... 2.15–2.16, 2.23

**Worker classification rules,
call for ... 10.13–10.14**

*Worker, Homeownership, and Business
Assistance Act of 2009* ... 3.20

TOP FEDERAL TAX ISSUES FOR 2013 CPE COURSE

CPE Quizzer Instructions

This CPE Quizzer is divided into four Modules. To obtain CPE Credit, go to **CCHGroup.com/PrintCPE** to complete your Quizzers online for immediate results and no Express Grading Fee. There is a grading fee for each Quizzer submission.

Processing Fee:	Recommended CPE:	Recommended CFP:
$56.00 for Module 1	4 hours for Module 1	2 hours for Module 1
$70.00 for Module 2	5 hours for Module 2	2 hours for Module 2
$84.00 for Module 3	6 hours for Module 3	3 hours for Module 3
$28.00 for Module 4	2 hours for Module 4	1 hours for Module 4
$238.00 for all Modules	17 hours for all Modules	8 hours for all Modules

CTEC Course Number:	IRS Program Number:	Federal Tax Law Hours:
1075-CE-0015 for Module 1	4VRWB-T-00355-12-S for Module 1	4 hours for Module 1
1075-CE-0016 for Module 2	4VRWB-T-00356-12-S for Module 2	5 hours for Module 2
1075-CE-0017 for Module 3	4VRWB-T-00357-12-S for Module 3	6 hours for Module 3
1075-CE-0018 for Module 4	4VRWB-T-00358-12-S for Module 4	2 hours for Module 4
		17 hours for all Modules

Instructions for purchasing your CPE Tests and accessing them after purchase are provided on the **CCHGroup.com/PrintCPE** website.

To mail or fax your Quizzer, send your completed Answer Sheet for each Quizzer Module to **CCH Continuing Education Department, 4025 W. Peterson Ave., Chicago, IL 60646,** or fax it to (773) 866-3084. Each Quizzer Answer Sheet will be graded and a CPE Certificate of Completion awarded for achieving a grade of 70 percent or greater. The Quizzer Answer Sheets are located at the back of this book.

Express Grading: Processing time for your mailed or faxed Answer Sheet is generally 8-12 business days. To use our Express Grading Service, at an additional $19 per Module, please check the "Express Grading" box on your Answer Sheet and provide your CCH account or credit card number **and your fax number.** CCH will fax your results and a Certificate of Completion (upon achieving a passing grade) to you by 5:00 p.m. the business day following our receipt of your Answer Sheet. **If you mail your Answer Sheet for Express Grading, please write "ATTN: CPE OVERNIGHT" on the envelope.** NOTE: CCH will not Federal Express Quizzer results under any circumstances.

Recommended CPE credit is based on a 50-minute hour. Participants earning credits for states that require self-study to be based on a 100-minute hour will receive ½ the CPE credits for successful completion of this course. Because CPE requirements vary from state to state and among different licensing agencies, please contact your CPE governing body for information on your CPE requirements and the applicability of a particular course for your requirements.

Date of Completion: If you mail or fax your Quizzer to CCH, the date of completion on your Certificate will be the date that you put on your Answer Sheet. However, you must submit your Answer Sheet to CCH for grading within two weeks of completing it.

Expiration Date: December 31, 2013

Evaluation: To help us provide you with the best possible products, please take a moment to fill out the course Evaluation located after your Quizzer. A copy is also provided at the back of this course if you choose to mail or fax your Quizzer Answer Sheets.

CCH is registered with the National Association of State Boards of Accountancy (NASBA) as a sponsor of continuing professional education on the National Registry of CPE Sponsors. State boards of accountancy have final authority on the acceptance of individual courses for CPE credit. Complaints regarding registered sponsors may be addressed to the National Registry of CPE Sponsors, 150 Fourth Avenue North, Suite 700, Nashville, TN 37219-2417. Web site: www.nasba.org.

CCH is registered with the National Association of State Boards of Accountancy (NASBA) as a Quality Assurance Service (QAS) sponsor of continuing professional education. State boards of accountancy have final authority on the acceptance of individual courses for CPE credit. Complaints regarding registered sponsors may be addressed to NASBA, 150 Fourth Avenue North, Suite 700, Nashville, TN 37219-2417. Web site: www.nasba.org.

CCH has been approved by the California Tax Education Council to offer courses that provide federal and state credit towards the annual "continuing education" requirement imposed by the State of California. A listing of additional requirements to register as a tax preparer may be obtained by contacting CTEC at P.O. Box 2890, Sacramento, CA, 95812-2890, toll-free by phone at (877) 850-2832, or on the Internet at www.ctec.org.

Quizzer Questions: Module 1

1. For tax year 2011 (forms filed in 2012), Form 1065, Schedule K-1 information:

   a. Is optional on the exempt organization's Form 990, Schedule H
   b. May be reported from the exempt organization's books and records
   c. Must be reported using the partnership's books and records
   d. Must be developed from the 2011 audit report of the exempt organization

2. Exempt organizations that have been in existence at least three years may submit Form 990-N, the e-postcard, if the organization has annual gross receipts of less than or equal to:

   a. $50,000
   b. $100,000
   c. $250,000
   d. $500,000

3. The Tax Court has been perceived as showing leniency in case decisions for conservation easements on land that is or is intended to be used as a _____.

   a. Boating launch and storage site
   b. Youth campground
   c. Private university sports field
   d. Golf course

4. The new proposed regulations on program-related investments (PRIs) do *not* illustrate:

   a. Activities conducted in foreign countries
   b. Investments with a potentially high rate of return
   c. Payments for lobbying that would benefit the exempt organization
   d. Examples of PRIs as requested by private foundations

5. Charitable contribution easements:

   a. Help permanently preserve outdoor lands and historical structures
   b. Have very quantifiable benefits to the public
   c. Are a charitable deduction area that has historically shown not to be abusive
   d. Exclude charitable "qualified conservation contributions" of partial interests to qualified organizations

6. The online search tool on which users can check certain tax status and filing information about exempt organizations is:

   a. Exempt Organization Select Check
   b. TIGTA Report on Exempt Organizations
   c. Foundation Tax Finder
   d. Auto-Revocation and Reinstatement Tool

7. Final regulations for accountable care organizations (ACOs) specify:

   a. The type of legal entity an ACO must adopt
   b. That a charitable can participate in the Medicare Shared Savings Program (MSSP) through an ACO
   c. That an ACO cannot conduct activities unrelated to the Shared Savings Program without losing its tax-exempt status
   d. That an ACO may not be organized as a Code Sec. 501(c)(3) entity to participate in the Medicare Shared Savings Program

8. To qualify for tax exemption as a Code Sec. 501(c)(3) organization, an ACO engaged in Shared Savings Program activities:

   a. Must engage exclusively in activities that achieve charitable purposes
   b. May select the partnership form of business entity
   c. May not provide electronic health record software and technical support
   d. May not be a single hospital or clinic

9. Under the proposed regulations for exempt private foundations, program-related investments (PRIs):

   a. Are considered a jeopardy investment
   b. May include charitable purposes such as fighting environment hazards or promoting the arts
   c. Are not qualified if the investments have a potentially high rate of return
   d. Are no longer subject to excise tax

10. A donor must get a qualified appraisal issued by a qualified appraiser for donated property claimed to be worth more than:

    a. $500
    b. $2,000
    c. $3,500
    d. $5,000

11. The *Foreign Account Tax Compliance Act* (FATCA) mandates that withholding agents withhold _____ of withholdable payments to a nonparticipating foreign financial institution (FFI).

    a. 10 percent
    b. 20 percent
    c. 25 percent
    d. 30 percent

12. Nonfinancial foreign entities are also subject to the withholding requirement unless they provide the withholding agent with:

    a. Complete informational listings of all owners associated with the payments
    b. Certification that the beneficial owners are not substantial U.S. owners or the U.S. owner's contact information and TIN
    c. Certification that the payments will not be transferred before January 1, 2017
    d. An FFI agreement showing that the account holder is not recalcitrant

13. Grandfathered obligations not subject to withholding under FATCA apply to those existing on:

    a. March 18, 2012
    b. January 1, 2013
    c. January 1, 2015
    d. March 31, 2017

14. The terms of a foreign financial institution (FFI) agreement apply to checking, savings, CD, and interest-bearing accounts determined to be United States:

    a. Agent accounts
    b. Financial accounts
    c. Substantiated accounts
    d. Attributable accounts

15. Foreign financial institutions participating in an FFI agreement must comply with due diligence and verification requirements under FATCA if a preexisting individual account contains at least _____ or an insurance or annuity contract is valued at _____ or more.

    a. $10,000; $100,000
    b. $25,000; $150,000
    c. $50,000; $250,000
    d. $100,000; $1 million

16. Preexisting entity accounts that have balances of $250,000 or less are not subject to the due diligence requirements for FFI agreements until the balance exceeds:

    a. $500,000
    b. $750,000
    c. $1 million
    d. $2 million

17. Registered or certified FFIs are exempt from withholding tax if they are:

    a. Nonparticipating
    b. Deemed compliant
    c. Unrestricted funds
    d. Nontreaty FFIs

18. An FFI that, under local law, cannot report or withhold as required under its FFI agreement is a(n):

    a. Limited FFI
    b. Passthrough FFI
    c. Unrestricted FFI
    d. Unlicensed FFI

19. To ensure that an FFI will be identified as a participating FFI and avoid withholding beginning on January 1, 2014, a participating FFI must enter into an FFI agreement by:

    a. December 31, 2012
    b. June 30, 2013
    c. December 1, 2013
    d. December 15, 2013

20. Withholding agents will be required to withhold tax on all withholdable payments made on or after:

    a. December 31, 2013
    b. June 30, 2014
    c. December 15, 2014
    d. January 1, 2015

Quizzer Questions: Module 2

21. Code Sec. 6694(a) imposes a penalty in an amount equal to the greater of _____ or ____ of the income derived—or to be derived—by the tax return preparer from the preparation of the return

    a. $100 or 10 percent
    b. $500 or 25 percent
    c. $1,000 or 50 percent
    d. $5,000 or 75 percent

22. Code Sec. 6694(b) imposes a penalty in an amount equal to the greater of _____ or ____ percent of the income derived—or to be derived—by the tax return preparer from preparing a return that understates a client's tax liability resulting from the preparer's willful attempt to understate the client's tax liability; or the preparer's reckless or intentional disregard of rules and regulations.

    a. $100 or 10 percent
    b. $500 or 25 percent
    c. $5,000 or 50 percent
    d. $10,000 or 100 percent

23. If both the Code Sec. 6694(a) and Code Sec. 6694(b) penalties apply to a tax return preparer:

    a. The 6694(a) amount must be multiplied by two
    b. The 6694(b) amount must be reduced by the 6694(a) amount
    c. The 6694(b) amount must be ignored
    d. The greater of the two amounts is used

24. What is the maximum penalty under Code Sec. 6695(f), Negotiation of Check, for each check issued to the taxpayer impermissibly endorsed or otherwise negotiated by a preparer?

    a. $500
    b. $1,000
    c. $2,000
    d. There is no maximum per-check dollar penalty

25. All tax return preparers who prepare returns for compensation must obtain and use a preparer tax identification number (PTIN) unless the returns are exempt by the IRS. The PTIN requirement applies as of _____.

    a. January 1, 2009
    b. January 1, 2011
    c. January 1, 2012
    d. January 1, 2013

26. Under *United States-Republic of Korea Free Trade Agreement Implementation Act of 2011,* the penalty for noncompliance with the Code Sec. 6695(g) earned income credit (EIC) due diligence requirements for tax returns for tax years ending on or after December 31, 2011 is:

    a. $100 per failure
    b. $250 per failure
    c. $300 per failure
    d. $500 per failure

27. Under Code Sec. 7216, the maximum penalty for tax return preparers who knowingly or recklessly make unauthorized disclosures or uses of information furnished in connection with the preparation of an income tax return is:

    a. Six months imprisonment or a fine of up to $500 or both
    b. One year imprisonment or a fine of up to $1,000 or both
    c. Two years imprisonment or a fine of up to $5,000 or both
    d. Five years imprisonment or a fine of up to $10,000 or both

28. The new designation for tax return preparers initiated as a result of an IRS oversight study in 2009 is:

    a. Registered tax return preparers
    b. Unenrolled agents
    c. Supervised preparers
    d. Enrolled tax return practitioners

29. A specified tax return preparer for purposes of mandatory e-filing is any person who prepares covered returns for compensation unless that person reasonably expects to file _____ or fewer individual income tax returns in a calendar year.

    a. 10
    b. 25
    c. 50
    d. 100

30. Circular 230's rules of practice are enforced by the:

    a. Financial Accounting Standards Board
    b. IRS Office of Professional Responsibility
    c. International Financial Reporting Standards Board
    d. Public Company Accounting Oversight Board

31. For fiscal year 2011, the IRS Enforcement and Service Results show that examinations of returns:

    a. Represented a 12-year high for individual return exams
    b. Exceeded 2 percent of business and corporate returns
    c. Were less frequent for individual than for business returns
    d. Focused on returns of taxpayers in lower adjusted gross income classes

32. Absent indications of fraud, the statute of limitations for assessing a deficiency of tax liability running from the date of filing a return is generally:

    a. One year
    b. Two years
    c. Three years
    d. Five years

33. IRS audit guidelines provide that examinations of individual returns generally should be completed within ____ of the date was due or filed, whichever occurs later.

    a. 12 months
    b. 15 months
    c. 24 months
    d. 26 months

34. A taxpayer's completion of Form 8821, *Tax Information Authorization (TIA)*, allows the IRS to:

   a. Issue an administrative summons to expedite the examination's determination
   b. Share confidential information about the taxpayer's return with the individual or organization chosen by the taxpayer
   c. Assign counsel for the taxpayer free of charge
   d. Initiate interviews with third parties about the taxpayer's income sources

35. An IRS examiner may consider any of the following factors while selecting the best examination technique for gathering evidence *except:*

   a. Less expensive alternatives to high-cost techniques
   b. Likelihood that the taxpayer may seek representation
   c. Benefits to be gained versus costs and burden of employing the method
   d. Effectiveness of the method in obtaining the necessary evidence

36. When an examiner has reviewed all audit evidence and found proper substantiation of items under review, the determination is termed a(n):

   a. Agreed
   b. Undisputed
   c. No change
   d. Unadjusted

37. If, following the taxpayer's appeal of a determination through a conference with the examiner's supervisor, the disputed assessment and penalties are unresolved, the taxpayer has _____ to respond with another course of appeal within the IRS.

   a. 10 days
   b. 25 days
   c. 30 days
   d. 90 days

38. An example of a prohibited *ex parte* communication between an IRS Office of Appeals employee and another IRS employee would be:

   a. An e-mail from a taxpayer representative to an IRS Office of Appeals employee
   b. A private discussion between an IRS Office of Appeals Employee and the IRS examining agent regarding the case's outcome
   c. A request from an IRS Office of Appeals Employee for legal advice from the IRS Office of Chief Counsel
   d. A letter exchange between two IRS Office of Appeals employees

39. When the IRS issues Letter 3219, Notice of Deficiency, in a correspondence audit, the taxpayer must pay the assessment or petition the U.S. Tax Court for judicial review within:

   a. 30 days
   b. 60 days
   c. 90 days
   d. 120 days

40. Teams of IRS specialists in the Market Segment Specialization Project prepare:

   a. Internal Revenue Manual revisions
   b. Audit Technique Guides
   c. Industry Issue Resolution procedures
   d. Compliance Assurance Process procedures

41. Self-assessed taxes are:

   a. Overpayments of current tax to create a reserve for a future tax liability
   b. Based on amounts reported on the taxpayer's tax return
   c. Based on determination the IRS makes after examinations
   d. Determined by the U.S. Tax Court

42. Unless the statutory period for collection is tolled or extended, the IRS generally has a collection period for an assessed liability of up to:

   a. 90 days
   b. 3 years
   c. 5 years
   d. 10 years

43. The Fresh Start Initiative created in 2011 improved IRS collection practices in all of the following ways **except:**

    a. Increasing the dollar maximums for liabilities qualifying for streamlined installment agreements
    b. Doubling the threshold for filing a Form 668(Y)(c), *Notice of Federal Tax Lien*
    c. Lengthening the time for requesting a hearing following notification of a tax lien
    d. Easing the process for obtaining a withdrawal of federal tax lien when a liability is paid

44. The IRS usually will withdraw its *Notice of Federal Tax Lien* if:

    a. The other creditors have priority over the IRS's tax lien in the taxpayer's assets
    b. The taxpayer enters an installment agreement to pay the liability
    c. The taxpayer disposes of the property subject to the lien
    d. The taxpayer declares a Chapter 11 bankruptcy

45. Which type of installment agreement may **not** be used by businesses?

    a. Guaranteed installment agreements
    b. In-business trust fund express agreements
    c. Streamlined installment agreements
    d. Installment agreements requiring financial analysis

46. Reasonable collection potential (RCP) is calculated for purposes of:

    a. An offer in compromise based on doubt as to liability
    b. An offer in compromise based on doubt as to collectability
    c. An offer in compromise based on effective tax administration
    d. Any case of individual or business taxpayers in which no financial records are available

47. For an offer in compromise, assets are valued using their:

    a. Net realizable equity
    b. Quick sale value
    c. Fair market value
    d. Market comparable value

48. Which of the following are the two general types of effective tax administration offer in compromise?

    a. Individual economic hardship and equity or public policy
    b. Streamlined and direct debit
    c. Doubt as to collectibility and doubt as to liability
    d. Future income and business economic hardship

49. Which type of collection appeal allows the taxpayer to appeal its decision to the Tax Court?

    a. Collection due process hearing (CDP)
    b. Equivalent hearing
    c. Collection appeals program (CAP) appeal
    d. No appeal may be made by taxpayers directly to the Tax Court but only to the District Court

50. A major difference between a CDP hearing and an equivalent hearing is that:

    a. The taxpayer may request an equivalent hearing before receiving notices of collection actions
    b. The information considered and procedures used by the Appeals Office differ in the two types
    c. The decision of the Appeals Office in an equivalent hearing is final
    d. The equivalent hearing addresses cases of lower tax liability than does the CDP hearing

Quizzer Questions: Module 3

51. A unit of property:

    a. Includes all property within a manufacturing plant
    b. Does not affect the analysis of whether an expenditure is a repair or capitalized expense
    c. Consists of functionally interdependent components
    d. Is not defined in the case of a building

52. Which one of the following expenditures is **not** capitalized as a betterment?

    a. A simple retail store refresh
    b. Environmental remediation costs attributable to environmental damage caused by a prior land owner
    c. Amelioration a material condition or defect that arose during a taxpayer's production of a unit of property
    d. The addition of a new wing on a building

53. In comparing when work on property is capitalized versus deductible:

    a. If a casualty loss is claimed, the cost of repairing the property may also be claimed as an additional deduction
    b. The cost of replacing an entire roof is deductible
    c. If a taxpayer replaces a component of a unit of property and properly claims a loss deduction for that component, the cost of the new component must be capitalized
    d. Rebuilding a machine to a like-new condition in accordance with a manufacturer's specifications is a deductible repair if the rebuild occurs after the machine's MACRS alternative depreciation system has expired

54. The routine maintenance safe harbor:

    a. Applies to activity that is necessary to keep a unit of property in its ordinary efficient operating condition as a result of the taxpayer's use of the property
    b. Applies to an activity that is only performed once during a unit of property's class life (i.e., MACRS alternative depreciation recovery period)
    c. Applies to rotable spare parts if the optional method of accounting for rotable spare parts is used
    d. Must be elected in order to apply

55. Which of the following is *not* a material or supply?

   a, A unit of property that has an economic useful life of 60 months or less, beginning when the property is used or consumed in the taxpayer's operations
   b. A component (whether or not the component is a unit of property) that is acquired to maintain, repair, or improve a unit of tangible property
   c. A unit of property that has an acquisition or production cost of $100 or less
   d. Fuel reasonably expected to be consumed in 12 or fewer months, beginning when used in   the taxpayer's operations

56. Which of the following elections applies to a material and supply?

   a. An election to treat units of property with an acquisition cost of $1,000 or less as materials and supplies
   b. An election to treat a material and supply as inventory
   c. An election to treat a material and supply as Section 1250 property
   d. An election to capitalize the cost of a material or supply

57. The *de minimis* expensing rule may only be used by a taxpayer:

   a. With an applicable financial statement
   b. Without any written accounting procedure that treats amounts costing less than a certain dollar amount as an expense for nontax purposes
   c. With annual gross receipts of less than $10 million
   d. With a net operating loss

58. The total amount that may be expensed under the *de minimis* rule is limited to the greater of: _____ percent of gross receipts reported for federal income tax purposes for the tax year or 2 percent of total depreciation and amortization reported on the applicable financial statement for the tax year.

   a. 5.0
   b. 0.1
   c. 10.0
   d. 20.0

59. If the optional method for rotable spare parts is *not* elected, the cost of a rotable spare part is deducted in the year that it is:

    a. Purchased
    b. Disposed
    c. Installed
    d. First repaired

60. The optional method for rotable spare parts:

    a. If elected, does not need to be applied to all of a taxpayer's rotable spare parts used in the same trade or business
    b. Does not apply to temporary spare parts
    c. May only be elected by corporations
    d. Allows a taxpayer to deduct the cost of a rotable spare part in the year it is first installed

61. Which of the following is generally *not* used in determining the adjusted depreciable basis of an asset?

    a. Code Sec. 168(k) bonus depreciation claimed
    b. Asset's fair value
    c. Code Sec. 179 deduction claimed
    d. Asset's cost

62. Under the temporary regulations, when a MACRS asset is disposed of by converting it to personal use:

    a. A loss is claimed, based on the asset's depreciated value
    b. A gain is reported, based on the asset's current fair value
    c. A gain is reported, based on the asset's replacement value
    d. No gain or loss is recognized

63. In ideal circumstances for deducting, a taxpayer will not choose _____ that results in a loss deduction when a repair deduction may be claimed.

    a. A structural component
    b. An interdependent component
    c. A bundle of components
    d. A level of granularity

64. A group of all functionally interdependent components is known as:

    a. A unified asset
    b. Structurally linked assets
    c. A unit of property
    d. Operable assets

65. The asset disposition regulations apply to tax years beginning on or after:

    a. January 1, 2011
    b. January 1, 2012
    c. January 1, 2013
    d. January 1, 2014, with transition rules applied during 2013

66. For a previously retired structural component of a building, a Code Sec. 481(a) adjustment and change in accounting method are required if:

    a. A taxpayer is currently depreciating the retired structural component
    b. A taxpayer files Form 4562, *Depreciation and Amortization*
    c. The retired structural component is fully depreciated
    d. The taxpayer makes a retroactive general asset account election for the building and does not retroactively elect to recognize a loss on the retirement as a qualifying disposition

67. The adjusted depreciable basis of a general asset account (GAA) is:

    a. Increased by all deductions and expensed items claimed in the tax period
    b. The sum of the fair market values of all assets within the GAA
    c. The cost of the assets in the account plus any Section 179 deductions claimed on the assets in the GAA
    d. The unadjusted depreciable basis of the GAA minus depreciation deductions and bonus depreciation claimed for the account

68. A taxpayer may make a GAA election on an amended return within _____ of the due date of the return (excluding extensions).

    a. 30 days
    b. 90 days
    c. 6 months
    d. 12 months

69. A late GAA election may be made by a calendar-year taxpayer in tax years that begin in:

    a. 2011 and 2012
    b. 2012 and 2013
    c. 2013 and 2014
    d. The late GAA election expired in 2011

70. When a taxpayer files amended returns for open tax years regarding pre-2003 assets in order to comply with the temporary MACRS regulations:

    a. A cumulative depreciation adjustment is allowed
    b. The change is not considered a change in method of accounting
    c. A Code Sec. 481(a) adjustment is required
    d. Bonus depreciation previously claimed is recaptured

71. All of the following are reasons that justify net operating loss (NOL) deductions *except:*

    a. Offsetting timing consequences of the annual tax period
    b. Deducting the expenses of earning income
    c. Stimulating investments by a new entity
    d. Offering refunds to taxpayers in tax years of losses

72. When more than one NOL amount is available for deduction, the taxpayer:

    a. Combines all of the amounts for a lump-sum deduction
    b. Starts with the amount in the earliest tax year
    c. Can only carry the combined amounts forward to claim in succeeding tax years
    d. Applies the largest NOL amount to the current tax year's return

73. Which of the following is *not* a circumstance in which an individual commonly has an NOL?

    a. Claiming a loss incurred by a spouse on a joint return
    b. Claiming a prior-year deduction for a bankruptcy estate loss
    c. Claiming a spouse's losses on a separate return
    d. Claiming expenses for improvements to rental property used to produce income

74. An NOL is claimed first for:

    a. The current tax year as long as the taxpayer has a loss
    b. The earliest carryback year for which the NOL is permitted
    c. All prior tax years in which the taxpayer had income
    d. Any future period up to the following 20 tax years

75. When a taxpayer carries back an NOL to a previous tax year, all of the following tax elements are recomputed *except:*

    a. Alternative minimum tax
    b. The charitable deduction
    c. Itemized deductions
    d. Casualty losses

76. The general carryforward period for deducting an NOL is:

    a. 2 years
    b. 5 years
    c. 10 years
    d. 20 years

77. Product liabilities, workplace liabilities, or environmental remediation are specified liability losses allowed a carryback period of:

    a. 2 tax years
    b. 5 tax years
    c. 10 tax years
    d. An unlimited number of tax years

78. A quick carryback claim is filed to claim:

    a. An election to waive the carryback period
    b. A tentative carryback adjustment
    c. A revision to an existing carryback amount
    d. A waiver for using a loss carryforward

79. In a corporate acquisition, the target corporation's NOLs:

    a. May not be carried back to the preacquisition years of the acquiring corporation

    b. May not be carried to the postacquisition period in the year of acquisition

    c. Are available to offset the acquiring corporation's current year income on an unlimited basis

    d. Lose their eligibility to be carried forward to succeeding tax years

80. An ownership change that triggers the loss limitation rules applies to a:

    a. 5-percent owner

    b. 10-percent owner

    c. 25-percent owner

    d. Majority share owner

Quizzer Questions: Module 4

81. The U.S. Supreme Court upheld the individual mandate (Code Sec. 5000A) in the Affordable Care Act by finding that it:

    a. Mandates only large employers to remit employer shared responsibility payments
    b. Mandates all employers to provide health coverage to employees
    c. Mandates individuals in grandfathered health plans to replace them with health insurance from state health exchanges
    d. Falls under the constitutional power of Congress to tax

82. The Affordable Care Act's shared responsibility payments for individuals are calculated on a _____ basis.

    a. Daily
    b. Weekly
    c. Monthly
    d. Annual

83. The Affordable Care Act's shared responsibility payments for employers are scheduled to be effective for months beginning after:

    a. December 31, 2010
    b. December 31, 2011
    c. December 31, 2012
    d. December 31, 2013

84. For-profit employers with 10 or fewer full-time or full-time-equivalent employees (FTEs) paying average annual wages of not more than $25,000 may be eligible for a maximum Code Sec. 45R credit of _____ for tax years beginning in 2010 through 2013.

    a. 25 percent
    b. 35 percent
    c. 50 percent
    d. 75 percent

85. The Affordable Care Act's employer shared responsibility payment generally applies to an employer that averages _____ or more full-time equivalent employees during the preceding calendar year, subject to certain limitations.

    a. 25
    b. 50
    c. 100
    d. 150

86. Free choice vouchers under the Affordable Care Act :

    a. Are available to qualified individuals after December 31, 2013
    b. Were repealed by the *Department of Defense and Full-Year Continuing Appropriations Act of 2011*
    c. Will be included in a taxpayer's Code Sec. 36B premium assistance tax credit calculation
    d. Cannot be greater than $1,500 per recipient

87. For tax years beginning after December 31, 2012, health flexible spending arrangements (health FSAs):

    a. May not allow employees to use employer flex credits
    b. Have a $2,500 annual limit for employee salary reductions
    c. Exclude payments for medical care items that are not medicines or drugs
    d. Allow payments for nonprescribed over-the-counter medicines

88. A covered entity must pay the Affordable Care Act's branded prescription drug fee when the entity's calendar year sales of the drugs total at least:

    a. $5 million
    b. $10 million
    c. $225 million
    d. $400 million

89. After December 31, 2012, the Affordable Care Act imposes an excise tax on the sale of certain medical devices in an amount equal to ____ percent of the sale price.

    a. 1.5
    b. 2.0
    c. 2.3
    d. 3.3

90. Health care coverage reporting to the IRS by plan sponsors and applicable employers under Code Secs. 6055 and 6056 applies to calendar years beginning on or after:

    a. January 1, 2013
    b. June 30, 2013
    c. January 1, 2014
    d. December 1, 2014

91. New taxes proposed as a means to raise federal revenues have included all of these types *except:*

    a. National retail sales tax
    b. Multinational corporate repatriation tax
    c. Value-added tax (VAT)
    d. Environmental tax

92. The President's Framework proposes to stimulate domestic manufacturing through all of these ways *except:*

    a. Reducing the corporate tax rate
    b. Increasing the Code Sec. 199 deduction to a special level for advanced manufacturing
    c. Eliminating double taxation of C corporation profits
    d. Expanding the Code Sec. 199 domestic production activities deduction

93. A worldwide tax system, rather than a territorial one, is favored by:

    a. President Obama
    b. The Deficit Commission report
    c. Republican party leadership
    d. Congressman Dave Camp

94. Recent reform proposals aimed at benefitting individuals include all of the following *except:*

    a. Turning certain deductions into tax credits to make them more equitable;
    b. Lowering the tax rate for capital gains and dividends to streamline investment decisions
    c. Improving the alternative minimum tax by allowing additional exclusions and deductions to protect a greater number of middle-class taxpayers; Increasing the amount of personal exemptions
    d. Collapsing the number of tax rates from six to two or three

95. The Deficit Commission's tax code reform proposal calls for lower tax rates, which would be partly paid for through repeal of several tax expenditures, including the deduction for:

    a. Retirement account contributions
    b. State and local taxes paid
    c. Charitable contributions
    d. Employer-provided health insurance

TOP FEDERAL TAX ISSUES FOR 2013 CPE COURSE   (4590-5)

Module 1: Answer Sheet

NAME _____

COMPANY NAME _____

STREET _____

CITY, STATE, & ZIP CODE _____

BUSINESS PHONE NUMBER _____

E-MAIL ADDRESS _____

DATE OF COMPLETION _____

CFP REGISTRANT ID (for Certified Financial Planners) _____

PTIN ID (for Enrolled Agents or RTRPs only) _____

CRTP ID (for CTEC Credit only) _____

Please go to **CCHGroup.com/PrintCPE** to complete your Quizzer online for instant results and no Express Grading Fee. A $56.00 processing fee will be charged for each user submitting Module 1 for grading.

If you prefer to mail or fax your Quizzer, remove both pages of the Answer Sheet from this book and return them with your completed Evaluation Form to: CCH Continuing Education Department, 4025 W. Peterson Ave., Chicago, IL 60646-6085 or fax your Answer Sheet to CCH at 773-866-3084. You must also select a method of payment below.

METHOD OF PAYMENT:

☐ Check Enclosed   ☐ Visa   ☐ Master Card   ☐ AmEx

☐ Discover   ☐ CCH Account* _____

Card No. _____ Exp. Date _____

Signature _____

EXPRESS GRADING: Please fax my Course results to me by 5:00 p.m. the business day following your receipt of this Answer Sheet. By checking this box I authorize CCH to charge $19.00 for this service.

☐ Express Grading $19.00   Fax No. _____

* Must provide CCH account number for this payment option

CCH
a Wolters Kluwer business

TOP FEDERAL TAX ISSUES FOR 2013 CPE COURSE   (4590-5)

Module 1: Answer Sheet

Please answer the questions by indicating the appropriate letter next to the corresponding number.

1. ___	6. ___	11. ___	16. ___
2. ___	7. ___	12. ___	17. ___
3. ___	8. ___	13. ___	18. ___
4. ___	9. ___	14. ___	19. ___
5. ___	10. ___	15. ___	20. ___

Please complete the Evaluation Form (located after the Module 4 Answer Sheet) and return it with this Quizzer Answer Sheet to CCH at the address on the previous page. Thank you.

TOP FEDERAL TAX ISSUES FOR 2013 CPE COURSE (4590-6)

Module 2: Answer Sheet

NAME _____

COMPANY NAME _____

STREET _____

CITY, STATE, & ZIP CODE _____

BUSINESS PHONE NUMBER _____

E-MAIL ADDRESS _____

DATE OF COMPLETION _____

CFP REGISTRANT ID (for Certified Financial Planners) _____

PTIN ID (for Enrolled Agents or RTRPs only) _____

CRTP ID (for CTEC Credit only) _____

Please go to **CCHGroup.com/PrintCPE** to complete your Quizzer online for instant results and no Express Grading Fee. A $70.00 processing fee will be charged for each user submitting Module 2 for grading.

If you prefer to mail or fax your Quizzer, remove both pages of the Answer Sheet from this book and return them with your completed Evaluation Form to: CCH Continuing Education Department, 4025 W. Peterson Ave., Chicago, IL 60646-6085 or fax your Answer Sheet to CCH at 773-866-3084. You must also select a method of payment below.

METHOD OF PAYMENT:

☐ Check Enclosed   ☐ Visa   ☐ Master Card   ☐ AmEx

☐ Discover   ☐ CCH Account* _____

Card No. _____ Exp. Date _____

Signature _____

EXPRESS GRADING: Please fax my Course results to me by 5:00 p.m. the business day following your receipt of this Answer Sheet. By checking this box I authorize CCH to charge $19.00 for this service.

☐ Express Grading $19.00   Fax No. _____

* Must provide CCH account number for this payment option

.CCH
a Wolters Kluwer business

TOP FEDERAL TAX ISSUES FOR 2013 CPE COURSE   (4590-6)

Module 2: Answer Sheet

Please answer the questions by indicating the appropriate letter next to the corresponding number.

21. ___	29. ___	37. ___	44. ___
22. ___	30. ___	38. ___	45. ___
23. ___	31. ___	39. ___	46. ___
24. ___	32. ___	40. ___	47. ___
25. ___	33. ___	41. ___	48. ___
26. ___	34. ___	42. ___	49. ___
27. ___	35. ___	43. ___	50. ___
28. ___	36. ___		

Please complete the Evaluation Form (located after the Module 4 Answer Sheet) and return it with this Quizzer Answer Sheet to CCH at the address on the previous page. Thank you.

TOP FEDERAL TAX ISSUES FOR 2013 CPE COURSE　　　　(4590-7)

Module 3: Answer Sheet

NAME _____

COMPANY NAME _____

STREET _____

CITY, STATE, & ZIP CODE _____

BUSINESS PHONE NUMBER _____

E-MAIL ADDRESS _____

DATE OF COMPLETION _____

CFP REGISTRANT ID (for Certified Financial Planners) _____

PTIN ID (for Enrolled Agents or RTRPs only) _____

CRTP ID (for CTEC Credit only) _____

Please go to **CCHGroup.com/PrintCPE** to complete your Quizzer online for instant results and no Express Grading Fee. A $84.00 processing fee will be charged for each user submitting Module 3 for grading.

If you prefer to mail or fax your Quizzer, remove both pages of the Answer Sheet from this book and return them with your completed Evaluation Form to: CCH Continuing Education Department, 4025 W. Peterson Ave., Chicago, IL 60646-6085 or fax your Answer Sheet to CCH at 773-866-3084. You must also select a method of payment below.

METHOD OF PAYMENT:

☐ Check Enclosed　　☐ Visa　　☐ Master Card　　☐ AmEx

☐ Discover　　☐ CCH Account* _____

Card No. _____ Exp. Date _____

Signature _____

EXPRESS GRADING: Please fax my Course results to me by 5:00 p.m. the business day following your receipt of this Answer Sheet. By checking this box I authorize CCH to charge $19.00 for this service.

☐ Express Grading $19.00 .　Fax No. _____

* Must provide CCH account number for this payment option

.CCH
a Wolters Kluwer business

TOP FEDERAL TAX ISSUES FOR 2013 CPE COURSE   (4590-7)

Module 3: Answer Sheet

Please answer the questions by indicating the appropriate letter next to the corresponding number.

51. ____	59. ____	67. ____	74. ____
52. ____	60. ____	68. ____	75. ____
53. ____	61. ____	69. ____	76. ____
54. ____	62. ____	70. ____	77. ____
55. ____	63. ____	71. ____	78. ____
56. ____	64. ____	72. ____	79. ____
57. ____	65. ____	73. ____	80. ____
58. ____	66. ____		

Please complete the Evaluation Form (located after the Module 4 Answer Sheet) and return it with this Quizzer Answer Sheet to CCH at the address on the previous page. Thank you.

TOP FEDERAL TAX ISSUES FOR 2013 CPE COURSE   (4590-8)

Module 4: Answer Sheet

NAME _____

COMPANY NAME _____

STREET _____

CITY, STATE, & ZIP CODE _____

BUSINESS PHONE NUMBER _____

E-MAIL ADDRESS _____

DATE OF COMPLETION _____

CFP REGISTRANT ID (for Certified Financial Planners) _____

PTIN ID (for Enrolled Agents or RTRPs only) _____

CRTP ID (for CTEC Credit only) _____

Please go to **CCHGroup.com/PrintCPE** to complete your Quizzer online for instant results and no Express Grading Fee. A $28.00 processing fee will be charged for each user submitting Module 4 for grading.

If you prefer to mail or fax your Quizzer, remove both pages of the Answer Sheet from this book and return them with your completed Evaluation Form to: CCH Continuing Education Department, 4025 W. Peterson Ave., Chicago, IL 60646-6085 or fax your Answer Sheet to CCH at 773-866-3084. You must also select a method of payment below.

METHOD OF PAYMENT:

☐ Check Enclosed   ☐ Visa   ☐ Master Card   ☐ AmEx

☐ Discover   ☐ CCH Account* _____

Card No. _____ Exp. Date _____

Signature _____

EXPRESS GRADING: Please fax my Course results to me by 5:00 p.m. the business day following your receipt of this Answer Sheet. By checking this box I authorize CCH to charge $19.00 for this service.

☐ Express Grading $19.00   Fax No. _____

* Must provide CCH account number for this payment option

.CCH
a Wolters Kluwer business

TOP FEDERAL TAX ISSUES FOR 2013 CPE COURSE   (4590-8)

Module 4: Answer Sheet

Please answer the questions by indicating the appropriate letter next to the corresponding number.

81. _____   85. _____   89. _____   93. _____

82. _____   86. _____   90. _____   94. _____

83. _____   87. _____   91. _____   95. _____

84. _____   88. _____   92. _____

Please complete the Evaluation Form (located after the Module 4 Answer Sheet) and return it with this Quizzer Answer Sheet to CCH at the address on the previous page. Thank you.

TOP FEDERAL TAX ISSUES FOR 2013 CPE COURSE   (4281-5)

Evaluation Form

Please take a few moments to fill out and mail or fax this evaluation to CCH so that we can better provide you with the type of self-study programs you want and need. Thank you.

About This Program

1. Please circle the number that best reflects the extent of your agreement with the following statements:

		Strongly Agree				Strongly Disagree
a.	The Course objectives were met.	5	4	3	2	1
b.	This Course was comprehensive and organized.	5	4	3	2	1
c.	The content was current and technically accurate.	5	4	3	2	1
d.	This Course was timely and relevant.	5	4	3	2	1
e.	The prerequisite requirements were appropriate.	5	4	3	2	1
f.	This Course was a valuable learning experience.	5	4	3	2	1
g.	The Course completion time was appropriate.	5	4	3	2	1

2. This Course was most valuable to me because of:

    ____ Continuing Education credit   ____ Convenience of format
    ____ Relevance to my practice/   ____ Timeliness of subject matter
    employment   ____ Reputation of author
    ____ Price
    ____ Other (please specify) _____

3. How long did it take to complete this Course? (Please include the total time spent reading or studying reference materials and completing CPE Quizzer).

    Module 1 ____   Module 2 ____   Module 3 ____

4. What do you consider to be the strong points of this Course?

5. What improvements can we make to this Course?

Evaluation Form *cont'd*

General Interests

1. Preferred method of self-study instruction:

    _____ Text _____ Audio _____ Computer-based/Multimedia _____Video

2. What specific topics would you like CCH to develop as self-study CPE programs? _____

    _____

    _____

    _____

3. Please list other topics of interest to you _____

    _____

    _____

About You

1. Your profession:

    _____ CPA   _____ Enrolled Agent

    _____ Attorney   _____ Tax Preparer

    _____ Financial Planner   _____ Other (please specify)

    _____   _____

2. Your employment:

    _____ Self-employed   _____ Public Accounting Firm

    _____ Service Industry   _____ Non-Service Industry

    _____ Banking/Finance   _____ Government

    _____ Education   _____ Other _____

3. Size of firm/corporation:

    _____ 1 _____ 2-5 _____ 6-10 _____ 11-20 _____ 21-50 _____ 51+

4. Your Name _____

    Firm/Company Name _____

    Address _____

    City, State, Zip Code _____

    E-mail Address _____

THANK YOU FOR TAKING THE TIME TO COMPLETE THIS SURVEY!